BUSINESS Superbrands

AN INSIGHT INTO BRITAIN'S STRONGEST B2B BRANDS 2003/04

America • Australia • China • Czech Republic • Denmark • Egypt • France • Germany • Hong Kong
India • Indonesia • Ireland • Italy • Malaysia • Morocco • The Netherlands • Norway • Philippines
Portugal • Saudi Arabia • Singapore • Spain • Sweden • Thailand • United Arab Emirates

www.superbrands.org/uk

AUTHORS
Rebecca Barnes
Alicia Clegg
James Curtis
Des King
Delwyn Swingewood
Mark Tungate

MANAGING EDITOR
Angela Pumphrey

EDITORIAL ASSISTANT
Emma Selwyn

BRAND LIAISON DIRECTOR
Annie Richardson

DESIGNER
Verity Belcher
Creative & Commercial Communications

ART DIRECTOR
Adam Selwyn
Creative & Commercial Communications

Special thanks goes to **Mintel** for providing a considerable
amount of market research material.

Other publications from Superbrands in the UK:
Consumer Superbrands Volume V ISBN: 0-9541532-1-9
Cool BrandLeaders Volume II ISBN: 0-9541532-4-3

For more information, or to order these books direct
from the publisher, email brands@superbrands.org or
call 01825 723398.

For Superbrands publications dedicated to: America, Australia,
China, Czech Republic, Denmark, Egypt, France, Germany,
Hong Kong, India, Indonesia, Ireland, Italy, Malaysia, Morocco,
The Netherlands, Norway, Philippines, Portugal, Saudi Arabia,
Singapore, Spain, Sweden, Thailand and United Arab Emirates
email: brands@superbrands.org or telephone: 0207 267 8899.

© 2003 Superbrands Ltd

Published by Superbrands Ltd
64 West Yard
Camden Lock Place
London
NW1 8AF

www.superbrands.org/uk

Contents

The role of brands is often dismissed in the business-to-business marketplace. This after all is the realm of logic over emotion, of thorough analysis over impulse, of large-scale purchases over the everyday. The Business Superbrands presented here give the lie to such thinking. Here are companies that have invested for the long term, in the veracity of their brand promise, in consistent delivery, and in doing things differently. As a result they have connected with their customers – and the wider community – both forcefully and meaningfully, and done so over time. The British Brands Group, as the voice for brands in the UK, is committed to building an environment in which such brands can flourish.

JOHN NOBLE   Director, British Brands Group

Does your company have a big idea?

Does your business strategy work around this idea? Does your CEO act as a champion of it? Does it focus resources and prioritise action? Does it inspire staff to live and deliver it? Does it drive customers to want and buy it? Does it encourage shareholders to value and invest in it?

Business Superbrands do. And as a result they have the best chance of creating exceptional value for both their customers and shareholders. This is the real challenge for every business and every marketer today.

At the Chartered Institute of Marketing, our big idea is to ensure that great marketing becomes great business, and that's why we are delighted to endorse this book and these great brands.

PETER FISK   CEO, Chartered Institute of Marketing

What are the secrets of success in business-to-business branding?

Where better to find out than in this third collection of Business Superbrands selected by some of the most experienced practitioners in the business. What sets them apart from their competition? Clarity of direction, self-belief, creativity, the ability to adapt to market needs, sustained marketing effort and investment. 'Thinking big' and for the long term. They set the standard for others to follow.

How refreshing to also see communications agency brands making the grade.

JANET HULL   Head Of Marketing, IPA

Angela Pumphrey

Managing Editor

Business Superbrands is published by Superbrands Ltd, the independent arbiter and authority on branding. In the UK, the organisation has been given permission to trade as The Brand Council. The organisation exists to promote the discipline of branding and pays tribute to exceptional brands around the world. The organisation promotes the discipline of branding through a number of channels including media comment, research, events as well as through a dedicated branding website. There are now Superbrands programmes operating in over 25 countries.

The organisation has concentrated on three main areas: Consumer Superbrands, Business Superbrands and Cool BrandLeaders. In the UK it has published five books addressing Consumer Superbrands, two previous volumes examining Business Superbrands as well as two books presenting the strongest Cool BrandLeaders. Only brands highly rated, as decided by the independent and voluntary judging panels (for each respective programme), are considered for inclusion in each publication.

Branding is well established in consumer marketing, but has been slower to become recognised in the business-to-business world. It is however now being seen as a key ingredient for success to an increasing number of organisations that operate in this field. This, the third edition of Business Superbrands, aims to highlight companies, across a wide range of sectors, that have applied branding techniques with precision and expertise. These brand owners have built confidence in their brand and, as a result, have reaped both the operational and bottom-line rewards for doing so.

All the brands that feature in the book have been awarded Business Superbrand status by the Business Superbrands Judging Panel. Made up of eminent figures from the world of business, each member has a deep appreciation of what makes an inspiring business brand and has born the following definition in mind when awarding this status:

'A Business Superbrand has established the finest reputation in its field. It offers customers significant emotional and/or tangible advantages over its competitors which (consciously or subconsciously) customers want, recognise and are confident about investing in. Business Superbrands are targeted at organisations (although not necessarily exclusively so).'

The Business Superbrands case studies explore the history and development of each brand, its placing within its market as well as presenting its marketing, advertising and design achievements. It is no accident that the majority of these brands have been built upon a high quality product or service, standing for something distinctive, generating considerable awareness. They share a defined and clear personality, consistently remain faithful to their brand values and live up to their brand promise.

There is no definitive formula for becoming and remaining a Business Superbrand. However, the following pages divulge many lessons that can be learned from those who have cultivated a successful formula.

How does being a Business Superbrand give competitive advantage?

In a challenging economic climate how does being a Business Superbrand give competitive advantage?
according to members of the Business Superbrands Judging Panel.

**Marketing Director
Accenture**

Claire Allen

"When the going gets tough, the tough get going", according to a 1980s classic soundtrack. Good advice? Not in branding. In fact, in branding, probably the reverse is true. If you're a Business Superbrand, it means that you've developed your company's image into an immensely strong bastion of reliable, differentiated and relevant experiences for your customers. And when your customers find themselves in difficult economic times, the last thing you want to do is to desert them. Rather, you need to actively demonstrate the solidity of your brand, and, if appropriate, to underscore the depth and longevity of your customer relationships. Ideally, a Business Superbrand should be seen by its customers as a safe-haven in difficult times, thanks to a shared and mutually beneficial history. Of course, you need to ensure your products are fresh and relevant, but the brand should be a constant, reassuring presence, that keeps its customers loyal and active in even the most trying of circumstances.

**Global Head of Advertising
UBS**

Deborah Keily

Unfortunately, between accepting her responsibilities as a judge and this book going to print, Deborah Keily is no longer able to sit on the Business Superbrands Judging Panel due to serious illness.

**Group Managing Director
Enterprise IG**

John Mathers

There are many phrases to sum up the challenging business world of today – 'the knowledge era', 'the information age', 'the global marketplace'. They capture part of the truth but there is one theme that consistently seems to separate the winners from the losers – 'Imagination'.

The secret of outstanding value creation doesn't lie in global scale, information access or knowledge per se – rather it lies in how well these things are used to create and seize new opportunities.

Business Superbrands understand this; they are imagination businesses. Sure, they recognise that cost cutting and efficiency are important, but they are not centre stage. To achieve top line growth they innovate, because it's the only genuine way to keep existing – and grow new – customers.

Innovation, of course, isn't easy. You need to marry knowledge and data to help create informed intuition and inspiring creativity. You need to flit between the seeming opposites of 'the big idea' versus the evolutionary step.

Chief Executive
J Walter Thompson
Simon Bolton

"Within any brand there's a product, but not every product is a brand. Behind every product there's a company, but not every company is a brand. By failing to communicate the nature of the corporate brand we may be failing to play one of our more powerful cards."

Telling words from Jeremy Bullmore and ones that all of us in the business of brand creation would do well to heed. By definition the businesses featured here have succeeded in playing that card, and pulled off the difficult alchemy of turning a company into a brand.

Their reward? In tough times there is no better defence than a Superbrand and here's why:

They have an in-built consumer goodwill factor – they can survive terrible times.

They endure, conferring their values on successive cycles of product innovation.

They act as talent magnets – they attract the best people often for less.

That's why Superbrands will see off the competition and continue to add shareholder value, even in challenging times.

Executive Director
Citigate Dewe Rogerson
Anthony Carlisle

Business Superbrand status means that within your sector and among your peers, you are the respected business. It's a reflection of the competitive advantage the company itself has worked for and already gained. The label Business Superbrand does not add to this – it simply tells people that, in poor economic times, these are the businesses likely best to be able to prosper. It's like a lot of things – success breeds success; recognition follows. The job of a Business Superbrand is to stay a Business Superbrand.

CEO, UK
Cable & Wireless
Royston Hoggarth

For years the received wisdom was that branding was not relevant in the business-to-business market place. Branding was, it was claimed, a phenomenon confined to the consumer sector which had no place in the highly rational world inhabited by those of us involved in making business decisions. However today, some of the strongest brands exist in the business-to-business space. As in the consumer market strong business-to-business brands provide the customer with a guarantee of quality and performance, reducing the 'misery of choice'. Secondly, as functional advantages become increasingly rare, particularly in the telecoms and IT sectors where product cycles are increasingly short, it becomes ever more essential to develop an offering that goes beyond the purely functional. Service brands, differentiated by their culture and brand experience, meet the changing needs of their customers, because they take time to understand them better. Those that make this transition first will become the leading brands.

President
Added Value, The Henley Centre, Fusion 5
Tamara Ingram

In my view there are five key things that make Business Superbrands most likely to succeed in tough times compared to the others:

Saliency: When there's less spare cash, there's less experimentation. People stick with what they know, so being a top of mind brand keeps you on all stakeholders shopping lists.

Unusual level of trust: Business Superbrands become 'super' when they are really trusted by the consumer. In uncertain times this trust holds consumer loyalty.

Positive intent: When you're a Business Superbrand most people think of you as a leader. So when times are tough customers are more likely to stick with you.

Employment: Business Superbrands not only have power externally but also internally, so that it is easier to attract the best and hold on to your stars.

Rich: Business Superbrands tend to be market leaders and therefore make more money and have greater flexibility. They can also gain competitive advantage by affording to spend in troubled times.

Managing Director
Management Today
Rufus Olins

Being a powerful brand provides competitive advantage because the powerful brands get noticed. This is not always good. People will not necessarily admire or choose to spend money on them, but they will at least be considered. At a time when people are looking for reassurance or even insurance for their decisions there is what is often called a flight to quality – sometimes this is just a flight to the familiar. Being a powerful brand means that you are a contender and if you have a recognised set of values you are not just fighting on price.

Editor
Marketing
Craig Smith

We know what the answer should be – Business Superbrand status equates to trust, and trust, when everything else is falling about your ears, is a bankable asset. The old ad line and now adage 'No manager ever got fired for buying IBM' is based on this premise – don't gamble the company's money, go with something you know.

The reality is that a challenging economic climate levels the playing field. Superbrands generally have the buffer of operational scale, while smaller, younger brands are presented with the opportunity to challenge industry convention – and a greater chance to achieve Superbrand status themselves. Trust is an asset, and should be treated as such by all organisations. It can easily be squandered through scandals of corporate governance, employee disputes or good old-fashioned complacency. It's not being a Business Superbrand that gives competitive advantage, so much as remaining one.

Chief Executive Officer
Mintel
John Weeks

The question isn't so much about brands, but about leading brands. After all, most markets are awash with brands – but in most, there is little notion of what they stand for, what they deliver, what distinguishes them.

Leading brands convey clarity. In B2B markets, it's no different.

As B2B marketers, we aim to transcend the functional aspects of our brand. These are taken as given. Most brands offer functionality – this is relatively easy to communicate. We want to develop our brand so that it gets under the emotional skin of our customers.
Prestige
Supremacy
Empowerment
Confidence
Enhancement …

At Mintel we believe there are emotional 'props' within our brand, working alongside our more traditional values, subtly reinforcing a client's decision to work with us. In good and bad times, the most successful brands consistently share these values with their clients.

Chief Executive
Hill & Knowlton
Marie Louise Windeler

Branding is more important than ever in a tough economic climate. That's the time when your brand equity, if it's been managed effectively, can pay dividends. We work with eleven of the 50 biggest selling fmcg brands (Source: Marketing magazine August 2003) in the UK and several FTSE 100 companies, as well as building new brands for younger companies. Hill & Knowlton understands very well the power of maintaining brand equity and that is why we see a clear advantage in being included in Business Superbrands. It's a sign of the strength, vibrancy and enduring value of our brand. And it puts us in great company. By keeping such good company, our teams are able to work with exciting clients and have rewarding careers at Hill & Knowlton. That's good business.

3M

Market

3M justifiably claims to be one of the most diversified companies in the world. 3M products are in use everywhere: in the home as well as the work place, in schools, hospitals and in the street. Its portfolio of 50,000 products includes pharmaceuticals, medical equipment, advanced optical solutions, safety and security systems, micro-abrasives, office productivity tools and a developing range of consumer products making home life a little easier. Originally known as the Minnesota Mining and Manufacturing Company, 3M has spread from its North American base, boasting operations in more than 60 countries and customers in nearly 200. Its vision is to be the most innovative enterprise and the preferred supplier. It achieves this by creating products which provide its customers with practical and ingenious solutions.

Achievements

3M, which celebrated its centenary in 2002, is a US$16 billion company with almost 69,000 employees worldwide. The St Paul, Minnesota, company is one of the 30 benchmark corporations comprising the Dow Jones Industrial Average and, as well as being a Fortune 500 company, is a component of the Standard and Poor 500 Index. In 2002 3M was voted the ninth most respected company in a Financial Times global survey. The company also ranked in the top quintile of the UK's first Corporate Responsibility Index carried out by Business in the Community. 3M's long-standing commitment to the safety and well-being of its employees was recognised in the UK with a gold award by the Royal Society for the Prevention of Accidents in 2003 in addition to nine UK

manufacturing sites gaining individual recognition of their performance. It is also listed on the FTSE4Good Index and the Dow Jones Sustainability Index.

3M was among the first to recognise that business has environmental responsibilities and

in 1976 created the Pollution Prevention Pays (3P) programme which has achieved impressive worldwide results in terms of energy and waste reduction. This achievement was further underlined in 1999 when it won an eco-performance award from the Hamburger Umwelt Institute. The company, which has been described as 'an ideas factory' by the influential US News and World Report and 'synonymous with innovation' by Fortune magazine was also a founder member of the World Business Council for Sustainable Development.

3M products also win awards. In 1999 Fortune included the Post-it® Note in its Products of the Century League and Scotch® Tape was listed among the century's 100 best inventions by Business Week. In 2000, 3M was one of a handful of companies to win more than one Millennium Product award from the UK's Design Council. The 3M™ Paint Preparation System (PPS) alone has won a number

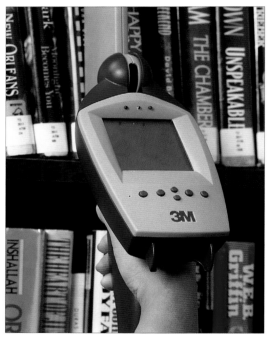

of international awards, including the 2002 'Best New Bodyshop Product or Service' from AutoTrade magazine. 3M's reputation as an innovator means that its expertise is frequently cited in case study material by educational institutions such as Harvard, INSEAD and London Business School.

History

3M has always focused on creativity and practicality as demonstrated in its 100 year history of solving everyday problems innovatively. The Minnesota Mining and Manufacturing Company was formed by five businessmen in 1902. The company's first commercial breakthrough came two years later with the production of 3M™ Wetordry™ Sandpaper, a product which revolutionised the industry. It is no coincidence that the company's growth was helped by the fledgling automobile industry which needed innovative materials in the production process. For example, developing 3M™ Scotchlite™ Reflective Tape as a practical solution for the car industry. By the mid 1940s 3M was listed on the New York Stock Exchange and during the 1950s the company introduced the concept of cross

pollination within its research laboratories, encouraging its scientists into a more fruitful collaboration in their quest for new technologies and solutions and securing 3M's reputation as a diversified technology company. The development of adhesive-backed surgical drapes was another milestone providing the foundation for the brand's health care business. Simultaneously 3M strengthened its home and office business range with the introduction of adhesives, sandpaper, scouring pads and tapes, for example Scotch® Magic™ Tape, virtually invisible when applied to books or papers and now used by countless millions in the home as well as the office.

New products continued to be part of the company's lifeblood. These included breakthroughs such as Scotch® Magnetic Tape, enabling the first recording of television pictures in 1957; 3M™ Steri-Strip™ Wound Closures; Data Cartridge technology which revolutionised the computer data sector and of course Post-it® Notes which were launched in 1980. More recent developments include the introduction in 1992 of 3M™ Flexible Circuits allowing electronic devices to be smaller and more powerful, CFC-Free Metered Doses Inhalers in 1995 and Aldara™ Cream in 1997.

Product

3M has more than 30 'technology platforms' representing the brand's innovative core manufacturing products ranging from adhesives, abrasives and coatings to fibre optics, drug delivery systems and fuel cells. Of its products 90% are designed for industrial or commercial use. 3M groups its brand portfolio across eleven customer centres: architecture and construction, creative communications, education, office, home and leisure, health care, manufacturing and industrial, electronics, telecoms and utilities, transportation and safety and security.

In the architecture sector 3M provides a variety of products including: the range of Filtrete™ Air Filtration systems; the revolutionary 3M™ Scotchtint™

Window Film which blocks out up to 99% of the sun's damaging ultraviolet rays; and, Scotch-Brite™ Cleaning Materials. As well as being a strong brand in its own right, 3M is very active in helping other companies build their brands. Scotchprint® Graphics provide high impact solutions wherever an advertising opportunity exists from commercial vehicles and public transport advertising to floor and pavement graphics as well as short term or seasonal promotional campaigns.

At home, 3M products are helping to make everyday jobs a little easier and more satisfying. The Scotch-Brite™ High Performance Cleaning Cloth can be washed hundreds of times and yet still removes greasy stains, without the need for additional cleaning sprays. 3M™ Command™ Adhesive Hooks and Clips help secure pictures and cables but can be easily removed without leaving a mark using its unique pull tab mechanism. For those little accidents you also have 3M™ Nexcare™ First Aid products, including colourful cartoon versions for kids. In the office, as well as a wide range of messaging and organisational products under the world famous Post-it® Brand, 3M offers a range of ergonomically designed products including the 3M™ Renaissance Mouse. Unlike the traditional palm down posture of most input devices this mouse uses an innovative 'handshake' design that keeps the user's arm in a more natural and neutral position significantly lowering pressure on wrist nerves and reducing the risk of discomfort.

Within the electronics sector, 3M™ Volition™ Fibre Optic Network Solutions is the first fibre-structured system that is a viable cost-competitive

alternative to copper. For the telecommunications industry, 3M offers an extensive range of copper, cable and fibre optic solutions and test units for telecommunications applications. 3M™ Scotchlok™ connectors for telephone and signal cables allow for wire branch connections without stripping or twisting. For those companies in the industrial and manufacturing arena, 3M offers the most advanced line of acrylic and rubber adhesive tape systems available. The systems offer customers high-quality shear performance, environmental resistance and long-term bond performance. For fine finishing needs, 3M™ Trizact™ Abrasives outlast any comparable grade of abrasive by at least three times.

In health care, 3M ESPE manufactures and markets more than 2,000 products to the dental industry worldwide. These products are designed to meet restorative, crown and bridge, preventive infection control, and cosmetic dentistry needs. On the data side of health care 3M Health Information Systems is the international leader in Diagnosis Group Related (DGR) classification and clinical information management. Products

range from health information coding systems to a comprehensive computer-based patient record system.

Since the introduction of 3M's first reflective sheeting product, Scotchlite materials have been keeping road users, pedestrians and emergency services personnel safe when out and about. From high impact road signs to high performance reflective materials used in the production of a wide range of high visibility clothing including children's trainers and overalls, 3M products are helping reduce accidents. For those employed in hazardous or noisy conditions, 3M helps ensure a healthier and safer working environment with a range of respiratory and hearing protection products.

3M doesn't just confine its products to landlubbers. It manufacturers marine products for the repair and maintenance of everything from canoes and powerboats to luxury cruisers.

Recent Developments
Innovation continues to be one of 3M's watchwords and the brand's diversified technologies enable it to meet the demands of the digital age. The 3M™ Vikuiti™ Display Enhancement system, which was unveiled in 2000 improves the clarity and impact of electronic displays on laptop computers, mobile phones and PDA's. The 3M™ Digital Wall Display combines the ability to bring multimedia presentation, teleconferencing, the digital white board and flip chart, into a single device.

In health care 3M™ Cavilon™ barrier creams, specifically formulated for use in hospitals, community and long term care facilities, are designed to keep skin healthy. Another breakthrough came with the introduction of a new class of pharmaceuticals, immune response modifiers, which stimulate the body's natural ability to fight virus infected and tumour cells.

The company has also introduced a variety of security solutions such as 3M™ Secure Express which offers custom security labels or seals to help in the fight against counterfeit products. Another system, 3M™ Secure Colour labels, offers immediate, clear-cut, overt authentication. While 3M™ Confirm provides enhanced security for passports and other legal documents.

Promotion
3M is a global brand and its distinctive logo is a precious asset used on all packaging and advertising worldwide. So too are 3M product brands such as Post-it® Notes, Scotch® Tapes, Scotch-Brite™ Cleaning Products and Thinsulate™ Insulation. The company's presence in a range of distribution and dealer channels serving business to business and consumer markets ensure that the 3M brand is seen by thousands of people every day.

Brand Values
In essence, 3M is viewed by customers and end consumers as an authority brand with a reputation

for quality, value and service. Its ongoing environmental, safety and social performance demonstrate that 3M believes that respect for the social and physical environment can complement the drive to provide investors with an attractive return through sustained, quality growth. With over a hundred years experience of capturing the ingenuity of its employees and transforming innovative ideas into commercial offerings, 3M is proving itself to be a company that employees are proud to be part of.

www.3M.com/uk

accenture
High performance. Delivered.

Market

The worldwide business consulting and information technology services market, excluding hardware support and processing services, is expected to grow from US$287 billion in 2000 to US$408 billion in 2003, a compound annual growth rate of 12.5%, according to market research company, International Data Corporation.

In this highly competitive market, Accenture maintains its position as one of the world's leading management consulting and technology services organisations. Accenture believes it is not how many ideas you have, but how you ensure your ideas deliver tangible benefits. Therefore, helping its clients turn innovative ideas into results is key.

With deep industry expertise, broad global resources and proven experience in consulting and outsourcing, Accenture can mobilise the right people, skills, alliances and technologies to help clients across all industries including automotive, energy, consumer goods and services and financial services, to quickly realise their visions.

With more than 80,000 people in 47 countries, from Australia to Venezuela, Accenture has extensive experience in eighteen industry groups in key business areas, including customer relationship management, supply chain management, business strategy, technology and outsourcing. Accenture also leverages its affiliates and alliance activities to help drive innovative solutions. Strong relationships with this network of businesses extend Accenture's knowledge of emerging business models and products, enabling the company to provide its clients with the best possible tools, technologies and capabilities. Accenture uses these to serve as a catalyst, helping clients anticipate and gain value from business and technology change.

Achievements

Accenture was launched as a brand and a new company on January 1st 2001 but the company's reputation as an industry leader has been built over the last decade. Since its launch, Accenture's rise has been truly outstanding. On July 19th 2001, Accenture shares began trading on the New York Stock Exchange. By becoming a public company, Accenture created opportunities for growth in the best interests of its clients, shareholders and people around the world.

Accenture entered Fortune's list of global brand leaders in 2002 at position number 53, and in 2003 rose to number 52. Accenture generated net revenues of US$11.6 billion for the fiscal year ended August 31st 2002.

History

Continuous reinvention and rapid transformation are themes throughout Accenture's history. It traces its roots back to 1953 when, as part of a larger organisation and under a different name, (Andersen Consulting) it installed the first computer for business application at General Electric. In 1989, the company was established as a separate and independent business unit, and at that point, Accenture started to evolve from a systems integrator to a global management consulting and technology services company.

In 1991, Accenture worked on one of its first major outsourcing arrangements when the company started managing British Petroleum Exploration's accounting, finance and support functions from a special centre that it established in Aberdeen, Scotland. In 1994 the company established the Accenture Technology Labs – then known as Centers for Strategic Technology – in Palo Alto, California, and Sophia Antipolis.

Chairman and CEO Joe W Forehand, a partner with 27 years experience, was officially named Accenture's managing partner and CEO in November 1999 and added the newly-created title of chairman in 2001. That same year, the company changed its name to Accenture.

Under Forehand's leadership, Accenture is helping clients deliver their vision to market ahead of the competition. It is now one of the world's leading management consulting and technology services companies, identifying new business and technology trends and developing solutions to help clients around the world enter new markets, increase revenues in existing markets, improve operational performance, and deliver their products and services more effectively and efficiently.

Product

Accenture's management consultancy and technology services and solutions business is structured around five global, industry-oriented Operating Groups– Communications and High Tech, Financial Services, Government, Products and Resources – which together comprise eighteen industry segments. Eight service lines support the global Operating Groups and provide access to the full spectrum of business and information technology solutions. Client engagement teams typically consist of industry experts, service line specialists and consultants with local market knowledge.

Accenture's Communications and High Tech Global Operating Group comprises three industry segments, Communications, Electronics and High Tech and Media and Entertainment. Communications serves many of the world's leading wireline, wireless, cable and satellite communications companies. Electronics & High Tech works with clients in the aerospace, defence, electronics, high technology and network communications industries. Media & Entertainment serves the media, entertainment and publishing industries.

Accenture's Financial Services Global Operating Group comprises three industry segments, Banking, Insurance and Health Services.

Accenture's Government Global Operating Group works with government agencies in 21 countries, focusing on defence, revenue, human services, justice, postal, education and electoral

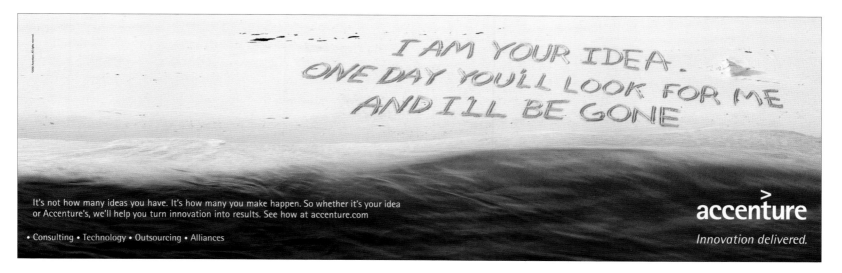

authorities. The company's Government clients typically are national, provincial or state-level government organisations, and to a lesser extent, cities and other forms of local government. Accenture advises on, implements and in some cases operates government services, enabling clients to use their resources more efficiently and to deliver citizen-centric services. It is also working with these clients to transform their back-office operations, build web interfaces and enable services to be delivered over the internet.

The Products Global Operating Group comprises six industry segments: Automotive, Consumer Goods & Services, Industrial Equipment, Pharmaceuticals & Medical Products, Retail and Transportation & Travel Services. Meanwhile, its Resources global Operating Group comprises five industry segments, Chemicals – serving half of the world's 100 largest chemical companies – Energy, Forest Products, Metals & Mining and Utilities.

Accenture also has specialised consulting and technology services in a number of business areas. Customer Relationship Management, for example, helps transform clients marketing and service capabilities, while Accenture Finance Solutions moves clients' back offices to Accenture's front office. Meanwhile, Finance and Performance Management helps Chief Financial Officers create value. Accenture's Outsourcing and Security Services remove many of the headaches for its clients and its Web Services turn commercial activities into web based services.

Recent Developments

Accenture's clients span the full range of industries around the world and include 92 of the Fortune Global 100 and more than two-thirds of the Fortune Global 500. In addition, 92 of its top 100 clients in fiscal year 2002, based on revenue, have been clients for at least five years, and 66 have been clients for at least ten years.

The company's most recent financial results show that new business for the third quarter 2003 were US$5.2 billion – US$2.2 billion of which was in consulting. This represents a 6% increase over new bookings in consulting in the third quarter of last year. And consistent with its growth strategy, Accenture continues to expand its outsourcing business, which now accounts for more than 30% of net revenues.

Among its new clients are Citizenship and Immigration Canada (CIC) which has awarded Accenture a contract to help CIC design, develop and deploy a global case management system

that will be used in Canada and at overseas missions to support the management of immigration and citizenship programs. Accenture is also working with the US Department of Defense's Federal Voting Assistance Program to design and build a new voting technology system for the SERVE project, which stands for Secure Electronic Registration and Voting Experiment. Using SERVE, thousands of absentee Uniformed Services personnel, their dependants, and overseas US citizens will have the opportunity to register to vote and cast their ballots over the internet from anywhere in the world.

Accenture has also recently announced an expansion of its global network of delivery centres with the opening of a facility in China, through which the company will deliver to clients a variety of technology services, including applications development and maintenance, systems integration, software re-engineering and business process outsourcing.

Promotion

Accenture's promotional strategy has evolved since its launch in 2001. The original emphasis was on generating awareness of the new Accenture name. Now that Accenture is established as a brand, the strategy is to establish its positioning in the market, using the line 'High Performance. Delivered'. This new positioning represents a positioning evolution for Accenture. Its previous positioning and advertising campaign ('I am Your Idea') sought to compel executives to turn all of their innovative ideas into business results – with Accenture's help.

The thought behind this campaign was that great ideas won't leave you alone. They exhilarate you with their potential but one of the greatest frustrations for senior executives is that good ideas may go unrealised. There is no shortage of ideas – but real, lasting competitive advantage only comes to those who fulfil and realise them.

Moving forward, in October 2003, Accenture launched a new positioning in the marketplace, that turns its focus towards the results and benefits of executing innovative ideas within an organisation, in order to help it become a 'High Performance Business'.

This is the key principle behind Accenture's new campaign which will run in 22 different countries, and which will build on the creativity of the 'I am Your Idea' campaign.

Through 2003 Accenture continued to promote itself through a combination of above and below-the-line techniques. Above-the-line, Accenture's advertising combines print and broadcast execution with strategic outdoor sites at major business airports. Below-the-line, Accenture's main activity is through its website, where many clients participate in Accenture's client-centric marketing channel, accessing specialised client-only insights and research. Accenture also continues to be associated with business events, such as the World Economic Forum. It has also continued its major brand building

event activities, including the BMW Williams Team, the Accenture Match Play Championship, and in 2002, the French Taste for Spanish Painting exhibition at the Metropolitan Museum of Art in New York.

Brand Values

Accenture believes that the brand is comprised of numerous facets, including the organisation's position in the marketplace, the work it does, its internal and external communications and the behaviour of its employees. The positioning of the organisation has evolved over time to ensure that the brand reflects the organisation's vision and remains closely aligned with its business strategy. The evolution of the brand positioning is guided by an understanding of the organisation's essential capabilities and its aspirations for the future.

www.accenture.com

AmericanAirlines®

Market

The international aviation industry is ultra-competitive, with over 260 airlines fighting to win a slice of the estimated 1.5 billion passenger journeys that take place every year. There are few industries where customers have so much choice, or where brands compete so vigorously.

With competition, especially from the new breed of budget operators, prices have plummeted, putting airlines' profitability under pressure. Figures from the International Air Transport Association show that the average air traveller is paying 70% less, in real terms, than twenty years ago.

Margins have also been squeezed in the aftermath of the September 11th attacks in the US. According to IATA, its members lost US$14 billion on their international services in 2001 and 2002. More recently, the industry has been further damaged by the war in Iraq and the Sars virus. All of this has created a business environment where only the fittest survive.

One way airlines have always tried to navigate their way through turbulent times is to maximise their share of the business market, which, although far smaller in terms of passenger numbers, is much more lucrative. According to IATA, slightly more than 14% of its member traffic is first and intermediate use business class. However, this small percentage provides almost 32% of revenue.

Despite the hardships of recent years, the airline industry is expected to return to growth at an annual rate of 4% over the next five years and, by 2015, the number of passengers will grow from 1.5 billion to three billion.

Achievements

American Airlines has built itself into one of the true giants of the international aviation industry, operating the world's largest commercial fleet with more than 700 aircraft carrying around 94 million passengers per year.

American Airlines has always been at the cutting edge of the airline industry and is responsible for many industry firsts, including major input in to the design of the DC-3 aircraft, and the introduction of the first airline loyalty scheme – AAdvantage®. Most recently, it has pushed back the boundaries of in-flight comfort for all classes on the aircraft.

The airline's achievements have been recognised in a number of prestigious awards. In September 2002, for the tenth consecutive year, it was voted Best North American Airline by readers of Business Traveller UK magazine and, in February 2002, Business Traveller US magazine awarded American Airlines three top prizes in its annual Best in Business Travel Awards.

History

American Airlines can trace its roots back more than 75 years. On April 15th 1926, the first regular scheduled flight of what would later become American Airlines took off with pioneer aviator Charles Lindbergh at the controls. Lindbergh, then chief pilot for Robertson Aircraft Corporation in Missouri, flew three planeloads of mail in a DH-4 biplane from St Louis to Chicago. It was one of the scores of companies that eventually consolidated to form the modern-day American

The American Way.. of getting places!

Airlines. The consolidation began in 1929 when the Aviation Corporation was formed to acquire young aviation companies, including Robertson. In 1930, the Aviation Corporation's airline subsidiaries were incorporated into American Airways Inc and in 1934, American Airways became American Airlines Inc.

American Airlines' first transatlantic venture was through a subsidiary called American Overseas Airlines (AOA), who were heavily involved in the Berlin Airlift after World War II. American Airlines' then went on to sell AOA to Pan American Airlines in 1950.

More than 30 years later, American Airlines stepped into the void when Braniff International Airlines abruptly suspended service between London Gatwick and Dallas/Fort Worth. On May 19th, just five days after Braniff had shut down, an American Airlines Boeing 747 took off on schedule from Dallas carrying passengers and a supply of Texan cowboy hats to pass out to English VIPs on arrival at Gatwick, the first-ever transatlantic flight operated by American Airlines.

Since then American has spread its wings across Europe and now flies to ten European cities in seven countries including London Heathrow and Gatwick, Paris Charles De Gaulle, Brussels, Frankfurt, Rome and Zurich.

Product

The airline has built its success on the tradition of providing great service to all its passengers both in-flight and on the ground.

Perhaps the most important aspect of its product is its route network. American competes in one of the fiercest markets, transatlantic from Heathrow, but it also serves Gatwick, Manchester, Glasgow, Paris, Frankfurt, Madrid, Zurich, Brussels and Rome.

American offers the most comprehensive network of flights across the US and to Mexico, Canada, the Caribbean, the Bahamas, South and Central America. All flights from Europe are timed to meet convenient connecting flights to a host of onward destinations.

On-board, American has set new standards for the quality of its service and the level of comfort. The most recent innovation is the Flagship Suite® on its Boeing 777 aircraft. The airline has extensively redesigned its First Class accommodation to offer a host of benefits to suit the business traveller. Not only does the seat turn into a 6'6" flat bed, and is wider than other airlines, it also swivels, so travellers can turn to face their companion.

A guest seat means someone else can join you to dine or work, and two large tables offer a bigger surface to work with. In the centre row, two Flagship Suites and their guest seats can turn into a table for four, for work or pleasure.

As well as this extraordinary flexibility, the traveller can further recreate the office environment with a laptop power port, satellite phone and modem connection.

The airline has also extensively improved its Business Class cabin. It has redesigned it to provide an extra 9-12 inches of space between seats, giving travellers five feet of personal space.

The seat can be moulded for each passenger, with controls for lumbar support, footrest and a six-way leather headrest. There is a personal

Fewer seats. More room to yourself.

American Airlines

video with ten-channel programming (on the Boeing 777) and a DVD player (on the Boeing 767).

As with First Class, there is also a laptop power port and satellite phone for the business passenger needing to work en route.

American Airlines has set a new standard in comfort for Economy Class passengers. The airline has removed seats from Economy Class, expanding space from the present industry standard of 31-32 inches, to predominantly 34 inches of space per seat.

American Airlines believes in being something special on the ground as well as in the air. It was the first airline to introduce a VIP lounge when it opened the first Admirals Club at New York's LaGuardia airport in 1939. Today the Admirals Clubs and Flagship Lounges form a network of 40 airport lounges. Open to First and Business Class transatlantic travellers, they offer a comfortable, quiet retreat away from the bustling airport terminal. Passengers benefit from office facilities, showers, and refreshments. American Airlines was also the first US carrier to introduce an Arrivals Lounge for passengers to use after a flight. American Airlines operates purpose-built arrivals lounges at London Heathrow and Paris Charles de Gaulle where passengers can grab a snack, a shower, use the conference area or business facilities and even work out in a fully-equipped gym.

American Airlines set another industry first with the introduction of the AAdvantage travel awards programme. It is the largest of its kind and was designed to reward frequent flyers of American Airlines. Launched in 1981 with 283,000 members, it has now grown to more than 45 million members worldwide. AAdvantage members can earn mileage credit by flying with American Airlines, American Eagle and other airline participants. Members can also earn mileage credit from other AAdvantage programme participants including hotels and car hire companies.

Recent Developments

American Airlines already makes extensive use of the internet, with its award-winning AA.com website, recognised as one of the largest e-commerce sites in the world. However recently, the airline has expanded its online offering by launching local websites in the UK, France, Germany, Spain, Switzerland, Italy and Belgium. The aim of these sites is to distil the huge amount of information available on AA.com and provide a site of relevance to the local user. Information on the local schedule, fleet, airport facilities as well as locally relevant offers is provided.

In the UK, travellers can now buy American's best fares in both Business and Economy directly online. Subscribers to American Airlines' e-mail service can also benefit from monthly alerts promoting special low fares, available at short notice.

The airline has also recently introduced some important operational changes from the UK. Almost all of the transatlantic fleet is now Boeing 777, including all flights from Heathrow and most flights out of Gatwick.

American has worked to improve its schedule times, particularly between New York and London. The airline now offers the first flight leaving Heathrow for New York and the last flight to leave New York for London.

Promotion

Over the years, American Airlines' marketing has attracted widespread acclaim, contributing to its Business Superbrand status. Its last advertising campaign, 'Fewer seats, more room', won several awards, including a Bronze at the advertising 'oscars' in Cannes and Gold awards in the Best Business Television and Best Multi-Media categories of the Chartered Institute of Marketing's Travel Industry Awards.

Much of this success is the result of careful research, conducted in the early stages of American Airlines' brand development in the UK. This research revealed that British business travellers enjoy the 'can-do' attitude, dedication to customer service and general feeling of freedom that the US offers.

Research has also revealed that the airline's customers see these values reflected in American Airlines. Consequently, they have been a recurring theme in the airline's advertising.

For example, in autumn 2002, American ran a press campaign to promote its New York schedule. Unusual and quirky images of New York captured a city that travellers could only experience if they were there early in the morning or late at night.

More recent research suggests that travellers appreciate emotional as well as physical room and that American, with its relaxed professionalism and American-style service can give passengers exactly this – namely more room to themselves.

The recent campaign launched in August 2003, is a natural progression from the previous two years' focus on 'Fewer seats, more room', in which American promoted the removal of seats from all its cabins to give passengers more room.

With this campaign, American reaches travellers through press, outdoor, online and ambient media. There has also been an extensive PR campaign, spearheaded by national research into where the

British public likes to go most when they need some 'room to themselves'.

The brand message is taken through the line, with direct mail and electronic marketing campaigns.

The campaign has been developed by a British creative team (at McCann Erikson) and was shot by a British photographer (John Offenbach) in New York.

Brand Values

With extreme competition in the marketplace of transatlantic travel, American offers an alternative to the national 'favourites', each with their own distinct characteristics.

Key values to the American Airlines brand are the best traditions of American hospitality (relaxed but always professional), a can-do attitude, innovative use of technology, and a desire for its customers to enjoy both a physical and emotional freedom on board. The airline sees air travel as a time to be your own person, to have some room to yourself, away from the demands of the world. It aims to be the airline that helps travellers achieve this.

www.americanairlines.co.uk

Things you didn't know about
American Airlines

American Airlines was the first US airline to recognise the importance of offering daily transatlantic flights from UK regional airports such as Manchester and Glasgow.

American Airlines introduced the world's first loyalty programme in 1981 with AAdvantage.

American Airlines' engineers drew up the specifications for a new aircraft in the 1930s, the DC-3. It became one of the most famous commercial airplanes in history and American Airlines was the first airline to fly it on a commercial service.

American Airlines developed Sabre in 1964, the first computerised reservations system in airline history.

On an average day American Airlines 113,000 employees will receive more than 338,000 reservation calls, handle more than 293,000 pieces of luggage, serve more than 200,000 meals and snacks, fly more than 2,400 flights and change more than 70 airplane tyres.

BARCLAYCARD

Market

Barclaycard, the UK's leading issuer and acquirer of credit, debit and commercial cards, operates in an increasingly complex market. The UK is the most developed credit and debit card market in Europe and second in the world after the US. Half the adult population has at least one card and the number is forecast to rise from 58.8 million in 2002 to 98.2 million by 2007 (Source: Datamonitor 2003). It is also one of the most competitive. Over the last ten years the range of issuers and products has increased dramatically.

In the early 1990s, some of the big American issuers such as MBNA and Capital One entered the market. From standard/classic cards, customers were then offered Gold and Platinum cards, each usually offering a range of exclusive services. Competition was further intensified as supermarkets started offering personal finance products and new online issuers, offered 0% interest on balance transfers.

A further feature has been consolidation. Although there are 2,000 different cards in the marketplace, there are fewer issuers behind them. Barclaycard, for example, also owns Monument (formerly Providian). The market also faces other

Barclaycard Merchant Services is one of Europe's largest acquirers and processors of plastic card transactions and in 2002 processed 1.4 billion card transactions giving it a 35% market share in the UK. In 1986 Barclaycard Merchant Services was the first operation to process transactions electronically through its PDQ brand. Today it is a leader in card payment technology and solutions. It boasts the UK's largest bank-owned PDQ Online electronic fund transfer network with 160,000 terminals in 230,000 outlets. Overall it authorises more than 300 transactions a second. Total group turnover in 2002 was more than £1.5 billion yielding pre-tax profits of £615 million.

The brand has won a string of awards especially for its humorous advertising. These include a Gold Lion at the prestigious Cannes International Advertising Festival in 1991 and a Gold at the IPA Advertising Effectiveness Awards five years later. Furthermore, in 2002 Business Moneyfacts magazine voted the brand best Company Chargecard.

History

Barclaycard became the UK's first credit card when it was unveiled in 1966, three years later

Barclaycard Merchant Services was also the first to enable credit card payments over the internet in 1997. The following year it launched the EPDQ – internet payment solution. A further key development took place in 2000 with the launch of 'Enable'. This service gave UK retailers and businesses the ability to trade online.

Product

Barclaycard can be used to pay for goods and services in more than 22 million outlets in over 200 countries and to withdraw cash from over 600,000 ATM's and banks worldwide. The Barclaycard portfolio consists of: Classic, Gold, Platinum, MasterCard, Student and Premiership. Each card offers services specifically tailored to suit the user. With Barclaycard Classic services range from up to eight weeks interest free credit to complimentary travel accident insurance.

Company Barclaycard allows simple, cost-effective management of business travel expenditure and frees staff from the paperwork often associated with expenses. It enables businesses to pay for travel expenses such as airline tickets, car hire, hotels and restaurants and provides a range of

issues such as the prospect of regulatory changes over card payments and fraud which, in a market worth £48 billion, is a serious problem.

Barclaycard is aware of the challenges it faces in this huge and busy market. But its pre-eminent position means it is clearly strongly placed to meet them.

Achievements

Barclaycard International is Europe's leading issuer of credit cards with 10.4 million customers and twelve million cards in circulation worldwide. It operates in 62 countries across Europe, Africa and the Caribbean and in the UK has over nine million customers which means one-in-five card holders carry a Barclaycard. Since 1999 the brand's primary focus has been Europe, concentrating on Germany, France, Spain and Greece. A successful Italian launch in May 2002 strengthened the brand's international presence.

The brand's commercial card subsidiary Company Barclaycard is the UK's leading issuer of Visa commercial credit cards. It services businesses of all sizes from multinationals and Government departments to small and medium sized enterprises (SME's). Company Barclaycard has more than 142,000 corporate customers and 500,000 cardholders.

The majority of card transactions are now processed electronically through a card acquirer.

it introduced its corporate brand Company Barclaycard. In 1986 Barclaycard launched Profiles, the UK's first loyalty scheme. Early on the brand recognised the potential of the internet and in 1995 was the first in the sector to go online with Barclaycard Netlink. It simultaneously notched up another first with the introduction of the online shopping mall BarclaySquare. Two years later the brand pioneered the payment of bills over the internet; as a result more than one million customers regularly use Barclaycard's online account services.

Company Barclaycard which became a stand-alone brand in 1974 was the first commercial card issuer to recognise the demand for gold and silver card variants in 1991. Seven years later it became the first issuer to develop a co-branded card for clients BTI UK Hogg Robinson and in 2001 was the first issuer to issue chip cards to businesses to protect against fraud.

Barclaycard Merchant Services first entered the UK payments market in 1966 when it signed up 30,000 retailers for the launch of Barclaycard. In 1986 it was the first to process transactions electronically using Barclaycard's registered PDQ brand. Barclaycard Merchant Services has remained a market leader and at the forefront of innovation in Point of Sale technology. Indeed, in 2001 Barclaycard Merchant Services launched both mobile and portable PDQ terminals.

added-value services. Company Barclaycard's product range has grown to meet the diverse demands of all UK business customers, from start-ups to the largest corporate. The card is carried by more than 500,000 UK business people, accepted at 660,000 places in the UK and 24 million outlets worldwide. The Corporate Card is designed for businesses with a high level of UK and international travel and entertainment spend, that need detailed management information. The Business Card has been developed for operations that need a card for everyday expenses while the Purchasing Card was introduced to help large organisations streamline their high volume, low cost procurement. In addition, the Lodge Account was created for larger organisations with a high level of travel expenditure, especially by air.

Card fraud is a major problem in the UK. Proceeds from card fraud are used to fund organised crime and the cost is felt by the retail and banking industries alike. Barclaycard Merchant Services is helping its retailers use a 'Chip and PIN' system to make it safer, quicker and easier to accept credit and debit cards. The company also provides the latest Chip-enabled point-of-sale equipment. It is thought that this will lead to a reduction in retrieval requests, less time spent checking signatures, a reduction in chargebacks and administration and, most importantly, protection from fraud for retailers.

Barclaycard Merchant Services was the first UK acquirer to provide its customers with '3D-Secure' – a technology which supports the secure ePDQ online payments system, Verified by Visa (VbV), which is a cutting-edge initiative to combat online fraud. With 3D-Secure technology now in place, Barclaycard Merchant Services can help retailers trade online without fraud liability.

85% of all newly purchased mobile phones are pre-pay, and it is estimated there are 33 million UK pre-pay customers. Barclaycard Merchant Services now offers 'E-Top Up' technology to help retailers boost sales, reduce theft and improve cash flow.

Recent Developments

Barclaycard continues to offer an innovative range of products which are competitively priced. In April 2001 the brand introduced the Price Promise. The service refunds the difference if branded goods are bought cheaper elsewhere. Twelve months later Barclaycard launched Nectar, a new loyalty scheme with partners Sainsbury's, BP and Debenhams as well as Ford, Thresher, Vodafone and adams. Nectar has become the UK's biggest loyalty scheme and boasts more than thirteen million active collectors. Barclaycard customers earn Nectar points by using their card and when shopping at partner outlets can therefore effectively earn double points.

The Barclaycard Premiership, a deal which secured the brand's global sponsorship of the FA Premiership until 2004, has helped to accelerate the brand's international and domestic growth.

In the competitive balance transfer market Barclaycard devised a new product offering 0% interest for the life of the transferred balance.

Its sponsorship of the FA Premiership has enabled the brand to offer a special card for football fans with a range of soccer related discounts and deals.

Promotion

Barclaycard has always used a broad range of media to communicate with its customers. For a brand

with no high-street or on-shelf presence, the salience resulting from high profile, popular advertising campaigns is vitally important. This presence over the years, from a number of high profile campaigns featuring Dudley Moore, Alan Whicker, Rowan Atkinson and Angus Deayton, has given the brand stature, international credentials and authority. This reassurance of customers and prospective customers is very important in a market where the dark side of debt leaves people looking to brands for security and confidence.

Over the years brand advertising has highlighted a variety of new products and services helping position the product as the 'added value' card against a growing number of low cost competitors.

The Purchase Cover commercial, for example, featured Atkinson as an accident-prone jet setter who, in one execution, set fire to a costly oriental rug.

Recent TV, press and poster advertising campaigns have highlighted the major launch of Barclaycard's involvement with the Nectar loyalty scheme and new pricing initiatives to help keep brand perceptions positive.

The high profile three-year £48 million sponsorship of the FA Premiership in 2001 gave Barclaycard the opportunity to enhance further its stature and salience, particularly amongst young consumers. The Barclaycard Premiership which opens a range of commercial opportunities for the brand also adds a set of highly competitive new values, injecting it with dynamism, relevance and prestige. The sponsorship and its associated benefits like the Premiership Barclaycard was

announced through poster and TV advertising, football programme ads and PR.

Against a backdrop of popular advertising and one of the world's biggest sponsorship properties, Barclaycard has expertise and experience in direct communication to its customers. Through statements, mailings and through its online channels customers are kept up to date with their account and the latest products and benefits the brand has to offer. While not often considered one of the 'new breed' of online cards, over one million Barclaycard customers are currently registered to the brand's MyAccount online service.

Barclaycard Merchant Services and Company Barclaycard have developed their own promotional blueprint to meet the ever changing demands of the brand's business customers. A broad range of marketing strategies have been employed to drive business in each sector. For SME's the Barclays Branch network and direct marketing remain the bedrock using customer data to identify core needs. For larger businesses, the strategy to target decision makers in finance/procurement functions incorporates press, exhibitions, PR and a dedicated sales team to manage the face-to-face approach required.

Brand Values

Barclaycard owns a set of highly distinctive brand values in the credit card market. The strongest of these and those which best set it apart from competitors are the brand's stature, worldly-wise authority and international credentials. Whilst a growing number of competitors are beginning to build brand values of their own these new entrants by comparison to Barclaycard are seen as less worldly, lacking heritage in credit and as a result, appear to many as less reassuring. Barclaycard, in contrast, is trustworthy and reliable.

www.barclaycard.co.uk

BARCLAYS

Market

Barclays is one of the largest financial services groups in the UK and competes in the banking, investment banking and investment management sectors.

It services almost a quarter of the UK business banking market, working for more than half of Britain's top 100 companies. It is also a major player in the small and medium sized business banking market, supporting over half a million SMEs in the UK. Barclays is also a leading provider of co-ordinated global services to multinational corporations and financial institutions worldwide; operating in over 60 countries with well over 70,000 employees.

Barclays is a leader in several other banking sectors. For example, Barclays Global Investors is the world's biggest institutional asset manager. It is one of the world's top five internet banks and, with Barclaycard, it has the leading credit card operation in Europe. It also has an increasingly strong presence in the global investment banking sector with Barclays Capital.

Achievements

Barclays has grown from a London partnership to a global bank represented in Africa, Asia, Australasia, the Caribbean (with FirstCaribbean), Europe, Latin America, the Middle East and the US.

It has been at the forefront of many important innovations in the banking industry, such as its launch of the UK's first credit card in 1966, the first telephone banking service Barclaycall in 1994 and online PC banking in 1997. It has also launched a raft of customised services, such as Barclays Private Bank and Premier Banking.

Barclays investment banking division, Barclays Capital, has been a particular success. Since its inception in 1997, Barclays Capital has focused on its key businesses in bonds, loans and risk management products such as convertible bonds, derivatives and commodities trading. The expertise it has developed has been recognised by the broadest spectrum of clients, including governments, multinationals, financial institutions and corporate borrowers.

Its strong performance has been reflected by some high-profile awards, including being named 'Loan House of the Year 2002' by The Banker magazine and 'Most Improved Investment Bank' in the Euromoney Awards for Excellence 2002.

Overall, the Barclays Group has won over 40 awards in 2002/03, including 'Best Service Provider' by Charity Finance in May 2002 and

'Bank Borrower of the Year' at the prestigious International Finance Review Awards, 2002. The bank was also named 'Best Leasing and Asset Finance Provider' in the 2002 and 2003 Business Money Facts awards.

Barclays' contribution to the community has also been a notable achievement. In 2002 Barclays' global commitment to the community amounted to £32 million, 1% of UK pre-tax profits. Activities such as this have helped make Barclays one of the UK's largest corporate community contributors.

History

Barclays origins can be traced back to a modest business founded more than 300 years ago in the heart of London's financial district.

In the late seventeenth century, the streets of the City of London may not have been paved with gold, but they were filled with goldsmith-bankers. They provided monarchs and merchants with

1959: Barclays is the first UK bank to buy a computer.

 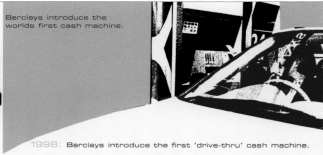

1967: Barclays introduce the worlds first cash machine.

1998: Barclays introduce the first 'drive-thru' cash machine.

the money they needed to fund their ventures around the world.

One such business was founded by John Freame and his partner Thomas Gould in Lombard Street in 1690. The name Barclay became associated with the company in 1736, when James Barclay – who had married John Freame's daughter – became a partner.

Private banking businesses were commonplace in the eighteenth century, keeping their clients' gold deposits secure and lending to credit-worthy merchants. In 1896, twenty of them formed a new joint-stock bank.

The leading partners of the new bank, which was named Barclay and Company, were already connected by a web of family, business and religious relationships. The company became known as the Quaker Bank, because this was the religion of the founding families.

The new bank had 182 branches, mainly in the East and South East, and deposits of £26 million – a substantial sum of money in those days. It expanded its branch network rapidly by taking over other banks, including Bolithos in the South West in 1905 and United Counties Bank in the Midlands in 1916.

In 1918 the company amalgamated with the London, Provincial and South Western Bank to become one of the UK's 'big five' banks. By 1926 the bank had 1,837 outlets.

Barclays acquired Martins Bank in 1969, the largest UK bank to have its head office outside London. And in 2000 it took over The Woolwich, a leading mortgage bank and former building society founded in 1847.

The development of today's global business began in earnest in 1925, with the merger of three banks – the Colonial Bank, the Anglo Egyptian Bank and the National Bank of South Africa to form Barclays international operations. This added businesses in much of Africa, the Middle East and the West Indies.

Barclays' global expansion was given added impetus in 1986 with the creation of an investment banking operation. This has developed into Barclays Capital, a major division of the bank that now manages larger corporate and institutional business.

In 1995 Barclays purchased the fund manager Wells Fargo Nikko Investment Advisers. The business was integrated with BZW Investment Management to form Barclays Global Investors.

Product

Barclays has a wide range of services and equally broad knowledge of its business customers' activities.

With this, it aims to provide the right support for businesses at each end of the spectrum, from helping entrepreneurs get a new company off the ground, to managing the complexities of a large blue chip organisation.

Barclays is organised into seven business groupings: Barclays Africa; Barclaycard; Barclays Capital; Barclays Global Investors; Barclays Private Clients; Business Banking and Personal Financial Services.

Barclays Capital is focused on minimising its clients' cost of funding and broadening their investor base in the process. It runs one of the largest inflation-linked bond franchises and devotes considerable resources to this important segment of the fixed income market. Already, it has earned widespread recognition for its expertise and innovation in this asset class.

Barclays' Business Banking works closely with

small and large businesses to provide practical business solutions and the highest level of customer service. There are a number of ways that Barclays' support can help businesses to prosper, such as providing tailored financing options, including working capital and finance for the acquisition of premises and other fixed assets. Choices include capital repayment holidays, fixed or variable interest rates and a wide variety of terms.

Barclays has a substantial range of financial products designed to help businesses ensure their money works harder over the short or longer term. An example is the recently introduced Business Base Tracker Account, designed for small and medium sized businesses.

Customers can also benefit from Barclays' electronic banking services, such as BusinessMaster, which provides direct access to bank accounts from a desktop PC. This gives customers an up-to-date picture of their banking position and enables many banking transactions to be initiated online.

For smaller businesses, Barclays has more than 1,500 specially trained staff dedicated to start-up and small business customers.

For medium sized businesses, customers can benefit from Barclays' extensive locally based expertise with both a dedicated relationship manager and support team.

For large businesses, customers gain from Barclays' extensive industry expertise. The bank serves over 40 industry sectors throughout England and Wales, from law and education to aerospace and property. Each sector has a dedicated team with three named points of contact, which understands customers' specific operating environments and adds value through specialist knowledge and expertise.

An important part of Barclays' service in this area is helping ailing businesses to recover. The Barclays Business Support unit has over 70 managers around the country focused on returning ailing business to financial health. In 2002, to help achieve this, the unit lent £200 million of new money.

Recent Developments
In 2002, working with NFEA, Barclays ran 379 Start-Right Seminars for people thinking about starting their own business, with a further 350 planned during 2003. These supplement the Kick-Start seminars which Barclays also run to

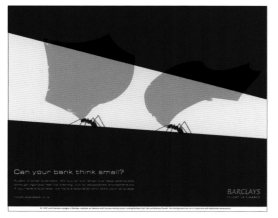

ensure that new businesses get off on the right foot and have access to free advice.

In 2001 Barclays further strengthened its product offering by forming a strategic alliance with Legal & General to sell life pensions and investment products throughout its UK network.

Promotion
Barclays has recently embarked on a new advertising approach which challenges the way that banks present themselves. The national campaign was deliberately thought-provoking; concentrating on what bank customers focus on most – money.

The advertisements, created by the advertising agency BBH, directed by top director Jonathan Glazer and starring Hollywood superstar Samuel L Jackson, revealed that people talk about money in many different ways – and Barclays understands them all because it is 'Fluent in Finance'.

Research revealed that UK people are highly advertising-literate, as well as sophisticated about their banking needs, Barclays deliberately adopted a thought-provoking, not hand-holding approach. It recognises that customers want to

Good things come in threes.

With Barclays Business Banking you can have three named contacts who know you and your business.

BARCLAYS
FLUENT IN FINANCE

talk to a bank which knows what it is doing and has the ability to 'make things happen'. The second phase of the Fluent in Finance advertising campaign was launched in April 2003, demonstrating how Barclays money expertise brings value to customers. The new campaign builds on the success of the first, and also stars Samuel L Jackson. It is fully integrated, comprising TV, press, and promotions. It encompasses the range of Barclays offerings in savings and investments, business banking and consumer banking.

The new campaign builds on the theme launched last year – that Barclays is expert at the management of money. This year the advertising illustrates how Barclays is 'Fluent in Finance'. In one of the most recent elements of the programme, Barclays unveiled the UK's largest ever station advertising installation at Bank tube station. The installation, which takes the form of an evolving educational exhibition exploring themes and thoughts to do with money, will last until June 2004.

Occupying 75% of the station the exhibition initially comprises of famous quotes about money – from people such as Henry Ford, Spike Milligan and George Bernard Shaw – a history of money and interesting money stories and facts.

As well as innovative projects like this, Barclays also builds its brand through sponsorship. In 2002

the company entered into a five-year agreement for the title sponsorship of The Barclays Scottish Open, played at the prestigious Loch Lomond Golf Club in the west of Scotland. The tournament is televised by BBC Television with a potential worldwide audience reach of 400 million homes and more than 500 hours of broadcasting.

Brand Values
The Barclays brand is built upon the breadth of its operations across many continents, servicing twenty million customers, and in the depth of its involvement with these customers.

Its experience, built up over 300 years, enables it to make the complex seem simple. This breadth and depth of experience, and the benefits it offers through being the banking sector's leading money expert is key to its 'Fluent in Finance' brand positioning.

Also central to the Barclays brand is the company's aspiration to be one of the most admired financial services organisations in the world, recognised as an innovative, customer-focused company that delivers world-class products and services, ensuring excellent careers for its staff and contributing positively to the community.

www.barclays.co.uk

BASF

Market

BASF is the world's leading chemical company. In 2002 it was sighted to be the world's most admired chemical company by Fortune magazine. In addition, Chemical Insight magazine ranked BASF as the number one chemical company in terms of sales for 2002.

BASF deals with customers in more than 170 countries and supplies approximately 8,000 products to a wide range of industries worldwide. Its products include high-value-added chemicals, plastics, colourants and pigments, dispersions, automotive and industrial coatings, crop-protection agents, fine chemicals, oil and gas.

Major customers for BASF products come from the agricultural, automotive, chemical, energy and construction industries. Important sectors also include the health, nutrition, electrical, electronics, textiles, packaging and paper industries.

BASF's strength is not only that it has an extremely broad product range, but it also supplies an extraordinary number of different industries. This balance makes the company relatively resilient to factors affecting individual industries.

BASF also supplies these individual industries with a wide range of products. The automotive and transportation industries for example, purchase coating systems and many types of plastics as well as antifreeze, brake fluids and fuel additives.

BASF has about 90,000 employees worldwide and operates production facilities in 38 countries. In 2002 worldwide sales totalled 32.2 billion euros.

In the UK, fibre intermediates, pharmaceutical active ingredients, printing inks, polyurethane raw materials, and vitamins and mineral premixes for animal feed are all manufactured at BASF plants.

Achievements

When Friedrich Engelhorn founded the company back in 1865, he had a vision – to bring dye research and production under one roof. Each production facility would be linked to other plants so that the products and leftover material from one plant could serve as raw materials in the next.

The original site in Ludwigshafen, Germany, is today the world's largest chemical complex. All 350 plants are connected to others by at least one product or process stage.

The crux of what BASF does is to take a few raw materials and use them to manufacture several dozen basic materials, which in turn are used to produce several hundred intermediates. After passing through a network of value-added production chains, these intermediates give rise to approximately 8,000 different products.

BASF uses raw materials, energy and intermediates efficiently, re-uses by-products and residual materials, and keeps the distances that substances need to be transported to a minimum. This reduces the impact on the environment and saves money.

The company also has a history of scientific innovation. It produced the first synthetic dyes,

including the indigo used to colour jeans, the first polystyrene and the first magnetic recording tape. Furthermore, a BASF employee won a Nobel Prize for helping to develop the process for synthesising ammonia, which led to synthetic production of nitrogen fertilisers. Today BASF is a world leader in new fields of development such as biotechnology and nanotechnology.

As a founding member of the United Nations' Global Compact initiative, BASF is committed to promoting and implementing the Compact's nine principles concerning the safeguarding of human rights, labour and environmental standards. As a sign of its commitment to the Global Compact,

BASF carries out partnership projects with public sector organisations and Non Government Organisations (NGOs).

In a joint project with the United Nations Environment Programme (UNEP) and the United Nations Industrial Development Organization (UNIDO), BASF is helping textile dye companies in Morocco to work more efficiently and in a more environmentally friendly way.

BASF withstood the weak business situation in 2002 and, contrary to the general trend, considerably increased income from operations due to a cyclically resilient portfolio and restructuring measures implemented in 2001. It has significantly reduced costs, streamlined the organisation and further sharpened its customer focus.

In sight of these achievements Fortune, one of the world's leading international business magazines, has ranked BASF as the world's most admired chemical company.

History

BASF, originally known as Badische Anilin & Soda-Fabrik, was founded in Germany in 1865 to produce coal tar dyes and precursors.

Soaring population growth led to strong demand for dyes, and within a few decades BASF had gained a leading position in the world dye market. It produced the first synthetic indigo in 1897, and in 1901 came another pioneering development, the exceptionally lightfast and wash fast indanthrene dyes which soon took over the supremacy of indigo in dyeing and printing.

Early research into nitrogen, and the development of the Haber-Bosch process between 1908-12, ushered in a new phase in the history of the company and of the chemical industry. This process allowed atmospheric nitrogen to be combined with hydrogen at high pressure and temperature, and with the use of catalysts, to form ammonia. This paved the way to the synthetic production of nitrogen fertilisers and opened up new opportunities in process engineering.

Following the success of the motor car in the 1920s, BASF invested heavily in the development of fuels, synthetic rubber, surface coatings, and other products for the automotive industry.

The 1930s saw the beginning of the plastics era. BASF produced the first polystyrene in 1930 and BASF researchers created a sensation with another pioneering invention: the Magnetophon, which had been developed in co-operation with AEG. This led to a 60-year period of manufacturing magnetic tape – BASF's most famous consumer product, until the business was sold in 1997.

The 1950s saw nylon become a bestseller and in 1951 BASF developed Styropor, a white rigid foam with an air content of 98%. Its light weight and high insulating capability made it an ideal insulation material in the construction industry as well as for packaging fragile goods and deep-frozen products.

In the 1960s, BASF began systematically building or acquiring production sites around the world, including several in the UK. It developed into a transnational company focused primarily on Europe, the US, Latin America and the Far East.

From 1965 onwards, company policy was geared to adding consumer products and other high value-added lines to the product range. Companies were acquired or founded to produce end products such as surface coatings, pharmaceuticals, crop protection agents and fertilisers. In the UK BASF acquired the pharmaceutical business of Boots, the polypropylene business of ICI and the textile dyes business of Zeneca.

In recent years portfolio rationalisation and a strategy of concentrating on core businesses has resulted in a number of divestitures, including the sale of the tapes business to Emtec in 1997 and the pharmaceutical business to Abbott Laboratories in 2000.

Product

BASF's products are organised in five segments – Chemicals, Plastics, Performance Products, Agricultural Products & Nutrition, and Oil & Gas.

The company uses its integrated approach to produce a full range of chemicals. BASF is one of the leading global producers of styrenics, engineering plastics and polyurethanes.

Its broad range of Performance Products includes high-value performance chemicals, coatings and

BASF is playing an active role in the development of fuel cell cars. A new high performance BASF catalyst helps to provide problem-free energy supply in the NECAR 5, DaimlerChrysler's prototype electric car. The catalyst converts liquid methanol into the hydrogen needed by the fuel cell.

Simple, safe, and environmentally friendly. Just one way that BASF, the leading chemical group, is developing alternative concepts to ensure continued mobility and sustainable energy.
e-mail: info.service@basf-plc.co.uk
Fax: 0161 488 4133, www.basf.co.uk

The Segments of BASF:
Chemicals, Plastics & Fibers,
Performance Products,
Agricultural Products & Nutrition,
Oil & Gas

Thinking innovatively. Acting responsibly.

BASF

functional polymers for the automotive, oil, paper, packaging, textile, sanitary care, construction, coatings, printing and leather industries.

In addition, BASF is a major supplier of agricultural products and fine chemicals to the farming, food processing, animal and human nutrition and personal care industries. In plant biotechnology, the company is developing plants that are less sensitive to drought or are more nutritious.

A BASF subsidiary explores and produces crude oil and natural gas. Together with a Russian partner it markets, distributes and trades natural gas in Central and Eastern Europe.

Recent Developments

Innovations are a decisive tool for BASF when it comes to shaping a promising and profitable future. Indeed, approximately 1.1 billion euros was invested in research and development in 2002. BASF is

among the top five companies in Europe for patent applications and currently the brand has more than 110,000 patents and patent applications.

To optimise its portfolio, BASF is expanding highly profitable businesses and concentrating on core competencies. Cost leadership is also crucial to the brand's long-term competitiveness, with integrated large-scale plants being one of the company's greatest strengths.

BASF aims to become a preferred partner through co-operation with key customers. In response to cost pressures in the commodities business, the brand is turning to e-commerce, while in its non-commodities business it is expanding customer services to create added value for customers.

Co-operative research and development agreements are also undertaken with innovative customers while building local production capacities in growth markets is also crucial to BASF's strategy.

In order to serve customers quickly and efficiently, European marketing and sales activities have been organised into regional operative units that are also responsible for production. The regional business centres that support strategic marketing activities work closely with these units and are also responsible for promoting synergies within the region and providing business services.

Promotion

BASF undertakes corporate advertising and communication worldwide. A European advertising campaign designed to strengthen the corporate brand has been running in the UK since 2001.

Ads in the national and business press promote the brand to decision-makers in business and industry, opinion formers and the financial community, as well as suppliers, customers, potential customers and customers' customers.

Recent ads have featured catalysts for hydrogen fuel cell cars, a project to reduce household energy consumption, and agricultural research based on nature.

The campaign, which uses the slogan 'Thinking innovatively. Acting responsibly', focuses on the fact that BASF not only has good ideas, but also puts them into practice in a responsible manner.

BASF has also been actively promoting its products to B2B audiences in the UK for many years. In addition to advertising in trade magazines, the company has been prominent at trade exhibitions and has produced a number of publications for customers, including plastics and coatings magazines as well as a long running magazine for farmers.

BASF has been involved in a number of sponsorships over the years in education, the arts and the industries it supplies. These have included awards for building and plastics design. BASF has been a sponsor of Manchester's Halle Orchestra for more than 30 years, and is also the sponsor of the BASF/Daily Telegraph Young Science Writer competition.

Brand Values

It is BASF's mission, as one of the world's most successful chemical companies, to be of value to people – to create value for the company, its customers, shareholders, employees, and the countries in which it operates.

BASF's corporate philosophy is based on the principle of sustainable development. Key to this approach is taking accountability for balancing business development with environmental protection and social responsibility.

By subscribing to the 'Responsible Care' initiative launched by the chemical industry, BASF has committed itself to steadfastly pursing improvements in the realms of environmental protection, health and safety as well as customer satisfaction.

In order to achieve this, it develops products, chemical processes and provides services of high scientific and technical levels to foster good partnerships with its customers. Economic considerations do not take priority over safety and health issues and environmental protection.

BASF is conducting a study of its corporate brand in order to assess how it is seen now and how the company would like to be seen in the future. Research has shown that 'sound', 'caring', 'reliable', 'trustworthy' and 'innovative' are among the images currently associated with the brand.

www.basf.com

Things you didn't know about BASF

BASF doesn't make tapes. It produced the first ever magnetic recording tape in 1934, and continued to manufacture tape until it sold the business in 1997.

Audio and video tapes never accounted for more than 1% of the turnover of this worldwide chemical company.

BASF made jeans fashion possible almost right from the beginning. The legendary German emigrant Levi Strauss had his riveted 'waist overalls' patented in 1873 at the time of California's great gold rush. In 1890, BASF was granted the patent to manufacture the blue synthetic (jeans) dye indigo on an industrial scale. Combined with the hard-wearing cotton fabric imported from the French city Nimes (de nimes = Denim), this added up to a fashion story with phenomenal success.

BASF supplies plastics, coatings and engine coolants to UK car manufacturers. BASF is the sole supplier of coatings to Rolls Royce Motors, and is also responsible for the flip-flop pigments that helps the TVR Tuscan change colour according to the angle at which it is viewed.

BASF's Carl Bosch and German chemist Fritz Haber won a Nobel Prize for their discovery in 1908 of a process for synthesising liquid ammonia. Agricultural historian Vaclav Smil, recently claimed that: "Industrial synthesis of ammonia from nitrogen and hydrogen has been of greater fundamental importance to the modern world than the invention of the airplane, nuclear energy, space flight or television".

Market

Since it was founded in 1982, BBH has demonstrated consistently strong year on year growth despite fluctuating market conditions and has grown during this time from one office in London's Soho to five offices, based in Singapore, Tokyo, New York and Sao Paulo with global billings of US$700 million. 2002 was another strong year for BBH which saw billings increase from £260 to £307 million in the UK through new business wins from ITV, Unilever, AEG, The Woolwich, Lindt, Sanford, Mentos and KFC. This was in stark contrast to the wider advertising industry which experienced a difficult year with expenditure on advertising falling for the second year running.

Achievements

BBH has a reputation for developing some of the industry's most creative advertising and after 21 years it is still working with its three founding clients, Audi, Interbrew and Levi's.

Creativity and effectiveness are the backbones of the business and the first of its ten beliefs which define the culture of the agency is 'The importance of creativity and the primacy of the idea'. Its work for Levi's is some of the agency's most famous, from the early TV ads such as Laundrette when Nick Kamen walked into a laundrette and took off his Levi 501s to the yellow puppet, Flat Eric and more recently, Odyssey which saw a girl and guy running through walls to classical music. Other famous work includes 'The Lynx Effect' campaigns for male body spray Lynx, the endline 'Vorsprung durch Teknik' for Audi, 'The Cream of Manchester' work for Boddingtons, the 'Play More' campaign for Xbox as well as the 'Fluent in Finance' campaign for Barclays featuring Samuel L Jackson.

Over the years BBH has won 32 IPA Effectiveness Awards, in each case demonstrating the contribution of advertising to its clients' businesses. In 2002 BBH won the IPA Grand Prix award for its work with children's charity Barnardo's as well as the coveted IPA Effectiveness Agency of the Year Award. In 2003 it won two Marketing Society Awards for marketing excellence on its Lynx and Olivio accounts and since 1993 has won nineteen APG Strategy Awards which recognise the importance of the development of brand strategy. BBH has twice won the Queen's Award

For Export for outstanding achievements in overseas earnings by a business in the UK.

Overall, BBH has been characterised by a consistency that few agencies can claim. Firstly, four of its founders are still active in the business today and its Departmental Heads each average nine years service. Secondly, BBH says that it is never satisfied. Although it has consistently won creative and effectiveness awards, it remains as hungry and ambitious today as it was in 1982 and is still committed to making its clients' brands famous.

truly outstanding work for like minded clients whilst having some fun in the process. A few months later they won the Audi, Whitbread Beer Company and Levi Strauss accounts which provided the foundation of their business. In 1986, BBH was also voted Campaign magazine's Agency of the Year, and won the title once again in 1993. In addition, BBH became the Cannes Advertising Festivals very first Agency of the Year in 1993 by winning more awards than any other agency. It also won the title again in 1994.

History

BBH was founded by John Bartle, Nigel Bogle and John Hegarty in London in 1982. The three had met eight years previously when they were each approached to start the UK office of TBWA. Having grown TBWA into one of the leading creative agencies in London and creating the winner of Campaign magazine's first ever Agency of the Year award, they decided to go it alone. Taking no business and just five people they set up BBH with the objective of producing

Throughout the 1980s and 1990s BBH won business from clients such as global players Unilever, Johnnie Walker and Polaroid as well as local UK clients like Barnardo's, Warburtons and Ginsters. 2000 to 2003 saw the agency add business from clients such as Barclays, Mentos, KFC, Woolworths, Bisto and Robinsons. Meanwhile it also opened offices overseas to service both global and local clients. The first was in Singapore in 1996 where BBH worked with clients such as Coca-Cola, Mercedes-Benz and Singtel locally, followed by

BBH New York in 1998. The agency works with clients such as ING Direct and Cantor Fitzgerald in the US, however the international nature of the company allows it to service global clients such as Levi's, Unilever and Johnnie Walker to name but a few. In 2003, BBH bought a minority share in Brazil's hottest advertising agency, Neogama, giving it a presence in each of the main global economic regions.

Product

BBH is an advertising agency structured to deliver through the line communications campaigns locally, internationally and globally. BBH aims to create fame for its clients' brands and to lead the world in creating shared noise and excitement around those brands to make them more valuable. In addition, it strives to create big brand ideas that drive hard business results. BBH is not a typical agency network. Instead it has an office in five key regional centres – London for Europe, New York for North America, Singapore and Tokyo for Asia Pacific and Sao Paulo for Latin America. These five regional hubs work collectively or independently, depending on the needs of the individual client. This five-office structure allows BBH the reach and

in-store music, through to music on video games. BBH has also hired a Director of Content to develop the area of advertiser-funded programming, a fast-growing new way for brands to engage with consumers by being part of TV programmes rather than just residing between them.

Promotion

BBH's own marketing is focused on the Business Development Unit which is responsible for internal and external communications. It is in charge of fostering new client contacts, using a number of tools such as direct mail, events and face to face

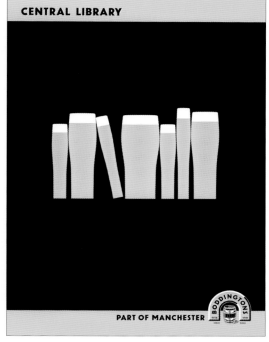

The right of everyone to be listened to.
The fundamental importance of effectiveness and accountability.
Processes that liberate creativity.
Client relationships that encourage equal status, allowing best advice.

operational efficiency to develop international or pan-regional communication solutions for brands. The priority is the creation of big ideas for brands; ideas that successfully engage, cross borders and unite consumers. Central to this model is the idea of operational flexibility. No two clients are the same so it develops solutions that are tailored to the needs of the brand and the client organisation. This is a major part of its competitive advantage and means that the agency is able to find solutions that have to be effective at any combination of global, regional and local levels. Currently 71% of the group's income derives from work which runs in more than one country.

Recent Developments

BBH also recognises the need to think to the future of advertising and has implemented a number of initiatives to take the agency into the next era of advertising, an era where consumers are ever more difficult to reach and where brands must engage and entertain rather than just interrupt consumers' media consumption. These include launching a music publishing arm, Leap Music which aims to make added revenue for BBH and its clients through owning the music tracks in ads. It has also launched Affinity Music, a venture which aims to build relationships between music and brands. Affinity works with advertisers to create music based marketing activity – anything from CD compilations to

meetings. It also looks after the agency's PR, building the agency's profile in the media. It produces a range of material to keep existing and prospective clients informed about the agency's work. These include the BBH website, booklets with information about the agency, a showreel of latest work, case histories on the work BBH has developed for its clients as well as PR cuttings books.

Brand Values

The first ad created by BBH was for the European launch of Black Levi's 501s. It featured a whole flock of white sheep walking in one direction whilst one black sheep faced the opposite direction and bore the legend 'When the world zigs, zag', encouraging individuals to think differently and to be aware that the obvious choice is not necessarily the best. For 21 years this has been BBH's mantra and it has aimed to forge a different path to that of other agencies. BBH do this in the way it approaches its own business, but more importantly it employs this philosophy in its approach to its clients' businesses. This has helped BBH produce category changing brand ideas and advertising.

At the heart of BBH is a set of ten beliefs which sums up the way the agency does business. Today they are etched in steel outside its meeting rooms. They are as follows;
The power of creativity and the primacy of the idea.
Encouraging ideas from any source.

An organisation without politics.
Providing opportunity, stimulation and consideration to all who work with us.
The need for honesty, decency and integrity in all that we do.
The obligations these beliefs place upon us.

www.bartleboglehegarty.com

Blue Circle™

Market

According to the latest figures from the British Cement Association, in 2002, over eleven million tonnes of cement were produced in the UK.

Lafarge Cement UK, the manufacturer of the Blue Circle Cement brand, currently supplies approximately 50% of the UK cement market with other key players in the UK including Castle cement and Rugby cement.

Lafarge Cement UK is part of the Lafarge Group, the worldwide leader in building materials with 85,000 employees in 75 countries. Lafarge also holds top-ranking positions in each of its four divisions, namely Cement, Aggregates & Concrete, Roofing and Gypsum.

Achievements

Lafarge Cement UK was awarded registration to the Eco-Management and Audit Scheme (EMAS) in 2001 – the first multi-site registration in Europe – in addition to accreditation to ISO 14001. Furthermore, Lafarge Cement UK was re-certificated under EMAS for 2002.

Aberthaw Works, Lafarge Cement UK's South Glamorgan plant, was 'runner up' in the Wales Environment Awards for companies with 50-250 employees in 2002. A reduction in its particulate emissions was also singled out in the Environment Agency's 'Spotlight on Business Performance' report in 2002. This reduction has been enhanced with the addition of a new dust filtering system, known as a Bag Filter, in January 2003.

Lafarge Cement UK was ranked in the upper quintile of the 122 companies featured in Business in the Community's Corporate Responsibility Index (known as the 'Premier League') with an overall score of over 83% by Business in the Community, compared to an average score of 67.87%. Lafarge Cement UK came equal first in the environmental category with a score of 100%.

Lafarge Cement integrates environmental considerations into all levels of its operations. The company's strategy is to achieve growth through efficient and sustainable development, setting new industry standards.

The core commitments in its environmental policy are to: comply with environmental legislation; continuously improve environmental performance; and contribute to long-term economic, environmental and social sustainability.

With the other members of the British Cement Association, the company was one of the country's first major energy consuming sectors to reach an agreement with the Government over reducing

its carbon dioxide emissions. The commitment is to cut emissions of greenhouse gases by more than a fifth of 1990 levels by 2010. Lafarge Cement plans to achieve the reductions in emissions through investment in new production equipment, increasing energy efficiency and increased use of alternative fuels such as scrap tyres and packaging waste which can be used in place of fossil fuels.

In addition, Lafarge Cements' operations are strictly monitored and controlled by the Government's environmental regulators.

History

Lafarge Cement UK has a history that stretches back to 1900, when 27 small cement manufacturers and their subsidiaries merged to form the Associated Portland Cement Manufacturers Ltd. The Blue Circle brand was introduced in 1928 and has become established as one of the most well-known cement brands in the world.

Since then, some of the UK's best known buildings have used Blue Circle Cement including The Channel Tunnel in Kent, Canary Wharf Development in London, G-Mex Centre, Manchester, The Tay Bridge, Dundee, The Millennium Stadium, Cardiff and The Foyle Bridge, Northern Ireland.

In 2001, Blue Circle Industries was taken over by the Lafarge Group to become part of the world's leading producer of cement and building materials. The UK cement making operations changed its company name to Lafarge Cement UK in early 2002, but retains the Blue Circle brand of cement which it manufactures and markets nationwide.

Product

Lafarge Cement UK produces a range of cement products throughout its nationwide network of

plants. The full Blue Circle product range includes:

Standard Cement – Blue Circle Ordinary Portland Cement (OPC) which is a general purpose cement suitable for all types of concrete, including structural concrete, mortars, renders and screeds. Blue Circle OPC is available in bags and bulk.

Enhanced Cement – this range mixes traditional cement with extra ingredients for specialist uses. Products within the range include Blue Circle Ferrocrete; Blue Circle Snowcrete; Blue Circle Sulfacrete; Blue Circle Phoenix; Blue Circle Lightning; Blue Circle Extra Rapid and Blue Circle Mastercrete Original.

Ready-To-Use – is a new range of products specifically designed to meet the requirements of builders and DIY enthusiasts by ensuring straightforward application and an excellent finish. Products in the Blue Circle Ready-To-Use range include Blue Circle Slablayer; Blue Circle Postcrete; Blue Circle Quality Assured Mortar Mix.

Renders – this includes a number of products for various uses, namely Blue Circle Rendaplus Colourtex S; Blue Circle Rendadash Backing Coat; Blue Circle Fibrocem GRC; Blue Circle Rendaplus; and Blue Circle Rendadash.

Recent Developments

In the past twelve months, Lafarge Cement UK has introduced a number of new product innovations into the market. For example, plastic packaging which is a pioneering bag design that protects bags and the products inside, from damage from water, mishandling and corrosive materials. Four Blue Circle products are now packed in plastic bags; Blue Circle Postcrete, Blue Circle Slablayer, Blue Circle Extra Rapid and Blue Circle Quality Assured Mortar Mix.

This revolutionary method of packaging cementitious products means that they can be stored outside, whether in a merchant's yard or on a building site. This offers significant benefits to merchants and end users alike. For merchants, there is the advantage of eliminating the need for extra waterproof protection when transporting products to the merchant yard. There is a minimal level of product wastage due to the high resistance these bags offer against damage by rain or tearing. Finally, the packaging provides the ability to cross-sell products by stocking the appropriate cementitious product outside alongside each other, for example, fence posts or paving slabs.

Benefits can also be seen by the consumers – the bags are easy to transport, alleviating concerns about bags being damaged. Furthermore, there

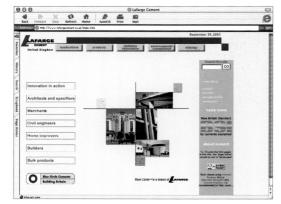

is no need for on-site storage as the bags can be left on site in all weathers. Cost savings are also made through reduced product wastage caused by damaged bags.

In June 2003, Blue Circle Quality Assured Mortar Mix was introduced to the range packaged in the innovative plastic bags. The product is designed to overcome the traditional problems caused by poor on-site mixing of mortar. As the latest addition to the Ready-to-Use product range, it offers a number of benefits to both merchants and end users. For merchants, it offers the benefit of being a quality assured product which requires minimal storage space compared to the separate elements required to mix traditional mortar.

Benefits for end users include the assurance of the high quality of the product, with no need for on-site mixing which leads to a reduced level of product wastage, usually caused by incorrect mixing. In turn this also guarantees consistent results.

In 2002, Lafarge Cement UK launched the Blue Circle cement Builder's Guide. This is a pocket-sized guide for builders that keeps them up-to-date on the latest Blue Circle product news as well as providing them with valuable application instructions.

The Guide includes a wealth of information for professional builders, such as facts on packed cement and pre-mixed products; guidance on appropriate applications for these products when used for concretes, mortars, renders and floor screeds; advice on recommended mixes; technical considerations during a project; as well as health and safety issues.

With the vast array of products available on today's market, the Blue Circle Builder's Guide is intended to help builders select the most suitable product for a specific job, and help them achieve the best results with it.

Promotion

Lafarge Cement UK supports the Blue Circle product range with ongoing promotional activity – in turn helping merchants to drive Blue Circle cement products through their stores and keeping end users up-to-date with the latest industry news.

Promotional activity typically covers a full range of media, including advertising in the trade press, carrying out direct mail campaigns, PR activities, in-store marketing communications and customer giveaways, as well as e-DM campaigns and website updates.

For the recent launch of Blue Circle Quality Assured Mortar Mix a four-month advertising campaign across the full spectrum of merchant and end user press was carried out in conjunction with the other promotional methods described above.

Blue Circle's latest advertising campaign again focuses on the benefits of the new Quality Assured Mortar and is designed to support sales of this

new product. The campaign is aimed at a range of audiences, from jobbing builders and housebuilders to those specialising in local authority work. The eye-catching advertisements, which launched in June 2003, appear in a range of leading trade titles to reflect the spectrum of the audience they are aimed at.

In conjunction with this, a high-profile public relations campaign was undertaken to highlight the product launch, helping to communicate the product benefits both to merchants and customers.

Direct mail is another important tool used in Blue Circle's promotional mix. A new direct mail campaign has therefore been devised to support the launch of Blue Circle Quality Assured Mortar. It comes in the form of a leaflet, which has been designed to introduce the product and explain its benefits. It was mailed to some 10,000 builders nationwide. The campaign includes a competition in which participants have the opportunity to win two tickets to the 2004 FA Cup Final at the Millennium Stadium in Cardiff, which was built using Blue Circle cement.

To support this activity, stockists of Lafarge Cement UK have unveiled a new range of colourful and informative point-of-sale dispensers, leaflets and posters. Each item aims to boost sales by focusing on the benefits that Blue Circle Quality Assured Mortar offers over traditional sand and cement.

To keep Blue Circle Quality Assured Mortar front-of-mind for end users, Lafarge Cement UK is giving away a number of promotional items, including branded lunch boxes, spirit levels, mugs and T-shirts.

Meanwhile online, the Lafarge Cement UK website, www.lafargecement.co.uk, contains up-to-date information on the launch of pre-packed mortar, as well as all other products in the Blue Circle range.

Brand Values

The Blue Circle brand stands for a number of values, most typically encapsulated by the words quality, trust, durability and the cement experts.

www.lafargecement.co.uk

bmi

Market

It is no exaggeration to say that the last few years have been unprecedented for the airline industry. General economic malaise was compounded by September 11th, which caused airline passenger figures to fall dramatically, leading to collapsing profits and mass redundancies. Even the most optimistic estimates speak of 100,000 job-losses industry-wide since the end of 2001.

The world's airlines are thought to have lost more than £7 billion from international services in the year after September 11th. American carriers, which have about half the world's aircraft, were the worst hit.

In addition, development and promotion costs which had escalated during the boom of the 1990s could no longer be sustained with the drop in higher-paying business customers, which opted to take economy tickets instead. In the late 1990s, business travellers accounted for just 9% of passengers, but generated 40% of revenues.

Since September 11th there have been wars in Afghanistan and Iraq, the Sars outbreak, and strikes by ground staff in the UK and France. Figures for April 2003 showed an 18.5% drop in global passenger traffic compared to the previous year, with Asia-Pacific carriers experiencing a 44.8% drop and North American carriers seeing traffic fall by 23.5%. However, European carriers fared better, seeing an overall fall of 4.8%. Both bmi and Virgin announced comparatively positive financial results, offering hopes of a slow recovery.

In Europe, a major factor in recent years has been the rise of low-cost airlines such as easyJet and Ryanair. These proved that travellers were more than willing to forego the usual 'trimmings' offered by airlines such as a free meal and drinks on-board and flights from major hubs if prices were slashed. This has kept passenger numbers healthy, but put pressure on mainstream airlines like BA and bmi to lower prices and launch their own low-cost services.

Achievements

In its 2002 financial results, bmi reported a record growth in passenger numbers and an improved operating performance in an exceptionally tough trading environment for the airline industry. A new segmentation strategy – which saw the launch of no-frills subsidiary bmibaby, as well as the further development of its regional service – resulted in an 11.9% increase in passengers to 7.5 million, compared to 6.7 million in 2001.

Although the group recorded a pre-tax loss of £19.6 million, against a pre-tax profit of £12.4 million in 2001, the new strategy plus additional cost cutting measures enabled it to generate a strong positive cash flow, with strong signs of recovery by early 2003.

bmi's success at providing quality products and services has been recognised by 50 industry awards since 1990. These include being voted best UK domestic airline twelve times (Travel Weekly), Best Short Haul Business Airline (Business Travel World), Best Short Haul Airline (Business Traveller) and Best UK Domestic Airline, Business (Conde Nast Traveller Readers Award).

More recently, the airline received a maximum five-star rating in the May 2002 edition of Business Traveller magazine, for its Manchester to Washington services.

History

The company started life as a flying school for RAF pilots, set up in 1938 by air ace Captain Roy Harben, a recipient of the Flying Cross. When the demand for pilot training diminished at the end of World War II, the company was transformed into a small cargo and charter service under the name Derby Aviation.

Derby Aviation grew slowly but surely throughout the 1950s, and changed its name to British Midland in 1964 – by which time the company had a fleet of several DC-3s and Canadian DC-4 Argonauts. It also switched its headquarters to the new East Midlands Airport. Soon it was running charter flights to Palma, Basle and Barcelona, and had acquired Manchester-based airline Mercury. When it won the right to run a service from Teeside to Heathrow, it was well on the way to becoming the London airport's second largest operator having acquired its first jets in 1970.

Today, bmi is the UK's second-largest full-service airline and has its main operational base at London Heathrow, where it holds 14% of all take off and landing slots.

Innovation has been a major factor in bmi's history. Its industry 'firsts' include vegetarian food on domestic services (1992); a separate business class (1993); internet booking and reservations (1995); participation in the Pet Travel Scheme (2000); an all-jet regional service (2001); and the installation and use of Tempus 2000, an integrated telemedicine service, on all its long haul flights.

Product

bmi operates over 2,000 flights a week with a fleet of 41 jet aircraft. It serves 28 destinations in ten countries and in 2002 carried over 7.5 million passengers. Through its membership of Star Alliance, a group of sixteen airlines offering seamless travel worldwide, it is also able to offer an international network crossing the globe. It is especially recognised for having helped to open the skies of Europe to competition, as well as making the transatlantic route more competitive.

Recent Developments

In August 2003 the bmi group carried 921,215 passengers – its highest-ever number of passengers in a single month, reflecting a 25% increase over the same period the previous year and eclipsing even the recording breaking 905,000 set in July when the important 900,000 mark was passed for the first time.

Probably the most significant development in 2002 was the launch of bmibaby, a no-frills service to nine destinations from the East Midlands. By the end of the year, it had carried more than 700,000 passengers to nineteen different destinations and by March 2003, the millionth passenger had checked-in. A second base was launched at Cardiff in October 2002 followed by a third base Manchester in May 2003. The fleet of Boeing 737s will serve 24 destinations and is on target to carry three million passengers in 2003. A fourth base at Teesside Airport was opened in October 2003.

In the same year, bmi introduced a one-way fare structure on its regular services, removing the 'Saturday night stay' requirement, thus stimulating high growth in passenger numbers. Also in 2002, bmi became the market leader on the Manchester-Chicago route, with passenger numbers rising 16% to a total 73% slice of the market.

The company made a £1.5 million investment in a new business lounge at Belfast City Airport, which opened in March 2003. New services were launched from London Heathrow to Venice and Alicante in April 2003, October sees the launch of East Midlands to Brussels services and in November it is due to launch the only direct service from Heathrow to Tenerife.

Promotion

With the introduction of a new pricing model in 2002, bmi could more easily compete with the low fares offered by the likes of easyJet and Ryanair. But it remained a full service airline, with all the associated benefits – such as being able to fly from Heathrow, check-in at Paddington station, and the inclusion of food and drink in the ticket price. In other words, bmi could offer customers great fares without the downsides of flying 'low-cost'. While it is still not the cheapest airline, it offers good value.

tasty hot breakfast

Heathrow – Amsterdam from £25
Heathrow – Edinburgh from £25
Heathrow – Paris from £25

book now at flybmi.com

those who know fly bmi

A STAR ALLIANCE MEMBER

Prices shown are one-way fares available only at flybmi.com and include all taxes and passenger service charges. Book using your Switch, Delta or Solo card and avoid a £3 credit card fee. Flights and fares are subject to availability. Conditions apply.

bmi's advertising campaign that broke in April 2003 was designed to bring this positioning to life. The commercials focused on fares and destinations, but underlined the added extras included in the price. In order to compete with high-spending, high profile brands – in order simply to get noticed – the ads needed to do more than merely impart

Heathrow - Milan from £35 one way

those who know fly bmi

A STAR ALLIANCE MEMBER
flybmi.com

information. bmi needed an advertising idea that not only stood out, but became a brand in its own right. Enter 'the bmi birds' – the avian brand spokesmen who choose to fly with bmi. The idea being that birds are the flying experts, so if they pick a particular airline, it must be a good choice.

The birds are also able to communicate fare prices and other information in a way that is charming and different.

The integrated campaign covered TV, posters, newspapers, the trade press, the web (including a computer game), and direct channels such as email.

Brand Values

bmi strives to offer the best possible customer service and value. It has set performance standards in every aspect of its business to enable staff to meet and exceed customer needs. In 2003, along with other major European airlines, it implemented a series of standards known as the Airline Passenger Service Commitment (ASPC).

Its commitments include offering the lowest available fares, honouring fares without springing last-minute taxes or other price increases on the customer, keeping travellers informed of delays, and assisting them if delays are unavoidable. Other commitments include the swift return of mislaid baggage, providing refreshments when aircraft are delayed, and speeding up the check-in process. It is also working with the industry and legislators to reduce the problem of 'overbooking' – when airlines calculate that a certain amount of travellers will not show up, but are then forced to deny passengers access to flights for which they have paid.

bmi also aims to provide the maximum information on journey times, destinations, airports and terminals during the booking process – as well as advising on sensitive matters like carry-on luggage limits.

Finally, through its customer feedback scheme, bmi strives to respond swiftly to passengers who have experienced difficulties during flights.

www.flybmi.com

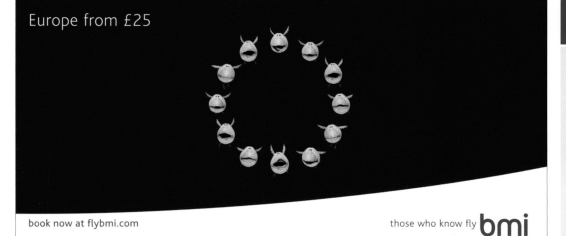

Europe from £25

book now at flybmi.com

those who know fly bmi

A STAR ALLIANCE MEMBER

Prices shown are one-way fares available only at flybmi.com and include all taxes and passenger service charges. Book using your Switch, Delta or Solo card and avoid a £3 credit card fee. Flights and fares are subject to availability. Conditions apply.

BRITISH AIRWAYS

Market

Air transport is one of the world's largest and most competitive industries. Airline profitability, however, is closely tied to the economic cycle and in 2001 and 2002 combined, member airlines of the International Air Transport Association (IATA) suffered a total net loss of £9 billion as war, politics and the economy took their toll. Despite the world economic slowdown and the uncertain geopolitical environment the global airline industry generated revenues of more than £190 billion in 2002 and carried more than half a billion passengers on international scheduled services (the corresponding figure in 1970 was 75 million).

British Airways is one of the world's longest established carriers and has always been regarded as an industry leader. In the 2002/03 financial year, some 38 million people chose to fly with the airline.

Privatisation and deregulation have undoubtedly helped stimulate the market for air travel. One feature has been the emergence of no-frills airlines, which have stimulated rapid market growth in the US domestic and short haul European markets. Analysts predict that the polarisation between international networks and regional, no-frills short haul carriers will become more pronounced. They also forecast that a radical restructuring of the industry's complex and outdated regulatory system is inevitable and long overdue.

Achievements

British Airways enjoys a world-class reputation for professionalism, high standards of quality and leading product development and consequently

industry including the Grand Prix at the International Design Effectiveness Awards and the Marketing Society's Award for Innovation. The company's marketing campaigns have also won numerous prizes at national and international competitions, including Gold Awards for Best TV Advertisement (Business category) and Multimedia Campaign of the Year among a total of ten awards from the Chartered Institute of Marketing Travel Industry Group.

History

British Airways can trace its origins to the pioneering days of civil aviation when its forerunner, Aircraft Transport and Travel Limited (AT&T) launched the first daily scheduled international air service between London and Paris. That initial flight, on August 25th 1919, carried one passenger and took two and a half hours. In 1924 AT&T's successor Daimler Airways merged with three other fledgling companies to form Imperial Airways Ltd, introducing services to Egypt, India, South Africa and Singapore during the 1920s and 1930s. Meanwhile a number of smaller UK air transport companies merged to form the privately owned British Airways Ltd which became Imperial's principal UK competitor on European routes. Both companies were nationalised in 1939 on the outbreak of World War II to form the British Overseas Airways Corporation (BOAC). Post-war continental European and domestic flights were operated by a new carrier, British European Airways (BEA). The 1950s witnessed the dawn of the passenger jet age and BOAC led the way by flying a Comet to Johannesburg in

In 1987 the airline was privatised. More than one million applications were received for shares making the flotation eleven times oversubscribed.

The company continues to expand its route network through alliances with other international carriers. The oneworld™ alliance came into operation in February 1999. oneworld combines the services of British Airways, American Airlines, Cathay Pacific, Qantas, Finnair, Iberia, Aer Lingus, LanChile and most recently Swiss, establishing it as the world's most global alliance serving more countries than any other. Taken together with its own extensive network, these partnerships increase the scale of British Airways presence in the major world airline markets.

Product

British Airways worldwide route network covers over 200 destinations in over 90 countries. Its main operating bases are London's two major international airports, Heathrow and Gatwick. The company operates more than 300 aircraft, including 56 Boeing 747's, 56 Airbuses and 60 Boeing 737s, making it one of the largest fleets in Europe. The airline takes great pride in delivering high levels of customer service and its offering is organised around a portfolio of products designed to meet customer needs. In January 2000 the company unveiled a £600 million customer service product update, the biggest in airline history.

FIRST assures every customer the highest standards of service and attention to detail at every stage of their journey. Each tastefully designed 'Demi-Cabin' provides comfort and

the carrier receives numerous plaudits from within and outside the industry. It has recently been voted Best Business Class, Overall Best Airline and Best Shorthaul Airline (all for the second year in succession) at the prestigious Business Traveller Awards 2003. Readers of Conde Nast Traveller also voted British Airways their favourite airline for business travel in their 2003 Readers' Travel Awards. The airline was the first carrier to introduce a seat that converts to a completely flat bed for business travellers. The revolutionary design led to a host of accolades from the design and travel

1952, halving the previous journey time. The next decade saw another world beater when BEA's Trident aircraft made the first automatic landing on a scheduled service, heralding the era of all-weather operations. In 1974 BOAC and BEA were formally merged to become British Airways. The new airline inherited its predecessors' pioneering path and in 1976 partnered by Air France launched the world's first supersonic passenger service. Concorde was heralded as an icon of style and a triumph of engineering which delivered the ultimate supersonic travel experience.

seclusion for work, sleep or relaxation. The specially trained FIRST crew will provide each customer with a discreet yet attentive service, ensuring that all their personal needs are taken care of.

Club World has redefined business travel for the twenty first century. More than £200 million has been spent to enable passengers to make the most of their time. From the calm of the lounges to the comfort of their own cocooned environment on board, Club World gives every customer the personal space, privacy and flexibility they need to sleep, work or simply relax. The award-winning seat converts into a six foot fully flat bed, providing a better night's sleep. And with in-seat laptop connection and telephone, Club World has all the facilities needed to catch up on work or stay in touch with colleagues and family throughout the journey.

Club Europe, the premium class for short haul travellers offers frequent and conveniently timed flights to key European business centres, with the option to get there and back in a day. Services such as dedicated check-in and Fast Track security are designed to save precious extra minutes for time-pressured travellers.

World Traveller Plus was launched just three years ago in October 2000, making British Airways the first airline to offer four cabin choices for long haul travel. World Traveller Plus offers extra space and comfort for an economy price, targeting the cost-conscious business traveller. Customers benefit from a more spacious dedicated cabin with a maximum of five seat rows to ensure comfort and relaxation. Each seat has an adjustable headrest, foot and legrest and lumbar support, with seven inches more legroom than World Traveller. Personal in-seat entertainment screens offer a wide choice of films, TV, interactive games and CD quality audio. Every seat is equipped with a laptop power point and telephone.

World Traveller represents excellent value for money. Everything has been designed to ensure a smooth and comfortable journey, from the ergonomically designed seats with foot and headrests, to individual seat-back screens (on all aircraft except Boeing 767s) offering a wide variety of entertainment, and the complimentary three course meal and bar service.

Short haul economy cabin Euro Traveller offers frequent flights to centrally located airports. Customers can sit back and relax with comfortable leather seats and a 31 inch seat pitch. A selection of complimentary newspapers is available on boarding. A complimentary bar service and contemporary 'All Day Deli' menu are served by friendly and highly trained crew.

The company has always been committed to providing a seamless travel experience for its business passengers, individual and corporate. British Airways is proud to be the preferred airline for many major companies, working in partnership

with them to develop bespoke arrangements which include specially negotiated fares and specific service benefits. Individual travellers can also benefit from the Executive Club loyalty programme which has more than four million members worldwide. Members can earn BA Miles when using the airline or any of its partner companies, which include Marriott Hotels and Hertz car rental. They can also collect tier points to enable them to progress to Silver or Gold membership, offering even more benefits such as lounge access and bonus BA Miles on every flight.

The On Business loyalty programme, specifically for small to medium sized companies, is designed to make travel budgets go further. On Business points are awarded to a company every time one of their employees flies with British Airways, which can then be redeemed by the company for benefits including free flights and hotel vouchers. Employees may also be members of the Executive Club, earning BA Miles for themselves as well as generating On Business points for their company on every flight.

The company was one of the first to introduce e-tickets as a flexible alternative to the traditional flight voucher, simultaneously providing time and cost savings to customers. The airline has a variety of check-in options tailored to the needs of the business traveller, including Online Check-in and Self-Service Check-in kiosks (available at selected airports), where you can check in for your flight, choose your seat and print your boarding pass in minutes.

Recent Developments

British Airways continues to offer new routes and services in response to demand from the business traveller. March 2003 witnessed the first British Airways flights from London City, where 70% of airport users are business travellers, to Paris and Frankfurt. New routes from London City to Edinburgh and Geneva are due to launch on October 26th 2003.

Research among British Airways business travellers has shown 75% of them carry laptops on flights and the majority are keen to have internet access on board. In February 2003 the airline embarked on an innovative pilot project, installing Connexion by Boeing in its FIRST, Club World and World Traveller Plus cabins on selected flights to New York. The broadband service not only allows passengers to surf the internet in-flight but also to send real-time emails at ten times the speed of traditional connections.

In July 2003 the company simplified the Executive Club loyalty scheme introducing better incentives and more ways of spending BA Miles. For example members can now use their BA Miles to upgrade to the next cabin on eligible flights or use a combination of cash and BA Miles to purchase an economy ticket.

One of the most difficult decisions was to retire Concorde and withdraw it from service at the end of October 2003. The aircraft enjoys a unique place in air transport history and served as the British Airways flagship for nearly three decades. Over its last months in service Concorde was celebrated with a programme of special promotions and commemorative activities. After retirement, Concorde will be preserved for posterity at some of the world's greatest aviation museums.

Promotion

British Airways has always been noted for its innovative and eye-catching advertising and marketing. In September 2003 the carrier launched a major tactical initiative for Club World by offering business travellers the opportunity to upgrade to FIRST if they have booked a full fare Club World return flight. The three month campaign, which appeared in the business press, was designed to encourage the business traveller to reappraise the superior and exclusive service offered by FIRST whilst leveraging British Airways extensive long haul network.

British Airways is also a major user of below-the-line marketing and its CRM-focused marketing strategy enables it to predict and cater for the

needs of its business customers. In addition to these mainstream marketing tools the airline has a dedicated B2B sales and marketing team which delivers bespoke solutions to corporate customers.

Brand Values

The brand has five distinct values which set it apart: reliability, safety, professionalism, responsibility and responsiveness.

British Airways has a global reputation as a reassuringly reliable and trusted brand with a strong focus on punctuality. Customers know they can always expect the best service and products.

British Airways is one of the world's safest airlines. Its safety record is maintained through the continual servicing and updating of its modern fleet which meets the strictest safety criteria.

British Airways status as one of the world's most respected airlines comes from its commitment to the highest standards of service. Years of experience have led to a reputation for professionalism that it strives to maintain.

In taking full responsibility for the travel experience British Airways customers can relax with the knowledge that everything is being taken care of for them by a company of substance.

British Airways aims to provide an appropriate response to any situation. The company's friendly ground and cabin crew will always try to make the customer's journey as smooth and comfortable as possible.

www.britishairways.com

Market

Founded in 1901, the BSI Group is a leading global provider of professional services to organisations worldwide. It is a group of complementary businesses, each with its own set of skills, working in parallel. Its services include independent certification of management systems and products, commodity inspection, product testing, development of private, national and international standards, management systems training and delivering information on standards and international trade.

The Group has over 5,000 employees in 110 countries and in 2002 its turnover was £232.8 million (US$145.5 million).

Businesses all over the world rely on BSI's integrity, authority and independence: 25% of companies listed on the FTSE 100 index and one sixth of Fortune 500 businesses utilise BSI's services. However, customers range from global companies to small local businesses.

The collective range of their products and services encompasses virtually every field of human endeavour including communications, banking, oil, engineering, electronics, food and drink, agriculture and consumer goods.

Achievements

The BSI Group has at its core the world's largest National Standards Body – producing an average of 2,000 new standards annually. BSI British Standards provided the model for other countries to follow and instigated the formation of the International Organisation for Standardisation (ISO) in 1946.

BSI is the world's leading provider of standardisation documents covering every aspect of the modern economy from protection of intellectual property and knowledge management to electromagnetic compatibility specifications, from guidelines on managing risk for corporate governance and standards on project management, to specifications on flood protection products.

In addition, BSI is the world's largest independent certifier of management systems, with 40,000 clients across the globe and is also North America's largest registrar.

Moreover the internationally accepted concept of management systems standards, was pioneered by the BSI Group. The ISO 9000 quality series – adopted, to date, by around 560,000 organisations in 159 countries worldwide – was also developed from British Standard BS 5750 which was first published in 1979. The most widely accepted environmental management system, ISO 14001, was derived from BS 7750 – established by BSI in 1992.

The BSI Group continues to innovate. In 2003 it became the first verification body in the world capable of offering verification to every entrant under the UK's Greenhouse Gas Emissions Trading Scheme.

History

The BSI Group was founded as the Engineering Standards Committee (ESC) in 1901. Among the first standards published was one which reduced the number of sizes of tramway rails from 75 to five, resulting in an estimated saving of £1 million a year. Standardisation was on its way.

In 1903, the British Standard Mark, now known as the Kitemark, was registered as a trademark and standardisation work gathered momentum: by 1918, 300 committees were in place with 31,000 standards being sold that year.

In 1929, what had been the Engineering Standards Committee was awarded a Royal Charter and in 1931, the name British Standards Institution was adopted.

World War II brought accelerated standards production, including over 400 wartime emergency standards. In the post-war era, the slow shift towards an affluent society created more demand for consumer standardisation work, characterised by

the 1953 introduction of the Kitemark's application to domestic products. By the 1960s, Government regulations were mandating compulsory Kitemarking of car seat belts and motorcycle helmets.

The next major development was the introduction of a standard for the quality of company management systems. BS 5750 was introduced to help companies build quality and safety into the way they work to meet the needs of their customers. In 1979 the Registered Firm mark was introduced to indicate that a company had been audited and registered to BS 5750 standard.

From 1994, BS 5750 became known as BS EN ISO 9000. From this point on a major part of BSI's work became registering companies to the world's most popular management systems series: ISO 9000.

In 1991, BSI Inc was established in Reston, Virginia in the US. The following year, BSI published the world's first environmental management standard, BS 7750. In due course, this was adopted internationally and in 1996 ISO 14001 was published.

In 1998 the BSI Group acquired Inspectorate – a global commodity testing business. This gave the group a foothold in around 100 countries, running over 170 facilities. With this acquisition, BSI virtually doubled its sales to around £170 million a year. Its total worldwide workforce grew to around 3,400, with a highly effective global reach, extending into emerging markets such as China, Eastern Europe and South America.

The BSI Group subsequently acquired CEEM, a leading American management system training and publication services provider in 1998, and in 1999, Rocky Mountain Geochemical, one of America's leading precious metals testing companies and Mertcontrol, among Hungary's leading inspection, testing and certification companies. It also acquired International Standards Certification Pte Ltd, a Singapore based certification organisation.

In January 2002, KPMG's ISO registration business in North America was bought, making BSI Group the largest standards body in the world and the largest registration body in North America.

BSI Group
Annual Review & Summary Financial Statements 2002

shape the future

As a result of these strategic acquisitions, and through more than a century of growth, the BSI Group can now provide a comprehensive service to its clients, helping them raise their performance and enhance their competitiveness worldwide.

Product

The BSI Group is made up of five key business units:

BSI British Standards is the world's leading provider of standards, covering every aspect of the modern economy from protection of intellectual property to technical specifications for personal protective equipment.

BSI Management Systems provides independent certification of management systems, including ISO 9001:2000 (Quality) ISO 14001 (Environmental Management), Greenhouse Gas Emissions Verification and BS 7799 (Information Security).

BSI Business Information exists to raise awareness and understanding of new standards and regulations through publications and training. It provides a comprehensive range of books, manuals, CD-ROMs and online services.

BSI Product Services tests products against standards, helps firms with new product development and provides third party certification. Product Services is the owner of the Kitemark brand, which was first registered as the British Standards mark in 1903.

Finally, BSI Inspectorate is a global commodity inspection and analysis company that joined the BSI Group in 1998. The core objective of BSI Inspectorate's global business is to minimise risk through independent inspection, analysis and testing of commodities.

Recent Developments

Since 1997, BSI has grown three-fold through acquisition and organic growth to become a global organisation. However, until recently it was not recognised as such because the Group operated under fifteen different brands. In July 2002 BSI decided to implement a new brand identity to leverage the power that global recognition and consistency can bring. The rollout activity covered product literature, online communications, corporate stationery, vehicles, uniforms, signage and an extensive internal communications programme.

To reflect the ambition and vitality of a complementary set of dynamic world-class businesses sharing the same intrinsic goals and values, a new strengthened and updated brand mark was adopted. This created a consistent and clear visual identity across the Group's global operations whilst retaining the brand's strong heritage. The BSI brand has evolved to reflect its global success.

Promotion

With the development of one unified brand, all BSI's marketing communications needed to

be focused on achieving the long-term goal of a coherent global brand identity. Two key creative challenges were identified. Firstly, to communicate BSI's transition from a UK-centric to an international organisation, as well as shift the public perception of the Group as a government institution to that of an independent, commercial enterprise. Secondly, bringing about understanding and buy-in of the BSI brand to all staff around the world, particularly those employees from recent acquisitions.

To meet the first challenge, marketing activities have taken on a more aspirational approach, through the use of carefully selected imagery and an emphasis on the brand's values and benefits.

BSI has also embarked on a strategy to raise brand awareness with senior decision-makers externally and communicate the new visual identity to them. The key channels for engagement are through press and public relations as well as direct marketing and the publication of a business magazine, Business Standards.

Sponsorship is another brand communication vehicle utilised by the BSI Group. The BSI Design Award scheme, run in conjunction with London's Royal College of Art (RCA), has evolved with the brand, from an award for standards in design into an environmental design award that positions the BSI group as on-message with contemporary issues. The BSI/RCA partnership reaffirms the thinking that good design, best environmental practice and profitability can work hand in hand.

The second challenge required marketing to internal customers. The core of this is a Brand Identity website developed to make the corporate guidelines and the various brand elements (such as stationery, presentation templates, logos and examples of on-brand communications) easily accessible to all staff and key suppliers around the world. In addition, the website provides a means of engaging BSI staff in a conversation on what the brand stands for and where it is going – a conversation which is critical to maintaining the fierce commitment that staff have to the brand.

Although the Group follows a carefully defined brand strategy, the business units tailor their marketing campaigns to meet the specific requirements of their individual customers. They utilise key elements of the marketing mix including print advertisements in key industry publications, posters, direct mail and exhibitions. Significant innovations have also taken place within e-marketing, with BSI's web presence now being a major channel for communications and marketing, supplemented with email marketing.

Brand Values

BSI has been building its brand for over a century, working and delivering to the highest standards and building a reputation for honesty. The Group's vision is to be world leader in advancing industry and business for a better quality of life. This vision is born from its core values of integrity, innovation and independence – values that define and drive all BSI operations from the services it provides and the benefits it delivers, to the goals BSI achieves with its clients.

www.bsi-global.com

Market

BT is one of Europe's leading providers of telecommunications services operating in one of the most competitive telecoms markets in the world. The company is the largest full service telecommunications operator in the UK and serves more than twenty million business and residential customers with more than 29 million exchange lines, as well as providing network services to other licensed operators.

In 2002, the telecoms market grew by 3% in overall revenue. In the year to September 2002, the UK telecoms market was worth approximately £47 billion (Source: Oftel).

In a market characterised by intense competition, brands carry particular importance, acting as potentially crucial influencers of choice. Telecom brands have to stretch their appeal and meaning – beyond simple voice communication over fixed lines and into the realm of mobile, internet and broadband services.

Achievements

BT has become a vital link in the smooth running and competitiveness of businesses at home and abroad. It has created networks which form the backbone of communication on which businesses rely and are capable of carrying massive volumes of critical data.

The company is a major force in spearheading the uptake of broadband services in the UK. BT passed a significant milestone in June 2003 when it achieved its initial target of one million wholesale broadband connections ahead of schedule.

On June 30th 2003, high speed broadband was available to 71% of the country. In July, trigger levels were set for a further 500 exchanges under the innovative demand registration scheme, which means that if the demand is there, ADSL (asymmetric digital subscriber line) broadband will be made available to 90% of UK homes and businesses. By the end of July, that availability had already risen to 73% and will top 80% by the end of 2003.

As well as signing up customers, BT is moving quickly to offer them inspiring new services. For example, new broadband services have been launched, offering music – Dotmusic on Demand, sport – Sportal on Demand, and education – the BT learning centre.

BT has made great strides in corporate social responsibility (CSR) and is committed to maximising its positive impact on society through leadership in CSR. BT believes that a well managed CSR programme supports the delivery of strategy and is in the best interests of the business, customers, shareholders and the community.

The Dow Jones Sustainability Indices rank companies for their success in managing those factors for competitive advantage. During the 2003 financial year, BT was ranked as the top telecommunications company in the Dow Jones Sustainability Index for the third year running.

BT also won the prestigious Queen's Award for Enterprise in recognition of its contribution to sustainable development.

History

BT was privatised in 1984 making it the only state-owned telecommunications company to be privatised in Europe. In 1991, British Telecom was restructured and relaunched as BT.

In May 2001, as part of a restructuring and debt reduction programme, BT announced a '3 for 10' rights issue to raise £5.9 billion – the UK's largest ever rights issue – and the sale of Yell for £2.14 billion. In November that year, BT Wireless – BT's mobile business, rebranded as mm02 – was demerged from BT.

The new BT is structured so that BT Group plc provides a holding company for the separately managed businesses which make up the group. These are BT Retail, BT Wholesale, and BT Global Services, each of which has the freedom to focus on its own markets and customers.

BT has seven strategic priorities:

To deliver the highest levels of customer satisfaction performance and reduce the number of dissatisfied customers each year.

To achieve organic profitable revenue growth, while constraining capital expenditure.

To put broadband at the heart of BT, expand the market for broadband services and create a media-enabled network.

To provide solutions and other value-added services for multi-site corporate customers in Europe.

To place all UK networks under a single management structure and to limit investment in legacy voice and data platforms, while migrating operations to new platforms.

To use the strength of the BT brand to move into broadband services for consumers and also into related markets, such as communications solutions and business mobility services for major business customers and information and communications technology for SMEs.

And finally for all of the above to be delivered by diverse, skilled and motivated people.

Product

BT Retail is the UK's largest communications service provider, by market share, to the residential and business markets and is the prime channel to market in the UK for other businesses in the BT group. The core portfolio covers traditional telephony products such as calls, analogue/digital lines and private circuits. New revenue generation is focused on broadband, mobility and ICT. The business has a comprehensive mobile strategy and provides a range of services for the business market. It is pioneering the take-up of public wireless broadband in the UK through BT Openzone. BT Openworld remains the leading internet service provider (ISP) for SMEs.

BT Wholesale provides network services and solutions within the UK, including ADSL, conveyance, transit, bulk delivery of private circuits, frame relay and integrated service digital network (ISDN) connections. It serves more than 500 communications companies, fixed and mobile network operators, including BT Retail and BT Global Services.

BT Global Services is BT's business services and solutions division, serving customers worldwide. BT Global Services provides integrated data and

value added services to meet the European needs of global multi-site corporates and the global needs of European corporates. BT's extensive global network and strong strategic partnerships enable it to serve customers in all key commercial centres of Europe, North America and Asia Pacific. The BT Global Services portfolio ranges from desktop and network equipment and software, transport and connectivity, IP-based e-business solutions, managed network services and systems integration to consultancy for complex global requirements.

Also part of the BT group of businesses is BT Exact which is BT's research, technology and IT operations business. It specialises in telecommunications engineering, leading-edge network design, IT system and application development and has extensive expertise in business consulting and human factors. Its knowledge helps its customers across BT Group and in selected other businesses to gain maximum advantage from their investments in communications networks and IT systems, develop new capabilities and open new opportunities. Backed by a team of over 6,000 technologists, it is active and influential in setting global standards.

Recent Developments

In July 2003, BT announced its return to the mass market for mobiles with the launch of a new service – BT Mobile Home Plan – aimed at families who want more than one mobile phone.

Quick calls home to the family land line are free with BT Mobile Home Plan. The line rental drops from £15 a month to just £10 for up to five additional 'family handsets' under the deal. There are bundled, fixed price packages of call minutes, which can be shared by the whole family.

The company also revealed it is to start immediate trials of a revolutionary mobile which allows users to make calls from home or the office via the cheaper and clearer land line network.

BT is conducting trials where users will be able to use their mobile normally when they are out and about, but when in a 'bluetooth site' their calls will be routed over the fixed network rather than the mobile network. This will mean that users will benefit from cheaper and clearer calls. BT's plan for the eventual product is that it should be a truly converged communications device allowing users to take advantage of Wi-Fi technology to surf the web or download files on the move.

BT's new directory enquiry services began operating in December 2002 well ahead of the cut off date for 192, which ceased in August 2003. By dialling 118 500 customers are not only able to find phone numbers but they can also search classified listings and new enhanced information services with all calls being answered by an operator in person. BT's International directory enquiry service is on 118 505.

Promotion

Marketing communications must both engage and inspire people about the benefits and possibilities that communications can bring.

BT is renowned for the excellence of its marketing, having won numerous plaudits such as the IPA Effectiveness in Advertising award. The breadth and depth of its marketing across its extensive portfolio makes it one of the largest

advertisers in the UK. In 2002, it spent around £100 million on advertising in the UK.

All BT marketing campaigns build from the brand communications platform, 'More connections, more possibilities'. BT provides the right connections that help businesses do better and the right connections deliver ease of use and integration. It identifies a clear offering from BT and shows that BT understands and has real business insight.

This links with the core thought that underlies every new communications platform for the entire BT Group: 'The more connections we make, the more possibilities we have'.

Brand Values

In April 2003, BT revealed a new corporate identity to replace the 'piper' logo. The new mark is the company's first visual identity change since 1991 and only the second since it became British Telecom in 1980. The piper did an excellent job for BT and became one of the country's most recognisable marks. However, it had become associated with some outdated perceptions of BT as simply a fixed-line telephone company.

BT strives to make all communications as simple as a telephone call, offering customers complete and easy to use solutions. BT's business and its culture are changing, so it is important to have a brand identity that represents the multi-faceted nature of the business. The new logo does the job. It represents BT as being in-tune with the multimedia age as well as communicating the company's international reach.

The newly launched BT promise sees the company committing to making every experience simple and complete. Underpinning the brand promise is a new set of values with the aim of being trustworthy, helpful, inspiring, straightforward, and acting with a real passion for what it does.

BT will manage implementation of the new identity over a three-year period in order to minimise costs.

www.bt.co.uk

Superbrands

CASIO®

Market

Casio is a leader in the global consumer electronics market, as well as providing productivity solutions to businesses and LCDs to other manufacturers. Times are currently hard for the industry as a whole since there are still limited signs of a pickup in the Japanese economy and the other industrialised economies are yet to emerge from this period of stagnation. Furthermore, consumer spending remains sluggish.

However, Casio is bucking the general market trend. By focusing on three key areas – digital cameras, Mobile Network Solutions and timepieces – it has enhanced its product appeal and sales have climbed 15.3% year on year for 2003. Casio says that it is determined to offer consumers, products, services and solutions of the highest quality and which represent value for money.

Achievements

As the creator of the enormously popular G-Shock range of watches and the first company to produce and market digital cameras with LCD viewing screens (QV10 in 1995), Casio has long maintained a reputation as a revolutionary electronics manufacturer. Its mission is to develop products in order to astonish consumers around the world with a glimpse of the future.

Since its inception in 1957, Casio has made it its mission to pursue 'creativity and contribution'. It uses ingenious concepts and state-of-the-art technology to create products and services that will make the lives of people throughout the world, more enjoyable and more comfortable.

Casio's achievements are marked by technological innovation, value and miniaturisation. The company has been responsible for a number of world firsts, including: the first all-electric compact calculator in 1956; the first inkjet printer in 1971; the first handheld PC (Cassiopeia with Windows CE) in 1996 and the production of the first CD titlers for office and home use. Its most recent development is the world's first dual band atomic timepiece – Wave Ceptor. It is the most accurate watch on the market as it receives wireless updates from the atomic clock transmitters near Rugby and Frankfurt. Casio expects it will appeal both to consumers and time critical businesses, where co-ordination of time is vital.

Casio says that its ability to lead the consumer electronics market is due to the fact that it does not simply incorporate new technologies into yesterday's products, but always aims to surpass users' highest expectations and go beyond what users can imagine. However, it does not believe in technology for technology's sake. "If it is of no use to consumers then there is no point in producing it," says Yoshio Ono, Managing Director of Product Development.

History

Casio was founded by Tadao Kashio, who grew up in a farming family in Nangoku City in Japan. Tadao loved creating things and was eager to start his own business. In 1946 he set up a firm making airplane parts. At a trade exhibition in 1949, he saw an electric motorised calculator

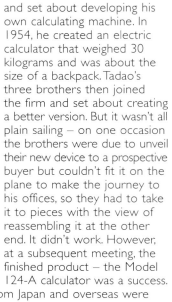

– the size of an office desk. It was operated by gears and extremely noisy. Tadao was convinced he could do better and set about developing his own calculating machine. In 1954, he created an electric calculator that weighed 30 kilograms and was about the size of a backpack. Tadao's three brothers then joined the firm and set about creating a better version. But it wasn't all plain sailing – on one occasion the brothers were due to unveil their new device to a prospective buyer but couldn't fit it on the plane to make the journey to his offices, so they had to take it to pieces with the view of reassembling it at the other end. It didn't work. However, at a subsequent meeting, the finished product – the Model 124-A calculator was a success. Manufacturers from Japan and overseas were impressed and Casio Computer Company went from strength to strength.

However, rival manufacturers, watching Casio's success began to create their own calculators which were smaller and easier to use. Casio responded in 1965, with the first solely electronic calculator. It also looked at expanding the market, by making the products available not only to businesses but also to better off consumers who could afford to pay around £80. By 1972, it produced the Casio Mini, which was an immediate success.

Casio focused on miniaturisation and in 1975, launched a digital watch called the Casiotron which is now highly collectable. January 1980 saw the release of the Casiotone 201, an electronic musical instrument. The company then applied its world leading LCD and power management technology to develop Pocket TVs and Japanese word processors.

More recently, its products have included the world's first mass-market digital camera and the Cassiopeia, handheld PC. Casio's mantra is "if it's not totally original, it's not Casio" and it's this spirit which drives the brand to find fresh ideas and innovative technology in order to make consumers' lives better.

Product

In Casio's utopia there would be one of its watches on every arm and one of its handheld devices in every pocket.

However, the company makes a huge range of consumer electronic products including digital cameras, TVs and digital pianos. It also produces mobile networking hardware, pagers, mobile phones and LCDs for other manufacturers.

Although famous for its consumer products, Casio is also a major player in the corporate market. It has sold cash registers and handheld data capture terminals for fifteen years. Now these product areas are uniting to provide innovative solutions such as 'queue busting' technology for clients such as the London Eye and WH Smith, mobile tills for Britannia Airline aircrew and wireless waitressing services for bars and restaurants. This application uses Casio touch screens, tills and handheld PCs which are connected together so that information is always up to date. The waiter takes a customer's order through the remote handheld terminal which sends the order to the kitchen or bar, processes the bill and accepts payment. Furthermore the waiter can be kept informed of specials and product availability.

Recent Developments

Casio is making maximum use of its expertise and has recently designated digital cameras, Mobile Network Solutions and timepieces as its core businesses.

The convergence of digital technologies means that Casio's traditional organisational structure is changing. The company focuses less on one product made by one division because there is now more crossover between different types of products. On the consumer side, this includes watches with built in GPS and digital cameras with MP3 players. For business, this is demonstrated by handheld PCs containing bar code scanner, digital camera and wireless communications. This has proved highly successful at the London Eye, which uses a Casio IT-700 wireless pocket PC as a 'queue busting' device so that London Eye staff can sell souvenirs, drinks and disposable cameras to people while they are waiting for their turn to board the giant wheel.

The company is also looking at ways it can extend the use of its products into new markets. For example, a major UK telecom company has chosen Casio's FX7400, a graphic calculator mainly used in education, as an effective 'productivity solution' for its 15,000 mobile engineers.

Some of the company's latest products include: Casio Projector World – a highly portable and powerful digital projector using state of the art DLP chip technology which Casio is confident will change the way meetings are conducted and presentations given; and the Wave Ceptor – a watch with atomic timekeeping – the most accurate form of timekeeping available.

Promotion

Much of Casio's promotional activity is focused on PR to build brand awareness – product placement, event sponsorship, conferences, case studies and media reviews – and highly targeted advertising to promote new products and campaigns. Traditionally, each product area has created its own promotion strategy, but as digital products converge more closely, Casio is running more joint promotions in order to leverage its brand. Subsequently even in the business arena, the promotional activity aimed at consumers has a benefit, as Casio feels that it is important to build an emotional attachment between user and product.

Sponsorship globally includes the football world cup and motor sport and in the UK, Casio has focused on rugby league, extreme sports and next year, the Global Challenge Round the World Yacht Race. With its range of fashionable products – Exilim cameras and G Shock watches – Casio is also targeting trendsetters and opinion formers through lifestyle events at cutting edge clubs.

On the business-to-business side, Casio runs a series of dealership conferences. It has developed a programme called Casio Mobility Partners which aims to formalise its relationship with systems integrators to ensure that Casio products are a key ingredient in any solution. The company also produces case studies to demonstrate its business solutions to its target business sectors.

Among recent awards for Casio's products are the European Image and Sound Associations Best Digital Camera 2003-4 for the Exilim Z3 which is the size of a credit card and has a 3x zoom, and the Best Design award for the twentieth anniversary G-Shock watch.

Brand Values

Casio believes that buying one of its products guarantees purchasers two things: trust and innovation. Trust is a central tenet of the company's ethos. Its products are reliable, rugged, durable

and accurate. Casio has always been a brand that the user 'takes with them', therefore Casio also focuses on ease of use and making its technology

'wearable'. In contrast to other consumer electronics companies that make products for use in the home, Casio has taken the lead in developing small, portable products that are worn by the users – the Casio Exilim wearable digital camera, pocket TV, digital wrist watch and pocket information devices. But none of this happens without constant innovation. Casio prides itself on pushing forward the boundaries of technology including miniaturisation, 'shock' and LCD technology as well as the convergence of innovations such as cameras with MP3 players and watches with digital cameras.

But at the same time Casio recognises its corporate social responsibilities particularly towards the environment and has strong green policies in place. Casio designs its products to be lightweight, compact and power saving, but also strives towards the three 'Rs' – reuse, reduce and recycle. Green products are now central to its product line and the company plans to expand their number with solar powered and radio controlled watches.

world.casio.com

CNBC EUROPE
a service of NBC and Dow Jones

Market

Our hunger for up to the minute news has never been greater, especially in business where having the right information at the right time, can help you stay one step ahead. CNBC Europe, a leading pan-European financial and business TV channel operates in a competitive market where companies such as BBC World, CNN and Bloomberg Television strive to bring their viewers exclusive news, round the clock.

A recent EMS survey of pan-European media, which measures the habits of Europe's top 20% income earners, shows that CNBC Europe has greater affinity with CEOs than any other channel. It has grown its weekly audience of CEOs by 15%, senior managers by 40% and influential opinion leaders by 6%. It is also significantly more efficient in reaching institutional investors than its general news competitors.

Furthermore, CNBC Europe's own research shows a particularly strong performance in the UK and Germany with year on year audience growth of 47% and 74% respectively. At the same time, because the channel broadcasts real-time financial information, 76% of its viewers say they act on information they receive from the channel.

Achievements

CNBC Europe is available in over 83 million homes on satellite, cable and digital platforms. It is also available in 340,000 four and five star hotel rooms and 1,400 financial institutions across Europe, the Middle East and Africa. Its team of expert business journalists and presenters deliver award winning programming to business people wherever they are – at home, in the office or travelling on business.

The round-the-clock CNBC Europe service breaks the major financial stories of the day and

History

CNBC was first launched by the National Broadcasting Company (NBC) in the US in 1989. NBC itself has been a pioneer in the television industry for more than 70 years and has a strong heritage of innovative television programming and technology. CNBC quickly led the market in television business news and broke new ground as

drawing on Dow Jones' editorial resources including Dow Jones Newswires, and NBC properties such as NBC News and MSNBC.

CNBC Europe was established in 1998. It is Europe's dedicated financial and business TV news network and provides an indispensable service for people who need to be informed about the latest business developments, with real time, up-to-the-minute data they can act and trade upon.

Product

CNBC Europe is the leading pan-European real-time business and financial TV channel, providing live and actionable market information and analysis. Broadcasting 24 hours a day, it delivers unrivalled coverage of breaking business news, in-depth analysis and interviews with business leaders from around Europe. The channel broadcasts directly from the major financial centres in Europe, the US and Asia and has bases in Amsterdam, Berlin, Brussels, Frankfurt and Milan providing up to the minute news on the financial markets.

CNBC Europe's programming sets it apart from its rivals. Coverage is clear and easy to understand even if you are in the office and have the sound turned down. One of its visual cues is the CNBC Europe real-time share ticker. It is specific to the channel and is one the most powerful trading tools via television, combining live data from all the leading Europe stock exchanges and giving immediate, real-time data on buying and selling activity.

CNBC also displays a stack on the right side of the screen which shows the main blue chip indices of the major markets and currency rates against the Euro. These indices automatically update and rotate with data in real time.

The company also has an 21 screen video wall which can display graphics and data from the European markets and industry sectors. It can be

provides up-to-the-minute market information as well as detailed analysis and interviews with business leaders. In Europe, CNBC Europe has bureaux in Paris and Frankfurt, with dedicated reporters linked to its London studios. It also has access to journalists in key cities around Europe, and a new operation in Brussels, which is of growing importance as a source of news on EU issues and announcements.

the first television company to broadcast directly from the floor of the New York Stock Exchange.

In December 1997, NBC and Dow Jones & Company entered into a global business television alliance, bringing together the most recognised business-news brands in the world – The Wall Street Journal, CNBC and Dow Jones. By teaming together, NBC and Dow Jones strengthened their international operations,

used as a large screen for interviewing guests across Europe and displays a map of Europe showing all the European exchanges and real time price changes, displayed in green and red to represent positive or negative positions.

CNBC Europe has an affluent and influential audience – traditionally one of the hardest for advertisers to reach. Its viewers include: senior corporate executives seeking in-depth and

10k@ 15.74 ▲ 0.05   Centrica 358k@ 177.50 ▼ 0.25   Deutsche Telekom 19k@ 13.36 ▲ 0.02   Tandberg 25k@ 31.6 ▼ 0.7   GSK 50k@ 1286.00 ▲ 1.00   ABB 29k@ 4.99 ▲ 0.15   Prudential 50k@

Telefonica ▲   Nokia ▲   Platinum 665.00 ▼ 4.00   Siemens ▲   Banco Pop Bergoma ▲   Amersham ▲   Opticom ▼   Olivetti ▲   Enel

analytical discussion of the news and trends affecting Europe's business community; the financial community who need access to real-time financial market information to make crucial business decisions; and active private investors who want discussion and expert opinion on investment strategies.

CNBC Europe offers a highly effective advertising sales environment for business-to-business advertisers, luxury goods advertisers and high-end travel and recreation advertisers.

It offers a range of advertising and sponsorship tools to make its clients' campaigns effective. Solutions are tailored to individual client needs and include traditional spot campaigns, promotions and sponsored features. It also offers sponsored programming opportunities such as sponsorship of the pan-European ticker, sponsorship of 'Hotboards' – customised market reports – and advertising around broadcasts of premier business events such as the World Economic Forum, CeBit and ITU Telecom World.

CNBC Europe's advertisers include – Airbus, Boeing, Barclays Bank, Chevron Texaco, Cisco Systems, Dubai Civil Aviation, Excel Capital, HSBC, Lacoste, Oracle, Rolex, State Street Global, Samsung, Saudi Aramco and UBS.

Recent Developments
CNBC Europe is building on its strong performance with programming developments which increase the depth of coverage and analytical discussion. It has introduced a series of primetime half hour programmes covering timely and topical discussion and profiles of business leaders. The company expects these changes will further increase its ratings in the coming months. It will also offer advertisers greater opportunities for sponsoring CNBC Europe programmes.

IN THE BUSINESS WORLD, CEOs COMPETE.
IN OUR STUDIO THEY COMBINE THEIR KNOWLEDGE.

Wednesdays 20:30 CET on CNBC Europe*

ADVANTAGE TECHNOLOGY
Solutions for CEOs

www.cnbceurope.com/advantage
*Repeated on Saturdays at 11.30 CET and Sundays at 20.30 CET.

In association with Sun microsystems

CNBC Europe is increasingly producing content for a multi-channel environment. It is working on an online subscription-based broadband streaming product of CNBC Europe. In addition, CNBC Europe video clips can be accessed via Cantor Mobile, the world's most sophisticated wireless trading service. These clips are delivered every hour to keep customers ahead of the news while they are on the move.

Other new initiatives include the launch of CNBC Europe Mobile, which provides recordings of the latest CEO interviews together with European and US financial market updates

straight to customer's phones. The channel has also recently agreed to provide content for Cabvision, a London-based Taxi company providing TV's in the back of taxis which launched in Autumn 2003.

Part of CNBC Europe's strategy is to provide viewers with access to its services wherever they are and also to provide news content in a number of increasingly important markets. To complement its pan-European English language main channel, CNBC Europe has also formed affiliate relationships with local

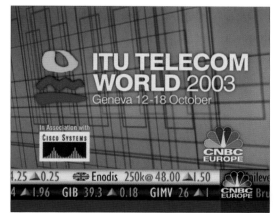

segments and make it the channel of choice for senior business executives, the financial professional and active private investors.

CNBC Europe interviews hundreds of CEOs every year about their latest financial results or company initiatives and this currently forms the basis of its advertising campaign which uses the strapline 'when CEOs aren't watching CNBC Europe they're appearing on it'.

CNBC Europe's print advertising appears in the FT, The Wall Street Journal Europe, and TIME magazine among others. It also runs a trade campaign using the same CEO themed ad in

TV channels. CNBC-E is a Turkish local language channel, while CFN-CNBC is in Italy and CNBC Arabiya is an Arab channel based in Dubai, catering for the business and investment communities. CNBC Europe is also providing news content for Russian language business news channel RBC-TV.

Promotion
CNBC Europe's marketing strategy is to build the brand profile amongst its key audience

a range of publications including M&M Europe, Media Week, the Internationalist and Campaign.

To build the brand, CNBC Europe actively participates in some of the world's premier business and industry events. In 2003 it was the official broadcaster at the World Economic Forum, Davos, Switzerland, the Thomson Extel Awards and the ITU World Telecom Event in Geneva. It also takes part in CeBIT, Europe's leading IT exhibition, the IMF – International Monetary Fund meetings in Dubai 2003, the World Travel Market in London and Dow Jones' CEO Summit in London in November.

Other promotional activity includes direct mail shots targeting international media buyers, newsletters and flyers as well as media agency roadshows which take the CNBC Europe sales team around media agencies, twice a year.

Brand Values
CNBC Europe aims to provide its audience with the most relevant, up to the minute news, real-time information, analysis and comment, 24 hours a day. Integrity is at the heart of its business. It is customer-focused and team driven. Its values are to question, to listen, to be responsive and to be flexible.

www.cnbceurope.com

COMPASS GROUP

Market

As more businesses and organisations outsource their catering requirements, the market for contract catering continues to grow at a healthy rate. Contract caterers are in demand for the increased range of benefits that they bring to a client's organisation – including management expertise, greater purchasing power, more sophisticated marketing and merchandising skills, and a growing appreciation of the benefits of food service branding.

Compass Group operates within this marketplace handling the outsourcing of food provision for major companies, organisations and institutions such as schools and hospitals around the world as well as operating concessions in airports, railway stations and at sport and leisure venues. Compass Group also offers clients vending services. Recent estimates indicate that the total global contract foodservice market is currently worth over £170 billion with a further £80 billion in concessions and vending. Furthermore, with

less than 30% of foodservice currently contracted out, there is plenty of opportunity for growth for the major players in the market.

There are over 4,000 companies registered in the UK involved in the business of contract catering. However, the market is dominated by Compass and Sodexho, which accounted for an estimated 80% of the market in terms of turnover in 2001 (Source: Mintel 2002). Aramark and Elior (Avenance) are also major players along with Initial, which is part of Rentokil.

Achievements

Compass Group may not be a household name but it is the world's largest foodservice company with annual revenues of over £10 billion and more than 375,000 employees in over 90 countries. It specialises in providing food and vending services on clients' premises often using foodservice brands that it either owns or franchises. In essence, it provides food to people where eating and drinking is not the primary purpose of the visit in locations such as offices and hospitals, schools, airports and railway stations, sports stadiums, the opera and concerts as well as prisons. Compass works in close co-operation with its clients and

because it is usually based at the client's premises, it becomes an integral part of their team.

The group has grown very quickly in recent years both organically and through a series of acquisitions – during the last ten years it has averaged one acquisition a month. It operates worldwide as one organisation through a senior international team. This has helped not only the acquisition process, but also the winning and operation of multinational and global contracts. Companies joining the Group during the 1990s brought a combination of strength of heritage and in-depth market awareness to give Compass market leadership through innovation.

Compass Group has introduced initiatives to ensure that the way the company does business is as environmentally friendly as possible. Stringent guidelines and policy requirements, often above those required by local regulations, have been applied across the Group – including waste reduction and recycling, water and energy conservation

(e.g. through the specification of environmentally friendly and efficient equipment – from cookers to cars), the use of environmentally friendly cleaning products, wide-ranging recycling and energy saving and the efficient use of machinery and transport.

History

The company was originally set up in 1941 and has since grown both organically and through acquisitions. Compass Group as we know it today, was formed in 1987 when the management bought out the catering business of London-based food and spirits giant Grand Metropolitan (now Diageo) for £158 million. The company went public the next year, listing on the London Stock Exchange. Believing that real growth in the catering industry could come from size and economies of scale, it began acquiring other companies.

In 1992 Compass bought Traveller's Fare (now Upper Crust), a railway caterer, from British Rail. The company expanded into airports the following year with the acquisition of Scandinavian Airlines System's catering operations. Then in 1994 Compass bought Canteen Corporation, the US's third-largest vending and food service company.

Compass achieved its goal of becoming the world's largest caterer in 1995 with the acquisition of France's Eurest International, putting it ahead of Sodexho and Granada.

By 1996 the company bought Service America, and then Daka International and France's SHRM in 1997. French subsidiary Eurest won the US$40 million contract to supply the staff restaurants at EuroDisney, one of France's top three catering contracts. The next year Compass consolidated its position in the airport markets with a five-year licensing deal for use of the TGI Friday's brand. It joined Pizza Hut, Taco Bell, Burger

In the education sector, Scolarest and Chartwells provides nutrition for pupils and students from pre-school infants through to primary, secondary and higher education establishments.

Morrison and Medirest service the health care and 'senior living' markets across the world.

Select Service Partner is the Group's specialist concessions company providing food at travel, shopping and leisure locations. The company also provides catering for high profile sporting, social and leisure events.

If you travel regularly on Britain's motorways then you are likely to have stopped at one of Compass Groups 48 Moto sites which provide food and fuel for people on the move. The Group also operates 22 further sites in mainland Europe.

Vending is an integral part of the business. People's eating habits are changing around the world and through its Canteen Vending and Selecta operations, Compass offers the convenience of vending in a diverse range of locations including shopping centres, schools and offices. Compass is the largest vending company in the world, servicing clients across the US and Europe.

Compass Group also owns a number of brands including Harry Ramsden's, sandwich chain Upper Crust and Caffé Ritazza. As well as its own brands, the group also franchises a number of international brands including Burger King, Pizza Hut and Krispy Kreme donuts.

King and Harry Ramsden's in Compass' range of branded airport outlets.

In 2000 the company merged with UK hospitality firm Granada Group and the company became Granada Compass.

In 2001 the companies demerged. In the same year Compass bought a US specialist health and senior care firm, Morrison Management Specialists; leading European vending company Selecta; and US health care management company Crothall Services. Late in 2001 Compass strengthened its presence in Japan with the £167 million acquisition of Seiyo Food Systems, Japan's number two food services group.

Product

Compass Group takes an individual approach to the marketplace through sector focused operating companies, which in turn have access to its strong portfolio of foodservice brands. It operates in six clearly defined market sectors through distinct operating companies.

In business and industry, Eurest operates employee restaurants and clients include local, national and international organisations as well as state and regional governments. Clients include the BBC, Ford, the European Parliament and British Airways. Eurest Support Services (ESS) provides specialist food service logistics to clients in the defence, offshore and remote sites sector at locations around the world.

Recent Developments

In 2002 Compass signed arguably the industry's largest contract ever, a US$200 million a year deal to feed Chevron Texaco employees around the world.

Compass works hard to provide its clients with the best possible service and enjoys a contract retention rate of more than 95%. Major new contract wins include GlaxoSmithKline, Volkswagen and Federal Express.

Compass has recently introduced a raft of forward thinking policies to ensure that it does business in the most environmentally friendly way possible and stringent guidelines above and beyond those required by law or local authorities are now in place.

Promotion

Compass Group does not promote its corporate brand externally other than to City and financial audiences. Individual operating companies and brands adopt promotional plans appropriate to their individual sector and/or market requirements.

Brand Values

The Compass Group focuses its business around five core principles in which it hopes to outperform the market. These are; customer and client satisfaction; market leadership; operational excellence; being a preferred employer and maintaining a strong financial performance.

Compass Group's vision is 'great people, great service, great results'. It aims to deliver outstanding service and with a commitment to quality that customers and clients have come to expect. Its brand values are simply stated as 'win through teamwork, embrace diversity, share success, a passion for quality and a can do attitude.'

To live up to these values, Compass Group focuses on attracting, training, developing and retaining the best people, offering the best possible services to its customers and really understanding what they need.

www.compass-group.com

Things you didn't know about Compass

The group has hundreds of famous companies and organisations among its clients but among the more unusual are Liverpool Football Club and The United Nations in East Timor.

Compass managed nearly all of the food serving operations at the 2002 Winter Olympics in Salt Lake City. It provided food for 3,500 athletes as well as 125,000 other people a day during the Games at fifteen venues spread over 5,000 square miles.

In one year, Moto sells 660 million litres of fuel and has over 120 million visitors. Also in this length of time, three million sandwiches, eight million cups of tea and 11.8 million litres of Coca-Cola are sold.

Compass Group serves over twenty million meals and snacks every day in over 30,000 locations.

conqueror

the art of communication

Market

Communication is key to any business, and is continually revolutionised by ongoing developments in technology. Increased use of the internet and email have brought previously unimaginable immediacy and worldwide access to business communications. This new technology has also brought opportunities for businesses involved in paper-based communication.

The speed, quality and increased affordability of computers, desktop printers and digital cameras, combined with ever more sophisticated graphics software packages, means that individuals can produce printed communications that would have been inconceivable ten years ago.

Despite the widely debated concept of the paperless office, paper continues to underpin business communications and still reflects trends in fashion and contemporary styling. Paper is used when communication objectives demand more than speed alone. Its tactile qualities and visual impact mean that it appeals to the senses and is a tangible form of communication through which style and creativity, professionalism and corporate image can be conveyed.

Conqueror, from ArjoWiggins, the world's leading brand of papers for professional business communications, has long been established as a premium brand within the corporate sector. Globally, Conqueror dominates the market with an estimated 56% market share and enjoys strong brand recognition with a high end-user awareness in the UK of 74%.

With its wide range of papers, boards and co-ordinating envelopes, Conqueror is primarily used as quality business stationery with guaranteed performance on all major print processes.

Achievements

Conqueror is one of the few paper brands requested by name and has become synonymous with quality business stationery. Stocked in over 100 countries, Conqueror is a truly global brand. Conqueror has been awarded Business Superbrand status for the second time in a row.

Throughout its 114-year history, Conqueror has embraced change and moved successfully from the era of pen and ink, through the advent of typewriters to the sophisticated world of digital communications.

Independent research conducted in 2002 put Conqueror firmly in the number one position, not only as the best known and preferred brand of paper, but also in blind testing. Conqueror was consistently chosen as the best quality and preferred sheet compared to a wide range of

other premium paper products (Source: Added Value Research 2002).

The Conqueror mill in Dover was the first UK paper mill to achieve BS 5750/ISO 9002 Quality Standard. Investors in People and other awards including the Process category winner of the Management Today Best Factory Awards, have also been achieved.

Conqueror's best-in-category performance and significant competitive advantage has been further enhanced by the development of a number of patented chemical formulations, which are now used in all Conqueror papers. These have led to partnerships with various manufacturers of printing equipment and have resulted in Conqueror being awarded the highest qualifications for paper capabilities and print quality.

History

In the late 1880s, Mr E P Barlow, a director of London-based stationer Wiggins Teape, became intent on producing and marketing a watermarked paper. His vision – an extremely high specification, quality paper called Conqueror London. He also decided what price he was willing to pay for it and had even written out his first order. However, that order was to remain on his desk for many months because the price was so low that no mill owner would accept it. Eventually the first order was taken by Henry Hobday who was struggling to rebuild his business at Buckland Mill, Dover following a disastrous fire. The first Conqueror paper rolled off the paper machine in 1888.

In 1890, Wiggins Teape purchased Buckland Mill. Demand for Conqueror was rapidly growing and in 1910 a dedicated Conqueror machine was installed, increasing the annual production capacity to 2,300 metric tonnes. At this time Conqueror was mainly used as a watermarked letterhead and ledger paper, and enjoyed strong sales in the domestic market with a burgeoning export business.

Production of Conqueror continued uninterrupted until 1940 when the mill received a direct hit by a Spitfire during World War II. From 1945 onwards, major changes in the production of Conqueror were introduced – cotton linter pulp replaced hand sorted and boiled rags, and quality control and specialised colour matching were also introduced. Subsequent investment focused on improving productivity, product consistency and production technology.

In 1990 the Arjo Wiggins Appleton group was formed from the merger of Wiggins Teape with the French paper manufacturer Arjomari and the US manufacturer Appleton Papers. Today, ArjoWiggins is the world's leading

manufacturer of technical and creative papers. Conqueror benefits from this excellence and plays an important part in the group's development strategy, reinforcing an image of the highest quality and innovation standards.

To meet growing worldwide demand for Conqueror, the majority of production was transferred to the larger, state-of-the-art site at Stoneywood, Aberdeen, in June 2000. Conqueror papers are also made at the Ivybridge mill in Devon and the Rives mill in southern France.

The watermark has been integral to the Conqueror brand since its inception in 1888, acting as a hallmark of quality and security. Starting life as simply Conqueror London, it has evolved over the decades to reflect the many developments in the brand. In the 1950s, the gateway image from the Wiggins Teape's logo was added and in the 1970s, 'London' was dropped as Conqueror's stature as a global brand grew.

In 1993 the brand logo and packaging were changed and a new watermark, which showed a horseman, representing William the Conqueror alongside the Conqueror name, was introduced. This remained the brand's visual identity until 2001, when it was replaced by a more contemporary watermark and logo. These focused on the sizeable equity in the Conqueror name and reflected the trend for simpler, uncluttered design and smaller and more discreet watermarks. Conqueror now also offers unwatermarked stock within each family, recognising the increasing trend for unwatermarked papers.

Product

All Conqueror products are suitable for a vast number of different applications including letterheads, business cards, compliment slips, documents, brochures, invitations and calendars. The factor uniting these disparate end-products is the desire to convey quality and a professional image.

The Conqueror range is sold through both trade and office/retail channels: the former concentrating on large size sheet sales to commercial printers and subsequently sold to the end consumer in a pre-printed format. The latter comprising smaller cut size sheets sold through office supplies dealers and retailers and then on to the end consumer in an unprinted format for use on desk top and office printers.

Conqueror papers sold through the commercial print channel include: Conqueror Smooth, a range of clean, fresh products; Conqueror Concept, a futuristic range for distinctly individual communications; Conqueror Digital, high performance papers, specially developed for

the latest digital printing technology; Conqueror Connoisseur for luxurious, understated and classic communications; and Conqueror Texture, with its traditional and tactile appeal, ideal for differentiated business correspondence. Recycled grades are also available within the Smooth and Texture families.

With an ever increasing need to stand out from the crowd, the new, innovative Office/Retail collection is currently being launched – designed to enhance a business image, making that all important first impression last. For the first time, customers can pick up a complete business stationery solution, straight from the shelf.

There are three families of products in the collection – Smooth/Satin, Texture and Concept/Effects – and each has a full choice of products available: A4 paper, envelopes, business cards, compliment slips and also document covers.

The Smooth/Satin range is crisp and contemporary, comprising of two finishes: the sharp and polished 'Ultra Smooth' CX22 and the rich and warm 'Wove'.

The Texture range is natural, with a totally distinctive touch. It comes in two finishes: the classic, traditional 'Laid' and the subtle, elegant 'Contour'.

When your customers want quality business paper, 7 out of 10 will think of **Conqueror.**

The Concept/Effects range is trend-setting and stylish, with three distinctive finishes to stand out from the crowd, namely, Iridescent, Metallic and Parchment.

Across both channels Conqueror provides not only a strong product range, but it also recognises that product guarantees are very important. All technical guarantees are tested and benchmarked to ensure Conqueror products are, and remain, 'the best in category'. Each component of the paper is tested and must conform to rigorous benchmarks at one of the company's dedicated research and development facilities.

Concern for the environment is a key issue. ArjoWiggins works towards reducing

the environmental impact of its manufacturing processes. This is reflected in the group's strict policy of using chlorine-free pulp only made from trees grown in sustainable forests, and its dedication to seeking methods of using energy and natural resources more efficiently.

All Conqueror mills have achieved International Environmental Management Standard (ISO14001) accreditation and heavy investment has been made in heat and power generation as well as water use and effluent processes. Water, a critical part of the papermaking process, is returned to source and treated so that it is clean enough to drink. Water from the Stoneywood mill in Aberdeen is fed direct back into the River Don, a class A salmon river.

Recent Developments

In 1999, ArjoWiggins undertook an in-depth strategic review of the Conqueror brand in order to meet the demands of its markets in the twenty first century. Extensive research and analysis considered all aspects of the brand and resulted in a complete global relaunch of Conqueror in May 2001. This represented a total overhaul of the brand positioning, image and promotion. The aim was to bring Conqueror to new audiences for a wider variety of applications without alienating its existing customer base or damaging its long-established reputation.

The relaunch of Conqueror included the introduction of innovative design-led products, a new Conqueror logo and identity and a simpler, modular brand structure, supported by a range of promotional events across the globe.

Since this relaunch, the brand team have worked hard to continually develop and evolve the range. In 2003, the new collection for Office and Retail channels is the latest advancement. In a world where the vast majority of papers are white, smooth and with minimal differentiation from each other, the new Conqueror Office collection offers a variety of products with highly distinctive features such as watermarks, textures and fashionable iridescent finishes. The collection has been designed to meet all external communication needs and promises to help businesses express their individual style and to really add weight to their message.

Packaging for the new range was key in its development to both engage the consumer and bring the range to life. FutureBrand in Paris designed the packaging to depict striking images of human eyes, which draw the user into the product, helping businesses identify the range that will represent the style and image they want to convey. The distinctive packaging will not only ensure impact and stand out on shelf and in catalogues, but retain a strong brand identity as well. The Office range will be on shelf in January 2004.

Promotion

The promotion of Conqueror focuses on the global communication of a consistent brand image and clear targeted messages to the key audiences of graphic designers, printers and business end users. In 2003, Conqueror launched a number of targeted promotions to business users, printers

and graphic designers alike. The aim: to improve awareness of the complete Conqueror product range and to broaden the appeal of the brand for applications beyond simply letterhead.

Conqueror is in the process of developing a fully integrated campaign to target business-to-business and consumer audiences. The current above-the-line activity focuses on the leadership position of Conqueror within the marketplace, for trade audiences. The copy is impactful and to the point: 'When your customers want quality office paper, seven out of ten will think of Conqueror… Is there any better reason to stock the UK's number one paper brand?'

Brand Values

Conqueror provides a high quality range of papers, which are image-enhancing for the user and can be specified with confidence globally for all professional business communications. The integrity of the Conqueror brand lies in its quality, assurance, wide choice, availability, consistency and reliable technical performance.

Constant development and testing ensures that Conqueror continues to meet the performance demands of both traditional printing processes as well as the latest digital technologies, while inspiring creativity through a range of contemporary and versatile products.

www.conqueror.com

Market

In today's truly global business market, there is more demand than ever for fast, reliable door-to-door delivery services. Helping business to run more efficiently, maintain international links and compete more sharply, the express delivery industry is a crucial facilitator of trade, productivity and investment.

According to a poll by the CBI, nearly one-third of SMEs said they would lose orders if they could no longer have access to international, next-day shipping services. Express services also help keep business costs down, by helping them refine 'just in time' logistics. According to the CBI, 40% of UK firms would have to hold increased inventories if next-day delivery were not available. In all, 87% of UK companies require suppliers to deliver shipments to them by express delivery.

The contribution of the express industry to the economy is huge. In the UK, again according to CBI, some 67 million shipments were carried to, from or within the UK during 2001. The industry supports 70,000 jobs and contributes £550 million per year to GDP. It transports £8.5 billion of UK exports per year – equivalent to 4.5% of total goods exports.

Express services are used by organisations from all sectors, but it is particularly important to the hi-tech industry and is a crucial driver of the new economy. The largest users are manufactures of electrical components, the telecoms industry and pharmaceutical companies. According to the CBI, 84% of new economy firms would be badly affected if next-day delivery services from the UK were no longer available, with 93% saying orders would be lost as a result.

Fuelled by this demand, the express industry is in a strong position and is expected to grow 7% per annum over the next decade, contributing £1.25 billion to UK GDP by 2011.

As one of the best-known and biggest international air express delivery companies, DHL is a truly global brand. Operating in over 220 countries and territories, DHL employs over 71,000 people and has over one million customers. In Europe, DHL is the largest express delivery company, with, according to Transport Intelligence, a 24% market share. The next biggest, TNT, has a 10% share.

Achievements

DHL is the original pioneer of the international express delivery industry, inventing the concept of international door-to-door delivery of time-sensitive documentation. It has perfected using a combination of speed, service and technological innovation to deliver on its well-known corporate objective of 'being there first'.

The secret behind DHL's growth over the last 30 years has been in delivering what its customers want – a factor supported by the fact that many of the companies that started doing business when it started operating remain customers today. The company, which was founded by three Californian entrepreneurs, has grown to be relied upon by many of the world's leading companies.

Throughout its history, DHL has made real breakthroughs – political and technological – on behalf of its customers. In the mid 1970s, it was the driving force behind postal reform in the US, championing the vision of tailored value-added services for business that were different to those offered by the postal monopoly. DHL's lobbying on behalf of its customers to challenge the monopoly was a crucial victory for business.

The company has also successfully harnessed technology to keep its service levels at the forefront of the market. In 1979 it developed one of the first word-processing computers in the world, the DHL1000, which greatly increased the efficiency of processing orders and documentation. In 1983, it was the first express delivery company to introduce a 'track and trace' system, helping customers to follow the progress of their important deliveries.

It has continued this record of remaining at the cutting edge of technology, and now DHL customers can trace their parcels using WAP services on their mobile phone. It is also using Bluetooth technology, so that each item has its own self-identifying radio tag. This means each DHL package is 'smart' – able to be automatically identified wherever it is on its rapid international journey.

History

DHL was formed in 1969, following a chance meeting in a car park between Adrian Dalsey and Larry Hillblom, who both worked for a small San Francisco delivery company, MPA. Hillblom was thinking of investing US$3,000 in stock market earnings in MPA, but Dalsey persuaded him to use the money to help them launch their own company. A real estate businessman, Robert Lynn, joined the two and together they set up DHL's first courier service, between San Francisco and Honolulu in Hawaii. Carrying the documents themselves on overnight flights, they established the concept of air express delivery.

Shipping companies and banks were DHL's earliest customers, excited by a service that could beat the postal system and was also safe and guaranteed. Before the days of electronic money transfer, customers often used DHL to transport cheques, worth millions of dollars.

The DHL Network grew incredibly quickly. The company travelled westward from Hawaii into the Far East and Pacific Rim, then the Middle East, Africa and Europe. In just four years, the

DHL has recently been re-organised into four divisions making up the 'New DHL'. These are: DHL Express; DHL Freight; DHL Danzas Air & Ocean and DHL Solutions.

Even without accounting for the additional infrastructure added to the DHL name following this re-structure, the DHL 'product' is a highly impressive network. With a fleet of 222 aircraft (modern Boeing 757s, acquired for US$1.3 billion in 1999), 18,000 vehicles, 33 distribution 'hubs' in key international locations, offices in 227 countries and 70,000 staff, DHL is a formidable operation.

Recent Developments
The management and divisional structure of DHL changed at the beginning of 2003 when Deutsche Post World Net decided to use one brand to represent all of its express and logistics business worldwide. As a result, the services of fellow group companies Danzas and Deutsche Post Euro Express are currently being integrated under the DHL brand. This has created a global superbrand in global logistics, with the 'new DHL' able to carry anything from a single document to a shipping container, by land, sea or air.

The re-organisation means DHL is now offering its new range of products and services on a one-stop basis, providing a complete range of express and logistics solutions from a single source. The company has expressed the formation of the new DHL with a new corporate identity. The distinctive yellow and red look will be applied across the newly integrated network.

In August 2003, DHL further strengthened its position in the US market with the £700 million acquisition of logistics and express delivery company, Airborne Inc.

Promotion
DHL is one of the best-known business brands in the world, which is partly due to a long heritage of high-profile marketing support. Speed has always been a central theme, such as a 1989 TV ad campaign depicting DHL vans speeding through the air, passing fighter jets and international landmarks on their way. Another famous campaign, emphasising DHL's 'superhuman' efforts to deliver on time, was a 1998 campaign featuring the Diana Ross song 'Ain't No Mountain High Enough'.

Recently, Deutsche Post World Net unveiled an £89 million marketing campaign to communicate the global rebranding of DHL, Danzas and Euro Express under the DHL umbrella. A Hollywood movie trailer-style TV campaign demonstrates the fast-paced and dynamic nature of the industry and familiarises customers with the newly merged group, and its new corporate identity.

DHL is also a major sponsor, and historically has continued the theme of speed in the events it works with. For example, until recently, it sponsored the Jordan Honda F1 team and in the mid 1990s it sponsored British Touring Car champion, John Cleland.

Another important promotional platform for the company – certainly as an internal marketing and team-building tool – is the long-standing DHL Euro Soccer Tournament. Founded in 1982, the competition started life as a small friendly soccer competition between colleagues from Holland, Belgium and the UK. Nowadays, it is an international, annual tournament with over 3,000 employees from all over the world competing.

Deutsche Post | World Net
DHL EXPRESS LOGISTICS FINANCE

More reach.

Nothing's beyond the new DHL. Because DHL Worldwide Express, global leader in air express, Securicor Omega Holdings, a leader in express logistics in the UK and Danzas, global leader in air and ocean freight have joined together under the name DHL to create a new global standard in express delivery, freight and logistics. We can now offer you more performance, more service and more options in more than 220 countries. So no matter who or where you need to reach, visit us at **www.dhl.com**

WE MOVE THE WORLD _DHL_

Brand Values
Perhaps the greatest testament to the DHL brand is that it has become a generic term around the world for sending an item in the fastest possible way. People rarely ask for their urgent items to be sent via international air express – they simply insist they are 'DHL'd'.

DHL has a 'can do' reputation for serving its customers as well as being a pioneer in the use of technology to constantly raise its level of service. Speed, dedication, precision, and investment in people are other key attributes of the brand.

The brand's focus on speed and reputation for being a pioneer are exemplified in its mission of 'being there first'.

www.dhl.co.uk

company had expanded to provide services to 3,000 customers with over 300 staff.

By 1977, it had extended its range of services and started to deliver small packages as well as documents. 1982 saw the first serious spurt of growth, with an additional 30 countries and territories added in this one year alone. The year after, it opened offices in Eastern Europe, the first air express company to do so, and in 1986 it started operations in China, again the first air express company to do so.

By its twentieth anniversary in 1989, DHL had offices in 175 countries and employed 20,000 people. A year later it underlined its international strength by signing a landmark deal with Lufthansa Cargo, Japan Airlines and Nissho Iwai, forming the first Global Transport Alliance and better positioning itself to meet the growing aspirations of its customers.

In 1993, it announced a US$1.25 billion investment in infrastructure and technology to help fuel its expansion, including doubling the capacity of its hub centre in Brussels – its biggest outside of the US. This was followed in 1996 by the opening of an Asia Pacific hub, in Manila, and an Express Logistics centre in Singapore.

In 1998, Deutsche Post AG became a majority shareholder in DHL. This led to DHL becoming wholly owned by Deutsche Post World Net (DPWN). DPWN also owns fellow global logistics giant Danzas, and Euro Express, the parcel and distribution network of Deutsche Post in Germany and Europe (known as Securicor Omega in the UK).

Product
DHL's core business is offering fast, responsive, and cost-effective, express deliveries, in addition to e-commerce fulfilment and intelligent logistics solutions.

Superbrands

Market

E I du Pont de Nemours and Company, to give the corporation its full name, is one of the world's oldest and largest companies and its products have shaped and influenced modern society significantly. World famous products such as Kevlar®, LYCRA®, nylon, and Teflon® all originated in the research laboratories of DuPont.

After starting the millennium under challenging market conditions, 2002 saw DuPont's earnings recovered dramatically from the previous year's low levels; putting aside the significant gain in 2001 from the sale of DuPont's pharmaceutical business. The performance placed DuPont at the top of the chemical industry and ahead of many leading companies in other industries. During the year, DuPont also continued to strengthen its portfolio with technologies and offerings that are significant to its customers – advancing the corporation's growth objectives and creating value for its investors.

Achievements

The effects of DuPont's achievements that span its 200-year history can be seen around the world today. It has developed significant materials that have helped grow the global economy by enabling rapid commercialisation with new and innovative products, such as nylon.

In 2002, for the second consecutive year, DuPont was ranked number one among chemical companies in the Fortune survey of 'America's Most Admired Companies'. DuPont was also selected as the chemical market sector leader of the Dow Jones Sustainability World Indexes; the first index family, tracking the financial performance of sustainability-driven companies worldwide.

History

E I du Pont de Nemours was founded by Eleuthère Irénée du Pont de Nemours in 1802 to manufacture gunpowder. The young du Pont and his family had emigrated to the US two years prior to this. Identifying a need for a good grade black powder and having been trained by the world famous chemist Antoine Lavoisier, du Pont believed he could make a better product. Construction of a factory along the Brandywine Creek near Wilmington, Delaware began in 1802 and the first powder carrying the DuPont label was shipped two years later.

The company underwent a change from family partnership to incorporation in 1899, with a complete reorganisation in 1902, the year of its 100th anniversary. When Eugene du Pont, then company president, died in 1902, three great-grandsons of the founder bought the company and began to expand and diversify. With the opening of the Eastern Laboratory in New Jersey in 1902 and the Experimental Station near Wilmington one year later, DuPont pioneered the concept of organised, applied scientific research in an industrial setting.

The first overseas office was opened in London in 1905 and was designed to serve as an observation post on developing European technology.

The modern form of the oval DuPont logo was used for the first time in 1907 and it looked very much like the trademark in use today – the name DuPont enclosed in an oval with no embellishment.

THE SPORT ALLURING – SHOOTING OFF A TIE

THE WINNING SCORES IN TRAP SHOOTING
ARE MADE WITH

DU PONT
Smokeless Shotgun Powders

The company was listed on the New York stock exchange two years later and has been quoted continuously ever since.

Much of DuPont's success can be attributed to the company's expertise in polymer chemistry: a pivotal discovery was made in 1926 when a DuPont research scientist was able to make cellophane moisture-proof. The packaging industry was revolutionised as a result and DuPont came to understand the importance of innovation.

The next key breakthrough came in 1927 when DuPont scientists developed an understanding of condensation polymers, which led to the invention and commercialisation of nylon in 1938. During that year, Teflon® fluorocarbons and Butacite® resin sheeting for safety glass were also invented. This launched the beginning of the modern materials revolution.

Where to find a 200-year-old company.

Celebrating 200 years of science and innovation in everything from automotive to crop protection.

DU PONT
The miracles of science
www.dupont.com

Between 1950 and 1980 DuPont continued to grow through the introduction of more new products such as LYCRA® elastane fibre, Corian® surface material, Kevlar® high strength fibre, and Nomex® aramid fibre, and subsequently increased its business outside the US.

During the 1970s DuPont turned its attention towards saving energy and renewing resources. For example, tough DuPont plastics resulted in lighter, more fuel-efficient cars, and nylon air-bags saw improved levels of safety. DuPont materials also helped miniaturize electronic circuits for use in cell phones, personal computers and the space shuttle.

As part of a business portfolio reshaping, DuPont divested its energy subsidiary Conoco in 1999, and at the end of 2000 announced the sale of its pharmaceuticals operation. Recently it acquired Pioneer Hi-Bred International, a leading seed producer, and Herberts paints, making it the leading supplier of coatings to the automotive sector. The company has also built up a research competency in biotechnology. This new strength is being integrated with traditional competencies in pursuit of renewable resources and less expensive routes to current products.

Product

Currently DuPont has a portfolio of over 2000 trademarks and delivers science-based solutions that make a difference to people's lives in food and nutrition, health care, clothing, home and construction, electronics, and transportation.

In 2002, DuPont realigned its businesses into five market and technology focused growth platforms, and created DuPont Textiles & Interiors (DTI), with the intent to separate DTI by year-end 2003.

The Agriculture & Nutrition platform leverages biotechnology and food value chain knowledge to increase the quality, quantity and safety of the global food supply. The platform has a broad portfolio of brands such as Pioneer seeds, and Solae soy protein as well as recognised brands of insecticides, fungicides, and high-value, low use-rate herbicides.

The Coatings & Color Technologies platform leverages DuPont technology and knowledge of the titanium dioxide, coatings and inkjet businesses to create added value for customers. DuPont is the world's largest supplier of coatings to the automotive OEM and after markets.

DuPont Electronic & Communication Technologies uses its strong materials and technology base to help advance the speed and reduce the size and cost of electronic and communication devices.

The Performance Materials platform provides high performance polymer materials, systems and solutions for demanding applications worldwide. Products include engineering polymers, flexible resins, and SentryGlas® Plus protective glass.

DuPont Safety & Protection integrates the corporation's technology, know-how and market presence to protect people, property, operations, and the environment. Nomex® fibre, trusted by fire fighters for more than twenty years, will soon be available for the consumer. Kevlar®, long recognised for its protection against bullets, is being introduced into commercial aircraft cockpit doors to improve pilot and public security. This platform also offers such products as Corian® and the new Zodiaq®, which provide attractive, easy-to-clean surfaces for medical facilities, offices, homes and public spaces. Tyvek® HomeWrap helps reduce moisture and prevent mould and mildew within well-designed and constructed walls in buildings.

DuPont Textiles & Interiors is the world's largest integrated fibres enterprise with manufacturing or marketing presence in every major market and region. It is a world leader in the supply of synthetic fibres for clothing. LYCRA® elastane fibre – known for adding the comfort of stretch and recovery to garments – is now being paired with leather to create more comfortable footwear. Durable and lightweight Coolmax® performance fabrics keep the body dry and comfortable while Tactel® nylon and Supplex® nylon, combine soft touch with strength and durability. On the other hand, durable Cordura® nylon is the choice for backpacks, footwear, and luggage.

In the home and construction sector, DuPont offers hundreds of products that add aesthetics, strength, and value. For example Tactesse® nylon fibres bring beauty and durability to Stainmaster® carpets. While for commercial applications, Antron® is the world's most specified carpet fibre.

Recent Developments

DuPont celebrated its 200th anniversary in 2002 and as it enters its third century in business, has been reinforcing its position as a premier science company and continuing its journey towards sustainable growth by linking modern biology with chemistry and physics.

With the growing importance of biological sciences, today's DuPont aims to put science work in global food and nutrition markets. DuPont biotechnology is making inroads in other areas such as the new fibres from renewable resources like corn.

DuPont science is also being applied to electronics. The company has for many years been one of the world's top suppliers of electronic materials, and DuPont scientists are on the leading edge of flat-panel display technology.

Meanwhile the company maintains its leadership in materials science with DuPont products continuing to change the clothes we wear, the vehicles we drive, the structure and decor of our homes and offices, and virtually every facet of our lives where materials provide comfort, aesthetics, performance and safety.

DuPont is also drawing on its heritage and technology to protect what matters most. One of the world's safest industrial companies, DuPont offers its knowledge of safety and

security to other companies and organisations.

What sets DuPont apart is not only its longevity, but its ability to adapt to changing circumstances. Because of its foundation in science – with an emphasis on discovery – change is very much a part of the DuPont culture. The ability to transform and reinvent itself several times during its history is a central reason why DuPont continues to be a competitive global company two centuries after its founding.

Transforming an enterprise as immense and complex as DuPont is no easy task. The key to the company's success during these major transformations has been its steadfast adherence to its core values of safety, health, environmental stewardship, ethical behaviour, and respectful treatment of people. With this successful heritage, DuPont begins its third century as a global industrial leader committed to putting science to work to help make the world a better place in which to live.

Promotion

DuPont was one of the first major industrial companies to understand the importance of the corporate brand. A key factor in building the strength of the DuPont brand has been the consistency of its communications. The corporate message associated with the oval – 'better things for better living through chemistry' – began as an advertising slogan on a weekly network radio show sponsored by DuPont, which debuted in 1935 in the US. The message remained unchanged until the acquisition of Conoco in 1981 and the words 'through chemistry' were dropped to reflect the broader scope of the DuPont enterprise.

The shortened slogan was then used until 1999 when the company undertook a change in corporate positioning to reflect a new strategic direction for its third century. The emphasis shifted from chemicals to science and knowledge-intensive offerings. After exhaustive testing among all stakeholder constituencies, the theme of 'miracles of science' was adopted. The concept behind this new slogan was to reflect the way in which DuPont helps bring the miracles of science to the market, to meet the needs of people worldwide.

The brand's new strap line, 'The Miracles of Science', encapsulated DuPont's commitment to being a worldwide premier science company. 'Miracles' was launched through a global communications campaign with TV, print and poster advertising and associated promotional and public relations activities.

Brand Values

DuPont believes that its ability to adapt to changing circumstances sets it apart from its competitors. DuPont began in the US in the nineteenth century as a manufacturer of explosives. In the twentieth century it became a global chemicals, materials and energy company and its third incarnation is as a broad-based science company.

Reinventing an enterprise as immense as DuPont is no easy task and the company attributes its success to a steadfast adherence to an enduring set

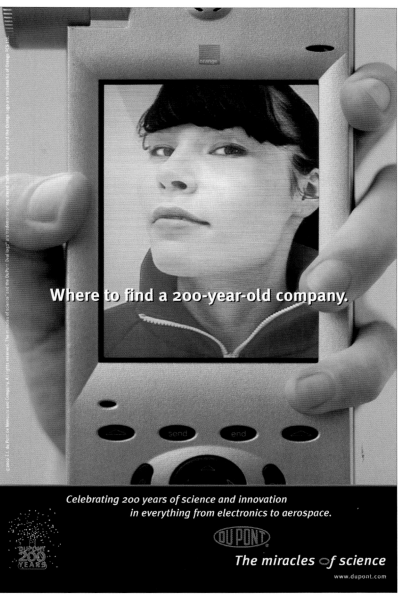

Where to find a 200-year-old company.

Celebrating 200 years of science and innovation in everything from electronics to aerospace.

The miracles of science

www.dupont.com

Where to find a 200-year-old company.

Celebrating 200 years of science and innovation in everything from aeronautics to sportswear.

The miracles of science

www.dupont.com

of core values. These include a commitment to all stakeholders as well as building the business without compromising future generations. It also places great importance on safety, health, environmental protection, ethical behaviour, and treating people fairly and with respect.

www.dupont.com

Superbrands

EARLS COURT AND OLYMPIA LONDON

Market

The UK exhibitions industry is worth tens of billions of pounds to the UK economy each year both through income generated directly at shows and also the indirect tourism income generated through hotels, restaurants, bars and other services. Exhibitions held at Earls Court and Olympia alone generate £1.27 billion each year. Additionally the industry supports more than 50,000 jobs, both full and part-time. Companies operating within the industry include exhibition organisers, hospitality providers, venues, contractors, stand manufacturers, designers, registration companies and market research organisations.

Over the last ten years exhibition space in the UK has grown by nearly 50%. In 2002 there were

Daily Mail Ski and Snowboard Show, RSVP and PLASA. But to talk about Earls Court and Olympia simply as exhibition venues does not do them justice. Conferences, conventions award dinners, sporting events and corporate events are all held at these leading venues.

Some of the biggest names of rock and pop, from Neil Diamond, Elton John and Paul McCartney to Coldplay, REM, Madonna and Oasis, have played at Earls Court.

Earls Court is also home to the BRIT Awards and Olympia to the annual International Showjumping Championships.

In 2002 Olympia was voted the best run venue at the AEO Excellence Awards, the industry's annual gathering. Despite industry wide concerns

gondoliers manning a fleet of gondolas which plied a maze of canals against a backdrop of the famous city. Royal approval of the Grand Hall coupled with such spectacular events served to increase the venue's popularity and the first show jumping event, held there in 1907, pulled in huge crowds. It became obvious that more space would be required and in 1923 the New Hall, subsequently renamed the National Hall, was added. Six years later the Empire Hall opened and was later named Olympia Two. Olympia's exhibition space was completed in 1959, when the West Hall, an extension of the Grand Hall was added. In 2003 the Grand Hall, with its impressive glass barrel roof designed by the Victorian architect Henry Coe and weighing

1,865 exhibitions and shows attracting 15.4 million visitors, around 250,000 of them from overseas (Source: Association of Exhibition Organisers).

Earls Court and Olympia (EC&O) offer just under 100,000 metres of floor space between them. These two London venues rank as the UK's third and fourth largest exhibition centres respectively after the NEC in Birmingham and ExCeL in London's docklands.

Broadly speaking the sector is divided between consumer exhibitions, which have been growing steadily over the last six years and trade shows. The former such as The Ideal Home Show, which has been held at either Earls Court or Olympia since its inception 95 years ago, comprised 44% of the sector in 2002 (42% in 2001). Trade shows like the Amusement Trades Exhibition International which has been staged at EC&O for more than two decades accounts for 55% of all major industry events (56% in 2001).

Achievements

The venues are renowned as home to many of the UK's finest trade and consumer shows and are immediately linked with names such as the Daily Mail Ideal Home Show, Daily Telegraph House & Garden Fair, The Baby Show, Urban Gardens, Spirit of Christmas, Destinations, Confex,

that show attendance is in decline, year on year conference bookings at EC&O rose by 25% in 2003 and the venues attracted 50 new shows. Among the newcomers were launch exhibitions such as the Autumn Ideal Home Show and events like the hospitality industry's RSVP and The Meeting & Incentive Travel Show which chose Olympia as a more convenient, central London venue with newly refurbished facilities. Simultaneously, attendance at almost all EC&O events held steady or grew in 2002.

History

From Buffalo Bill to Bruce Springsteen: EC&O has seen it all. Since Olympia's Grand Hall first opened in 1886, some of history's most famous figures have taken to the stage at the two central London venues together with a cast of millions at the trade fairs, consumer shows and special events that make up the history of these world famous centres.

The venues story began on Boxing Day 1886 when the Paris Hippodrome Circus opened to the public in the Grand Hall at Olympia. The following year Buffalo Bill and his Wild West show drew the crowds in their thousands. Olympia's most spectacular event was Venice in London which ran from 1891 to 1893 and boasted one hundred

1,360 tons, became a Grade II listed building.

In 1937 the attention of the events world was focused on a new centre in West London when the ground breaking Earls Court One was opened. The 43,000 square metre hall had taken just eighteen months to complete using a workforce of 3,500 at a cost of £1.5 million. One of the earliest shows Winter Cavalcade which featured a 100 foot high ski slope packed with hundreds of tons of crushed ice attracted 350,000 visitors. The venues were commandeered by the Government during World War II, but for Christmas 1946, Bertram Mills' Circus returned for Olympia's first post-war event. Earls Court was derequisitioned the same year. The two centres were run independently of each other until 1974 when they were combined under the common ownership of the Sterling Guarantee Trust which subsequently merged with P&O in 1985. In 1991, Earls Court One was joined by Earls Court Two which offered 17,000 square meters of column-free space beneath Europe's biggest unsupported roof-span. Conference centres were opened at Olympia and Earls Court in 1987 and 1993 respectively.

The latest chapter of EC&O's history began in September 1999 when a consortium of Candover Investment and the Morris Family Trust bought the venues from P&O for £183 million and embarked on a £60 million refurbishment programme designed to transform the buildings and make them more flexible, attractive and well-equipped for the needs of today's show organisers.

Product
Earls Court and Olympia can accommodate a wide range of events, from exhibitions and conferences to pop concerts, family spectaculars and sporting events. For example, for a six-week run in the 2003 pre-Christmas period Disney on Ice, Radiohead, Capital Christmas, Justin Timberlake and The Stereophonics were all booked to take centre stage.

Earls Court has been hosting world-class events and exhibitions for more than 60 years earning a worldwide reputation for delivering high attendance figures and excellent organisation. The impressive art-deco architecture venue which boasts 60,000 square metres of prime space and attracts a million visitors annually makes it one of the capital's major attractions.

Earls Court One offers more than 43,000 square metres of floor space with thirteen hospitality rooms and eleven public catering areas making it the venue of choice for many leading trade and consumer shows. Legends of rock and pop have played at Earls Court which is Europe's biggest live music venue with seating for between 10,000 and 20,000 spectators.

Earls Court Two is the smaller venue offering 17,000 square metres of floor space and six

Recent Developments
EC&O has a customer focused approach and has introduced a range of service initiatives. These moves have seen the company become more entrepreneurial in style with a flatter management structure, where the voice of all employees is heard. A revolutionary Customer Services team which brings the operational and support functions provided by the venues under one umbrella means EC&O is able to offer a proactive after sales service. Inside the venues the Venue Improvement Programme has been

throughout the UK, tough competition means that the company knows it cannot afford to rest on its laurels and so puts considerable resources behind marketing activities. As well as promoting the actual venues EC&O's in-house marketing team works with exhibitors to promote their shows so providing a halo-effect for the centres. In addition to VENEWS, a quarterly magazine which keeps business abreast of what is happening at EC&O, the company has produced a free guide for the 30,000 exhibitors who visit the venues each year titled 'Exhibiting made easy'. This is specifically designed to make the experience of exhibiting more effective and enjoyable, while the website, www.eco.co.uk, has been specially designed to be of use to both exhibitors and consumers. In 2003 the group developed a new visual identity for its literature, advertising, direct mail and website. Within the venues themselves EC&O has upgraded advertising sites with LED and plasma screens providing a variety of new opportunities for exhibitors to promote their shows.

Brand Values
EC&O Group provides versatile venues which are capable of creating exciting settings for an array of events. Clients can trust the brand's excellent reputation and considerable expertise in hosting first class events. The EC&O aims to provide the backdrop for a wide range of stylish,

hospitality rooms with four public catering rooms.

Olympia, which features original Victorian architecture, has three halls, comprising almost 40,000 square metres of floor space and attracts more than one million visitors a year. As London's busiest exhibition venue it provides a home to around 40% of exhibitions held in the capital providing a spectacular setting both for established shows and those shows that are growing and will need more room for future growth. Olympia's space, height and viewing galleries gives it the edge for many sports events. Premiere parties, gala awards and new product launches have however also been staged in the venue.

Each venue has its own dedicated, purpose built conference centre. The Earls Court centre is a modern and elegant venue, which can accommodate between 90 and 250 delegates. It can also be used for training courses, corporate roadshows, seminars, product launches and presentations. Olympia's state-of-the-art centre can cater for between 250 and 449 delegates. In addition to a raked auditorium with built-in stage it offers two breakout and five seminar rooms and a 988 square metre exhibition hall.

Each centre provides specialist in-house audio-visual, telecommunications and catering services which are co-ordinated by a dedicated manager.

accelerated and a new retail strategy has resulted in quality high-street brands such as Pret, Dash, Pizza Express, Soup Opera and Costa Coffee opening outlets on the premises. A new hospitality catering brand x-est has been developed by Searcy's to bring a modern and innovative approach to banqueting at both venues. The company has some of London's most talented chefs at its disposal who have been charged with creating exciting and enticing menus for exhibitors and guests. Leading edge technology has always played a role in the two venues operation. Recent innovations have included the £1 million hall dividing system which was specially created for Earls Court One, and opened in 2000, to allow smaller events to feel at home in its massive space. The same year the centres became the first exhibition venues in the UK to trial BT's wireless network. As part of its multi-million pound improvement programme EC&O has invested £400,000 in upgrading car parking including an online booking service designed to enhance the service provided to organisers, exhibitors and visitors.

Promotion
Although the legendary Earls Court and Olympia brand names often act as a magnet for shows and exhibitions and enjoy 90% brand recognition

charming, buzzing and imaginative events. The brand values also trade on the venues' 117 years worth of history, having witnessed some of the UK's most spectacular legendary moments.

www.eco.co.uk

Market

The European car rental market is a massive industry, worth over £3 billion annually. Traditionally, it has been dominated by leading players such as Avis, Hertz and Budget – in fact, according to Euromonitor, the four largest rental firms hold over 60% of the European market. Avis Europe, the largest, has a 18% share.

Although demand for car rental has increased as more people travel by air, the overall market is growing relatively slowly. For example, in the UK, the market is expected to grow from £571 million in 2003 to £670 million by 2007 (Source: Euromonitor).

Business rental is the biggest sector, accounting for around 40% by value in the UK in 2002. As for

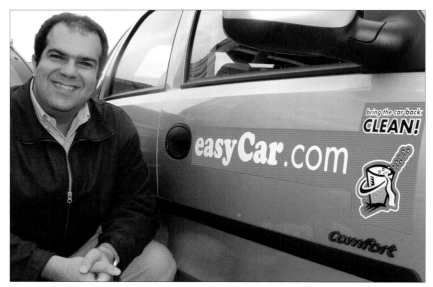

distribution, non-airport rentals are the dominant channel, accounting for 70% of all UK transactions in the UK in 2002.

Although the well-known and biggest multinational rental companies command a large share of the market, the sector has become more fragmented and price-competitive, especially with the entry of price-led brands like easyCar.

easyCar's revolutionary pricing structure and product offering means that it is not only competing against other car rental firms, but also alternative forms of transport. Part of the company's challenge to the car-user is to consider renting a car instead of taking public transport, or even hiring a minicab. Because of this, easyCar's 'competitive set' is potentially very wide indeed.

Achievements

No car rental company has challenged the status quo or changed the business model of the industry as much as easyCar did when it entered the market in 2000. easyGroup founder Stelios Haji-Ioannou set about doing to the car rental industry what he did to the airline industry with easyJet – dramatically reducing prices charged to customers by introducing efficiencies and innovations never seen before.

Offering online booking and following the guideline of the earlier you book the less you pay, easyCar set about reducing prices with a dramatically different business model.

For example, it saved maintenance costs by offering a uniform fleet of vehicles, saved on marketing costs by blazoning the cars with the easyCar brand name and web address, and shunned expensive airport locations in favour of cheaper city centre outlets.

The company stunned the business world when it launched, offering rental for as little as £9 per day. Not only was this cheap enough to raise the possibility for the first time of rental being a cheaper alternative to owning a car, but it did so without compromising on product quality. Observers couldn't believe that the 'standard' car being offered by easyCar was not a basic model, but a Mercedes A-Class.

Over time, easyCar has continued to innovate. Customers can now rent a car for as little as an hour and at as short notice as an hour. That makes car rental a realistic alternative to travelling by taxi, train or bus and further underlines the affordability of rental compared to ownership – especially for people who live in the city.

The fact that 70% of easyCar's customers have not considered using another car hire company is testament to the fact that it attracts a lot of people who are using it for non-traditional car hire purposes.

easyCar also pioneered the concept of giving customers cheaper hire rates if they clean and fuel their own cars. The 'empty to empty' fuel policy saves the cost of easyCar operating a refuelling service while the 'bring it back clean' initiative also saves on the number of people employed at each site.

The cost of opening new sites is also kept to a minimum. Instead of building stand-alone premises, the company rents space, often in a town-centre car park, where they may need as little as fifteen spaces, despite running 150 cars from each site. This high level of utilisation – usually over 90% – also saves money for the customer.

The concept has been enthusiastically received, with easyCar voted Best Car Hire Company in the Telegraph Travel Awards, 2001. Success has also brought expansion, with easyCar growing from its original UK base with

4,000 cars to 8,000 cars, available at 50 European sites. EasyCar is currently studying the possibility of incorporating franchising as part of its continental European business model.

History

Stelios Haji-Ioannou launched easyCar.com (originally called easyRentacar.com) in March 2000. Thanks to a deal struck with Mercedes-Benz, the company launched with a 4,000-strong fleet, based in London, Glasgow and Barcelona.

With the idea to expand to the destinations served by easyJet, the company quickly spread, setting up in Malaga, Amsterdam and Nice.

In July 2001 easyCar secured £26 million of expansion funding from a consortium comprising Bank of Scotland Corporate Banking and NBGI Private Equity. The funding was an important milestone. Not only was it the third easyGroup venture successful enough to attract outside capital, but it also gave the company the leverage to expand its low cost model further around the UK and Europe. Later that year, it opened new rental locations in Geneva and Paris.

In April 2002, easyCar signed an agreement with Vauxhall to add the Corsa to its rental fleet. Starting in London, the Corsa allowed easyCar to offer even lower prices, costing just £7 per day, with the Mercedes A-Class remaining at £9. The fleet has since expanded to include a range of other vehicles.

Product

The easyCar product is based on providing a reliable service at a low price. It achieves this by simplifying the product, and passing on the benefits to the customer in the form of lower prices. easyCar is committed to offering the lowest car rental prices amongst all of its competitors.

The company structures its prices using the 'yield management' system. Based on supply and demand, prices usually increase as more cars are rented at each location. So, generally speaking, the earlier customers book, the cheaper the rental price will be.

The easyCar booking system continually reviews the number of cars rented for each location and tries to predict how popular each day is likely to be. If the rate at which cars are being rented is higher than normal, then the price will go up.

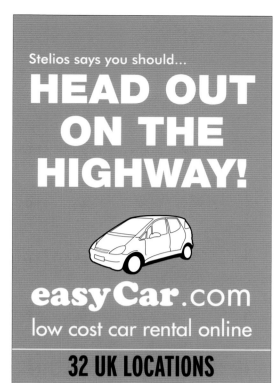
While most rental companies incorporate the cost of preparing a vehicle for rental into the basic cost – which effectively means those people renting cars for a longer period of time subsidise those people renting for a shorter period of time – easyCar separates these costs out. The cost of preparing the car is the same whether the rental is for one day or one week.

This system of preparation charging is connected to the 'Bring it back clean!' idea, whereby, if customers bring their vehicles back clean there is no charge. Alternatively, for customers who do not wish to clean their own vehicles there is a £10 charge which is the cost of ad hoc cleaning. 85% of easyCar customers chose to bring their cars back clean.

Rental costs are also kept down by not offering one-way rentals, collection or delivery.

It also operates a much wider fleet than before. The availability of different models depends on the locations they are rented from, but, currently rental options include Mercedes A-Class, Vauxhall Corsa, Vauxhall Zafira, smart, Renault Clio, Renault Kangoo, Toyota Yaris and Ford Focus.

Cars can either be booked online at the company's website, easyCar.com (over 95% of bookings are made this way) or through the call centre. This direct approach also helps keep

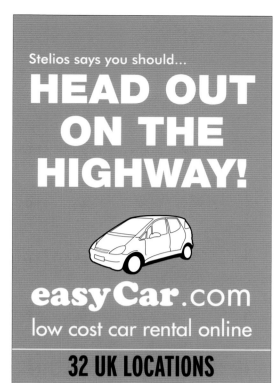
costs down as it avoids paying commission to middlemen such as travel agents.

In the future, easyCar will seek to expand its product, and further reduce prices, by allowing more of its outlets to be run as franchises. This concept has also worked well in the easyInternetcafe business and the company sees strong potential for it to succeed with easyCar.

Recent Developments
A major new product from easyCar was the introduction of 'car club' in March 2003. Designed to bring cheaper and more efficient car hire, the car club operates a staffless site where customers' cars are unlocked and immobilised remotely as customers arrive and leave.

The system, which launched initially in London but is planned for expansion, is available to customers who have already used easyCar at least three times.

When customers arrive at the car club site – having pre-booked online – they call the dedicated car club number with their mobile phone and the car is opened remotely, with the keys already in the car. Upon returning the car to the car club site, the customer calls the dedicated telephone number again, and the car is immobilised.

The advantage to easyCar customers is that they benefit from no transaction fee, a faster and easier car collection and drop-off, and even cheaper prices. easyCar costs are reduced by having a staffless car club with automated procedures. This cost advantage is passed on to customers in the form of cheaper prices.

This is the first time that off the shelf, consumer technology has been used in this way. Standard GSM technology, as used in mobile telephony, powers the easyCar car club which gives the company a huge cost advantage over other car hire companies and other car clubs.

Another important recent development was the appointment of Steve Maltby as chief executive officer, in September 2003. Maltby has more than 25 years experience in the car rental industry gained with Avis and Europcar. At the same time, easyCar announced another senior appointment, of Andrew Brandon as chief financial officer. He joins from Hertz Europe where he was Business Planning Director.

Promotion
The principle marketing channel used to promote the easyCar brand are the cars themselves, as they carry the distinctive orange company logo and contact details. Adopting the same approach as easyJet, which was one of the world's first airlines to display the booking telephone number and web address on the fuselage of its aircraft, this approach helps the company keep prices low by saving on expensive media costs.

However, the company also advertises using traditional advertising, such as newspapers, radio, posters and public transport. Many of the ads are tailored to be relevant to different cities. For example, a recent campaign in London carried the line, 'London's alternative transport' in order to raise awareness of easyCar's cheap prices.

Brand Values
A key aspect of the easyCar brand – and its sister companies within the easyGroup stable – is price transparency. Much of the success and appeal of the 'easy' concept has been to lay open a business sector and challenge competitors to justify their high prices. easyCar is a classic example of this, ingeniously re-engineering the traditional approach to the car rental business, offering dramatically lower prices, and then positioning itself against higher-cost competitors as the consumers' champion.

easyCar does not set out to be a small Hertz or Avis, but a company taking a completely different approach to the car hire business.

www.easyCar.com

Superbrands

Market

Eurostar, the stylish and fast international train service, has transformed business and leisure travel between the UK and the European mainland. Nearly a decade after it began passenger services through the Channel Tunnel, Eurostar carries more passengers than all of the competing airlines put together – it now has 60% market share between London and Paris, and over 45% market share between London and Brussels. Having carried over 50 million passengers since its 1994 launch, it can justly claim to have transformed links between probably the three most important capitals in Europe.

At 186mph (300 k/h), the high speed passenger trains provide fast and reliable connections between London, Paris and Brussels. Yet, Eurostar also provides direct trains from London to Disneyland Paris, and, during the winter ski season, to Bourg St Maurice in the French Alps. Some trains stop en route at Ashford (Kent), Calais and Lille in northern France.

The direct service to Avignon in the south of France, introduced in the summer of 2002, was an immediate success with virtually every train running full. Covering the 722 miles in just six hours and fifteen minutes, this service ran for an extended season in 2003 from May to October.

Competition in this market mainly comes from airlines and Eurostar competes with them head to head, both with the established airlines and the low-cost alternatives.

For the business traveller, Eurostar has a service which is frequent, direct, centre to centre, uninterrupted and smooth, an automatic choice for travel to Paris or Brussels. In the case of leisure travellers, Eurostar competes in an altogether broader area, faced with the competing attractions of other destinations or, indeed, with other leisure activities. What Eurostar offers is, to many, an altogether superior experience to air to numerous destinations –nine direct and over eighty more by simple connections onto continental high speed trains. Because of its simplicity of service, the Continent is so accessible by Eurostar.

Achievements

In 2003 Eurostar took a major leap forward with the opening of the first section of the Channel

Tunnel Rail Link at the end of September. This has shortened journey times by twenty minutes so that London and Paris are now only two hours and 35 minutes apart and London and Brussels two hours and twenty minutes. Lille is a mere one hour 40 minutes from London. Now, the trains can travel in Britain at the same speed as they do on the continent, at a maximum speed of 186 miles per hour (300 km/h). And just for good measure, Eurostar celebrated by achieving no less than 208 mph (334.7 km/h) with a test run on the new line on July 30th 2003. This shattered the previous UK rail speed record of 162 mph set in 1969.

The Channel Tunnel Rail Link will bring significant benefits to passengers but it also represents a major engineering achievement for the UK, and is an example of a successful public/private partnership, having been constructed on time and on budget.

Moreover, by further increasing the attractiveness of rail travel over short haul air, it has the potential to relieve substantial congestion building up at airports, particularly in the South East.

Judging by its long list of awards, Eurostar's claim to have revolutionised travel between London and the continent is without exaggeration. Before its launch in November 1994 about five million passengers per year were carried by air between London and Paris and London and Brussels, but now Eurostar on its own carries over seven million passengers annually. Eurostar has been responsible for developing the short break market, to the benefit of the tourism industry in all three countries, while opening up more travel opportunities for the public. Indeed, Eurostar doubled the overall market in its first five years of operation.

Eurostar has achieved this leadership by a combination of convenience, speed, comfort, reliability and frequency of service, while striving to provide the best levels of customer service in the industry.

With a wide appeal, Eurostar is used by people from all walks of life, from royalty and senior politicians to stars of stage and screen to families, and to the student backpacker. Its passengers come from every country in the world and it is an important link in European tours for visitors from regions such as North America and the Far East.

Eurostar has received awards from a range of organisations including the Royal Institute of British Architects, National Heritage Arts Sponsorship, the Civic Trust, English Tourist Board, Queen Elizabeth's Foundation (for disabled access), French Chamber of Commerce and numerous awards from trade and national press for the quality of the service provided.

History

Eurostar traces its origins back to 1981, when the British and French governments announced the studies for a fixed link under the English Channel. By 1986 the decision in favour of a rail tunnel was taken and planning started on linking the three capitals of London, Paris and Brussels by what was then known as the 'Trans-Manche Super Train'. This was based on the successful French TGV (train à grande vitesse or high speed train), which by then was starting to capture the imagination of travellers on the continent and in Britain.

Following construction of the Channel Tunnel, commercial services started on November 14th 1994 with just two trains per day each way on each route. However, the timetable was soon expanded; the millionth customer travelled in May 1995, after six months' service, and Eurostar has now carried well over 50 million passengers. Subsequent enhancements to the service included: the opening of Ashford International station, Kent; the inauguration of direct trains to Disneyland Paris, the introduction of business lounges at terminals and the frequent traveller programme. The opening of the high speed line in Belgium in 1997 reduced the London-Brussels journey time from three hours fifteen minutes to two hours 40 minutes, and through services started to the French Alps.

The UK arm was privatised in 1996 and, in 1999, the three operators (Eurostar UK Ltd, SNCF and SNCB) created Eurostar Group, a centralised company responsible for determining the commercial direction and development of the Eurostar service. Plans are now in hand for the creation of a single corporate entity, to be called Eurostar International, which will be responsible for running the service and will make its own decisions on the service specification, including investment programmes.

Product

The Eurostar product simplifies travel – a smooth and seamless train journey connecting people from one capital to another. You step on in one city and step off in the other.

During 2002, Eurostar embarked on a £35 million programme to renovate all aspects of its product – terminals and train interiors, on-board service and catering, signage, staff uniforms, literature, its website – all points where there is customer interface. The French designer Philippe Starck was appointed Artistic Director of the project. During 2002/03, there were substantial changes to the terminals at Waterloo, Paris Gare du Nord and Brussels Midi, with new dedicated business desks and check in points and, most notably, dramatic new business lounges. Eurostar lounges boast work stations with laptop points and internet access, telephone charging points, televisions, as well as free newspapers, magazines and refreshments.

Eurostar has now revealed Starck's design concepts for the train interiors which will be

Now 2h35 to the heart of Paris. fly eurostar
eurostar.com *Fastest timetabled journey quoted.*

implemented between 2004/05. These will create a still more comfortable and stylish environment for passengers in both standard and first class.

For customers, often the first contact with Eurostar will be at its award-winning call centre, which takes the majority of bookings direct from the public. Meanwhile, Eurostar's easy-to-use website, recently redesigned, is taking an ever increasing share of the total tickets sold.

Passengers arriving at any of Eurostar's modern terminals will find Eurostar's service is much more 'hassle-free' than airlines. Standard class passengers need check in only 30 minutes before departure, or, in the case of passengers travelling on fully flexible tickets, just ten minutes.

On board, Eurostar offers two classes of accommodation, First and Standard. On the London-Paris route within First Class, a Premium First service offers a range of additional benefits. All passengers benefit from air conditioned coaches and the articulated design gives an exceptionally smooth ride even at maximum speed. The benefits of First Class include wide reclining seats, complimentary newspapers on board, aperitifs, and a meal appropriate to the time of day served at your seat. Premium First includes automatic access to lounges at Waterloo or Paris Nord, a superior on-board meal service with four courses and fine wines, and the benefit of a complimentary car to take customers to their final destination.

Eurostar's multilingual sales and customer service staff are a very visible part of the product. On board there will be two train managers and a catering crew to meet and greet First Class passengers, provide the meal service and staff the two buffet cars. Staff are available at all terminals to help passengers with enquiries and particularly to attend to the needs of special needs passengers. Eurostar is highly accessible to those passengers with disabilities, and assistance can be given to wheelchair users, blind or elderly passengers and those with children.

Recent Developments

Apart from the major service improvement afforded by the UK high speed line, Eurostar has improved its service to passengers in a number of areas in the last few months. For business passengers, check in time has been reduced to a rapid ten minutes, there is a new flexible price structure, and the improvements at Paris Gare du Nord check in area have been completed.

Refurbishment of the train interiors will start in the summer of 2004.

Promotion

In a highly competitive marketplace, saliency is key, as is delivering communications activity which drives preference for travel with Eurostar.

For the Business market, Eurostar is tasked with driving improved relationships with its target markets: the travellers themselves, bookers and influencers.

The opening of the new high speed line in September 2003 presents a new impetus to re-instate Eurostar's superiority position in the marketplace and tip the balance for many who still believe air travel to be more convenient. Coupling the new journey times with the centre to centre benefit makes for a powerful argument.

With a smaller universe than that of the Leisure market, business communications is more targeted with much one-to-one marketing used, along with hard-hitting messages placed on airport routes or in key business hubs and interchanges. Eurostar also communicates to its most valued business customers through the Frequent Traveller scheme.

Eurostar has a high public relations profile and is regularly featured in films, print and broadcast media. Eurostar is frequently used as a tangible visual symbol of links between Britain and Europe.

Brand Values

At the heart of the Eurostar brand is a simple but special travel experience, connecting like-minded people between three of the top capitals of the world. Fast and frequent, transport taking passengers smoothly from the heart of one city to another.

Eurostar's personality embraces an independent spirit, is playful, stylish and cosmopolitan, whilst also being professional and trustworthy.

In its short history, Eurostar has succeeded in appealing to a wide range of people, is highly salient, and has established itself as an aspirational brand without being exclusive.

www.eurostar.co.uk

Market

Over the past four years, the investment management industry has continued to face a challenging and competitive environment, with sweeping regulatory change across most major markets, prolonged weak stock market performance, the penetration of new products and the entrance of more fund providers.

Against this backdrop, both retail and institutional clients are becoming more demanding. So the importance of a strong, well recognised and trusted brand across all market segments is even more critical.

Fidelity International Limited's principal business activity is to provide investment products and services to individuals and institutional investors outside North America.

It has a presence in all the major financial centres in the world and a range of funds covering all regions, industrial sectors and asset classes. Fidelity believes that its research resources are unrivalled within the industry and that it offers customers solid investments based on thorough research, and the security of investing with one of the world's leading investment houses.

Achievements

Fidelity is the world's largest independent fund management company with more than 50 years' investment experience, seventeen million investors worldwide and over £600 billion assets under management.

In the UK, Fidelity leads the mutual fund industry with a market share of 8% and over £19 billion of assets under management.

Few other investment houses can rival Fidelity's long-term performance record which is built on its recognised 'house style' of bottom-up stock picking.

Fidelity's approach to fund management brings results. It has won a string of major awards as well as coming out top in two rating systems published by Standard & Poor's – an independent company that monitors thousands of funds all over the world. Standard & Poor's Micropal Star Rankings reflect a fund's average risk-adjusted performance over the past three years. The highest rating is five stars and Fidelity has received a five-star ranking for seven of its funds – a higher proportion than any other company.

Meanwhile, Standard & Poor's Fund Management Ratings reflect quality and consistency of fund management, as well as performance. The highest rating is AAA and 67% of Fidelity's funds have achieved these ratings – more than any other investment company with twenty or more funds under management.

History

Fidelity Investments was founded in Boston in 1946 under the name of Fidelity Management & Research Company (FMR Co). Today FMR Co is a subsidiary of FMR Corporation. The company believes, as it always has, in the long-term investment potential of international markets.

Largely as a result of this global perspective, the company expanded rapidly. Fidelity International was set up in Bermuda in 1969, to act as a management centre for Fidelity's offshore funds. In the same year, FMR organised a Tokyo

subsidiary to advise on potential investments in Japan. A London office followed in 1973 to cover the UK and European markets.

By 1979 it was clear that the best way for Fidelity International to achieve its goals was to be independent of FMR Corporation. As a result, Fidelity International Limited (FIL) was established to work with Fidelity's clients outside North America. There are still strong links between Fidelity International and FMR Corporation, particularly in the area of research, on which they co-operate.

Fidelity's London office began selling unit trusts in 1979 and developed into a full investment management, marketing and administration group. The years since then have witnessed continuous expansion, with new offices opening all over the world.

Fidelity in the US and FIL together now form the world's largest independent investment management organisation, with over seventeen million clients and customers and US$995.5 billion assets under management.

In 1979 assets under management within the international group amounted to US$0.5 billion; today they amount to US$127.5 billion, illustrating the growth of investors' interest in global diversification of portfolios.

Product

Fidelity in Europe offers a range of products and services including equity funds, fixed-income funds, money market funds and institutional portfolio management.

It was the first investment organisation to launch a 'PEP' wrapped product, and now offers a range of ISAs (which replaced PEPs in 1999) to UK investors. Fidelity is also the third largest provider of ISA products, and the second largest provider of PEP products.

Fidelity distributes its products through a number of channels: direct to the consumer, via Independent Financial Advisers and Asset Managers, and in partnership with banks and life insurance companies. Fidelity is proud of the fact that it can work well with other organisations and that – as partners – both brands can build on each other's success.

One of Fidelity's innovative services is FundsNetwork – an investment supermarket – which allows consumers and their advisers to choose and manage investments online. Customers can open an ISA, invest outside an ISA and transfer PEPs and ISAs into a choice currently of over 840 investment funds, provided by 54 leading companies.

FundsNetwork makes investing quick and easy. It has incorporated news and information services in the system so that consumers can compare funds easily on screen. It takes a matter of minutes to choose investments, place an order or application with payment made through the secure online system or, if consumers prefer paper, by application form. All investments can be viewed in one place and as such, consumers and their advisers can create online valuations and breakdowns covering entire investment fund portfolios, 24 hours a day, seven days a week. Furthermore, they receive a single, consolidated paper statement in the post.

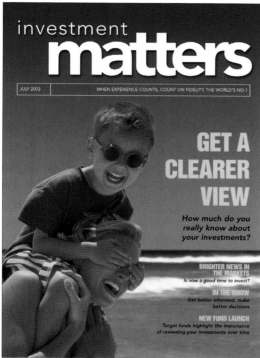

Recent Developments

Customers that invest to grow their money for the future, or for a high, regular income, first and foremost want a company that can consistently perform well over the long term. Fidelity has consistently done this. Its success is recognised with a long list of prestigious awards that it has recently won.

In the Institutional Investor Reuters Survey of European Companies, Fidelity won the top spot for the strength and depth of its European Research for the second year in succession. Fidelity was also the winner in the Survey of Asian Companies. The 2003 Reuters Institutional Investor rankings are based on appraisals of a firm's investment analysis acumen. Theses awards are great accolades for Fidelity's investment team, whose research expertise is fundamental to its stock picking success.

Fidelity received awards for Best Investment Provider (for the third consecutive year) and

Overall Provider of the Year at the Financial Adviser IFA & Provider Awards 2003. It was rewarded for its consistency of performance and for maintaining high standards. In addition, Fidelity was voted Best UK Investment Management Group of the Year in the Standard & Poor's 2003 awards, and Best Investment Provider of the Year in the Money Marketing Financial Services Awards 2003.

Fidelity also won Investment Trust magazine's Best Group award in 2002, the Best UK mainstream trust for 2002 in the Money Observer awards and Fidelity's website was highly commended for 'Best Fund Supermarket' and 'Best online Investment Provider' by the Online Finance Awards 2002. The judges were principally impressed by the comprehensiveness of its product range. Previously, the site has also been highly commended for Best Online Fund Provider in 2001 and won the same award in 2000. In fact, Fidelity has won a plethora of other awards from publications – more than 50 in the past year – for its overall investment capabilities and also for individual funds and managers.

Promotion

Since it first started promoting its products and services in the UK in 1979, Fidelity has had a heavyweight advertising presence in the personal finance pages of the national press, and in the trade press for financial advisers. Since the mid 1990s it has also built the brand through posters on roadside and rail networks and through advertising the lifestyle benefits of its products in weekend colour supplements.

Another key element in the promotional mix is direct mail, sent to both advisers and investors. This is often educational and includes regular newsletters, as one of Fidelity's aims is to keep people informed in bad times as well as good. Events such as road shows and workshops have also become an important way of communicating with Fidelity's stakeholders.

Fidelity has always taken pride in being at the cutting edge of technological innovation. It has had a transactional website since 1997 and the internet is an increasingly important method to communicate with its intermediaries and investors and for them to conduct business. In fact, around a third of its new business is via the internet.

Seven years ago, Fidelity adopted a new UK corporate identity – red, white and blue – and with a punchy and straight-talking tone of voice to reflect its American heritage. This look and feel has been rolled out to all the markets in which it operates throughout Europe and Asia. Fidelity is now a strong and recognisable global brand. The 2003 European Survey by Sector Analysis which is a poll of 500 distributors of investment products – top banks, insurers and financial intermediaries – showed that Fidelity is both the best known and the most highly-regarded fund manager.

Brand Values

Fidelity is committed to providing money management excellence to millions of customers around the globe, through hiring the best people and investing in research and technological innovation.

One of its key messages is leadership – it provides the best people, best products and best tools in the industry. It also has 50 years of innovation in products and technology and is trusted by more people with more money than any other investment house.

Fidelity is also totally dedicated to investment management – it is all it does and all it intends to do. It has unrivalled resources devoted to company analysis and portfolio management and a consistent, award-winning record of out-performance.

The company strives to understand the issues faced by investors, intermediaries and institutions and helps them to plan wisely and make the right decisions and customers and partners are educated and informed, in good times and in bad.

www.fidelity.co.uk

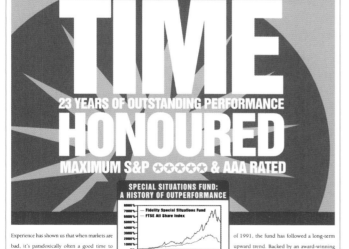

Market

As the business world faces its worst advertising recession for 30 years: a recent war in Iraq, the global threat of terrorism, corporate scandals, turbulent stock market movements and the ensuing loss of business confidence, the demand for independent, authoritative and accurate business and financial news is greater than ever.

Achievements

Whether the FT is targeting its readers, its website users and subscribers or its corporate clients, the FT's reach has never been stronger. The combination of the FT's newspaper circulation, FT.com traffic figures, and the number of people viewing FT content via corporate content sales and syndication services, ensures that more people than ever before now rely on the FT brand.

FT.com won the Media Prize at the New Media Age Awards in July 2003 for the launch of subscription services. Also in 2003 the website won Best Internet Special Feature at the Eppys, Best Marketing Information Service at the Legal Marketing Awards and Best Investigative Reporting at the Netmedia European Online Journalism Awards.

In addition, the FT supplement, How To Spend It Magazine, won Heatset Colour Supplement of the Year at the 2003 Newspaper Awards.

Throughout 2003, FT editorial also gained accolades. At the British Press Awards 2003, Adrian Michaels and Peter Spiegel won Business and Finance Reporters of the Year and David Buchan and Tobias Buck won Business and Finance Writers of the Year. The Business Journalist of the Year Awards 2003 saw Richard Tomkins being not only named Business Journalist of the Year but also given the award for the Best Marketing, Branding and Design piece. Meanwhile, Martin Wolf was presented with the Decade of Excellence Award and John-Paul Fintoff came away with the Best Management and Business Education Award.

David Gardner, FT international affairs writer, was also awarded the David Watt prize for Political Journalism.

History

The Financial Times launched in 1888 as the 'friend' of the 'Honest Financier and the Respectable Broker'. However, it wasn't until 1893 that the FT began printing on pink paper. This was done through a stroke of early marketing genius by Douglas Macrae to distinguish the paper from its rivals.

In 1919, Berry Bros, owners of The Sunday Times, and later The Daily Telegraph, took control of the FT. Developments took place over the course of time, for example in 1935 the 30-share index was introduced to the Financial Times for the first time.

The Financial News, which was established in 1884, finally merged with the FT in 1945 when its chairman Brendan Bracken bought the

company. The paper did however retain the name Financial Times as well as its signature pink paper.

In 1953 the 20,000th issue of the FT was celebrated. To reflect the increased scope of the newspaper an arts page was launched and 'Industry' 'Commerce' and 'Public Affairs' were added to the masthead.

Four years later the paper was taken over by Pearson and the business moved in 1959 to Bracken House, Cannon Street. Following this, further improvements were made and in 1960 the Technical page (now Technology), Executive's World page (now Inside Track) and the Saturday paper's 'How To Spend It' page were all introduced. By the following year, average circulation exceeded 132,000. Developments continued, with the European edition being printed in Frankfurt for the first time in 1979.

Circulation of the FT in the UK had increased significantly and in 1986 passed the 250,000 mark with the aid of the 'No FT…No Comment' ad campaign. In the same year, technological advancements also took place when printing processes moved from hot metal to cold set printing.

In 1987, the FT published the first world share index and, two years later, the FT Group Head Office relocated to Number One Southwark Bridge. Under the new editor, Richard Lambert who joined the company in 1991, several new initiatives were introduced, including the first edition of 'How To Spend It' magazine in 1994. One year later, the international edition was relaunched and FT.com, the Financial Times website, was created.

In 2000, Creative Business was introduced as a supplement with the UK edition and the European edition was relaunched. 2001 saw the launch of Global Investing pages in the US edition, Richard Lambert named Business Journalist of the decade and the FT reached the 500,000 copies mark. In addition, Andrew Gowers, former founding editor of Financial Times Deutschland, was appointed editor of the FT.

In 2002 significant events for the paper included the launch of the FT Fund Management supplement as well as the relaunch of FT.com with additional features such as subscription services. Unique monthly users of the site reached 3.2 million and page views exceeded 50 million by December of that year.

In terms of the FT's international development, its first move abroad took place as far back as 1979 when a European edition, printed in Frankfurt, was launched. By the end of 2002, the FT newspaper was being printed in nineteen cities across the world, including New York, Paris, Tokyo, Madrid, Stockholm, Los Angeles, Hong Kong, Milan,

Kuala Lumpur and Seoul. Indeed, these operations have been so successful that international circulation sales now exceed that of the UK. International expansion has continued, with the FT now being digitally printed in South Africa.

Product

The FT is firmly established as one of the world's leading business information brands and is internationally recognised for its authoritative, accurate, and incisive news, comment and analysis. Whether in print or online, the Financial Times is essential reading for the global business community.

The Financial Times is one of the world's leading English language newspapers. Following the launch of a digitally printed version in South Africa, and the opening of a new site in Dubai, the newspaper is now printed in 21 cities across the world. With a daily circulation of over 460,000, the Financial Times has a readership of more than one million people and is available in 140 countries.

FT.com is one of the world's leading business information websites, and the internet partner of the Financial Times. The site reflects the values and authority of the Financial Times newspaper, with the immediacy and interactivity of the internet. Since its relaunch in May 2002, the website has continued to be the definitive home for business intelligence on the web, providing an essential source of news, comment, data and analysis for the global business community.

FT.com's 3.6 million unique monthly users generate 55 million monthly page views, delivering a premium audience to advertisers. On top of this FT.com also has 56,000 subscribers. The website combines agenda-setting editorial content with comment and analysis, financial data, discussion groups, and a range of tools to search the web, manage the working day and seek out leisure opportunities. At the core of the site is authoritative news and analysis, updated throughout the business day by journalists in the Financial Times' integrated newsroom and by the FT's large network of correspondents around the world.

Recent Developments

In 2003 the FT expanded into Asia. In the third quarter of the year, an Asia edition of the paper was launched, following on from the success of Zhongwen, the Chinese language business service on FT.com.

In April 2003 the FT underwent a revamp. In the weekday edition changes included extended UK news coverage, more British business news, a daily sports page, and bigger and broader features pages. The weekend edition was reorganised into three clearly defined newspaper sections – news, Money and Business, and Weekend, as well as a new glossy weekly magazine, Financial Times Magazine.

FT's subscription services include Lex live, an intra-day email building on the newspaper's famous 'Lex' investment column, an improved Power Search facility with fast, intelligent information retrieval from over 500 worldwide publications, increased company data with the World Company Financials package, the view print edition service enabling readers to view a printable pdf of all editions of the FT newspaper, the night prior to publication. Personal Office is a fully personal administration system, which includes a reading and sending email facility and calendar tools.

In 2002, FT Fund Management (FTfm) was launched as a weekly supplement. FTfm has the world's largest circulation of any fund management title, and offers one of the most comprehensive pricing services for funds. Covering a wide variety of industry news, analysis, trends, opinion pieces, fund performance reviews and a full listing of managed funds, FTfm provides essential insight and analysis of the fund management industry and the people behind the scenes.

Promotion

The revamp of the UK edition of the Financial Times was complemented by an extensive brand and marketing campaign. The multi-media campaign included outdoor, radio, TV, financial press and trade press advertising. It also successfully boosted brand salience and awareness – reminding the UK that the FT is unrivalled when it comes to business insight and analysis for readers both

at work and at leisure. The revamp has refocused the offering for advertisers and promoted the FT brand – despite the economic downturn.

Brand Values

The FT aims to be the world's business information brand. Its goal is to become essential reading – both in print and online – for business leaders and other decision-makers, through the quality of its editing and reporting. The FT is now a truly global news organisation, seeking to explain how events in one area of the world are likely to have an impact on institutions and economies in other regions, looking for trends and common patterns, context and connections.

The FT is distinct by virtue of its commitment to accurate, impartial and authoritative reporting, which is always of the highest quality.

www.ft.com

Things you didn't know about
FT

The FT turned pink in 1893 – a stroke of marketing genius by Douglas Macrae to distinguish the paper from its rivals.

The Financial Times is believed to be the only daily newspaper with a greater circulation outside of its home market.

The FT is the only non-US newspaper to be delivered to the White House on a regular basis.

The Financial Times and FT.com are read in more than 140 countries.

The FT has 500 reporters worldwide, working in 100 news bureaux.

James Bond masqueraded as a Financial Times reporter in 'Live and Let Die'.

Market

Goodyear is a truly global tyre and rubber company marketing world class products in a number of different market sectors. Best known for its leading position in tyre development, with some 200 million tyres sold every year, Goodyear are also a major retailer with a network of fast fit outlets across the world, as well as being a major producer of chemicals and industrial rubber components.

Goodyear products are fitted by the leading original equipment vehicle manufacturers such as Ford, Renault, DaimlerChrysler, Fiat, Volvo and Peugeot and are trusted by millions of motorists for safety, durability and high performance.

In the UK, Goodyear holds a leading position in all market sectors, and is working in conjunction with UK vehicle manufacturers such as Mini and Land Rover in the development of new tyre technologies, such as Run Flat.

Although Goodyear has its own tyre retailing network in the UK, Goodyear tyres are available from almost every tyre dealer in the country, proof of the brand's high regard in the trade and high acceptance amongst consumers.

Achievements

All tyres may be black and round, but the level of technology contained within is staggering. Goodyear have led the way in tyre development

History

Charles Goodyear was a man who changed the world. In 1839, he discovered 'vulcanisation', the process that turns rubber into a versatile, weatherproof material. Goodyear died a pauper, but his name lived on when Frank Seiberling immortalised his name when founding the Goodyear Tyre and Rubber Company in 1898 in Ohio.

With just thirteen workers, Goodyear production began on November 21st, 1898, with a product line of bicycle and carriage tyres and horseshoe pads.

Ten years later Goodyear introduced the first all weather tyre, with its famous diamond tread design. In 1912, Goodyear launched its first ever airship, or blimp. These became an icon of the skies, aerial ambassadors for a proud brand.

In the early days, Goodyear manufactured blimps for commercial and military use.

Over the years, Goodyear built more than 300 airships, more than any other company

materials for more than 2,000 artificial reefs and floating breakwaters, protecting harbours and providing habitats for marine life. In 1981 Goodyear introduced its new family of Eagle high-performance tyres. For its innovative and highly successful work in hazardous waste disposal, Goodyear received the Environmental Industry Award from the White House.

In 1999, a global strategic alliance with Sumitomo Rubber Industries, owners of the Dunlop tyre brand, confirmed the organisation's global leadership.

Product

On the road, on the track; on tractors, on earthmovers, on trucks, whatever the vehicle, whatever the terrain, Goodyear pride themselves on offering high performance tyres for all applications.

Many high performance car drivers choose the Goodyear Eagle F1 as it brings race proven technology to the street. A stunning directional tread pattern gives the roadholding of a racing slick in the dry and new levels of security and traction in the wet.

Goodyear lead the way in developing run flat tyres. Cars as diverse as the Chevrolet Corvette and Mini Cooper are available with Goodyear Run Flat tyres – an incredible technological development that allows the driver to continue for up to 50 miles after a puncture.

A tyre has to cope with many demands. It has to reduce road noise, provide passenger comfort,

INTRODUCING THE GOODYEAR EAGLE F1 NOW YOU CAN DRIVE THE MOST EXHILARATING RACING CIRCUIT IN THE WORLD»

THE WORLD.

THE NEW EAGLE F1 WITH RACING SLICK TECHNOLOGY.

for over a century. The company took only 28 years to become the world's largest tyre and rubber company and have made a habit of passing milestones ever since.

Goodyear led the way in the use of nylon, synthetic materials and more recently introduced the run flat tyre to the mass market, bringing safety and peace of mind to a new generation of motorists.

Goodyear believes in proving its ability at the cutting edge. The result? More Formula One Grand Prix victories than any other tyre manufacturer and a road tyre range that developed from this success.

With manufacturing bases across the world and sales operations in most countries, Goodyear prides itself on its diverse team of some 90,000 associates and its commitment to quality. In the UK alone, the company employs over 3,000 people, with three UK group factories.

in the world. Akron, Ohio, the company's world headquarters, was the centre of blimp manufacturing for several decades.

During World War II many of the Goodyear-built airships provided the US Navy with a unique aerial surveillance capability. Modern surveillance technology eventually eclipsed the advantages of the airship fleet, and in 1962 the Navy discontinued the programme. Since then, the Goodyear blimps have been regular sights at major sporting events around the world.

In 1927, Goodyear started making tyres in the UK. This was Goodyear's first non-US plant, and in the years to follow the company expanded in every corner of the globe. By 1963 the company had made its one billionth tyre but kept a handle on its conservational concerns. In 1978, Goodyear pioneered new uses for old tyres as construction

4,000 MILES. 33 DAYS. 16 TEAMS. 4 TIME ZONES. 3 CONTINENTS.

1 TYRE.

GOODYEAR - OFFICIAL TYRE SUPPLIER TO THE 'LANDROVER G4 CHALLENGE'

The Land Rover G4 Challenge is the ultimate global adventure. That's why the rugged Goodyear Wrangler MT/R from Goodyear has been selected as control tyre for every challenger!

With its unique, 'Durawall', puncture-resistant sidewall compound and a superb all-season tread Wrangler MT/R is designed to get to grips with the toughest terrain on the planet.

But for less demanding, everyday use Wrangler AT/R offers all the grip and traction you'll ever need. And it's just one of the outstanding tyres in our comprehensive 4x4 range.

So for performance you can count on wherever you tread – stick with Goodyear, the world's No.1.

GOODYEAR
We discover. You explore.

For further information on the Goodyear 4x4 tyre range and details of your nearest stockist call 0845 367 6869

offer maximum grip, and of course, be durable and safe. Goodyear's experience in research and development, at the forefront of racing, and working with all major car manufacturers, means that Goodyear products can be trusted, day in, day out.

Off the road, the latest Goodyear Wrangler MT/R is a real tough act. It was developed to withstand the most extreme off road driving – and was chosen by Land Rover as the official tyre for the inaugural Land Rover G4 Challenge.

In the UK, Goodyear is the market leader in the agricultural tyre market. British farmers can rely on Goodyear for durability and traction but also for innovative technology that reduces soil damage and compaction – which results in greater productivity and yields.

In the fleet market, Goodyear know that fleet managers require good service as well as quality tyres. Truck Force is Goodyear's pan-European service network for truck operators, and keeps

fleets moving day and night. The Truck Force offer includes online fleet tyre management systems, part of Goodyear's commitment to developing e-commerce solutions. This is evidence of the company's reinvention as a true service led organisation.

Recent Developments

As the world's tyre industry leader, Goodyear is committed to protecting the environment and

the health and safety of associates, customers and the communities in which the company operates.

Environmental initiatives are an integral part of Goodyear's strategy. Policies for responsible tyre disposal and recycling are part of the ethic behind a major manufacturer and leading retailer of tyres across the world.

A commitment to discovery is part of the brand's mindset. The Goodyear GT3 tyre features a constituent which Goodyear's technical staff developed from ordinary corn. This revolutionary tyre development from

Goodyear is a benchmark in the world of eco-friendly engineering. This is because the GT3 family car tyre is the first on the market using a new starch-based filler substance called BioTRED.

Goodyear are also committed to delivering the highest service levels to their customers. The company's recent multi million pound investment in the TyreFort building in Birmingham has created the largest tyre distribution centre in the UK, capable of holding one million tyres for nationwide next day delivery.

Promotion

The Goodyear brand has built its strength through constant investment and innovation in integrated marketing campaigns. Periodic heavyweight advertising campaigns have reinforced the brand message supported by regular promotional activity in tyre dealerships. Indeed, the brands first television advert was as early as 1948.

Goodyear believes that the best way of promoting its product is to show them perform. Following years of unparalleled success in Formula One, Goodyear are still at the forefront in motorsport, as the tyre of choice for NASCAR, the world's fastest saloon car racing championship.

In addition to above-the-line advertising campaigns, Goodyear regularly exhibit at major UK exhibitions, are involved in a diverse range of sponsorship programmes and support this activity with hard hitting, targeted below-the-line activity such as direct marketing.

And of course, one can't forget that Goodyear has a distinctive brand icon in the form of the Goodyear Airship which performs a powerful advertising role for the brand around the world.

Brand Values

Brand Values are not just a superficial afterthought for Goodyear. The company's motto is 'Protect Our Good Name' and this message adorns the offices of every Goodyear location and is a key part of every Goodyear employee's job description.

This is brought to life through a developing culture in which a committed and competitive team can excel.

The Goodyear brand stands for many things. But the dominant brand values stem from the product excellence, superb all weather performance, the highest levels of safety, reliability and durability and a commitment to lead the way in discovering eco-friendly solutions for the future of motoring. This is what drives millions of motorists, and this is what drives Goodyear.

www.goodyear.co.uk

Heathrow **express**

Market

Heathrow is the world's busiest international airport as well as one of the busiest cargo ports. Handling over 63 million travellers per year and with over 90 airlines, Heathrow is regarded as one of the world's leading hubs.

Heathrow Express is the high-speed rail-air link between Heathrow Airport and central London, providing a fifteen-minute journey every fifteen minutes throughout the day. Carrying an average of 15,000 passengers a day, the non-stop service has gained market share over the tube and taxi since it launched in 1998.

The continuing success of Heathrow Express has resulted in the removal of over 3,000 journeys from the regions roads every day, and has made savings to the UK economy in terms of time, compared to the use of tube, taxi or bus of over £444 million.

Achievements

Heathrow Express has won an enviable number of awards and accolades in its relatively short life. In a little over five years, Heathrow Express has won awards from its peers in the rail, tourism, leisure, and marketing sectors for its innovative approaches and high standards of service.

History

Heathrow Express was officially opened by the Prime Minister, the Rt Hon Tony Blair MP, on June 23rd 1998.

A wholly owned subsidiary of BAA, Heathrow Express is a £450 million initiative which aims to increase the use of public transport to and from Heathrow Airport by providing a fast and efficient rail-air link with central London.

BAA invested a further £25 million to enhance the Heathrow Express service by providing a remote airline check-in facility at Paddington Station. Opened in June 1999, the facility allows passengers to check in with their airline up to two hours before their flight and receive their boarding card, allowing them to travel in luggage-free comfort to the airport on the Heathrow Express. Over one million passengers have used the check-in facility since launch.

Heathrow Express also introduced its Taxi Share scheme in 1998, in conjunction with the Licensed Taxi Drivers Association to enable passengers to share a taxi on their onward journey from Paddington Station. The lower fares and shorter waiting times generated by the scheme allow 40-75% more people to leave Paddington by taxi during peak hours. Over 305,000 travellers have shared a taxi so far, saving about 775,000 taxi miles and so helping to ease the pressure on London's roads during the rush hour.

Fast returns guaranteed.

Central London to Heathrow in 15 minutes; every 15 minutes; And the same on your way back.   Heathrow **express**

*Average journey time for trains from London Paddington to Heathrow terminals 1, 2 and 3 (approx 8 minutes more to terminal 4) between 05.10 and 23.10. ¹Later trains subject to different timings.   www.heathrowexpress.com   Timing is everything

Product

Heathrow Express provides a dedicated, non-stop, high-speed rail link between Heathrow Airport and central London, with a journey time of only fifteen minutes. There are two dedicated stations at Heathrow: Heathrow Central (serving Terminals 1, 2 and 3) and Terminal 4, which is a further 6-8 minutes away. The inter-terminal service also provides an additional option for passenger movement around the airport, offering free travel between the two stations.

The design of the Heathrow stations ensures that they offer customers swift, convenient access to the ultra-modern train service. For people with special needs, the service includes dedicated seating areas in trains. The dedicated platforms at Heathrow and London Paddington are level with train floors to ensure completely step-free access.

The purpose-built trains, capable of travelling at 100mph, run between 5.10am and 11.30pm from Paddington Station 365 days a year (the only exception being on Christmas Day when the service usually runs every 30 minutes). The carriages are air-conditioned and have ergonomically designed seating, generous luggage areas and exclusive Express TV keeping passengers up to date with international news issues. There are Quiet Zones on the trains where the use of mobile phones is prohibited and Express TV is not in use.

Heathrow Express enjoys a loyal customer base and carries approximately 15,000 customers each day. Research by the company indicates a high awareness level among potential users of the service, with the majority of these travellers stating they would consider using Heathrow Express in the future.

Heathrow Express is a key member of Airport Express, a joint alliance between BAA plc and National Express Group which promotes and markets the Heathrow, Gatwick and Stansted Express rail services. The alliance brings together the sales and marketing activities of all three operations to create a single point of contact for travel trade agents and tour operators.

Recent Developments

Steadily increasing passenger numbers, totalling over 22 million in the past five years, has led to further investment to provide increased capacity on board.

In July 2001 Heathrow Express placed an order for five new carriages, costing a total of £6.5 million, which has resulted in an additional carriage to each Heathrow Express train set-up providing a 14% increase in seat capacity. The new nine-car trains were brought into service in a rolling programme which is now fully complete.

In addition to the purchase of additional rolling stock, Heathrow Express also announced

details of a multi-million pound project aimed at delivering a robust ticketing and revenue system using the latest ticketing system technology. The project involved the replacement of 23 Automatic Ticket Vending Machines (ATVMs) and eight Ticket Office Machines (TOMs) at Paddington and Heathrow Airport. It also includes sales of tickets over the internet and the introduction of SMART card technologies.

Heathrow Express had already implemented many of the recommendations detailed in the Cullen Inquiry into the 1999 Paddington rail disaster, including the introduction of photoluminescent marking around emergency evacuation windows and an evaluation of a low-level escape lighting system, as part of a fleet wide refurbishment of its rolling stock.

Other upgrades introduced in the refurbishment included the upgrading of the flat screen televisions, incorporating state-of-the-art technology to provide a clearer, sharper picture; new reinforced luggage shelves; improved lighting system and the refreshment of interior fabrics throughout the trains.

A new development for 2003 is Webtod. This enables customers to book and pay online in one simple transaction. Customers are given a reference number, which they simply type into one of the Heathrow Express ticket machines or insert the credit card used to make the booking to retrieve their ticket at the point of departure.

Promotion

Heathrow Express primarily uses press, outdoor activity and radio to execute its promotional strategy. The company launched an advertising campaign called Back to Business for 2003/04, which highlights the convenience and speed of the Heathrow Express service. The campaign is directed at the business market, particularly within the UK, and aims to communicate the key benefits of the service. The objective is to encourage trial among prospective business passengers by focusing on the core business messages – speed, frequency, and convenience.

The campaign was based around the 'Timing is everything' message and included dramatic images of time crucial activities

such as cricket and stunt performing. To encourage interaction with the brand, a number of online creative executions were also developed, which were placed on a number of large corporate systems in the City of London.

The focus for below-the-line activity is working and developing relationships with airlines at Heathrow. Frequent travellers are the focus of joint initiatives run in conjunction with key airlines, where complimentary upgrades to First Class on Heathrow Express are offered. Key benefits of service and the airline check-in facility at Paddington Station are promoted through airline frequent flyer programmes.

To stimulate the leisure market, Heathrow Express uses 'two for one' style promotions which are executed through a number of channels including Time Out magazine and with a number of travel partners.

In addition, customer relationship marketing ensures consistent and frequent communication with the Heathrow Express customer base, giving news, promotions and information about new products. An awareness campaign also exists across all four terminals at Heathrow Airport communicating key benefits of use and directional 'way finding' which steer customers in the direction of the Heathrow Express platforms.

Heathrow Express has listened to and met the needs of their loyal customers by offering convenience in the form of a new product called Carnet, which offers travellers twelve single tickets for the price of eleven. Other activities include advertising in in-flight media and in-flight promotions.

Brand Values

The key brand values are speed, frequency and certainty. Recent research by Heathrow Express has shown that these key benefits are recalled most by its customers.

For both business and leisure customers, Heathrow Express aims to provide the excellent levels of comfort and customer service that air travellers have come to expect. However, different aspects of the brand's personality are highlighted for the business and consumer

markets to reflect the most desirable aspect of the brand for each of these segments.

For the business traveller, the brand is portrayed as fast, frequent, reliable and convenient, efficient, comfortable as well as stress-free, professional, modern and stylish.

When speaking to the leisure market, the brand is reflected as not being overly formal or austere while being fast, reliable, convenient (customers can check-in at Paddington), approachable, family friendly, comfortable and providing a stress-free start to the family holiday.

www.heathrowexpress.co.uk

Click to jump

Heathrow express

HILL & KNOWLTON

Market

The practice of public relations (PR) is about creating reputational or business impact through creative and targeted communication with a number of audience groups – from employees to shareholders, from governments to customers. PR's power is essentially in persuading others to tell your story in a compelling manner, corroborating the quality of products, services and activities by lending third party credibility.

The PR industry as a whole in the UK is worth an estimated £1.2 billion – on a global scale, ranked second only to that of the US. There are approximately 2,800 PR consultancies in the UK, of which the 150 largest have a combined fee income of over £600 million. An estimated 30,000 people are employed in public relations throughout the UK, with PR positioned as one of the top three career choices for graduates.

Hill & Knowlton is one of the UK's top three agencies and has consistently grown faster from organic growth than any other major agency in recent years. It is the leading multi-specialist agency and has been consistently ranked as the number one consumer agency for the past five years, advising eleven of the 50 biggest selling brands in the UK (Source: Marketing Magazine August 2003). It also ranks within the top three UK PR agencies serving the B2B; financial services; healthcare; and technology and corporate sectors.

As part of the WPP Group Hill & Knowlton has been responsible for the instigation and development of many of the key techniques and strategies that currently form accepted public relations practice.

On a worldwide basis, Hill & Knowlton has 72 wholly owned offices in 38 different countries, as well as operating via an extensive network of associates in an additional eleven geographical markets.

Achievements

The focus Hill & Knowlton places on its client work has resulted in many industry leading PR campaigns including adidas (World Cup communications and extensive work with its icons including David Beckham, Tim Henman and Jonny Wilkinson), UBS Americas Cup (international communications and sponsorship exploitation support for winning Team Alinghi), American Express (sponsorship exploitation), HP (support for CeBIT) and United Biscuits (corporate support).

To ensure a continued level of excellence, over the last six years Hill & Knowlton has recruited more graduate talent than any other marketing services company in the UK. The company also

has Consultancy Management Standard accreditation from the Public Relations Consultants Association (PRCA). As a demonstration of its international effectiveness, Hill & Knowlton has been chosen as Holmes magazine's International PR Agency of the Year for the last two years.

History

Hill & Knowlton was originally founded by ex-journalist John W Hill in 1927. Based in Cleveland, Ohio, Hill's early clients were banks, steel manufacturers, and other industrial companies in the Midwest. Hill then formed his partnership with Donald Knowlton, the PR director of a client's bank, as America entered into the Depression.

The firm's headquarters moved to New York in 1934, to be closer to its client the American Iron and Steel Institute, and where Hill stayed on to manage the firm until 1962. In the meantime, Knowlton stayed in Ohio to operate Hill & Knowlton of Cleveland.

Hill & Knowlton grew rapidly through the

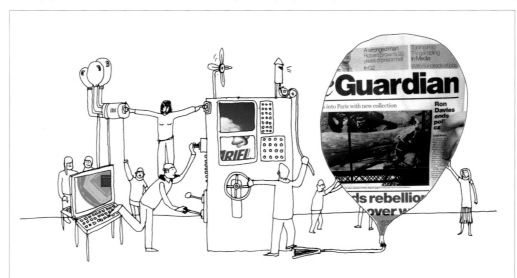

1940s, attracting major corporate clients including leaders in the steel, aircraft manufacturing, petroleum and shipbuilding industries. In 1952 Hill & Knowlton began to assemble a network of affiliates outside of the US, which by the middle of the decade had led to it becoming the first American public relations firm to have wholly-owned offices in Europe.

Hill & Knowlton evolved into the original multinational PR consultancy, an audacious business move closely followed by Burson-Marsteller, and

one that brought huge new revenues. Throughout the 1980s and early 1990s the two consultancies jockeyed for position as the world's number one PR agency.

Hill & Knowlton also led the way towards the extension of PR into lobbying services, which it was directly instrumental in establishing as an accepted and respectable business practice.

Hill & Knowlton was acquired by the J Walter Thompson advertising agency in July 1980. A further period of overseas expansion ensued, initially into Eastern Europe through the development of offices in Budapest, Hungary, and in 1984 as the first US consultancy to establish a presence in the People's Republic of China.

On the subsequent acquisition of JWT, the company became a key independent component of the WPP Group in 1987.

Product

Clients are drawn to Hill & Knowlton for a variety of reasons. For example: to launch a new product or revive an existing one; to reposition their company or communicate better to their stakeholders; to tackle an external issue posed by regulation or Government; to create and manage major sporting bids, or to renegotiate sporting contracts; to communicate unprecedented change; or to repair their reputation in the wake of disaster. Whilst these catalysts have largely remained consistent, the conditions within which corporate communications are successfully managed has never before required such an advanced degree of skill and expertise.

The arena in which reputation management must take place has changed dramatically. Technology and increased expectations have ensured that there is no hiding place and that news is instantaneous. Corporate shortcomings have driven an accelerating need for political and economic transparency. The increased power of pressure groups has forever changed the stakeholder landscape.

Hill & Knowlton's enviable positioning within the PR sector is based upon its capability to provide a holistic approach to communications issues, integrating campaigns from an extensive range of specialist services in Marketing Communications; Consumer Technology; Corporate and Business Communications; Change and Internal Communications; Public Affairs (including regulatory communications); Financial Communications; Interactive Communications (Netcoms); Sports Marketing and Sponsorship; Health and Pharmaceutical marketing; Issues and Crisis Consultancy and Media and Presentation Training.

Core to all Hill & Knowlton planning activity is its proprietary ComPASS methodology, which systematically assesses client needs in terms of existing and potential performance in order to determine the most appropriate and measurable PR strategy. The company has also recently introduced Dashboard™, a proprietary online service that helps clients to benchmark their performance in the media across internal and external communications, in real time.

Additional management tools include the STAMP intranet-based account management system; a proprietary digital intelligence system to monitor online issues and trends (RADAR); and a specially customised version of Brandz™, the WPP Group's international brand equity study based on over 170,000 customer interviews, and which covers more than 8,000 brands and their relationships with consumers in every one of the world's major economies — the largest, most in-depth, actionable study of its kind ever carried out. Hill & Knowlton is also one of the founding partners of SPORTZ™, a WPP research initiative conducted across eight countries, 45 sports and 60 sporting events. Targeting more than 21,000 sports fans, SPORTZ™ is the only international study of consumer attitudes and behaviour towards sport and how it impacts on brands, including both sponsors' and sporting brands.

In conjunction with other WPP Group companies: MindShare, Millward Brown and Millward Brown Precis, Hill & Knowlton also developed and operates its PRecision™ planning and evaluation methodology that measures the incremental impact of a PR campaign on a specified target audience — a major advance towards establishing true accountability within the PR industry.

Recent Developments

Hill & Knowlton's substantial growth over the last ten years has been largely based upon its clear focus upon increasing sector and service specialisation. This is complemented by a system where a designated senior director at Hill & Knowlton has a clear responsibility for an assigned global client through its Key Client Relationship Manager (KCRM) programme, thereby ensuring the needs of clients are met consistently and efficiently throughout the world.

Reflecting the increasingly global nature of current business issues, specialist 'Asset Groups' have also been established to provide best counsel to clients internationally.

The company has also invested in state-of-the-art technology with leading online account management tools maximising the time its consultants spend working with clients.

As well as forming best-practice teams internally, Hill & Knowlton is committed to a policy of partnering with respected external specialists to benefit clients. In the UK these

include not only other WPP Group companies such as Mindshare, Henley Centre as well as advertising agencies like JWT, but also the Leatherhead Food Research Group, who provide food and beverage clients with the most up-to-date thinking in food and nutrition. The company, for the first time, has also created a Global 'Cool Hunt' involving Hill & Knowlton people in 27 of its offices. This looks at young people, their behaviour and attitudes, and how communicators can better influence this audience.

Within the retail arena, Hill & Knowlton is an active participant in The Store, a virtual global community of WPP's retail specialists.

Promotion

Hill & Knowlton's in-depth reach across all major sectors has ideally positioned it to publish regular authoritative critiques and assessment reports on Governmental legislation, annual Budget statements and white paper topics. Subjects recently covered include the Disability Discrimination Act; the Comprehensive Spending Review; and the role of NGOs; and a discussion paper prepared by the Hill & Knowlton Brussels office on the new EU constitution and how it will impact on business.

The company organises frequent discussion forums for senior managers regarding current and predicted business challenges, and also stages regular events to present new tools and techniques such as account planning systems, evaluation techniques, trends in the media and audience segmentation systems.

Hill & Knowlton maintains a constantly updated global web presence at www.hillandknowlton.com, with direct links through to all of its locally based subsidiaries.

Specialist sector publications include i-Ball

that covers consumer technology, Fusion, which covers technology and Thirds which covers examples of Hill & Knowlton's work for its clients.

All of these services are freely available to both existing and potential clients; likewise, many Hill & Knowlton consultants are asked to act as commentators in the media or to speak at industry events on the role and impact of communication.

Hill & Knowlton maintains an ongoing Quality Service Programme built upon regular client feedback after every project and on an annual basis. This service, highly rated by clients, offers clients the opportunity to openly commend or criticise Hill & Knowlton's work and encourages the agency to continue to demonstrate increased value and results.

A new global corporate identity was introduced in February 2003, as a result of an extensive process of brand research with focus groups among employees, partners and clients. Developed by one of WPP's leading design agencies, The Partners, it marks a renewed focus on Insight, Expertise and Impact.

Brand Values

Hill & Knowlton's unbroken run of initiating and managing successful communications campaigns over a 75 year period is based upon its ability to deliver strategic thinking and creative solutions in one cohesive package.

The company prides itself on a willingness to innovate in the furtherance of its commitment to a central belief in the power of communications to bring positive change, and offers diversity of talent, passion, creativity, innovation, the desire to make a difference, integrity, and consistently high standards to a client base that includes high profile blue-chips such as adidas, Allied Bakeries, American Express, B&Q, BT, Gillette, HP, Kellogg's, Motorola, Nestlé, Roche and UBS.

www.hillandknowlton.co.uk

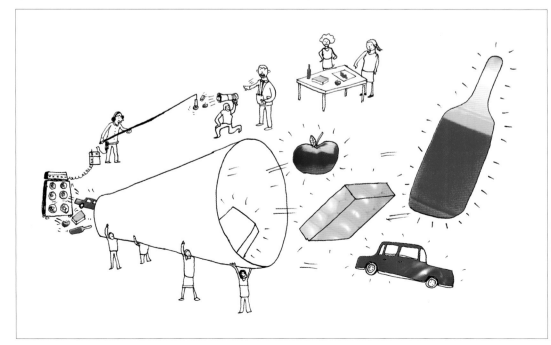

intel ®

Market

Intel is the world's largest manufacturer of computer chips and due to its enormously successful marketing strategy, most people in the UK are aware that a great deal of hi-tech equipment has 'Intel Inside®'. Recently, Intel has taken its marketing strategy onto an important new stage, becoming a pioneer in the field of wireless (or wi-fi) computer technology with its Intel® Centrino™ brand. Already, those with wireless computers can send emails or access the internet in growing numbers of airports, train stations, cafés, and even tourist attractions.

The world is becoming increasingly mobile. Intel's own research among 800 IT managers of companies with more than 100 employees in Germany and the UK showed that as many as 44% are 'hot desking' – moving from place-to-place using laptops. Furthermore, an article in Business Week in April 2003 predicted that two-thirds of the worlds 1,000 biggest companies would be using WLAN (wireless) networks by the end of 2004. In addition, researcher Gartner estimates that by 2007 there will be more than ten million frequent users of European public WLAN hot spots, and over twelve million infrequent users.

Achievements

When Intel was founded in 1968, it had twelve employees, operated out of a leased building in a quiet corner of California, and earned revenues in its first year of US$2,672. In 2002, it announced net revenues of US$26.8 billion.

Intel's success can be ascribed to a series of scientific breakthroughs and well-timed alliances. It came up with the first microprocessor, the 4004, in 1971. Ten years later, IBM chose the company's 8088 processor for use in the first ever PC.

By 1993 Intel had introduced its first Pentium® processor. Since then, the company has continued to render its own products obsolete almost every year – a strategy unheard of in any other business. As founder Gordon Moore comments; "If the auto industry advanced as rapidly as the semiconductor industry, a Rolls-Royce would get half a million miles per gallon, and it would be cheaper to throw it away than to park it."

History

In 1968, computer boffins Robert Noyce and Gordon Moore created Intel with the aim of creating a more efficient computer memory, based on semiconductor technology. They came up with the 1103 in 1970, and it became the world's biggest-selling semiconductor device by the end of 1971.

However, their most significant breakthrough came when a Japanese company called Busicom asked them to design twelve chips for a range of calculators. At the time, each electronic product required its own individually tailored chip. But Intel engineer Ted Hoff felt that it might be possible to create a single chip capable of carrying out a wide range of different functions – an advanced computer 'brain'.

The invention worked, and Intel realised that it had created a product with almost limitless applications. There was a problem, however – under the terms of the original contract, Busicom held the rights to the product. Moore and Noyce therefore bought them back for US$60,000.

Originally known as a 'microcomputer', Intel's first microprocessor – the 4004 – went on the market in 1971. By the time the company introduced the 8008, a few years later, its early predictions had begun to materialise: the chip revolutionised supermarket cash registers, traffic lights, petrol pumps, airline reservation systems and arcade games. As fast as its chips were installed, Intel created smaller and more powerful versions.

MOBILE TECHNOLOGY

In the early 1980s, IBM began tentative talks with Intel over the possibility of using its 8088 processor for an undisclosed new product. The details were shrouded in secrecy, and only when the deal was finally struck did Intel realise it was providing the brain of the first PC.

Intel continued to develop ever more efficient microprocessors, including the Pentium processor in 1993, which became its most famous brand name. In 1997 it made another breakthrough – although in a different field – by deciding to market itself as the brain behind a number of electronic products. Intel is now the best-known manufacturer of microprocessors. Its Pentium 4 processor is more powerful than Robert Noyce and Gordon Moore could ever have imagined.

Product

Intel produces the chips, boards, systems, software and communication equipment that make up the architecture of the high-tech world. But through its 'Intel Inside®' campaign, it is primarily known for producing microprocessors.

Microprocessors are the tiny brains that control the central processing of data in personal computers, servers, workstations and myriad other electronic devices. Intel's first branded processor was the Intel Pentium Processor, introduced in 1993. Alongside the Pentium, it has three other main brands for its processors: the Itanium, the Intel Xeon and the Intel Celeron brands. Over the years there have been many sub-brands, the most recent being the Intel Pentium 4 Processor and the Intel Itanium 2 Processor.

The launch of the Intel Centrino brand marks a new departure for the company, as it is the first time it has brought together a whole set of technology under a single brand name – from the microprocessor right through to the equipment, which allows wireless connections to be made.

Recent Developments

The Intel Centrino brand is by far and away the most important recent development for Intel. The multi-layered strategy involves pioneering the technology that makes wireless communication possible, developing an international network of wireless 'hot spots'. With wireless technology, business people will be able to check traffic and flight delays, forward mails to their teams back at base, and access street maps as they head for meetings and conferences. Leisure applications include being able to check news and sports results from home, wherever in the world you may be, or book a table in a restaurant. Eventually, consumers will be able to beam live pictures of important moments of their lives – weddings, christenings, graduation days – to relatives on the other side of the world.

Promotion

The rise to recognition began in 1989, when Intel launched a small campaign aimed at promoting its 386SX microprocessor to IT managers. The campaign was successful, but consumers remembered the processor and not the company's name. The main challenge was the fact that Intel was not a standalone product – it was a component, buried deep inside another device. Its advertising agency Dahlin, Smith and White came up with part of the solution – the slogan 'Intel. The computer inside.' This was later contracted into the famous 'Intel Inside®'.

At the same time, Intel began approaching computer manufacturers with the idea of a co-operative marketing programme whereby Intel would share the cost of any ads that showed its

logo. In the first year, 300 companies took it up on the offer. Meanwhile, in 1995, Intel embarked on TV ads promoting its product. These included an animated logo and the now familiar five-note melody.

Together with the high-profile launches of the Pentium and Pentium Pro processors, the campaign achieved strong results. According to research carried out by Intel in 1991, only 24% of European PC buyers were familiar with its logo. One year later that figure had risen to 80%, and by 1995 it had reached 94%.

Now more than 2,500 computer manufacturers are licensed to use the Intel Inside logo and the Intel name has a status akin to that of Coca-Cola. The company has spent almost US$8 billion on promoting the brand since 1991 and continues to invest. With the Intel Centrino brand now high on its list of priorities, it is helping to build an infrastructure of wireless 'hot spots' and promote them through press relations and print advertising. It is educating corporate users about the benefits of wi-fi, and

has already deployed wireless technology in its own network, equipping 80 buildings worldwide. Almost all of Intel's employees will be wirelessly enabled by the end of 2003. It has also been involved in helping to deploy public networks such as a citywide WLAN network in the historic city of Zamora, Spain, and public hot spot services in Brussels airport.

Intel Capital has invested more than US$25 million in more than ten wireless networking companies since 1999. The fund will invest in companies developing hardware and software products and services that enable easier-to-use and more secure wireless network connections. The US Cometa Networks was the first to benefit from this drive.

Brand Values

Intel's external brand values are evident from its advertising, which emphasises groundbreaking technology, quality and reliability. But Intel has always striven to underline its corporate culture. A victim of its own success, carefully watched by regulators and anti-globalisation campaigners, it is conscious of presenting itself as a forward-thinking company – a giant with the soul of a start-up.

Intel also aims to be open, egalitarian and disciplined. When Robert Noyce and Gordon Moore were building Intel, they were keen to banish hierarchies within the organisation and did not want to look at the company structure and see a complex set of hurdles. They preferred a company with no social hierarchy, no executive suites, no pinstriped suits and no reserved parking spaces. Intel aims to keep the spirit of its founders alive.

www.intel.co.uk

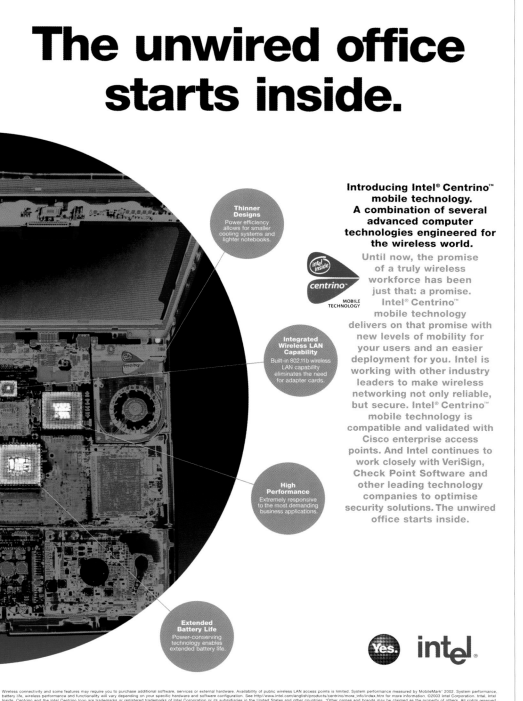

intel.co.uk

The unwired office starts inside.

Thinner Designs
Power efficiency allows for smaller cooling systems and lighter notebooks.

Integrated Wireless LAN Capability
Built-in 802.11b wireless LAN capability eliminates the need for adapter cards.

High Performance
Extremely responsive to the most demanding business applications.

Extended Battery Life
Power-conserving technology enables extended battery life.

Introducing Intel® Centrino™ mobile technology. A combination of several advanced computer technologies engineered for the wireless world.

Until now, the promise of a truly wireless workforce has been just that: a promise. Intel® Centrino™ mobile technology delivers on that promise with new levels of mobility for your users and an easier deployment for you. Intel is working with other industry leaders to make wireless networking not only reliable, but secure. Intel® Centrino™ mobile technology is compatible and validated with Cisco enterprise access points. And Intel continues to work closely with VeriSign, Check Point Software and other leading technology companies to optimise security solutions. The unwired office starts inside.

Yes. **intel.**

Wireless connectivity and some features may require you to purchase additional software, services or external hardware. Availability of public wireless LAN access points is limited. System performance measured by MobileMark™ 2002. System performance, battery life, wireless performance and functionality will vary depending on your specific hardware and software configuration. See http://www.intel.com/english/products/centrino/more_info/index.htm for more information. ©2003 Intel Corporation. Intel, Intel Inside, Centrino and the Intel Centrino logo are trademarks or registered trademarks of Intel Corporation or its subsidiaries in the United States and other countries. *Other names and brands may be claimed as the property of others. All rights reserved.

Things you didn't know about
Intel

'Hot spots' verified on Intel Centrino mobile technology in the UK include Heathrow and Gatwick airports, Claridge's Hotel in London as well as Starbucks in Fleet Street.

Intel founder Gordon Moore was asked in the 1970s why microprocessors could not be sold with keyboards and monitors, for the home market. He said that he could not see the point – 'apart from a housewife to keep her recipes on it'. He missed out on inventing the PC ten years early.

Some unusual products that contain microprocessors include electronic dartboards, fish finders (which are small sonar systems that use LCDs to locate shoals of fish and are used on fishing boats) and Cheetah trackers (which consist of a chip inserted under the animal's skin to monitor its breeding habits).

The Pentium 4 processor contains 75 million transistors on a piece of silicon the size of a thumbnail.

Market

The Institute of Directors (IoD) is one of the UK's leading business membership organisations. Founded in 1903 to support and promote the interests of directors, it soon afterwards gained a Royal Charter in 1906. The IoD has a growing worldwide association of members and provides a network that reaches into every corner of the business community. With approximately 55,000 individual members from companies of all sizes, types and geographical locations, membership spans the whole spectrum of business leadership, from the largest companies to the smallest private firms. 60% of IoD members are from small and medium-sized enterprises (SMEs), while it also has members on the board of 92% of the UK's FTSE 100 companies.

The IoD is recognised for its influence, integrity and is a respected authority on corporate governance issues. By championing the entrepreneur, the Institute seeks to establish an environment conducive to business success. For any company to prosper, its directors will be continually engaged in making entrepreneurial decisions involving innovation, risk and investment. Entrepreneurial activity needs to take place within a framework of business plans, financial controls, resources and market intelligence. Informed decisions depend upon knowledge and experience. The IoD has always been dedicated to providing directors with the information and advice they require while developing the business environment enabling them to succeed and grow.

Achievements

The IoD contributes significantly to influencing policy; it responds to over 80 government consultation documents a year which help in shaping the business environment. Recently the IoD provided valuable input into the Higgs review, which, after a thorough examination of the role and contribution of non-executive directors, called for positive measures to spread best practice.

Over the last five years, membership of the Institute has grown by over 11,000 and now includes directors from many sectors of the economy – from media to manufacturing, e-business to the public sector.

The IoD has also had many high profile speakers at its events, such as Jack Welch, Ronald Reagan, Sir Richard Branson, Bill Gates and Baroness Thatcher to name a few.

The IoD has been running courses for directors since the early 1980s. In March 1999 it was granted

approval from the Privy Council for new by-laws to enable it to establish a professional qualification for directors, Chartered Director. The new status is increasing in recognition across the world as a stamp of professionalism.

History

The IoD was formed in 1903 and throughout its 100-year history, the IoD has endeavoured to meet the needs of the directors of the day. With just 334 applications for membership in 1904, membership has grown significantly and there are now approximately 55,000 members.

In 1903, the head of a family run accountancy firm became the first founding pioneer of the IoD. W A Addinsell set up the Institute on his company premises and brought together ten other directors well known in the City from a range of disciplines including law, banking and insurance.

It was on April 29th 1903, that a group of 23 senior directors and chairmen of British companies met in a room at the Institute of Chartered Accountants in London, to form the first 'Council of The Institute of Directors'.

The stimulus to the IoD's creation came from the company legislation of 1900-1901, which included details of concern regarding the responsibilities and liabilities of directors. Their initial objective was to inform directors about the legal implications of the directorial role and to exchange experiences. A legal committee was also established to scrutinise legislation and liase with MPs in order to develop a legal framework which was conducive to an ethical and profitable economy. The success of this initiative has enabled the Institute to be a fore-running advocate of best practice in corporate governance across the globe today.

In 1947 Director magazine, was first published, providing information, inspiration and best practice advice to Britain's business decision makers.

The London headquarters of the IoD are housed at 116 Pall Mall, a Grade 1 listed building. This landmark of London's great Georgian heritage is now one of the country's most popular business venues with thousands of IoD members visiting the premises every week.

Product

The IoD is dedicated to creating an environment in which business can flourish. It not only represents the business community to government, regulatory bodies and the media, it also provides a wide range of products and services to support the needs of the individual director. These cover:

Free provision of exclusive premises in seven cities; London (116 and 123 Pall Mall), Belfast, Bristol, Birmingham, Edinburgh, Manchester and Nottingham for meetings and entertaining.

Free Business Information Services providing invaluable support ranging from extracts from competitors' company reports or market research, through to legal and tax telephone helplines.

The IoD represents members' interests to national and local government.

The IoD has a unique offering of training products and services to help facilitate professional development, whatever stage a director is in their career.

Members also have the opportunity to qualify as a Chartered Director – the professional qualification for directors.

Members are affiliated to one of the 28 branches, these are also divided into regions which allows for local and national networking, providing members with even greater opportunities for developing business interests in all sectors.

Members receive a free subscription to Director magazine, Director's Guides and pocket books, in addition to a whole range of affinity products including Director's Personal Indemnity Insurance and free access to fifteen executive airport lounges across the UK.

Recent Developments

IoD International was launched in 2003 as it was called upon to raise professionalism across the world. It develops professional excellence in the boardroom by training and is currently working with the World Bank and the Organisation for Economic Co-operation and Development (OECD) to create a corporate governance framework.

In 2001 the IoD joined forces with Stonemartin plc to expand the Institute's facilities, from five premises to eight to date. IoD hubs have opened in Bristol, Birmingham and Manchester, increasing the IoD's presence and influence across the UK.

123 Pall Mall was designed to reflect the growing number of younger directors. The premises were officially opened by the Right Honourable Prime Minister, Tony Blair on July 26th 2001.

Promotion

The Institute is promoted through a variety of mediums. Via direct marketing, both paper-based and electronic, members and non-members are kept abreast of major developments in the Institute's product portfolio. Direct sales of membership itself has increased substantially via a strategic integrated acquisition campaign to targeted directors, which include above and below-the-line marketing.

Over the last few years, the Institute has created one of the country's most successful 'opt-in' email communities with over 50% of its members choosing to be kept up-to-date with relevant issues by electronic communication.

Perhaps one of the most significant promotional messages benefiting the Institute is its consistent presence in the nation's editorial space. The IoD

distributes regular press statements on a variety of business issues with a view to representing its members' surveyed views on relevant issues. Local and national coverage in all media is generated on a daily basis and Ruth Lea, Head of the Policy Unit, is a frequent guest in broadcasted political debates. This coverage continues to keep the Institute's brand and identity in the forefront of the business arena.

Another significant promotional channel the Institute can capitalise on is via members' considerable brand loyalty. One of the most successful recruitment channels the IoD enjoys is word-of-mouth, where members consistently recommend the Institute to colleagues and friends.

Brand Values

The IoD was originally formed to protect the interests of directors and to support and set standards for all directors.

Lord Avebury, the first President defined the Institute's objective in 1904 as:

"...to protect the interests of directors. It is much more important that it should enable directors to carry out the great

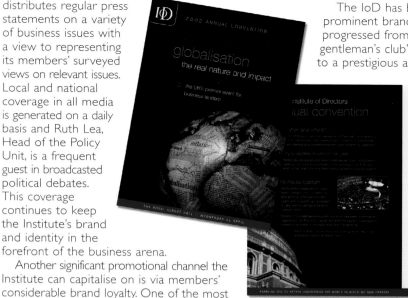

responsibilities which they have undertaken; that it should be the centre from which they might obtain information upon various points of interest; that it should be the meeting ground on which they might consult together." This still holds true today.

The IoD has been an established, prominent brand for 100 years. It has progressed from being considered 'a gentleman's club' for business leaders, to a prestigious and influential organisation with key brand strengths of heritage and authority.

To enhance the Institute's perceived relevance in the twenty first century, while maintaining these core strengths, the IoD's corporate identity was refreshed in 2001. All promotional collateral was revamped and standardised, with the introduction of contemporary imagery and simple, clean typefaces to maintain a consistent, meaningful presence in the business market.

The brand's repositioning is reflective of British business: incorporating past successes with innovation. The headquarters of the IoD, 116 Pall Mall, reflect the traditional, classic philosophies of the IoD while the contemporary 123 Pall Mall facilities allow for informal meetings; The two facilities complement each other and also reflect the multi-dimensional features of the IoD brand.

www.iod.com

the flight guides
the body supports
the point is business leadership

Superbrands

J Walter Thompson

Market

J Walter Thompson is one of the foremost brands within the global communications marketplace. The industry as a whole has, in the last couple of years, faced the worst advertising slump since the Great Depression. But while many of its competitors have faltered, J Walter Thompson has used hard times to create opportunities of its own. In 2002, it added over US$800 million in estimated net new billings worldwide, welcoming new clients and gaining significant new assignments from existing clients.

While above-the-line advertising continues to be important for many clients, the marketplace has evolved in recent years to reflect clients' changing needs. Communications groups such as Omnicom, Havas and Interpublic have broadened their offerings, while WPP Group, which owns JWT, has launched a wide range of integrated solutions to meet its clients business needs.

Achievements

JWT is consistently the UK's leading agency as judged by the client community and has been voted number one in Marketing Week's annual survey, for nine out of the last twelve years.

In terms of IPA Effectiveness Awards, it is the second most awarded agency ever, and in 2003, Marco Rimini, the agency's Director of Strategy, was the Convenor of Judges. Marco continues a long JWT tradition of outstanding industry-leading thinking and follows alumni such as Stephen King, the father of the account planning discipline and Jeremy Bullmore, one of the greatest creative thinkers of today.

In 2003 JWT won the global Vodafone account as well as Triumph Motorcycles, Reckitt Benckiser, RNIB, Golden Wonder, AXA, B&Q and Quorn accounts. This represents an additional £60 million in billings taking JWT to the number two position in the Campaign new business league.

JWT has a reputation for FMCG expertise, and for the second year running, won the GRAMIA FMCG agency of the year title in 2003, along with the agency of the year award (FAB) from the food and beverage industries. Together they recognise the agency's work on Yorkie, After Eight, Persil, SMIRNOFF, Kenco, Dairylea, Kellogg's Corn Flakes and Lipton Ice.

One of the reasons why JWT is proving to be consistently attractive to new prospects is that it has not stood still. Under the leadership of Simon Bolton, CEO, at its entirely open plan offices at one, Knightsbridge Green, London JWT has adopted a highly flexible, tailored client-centric way of working.

JWT operates collaboratively and transparently. 1KG is home to a community of strategy, advertising, direct marketing, digital recruitment, print, TV production and post production specialists, all of which can be configured in multi-discipline teams to suit any client's particular needs.

History

JWT is the world's oldest advertising agency. It was founded in 1864 when William J Carlton and Edmund A Smith set up a business in New York selling advertising space in religious journals. James Walter Thompson joined the business two years later as a bookkeeping clerk. He later bought the business for US$500 and put his name over the front door. A London office was set up in 1899. By 1916, when Thompson sold the business on, it had five offices and billings of US$3 million.

JWT was the first agency to focus on in-depth market research for clients. It was also the first to have its own recording studios. During World War II, JWT was responsible for many of the morale-boosting 'home front' campaigns. In 1944, it moved into 40 Berkeley Square – originally a block of luxury flats popular with showbiz legends including Frank Sinatra.

With the arrival of commercial television in 1955, JWT was the first agency to have its own casting department and the first to persuade top film and TV directors to make commercials. On the opening night of commercial TV, it produced spots for Kraft Cheese Slices and Lux toilet soap.

JWT became part of the WPP Group in 1987 and its media department merged with that of Ogilvy & Mather in 1987 to create MindShare. The agency moved from its Berkeley Square home to new premises at One Knightsbridge Green in 2002.

Incorporated into 1KG now is Specialised Communications, JWT's recruitment advertising brand which consistently bills in the top five in the UK market, and RMG Connect which alongside Black Cat, provides JWT's digital, direct and relationship marketing capability. Black Cat and RMG Connect's major clients include DaimlerChrysler,

British Horseracing Board, Shell, Avis, Microsoft, Pfizer and Boots.

Another first for JWT includes the in-house K-Post TV production facility. This provides top Soho post-production facilities within the Knightsbridge Green office, including Henry and Avid edit suites, and playout facilities delivering greater control, time saving, and convenience to creatives and clients.

Product

JWT creates enduring brands. Its aim is to understand people better than any other agency, using these insights to ignite powerful ideas that build long-lasting brands that consumers love.

It has created and sustained more brand leaders than any other agency. Currently, 26 of its clients' brands hold the number one or two position in their category.

JWT produces ideas, not executions, that can be delivered through the full range of communication channels in an integrated way. Thompson Total Branding, JWT's bespoke strategic planning tool, used across the global network since 1996, ensures integrated thinking.

JWT UK employs 441 staff – 350 in London and 91 in Cheetham Bell/JWT Manchester. JWT London is part of a global network of 311 offices in 155 cities in 90 countries.

Recent Developments

JWT recently recruited Nick Bell as Executive Creative Director. He has a formidable creative reputation and has won the Cannes Grand Prix award for his work on Mercedes-Benz, seven Cannes Gold and two D&AD Silvers. In his position as one of the creative industry's leading figures, Nick is also the president of D&AD, the body that inspires and drives creative standards in UK Design and Advertising.

JWT has developed a number of specialist brands within the agency to answer specific client needs. Label, led by Nicola Dicketts, offers consultancy and brand communications for fashion, beauty and lifestyle brands. Notable successes include Rimmel, which recently regained the number one spot as the UK's favourite cosmetic brand. Label also launched Glamour magazine into the highly competitive women's magazine sector, for Condé Nast. It has knocked Cosmopolitan off its long held top spot, and Glamour is now market leader.

As JWT's retail clients grow, High Street @ JWT has been established. This unit understands the particular needs and pressures of the retail environment, and is equipped to produce point of sale and display materials as well as above-the-line brand communication. High Street's most recent win is the 320 strong Vodafone retail network.

Have a break. Have a KitKat

Also launched this year is JWT's Ignition Tools. This is a range of ten consultancy products, each designed to give brands some added spark. They are practical, concise and robust and involve one day workshops to allow existing and new clients to tap into the depth of JWT's expertise on a very specific project basis. The tools cover communications planning, brand innovation, NPD, war gaming, cultural trend analysis, campaign brainstorming, and training and development.

Major campaign developments this year include the provocative and much talked about 'It's Not for Girls' campaign for Yorkie. This has reclaimed chocolate for men, and in doing so, has increased brand sales by 40%. Kit Kat launched a major new campaign, fronted by Jason Stantham of Lock Stock and two Smoking Barrels, which urges the nation to understand the benefits of the break. 'Remember, You Are Not a Salmon' is set to enter the vernacular alongside 'Have a break, have a Kit Kat'.

Smirnoff Ice, launched by JWT in 1999, is the number one brand in the dynamic Premium Packaged Spirits market (PPS). It now dominates

a market of 40 brands and has done this on half the spend of its nearest rival, Barcardi Breezer, delivering outstanding ROI, and driving Diageo's profits.

Kenco Rappor meanwhile, extols the virtues of staying awake and shook up the coffee advertising genre by displaying a laddism normally associated with beer advertising.

Promotion

JWT's Marketing and New Business department focuses on developing individual relationships with prospective clients. Beyond this, JWT regularly hosts exclusive events which, in line with the

HIGH VOLTAGE

NEW SHINE TEMPTATION STARS LIPSTICK
Super-charge your lips with one of ten high sparkle finish lipsticks.
Create some electricity and watch the sparks fly.

RIMMEL
LONDON

brand's values, bring together inspiring thinking from a wide range of sources. Past speakers have included Estelle Morris, Adam Crozier, CEO of Royal Mail, Greg Dyke, Director General of the BBC, Virgin's Richard Branson and Olympic gold

Andrex

medallist Lord Coe. Original research and insights into marketing trends are also a key feature. These include Fab Fifties – understanding marketing to the over 50s, and 'From Under the Mattress to over the Internet' exploring changing attitudes to money across Europe. JWT also enjoys just having some fun with clients and prospects, whether hosting a live broadcast of an England game with sports celebrities and guest TV soccer pundits; pre release film screenings or the much anticipated annual childrens' Christmas party.

Brand Values

JWT believes that it can attribute its strong position within the market to its clearly defined values. JWT also trusts in intellectual rigour and imagination to uncover insights that can be applied in a practical way. The result being memorable ideas that ignite brands that people feel great affection towards.

JWT values openness, collaboration and creating a supportive and secure atmosphere for staff and clients. It is proud to be thought of

throughout the industry as a 'clever' agency, but just as importantly, as a nice agency to work for and with. This is reflected in the long-standing relationship it has with its own people and with so many of its clients. For example, Unilever celebrated its centenary with JWT in a memorable celebration at Tate Modern in 2002.

JWT offers its staff innovative contracts to support a better work/life balance, and on a day to day level, little 'extras', from the Hyde Park running club through to the weekly in-house massage, themed bar evenings and comedy nights.

JWT continues to invest significantly in training and development. It was one of the principal architects of the industry's ground breaking IPA Continual Professional Development programme, which supports learning for all staff in every department, throughout their career. JWT won a Gold in the inaugural IPA CPD Awards for its Business Kinetics online learning programme.

www.jwt.co.uk

kall kwik ®

business design + print

Market

Print, creative design and graphics to a very high standard are now readily available, with the quality of reproduction underpinned by the steady advance in digital technology as an increasingly viable alternative to conventional printing techniques. Furthermore, the capabilities of digital technology have had a direct impact upon lead-times for delivery and wastage in terms of redundant promotional material, with the quality of the end-result increasingly comparable to that achieved by conventional printing techniques.

These technological advancements are reflected in the services that Kall Kwik now offers with 100% of Centres having digital colour, as well as 100% digital black & white and over 50% large format. Kall Kwik has also increased numbers of Centres with ADSL technology, four and five colour presses as well as computer to plate technology.

Kall Kwik's growth path is in itself a barometer reading to the pace of change within business.

With its 7% market share, Kall Kwik is the leader of the UK market for Print on Demand which is estimated to be worth around £1 billion per annum. The brand's growth has been achieved via a franchise operation backed up by centralised training and marketing support. Average annual sales turnover is currently just in excess of £400,000. Four Kall Kwik Centres are now achieving in excess of £1 million in annual sales, with one in the £2 million sales bracket.

Achievements

Maintaining nearly 170 outlets located throughout the UK, Kall Kwik's principal success has been in making on-demand print equally as accessible to both small businesses and corporate users; the latter sector – including high profile blue-chip customers such as David Lloyd Leisure, Marriott Hotels, Office Angels and Safeway – account for a significant majority of the brand's approximately £70 million annual turnover.

David Lloyd is one of Kall Kwik's principal national accounts. For each David Lloyd Leisure club, its local Kall Kwik Centre provides print, design and fulfilment, including the management of direct marketing campaigns.

Celebrating its 25th anniversary in 2003, Kall Kwik has a history of winning awards for both the quality of its print product and the commercial success of its franchising operation.

Kall Kwik has appeared within the British Franchise Association (BFA) annual franchise awards eight times in the past fourteen years, being recognised as Franchisor of the Year in 1989 and runner-up ten years later. Kall Kwik Edinburgh was awarded BFA Franchisee of the Year 2003 in October, following on Kall Kwik Middlesbrough's identical achievement in 1990. Kall Kwik Centres have been awarded second or third placed status on four

other occasions. Kall Kwik was the first UK company to be so recognised within both the franchisor and franchisee categories.

Kall Kwik Middlesbrough has subsequently followed its BFA Franchisee of the Year award by being recognised as Printer of the Year in 2002 by the British Association for Print and Communication (BAPC).

Additional awards in recent years include Marketing magazine's 'Connections 2000' for best use of an intranet; and the telemarketing award presented by the same publication in 1997.

History

Kall Kwik was founded in the UK in 1978 by Moshe Gerstenhaber, who purchased the master franchise from the US Kwik Kopy Organisation. The first Centre opened in Pall Mall in 1979.

The Kall Kwik group of franchise outlets now extends from as far north as Aberdeen down to Truro in South West England.

Kall Kwik was acquired in 1999 by Adare Group, the leading provider of print, mailing and data management solutions throughout the UK and Ireland.

In May 2001, On Demand Communications Limited (ODC) was established as a service company to provide further comprehensive support in the key areas of corporate sales, technology, training, IT and financial back-up from the Ruislip, Middlesex offices it shares with Kall Kwik UK. The 50 strong ODC team is focused on delivering innovative and robust solutions and services in order that Kall Kwik can continue to meet the needs of its customers throughout the country.

Product

Kall Kwik offers an extensive range of print, digital and design services for commercial applications, which range from brochures, leaflets, presentation documentation to direct mailing literature, posters and exhibition graphics. Scanning and archiving is a relatively new service which is becoming a popular solution for many customers. A key to the overall group's marketing and sales strategy has been to approach all client requirements on an individual basis in order to provide the optimum print solution to match specific needs.

As a tailored communications solutions provider, Kall Kwik has been a leading proponent of digital technology, enabling it to create a substantial market in cost effective short-run print from original creativity to final output. Established industry suppliers include leading players such as Canon, Xerox, Océ, Ricoh, Heidelberg and HP Indigo.

In exploiting the opportunities afforded by the digital output process, and being able to dispense with pre-press work, Kall Kwik has built a reputation for much faster turnaround times. Digital technology also enables the inclusion of variable data, helping

clients to successfully target individual customers more closely.

Litho printing, with its unmatched quality, remains a core offering. Although there are set-up costs, unit costs can be much lower than for digital printing and as a result longer runs (typically 500+) can be more cost-efficient. The higher running speed of the machines also means that longer runs can be completed faster.

Kall Kwik has achieved its leading positioning within the sector by being able to address customer issues on a localised basis, whilst benefiting from strong corporate brand awareness – also enabling it to print and distribute when required via a national intranet network.

Recent Developments
In January 2004, Kall Kwik is launching a brand new corporate identity. The logo at the heart of this identity (which heads up these pages), has been designed by Kall Kwik Winchester, to project the modern and highly creative focus of Kall Kwik today. The fresh, contemporary feel is also targeted to appeal to business clients, demanding of the highest standards of service and professionalism.

Kall Kwik Centres are increasingly collaborating on a network of regional production centres in order to optimise the use and investment in new high volume litho and digital equipment.

The most recently introduced Kall Kwik Digital Business Centre – strategically located in Cornhill at the heart of the City – occupies a 1,400 square foot site which includes a consultation area where clients can discuss their requirements with a digital specialist. It is targeted to achieve a £1 million plus turnover in its first year of operation. The client list includes companies such as Bloomsbury

Publishing, Great Ormond Street Hospital, ITN, London Weekend Television, NASDAQ, Pret A Manger, Prudential, the Royal Opera House and Sainsbury's.

The Cornhill DBC is equipped with a large format Canon BJW9000 digital colour printer for poster work; Canon black and white IR105 and IR8500 digital printers; a Xerox DC 2060 and DC12; and a Ricoh wide format black and white Aficio 470W for plan printing.

Kall Kwik has also strengthened its support of the franchise network through the introduction of significant corporate initiatives such as '21st Century Service' and formalised 'Business Planning'. '21st Century Service' is an integrated package of elements to assist Centres in providing consistently excellent levels of service. The results of the auditing process at its core are benchmarked against the rest of the network, and form a key input to Centres' quarterly Business Planning reviews.

The future is digital and it's looking good

solutions as **unique** as your business

Kall Kwik PRINT COPY DESIGN

---

earning
not
yearning

Live in the lap of luxury

Owning a Kall Kwik franchise won't always be plain sailing, however with effort and commitment the rewards can be significant. Average Centre sales are among the highest in the sector. Top Centres achieve sales well in excess of £1 million.

With substantial net profits available, a Kall Kwik franchise can deliver the wealth to fulfil your personal ambitions. To find out how you can start living the dream

call **0500 872060** or visit our web site www.kallkwik.co.uk

unique opportunities for **unique** individuals

Kall Kwik PRINT COPY DESIGN

Promotion
Despite the fact that Kall Kwik is naturally protective of its brand integrity, franchisees initiate promotion in support of individual Centres, albeit in accordance with strictly maintained guidelines.

Direct mail is Kall Kwik's preferred promotional medium, with the franchisor itself distributing in excess of 28,000 leaflets as well as 90,000 awareness cards and 92,000 'Business Bulletin' newsletters during the course of its 'Relaxing Rewards 2' marketing programmes. Nearly one-third of the mailers resulted in appointments, an extremely high conversion ratio for any business-to-business proposition. This positive indicator to the brand's strong level of awareness further underlines the universal requirement within the corporate sector for Kall Kwik's portfolio of services.

Further support to franchisees is facilitated through the distribution of Centre-customised variants of nationally distributed press releases.

In-Centre promotion is achieved through the use of POP material, merchandising and corporate attire all conforming to the corporate image.

Brand Values
Underpinning the Kall Kwik proposition is the ability of each of its franchisees to provide a range of products for which there is a growing demand at a level of service ahead of its competition.

Kall Kwik's mission through service excellence is to be the first choice provider of business-to-business communication solutions using the brand's skills in print, copy and design. This is translated via the positioning statement: 'Solutions as unique as your business.'

Kall Kwik regards its franchisees as being brand ambassadors – from the quality of print, digital and design produced, to the levels of service provided.

www.kallkwik.co.uk

London Business School

Market

London Business School is one of the most prestigious business schools in the world. For corporations, premier institutions like London Business School are invaluable, grooming the business leaders of tomorrow from the 800 or so students who graduate each year. The fact that London Business School has signed executive education contracts with companies such as BG Group, Vodafone, Roche Pharmaceuticals, Nestlé and Electronic Arts gives an indication of its reputation for academic excellence among the business community.

Reflecting trends in global business, the best business schools have a truly internationalist stance, and this is certainly the case at London Business School, where over 80% of the students and 70% of the faculty are non-British.

London Business School stands extremely well against its peers. The School's full time MBA programme is ranked seventh in the world in the Financial Times annual survey, while the Executive MBA programme was ranked fourth in the world in the paper's ranking of EMBA programmes in 2002. The School has also been ranked as the top business school outside the US in 'intellectual capital' by Business Week in its ranking of Best Business Schools in 2000.

The School has a reputation as the platform for international business and political leaders to present key note and policy speeches. Among these have been Bill Gates, the Rt Hon Tony Blair, Michael Dell and Michael Bloomberg.

In July 2003, the School held its first Global Leadership Summit featuring panel debates, keynote speakers and numerous days of networking opportunities. An enormously successful event, the Global Leadership Summit offered delegates a window into the world of international leadership success.

Achievements

The achievements of London Business School and its internationally renowned faculty are remarkable. For example, Leonard Waverman, Professor of Economics, was appointed director of a major new Economic and Social Research Council (ESRC) research programme into the e-society. The programme has a substantial research budget – £6.5 million over six years – for path-breaking and informative multi-disciplinary economic and social research on the e-Society and how institutions and practices are being restructured for the digital age.

Another member of London Business School's faculty, Elroy Dimson, Professor of Finance, won first prize in the 2002 Inquire UK (Institute for Quantitative Investment Research UK) competition for his paper, co-authored with Andrew Jackson, 'High Frequency Performance Monitoring', in the Journal of Portfolio Management.

Richard Portes, Professor of Economics, received a CBE (Commander of the British Empire) in the New Years Honours list 2003 in recognition for his services to Economics.

In January 2003, London Business School became the host of the Advanced Institute of Management (AIM), an £18 million management research initiative funded by the ESRC and the Engineering and Physical Sciences Research Council.

The Advanced Institute of Management is a major research project that will bring together academics, businesses and government policy advisers to provide new support for British competitiveness and address the productivity gap in terms of market output per hour between the UK and other economies.

In June 2003 it was announced that five of London Business School's eminent professors engaged in research in management had been awarded prestigious AIM Fellowships. The

Fellowships, which are valid for three years, have been awarded to: Julian Birkinshaw, Associate Professor of Strategic and International Management; Sumantra Ghoshal, Professor of Strategic and International Management; Lynda Gratton, Associate Professor of Organisational Behaviour; Chris Voss, Professor of Operations and Technology Management and George Yip, Professor of Strategic and International Management.

The School's standing as the UK's most international higher education institution bears testament to its ability to attract the highest calibre faculty members and students from all over the world. Each year, the School attracts over 1,000 students from more than 60 countries, as well as over 5,000 executive education participants on short courses from over 75 countries. Its 100 faculty members represent 30 countries and the School has important strategic alliances with Columbia Business School in New York and the Indian School of Business in Hyderabad.

London Business School has established a reputation as Europe's leading training ground for entrepreneurs, offering over 80 individual entrepreneurship electives on its masters programmes alone. Its skill in this area was recognised when London Business School was awarded the 2001 Queen's Award for Enterprise in the International Trade category. It was the only business school among the 133 organisations which received the award.

History

London Business School was founded in 1965 as a graduate school of the University of London. The School's early years in Northumberland Avenue saw the introduction of the MBA, PhD and the Sloan Masters programmes. Following rapid expansion, the School moved to its current location, a nineteenth century Nash terrace overlooking Regent's Park, in 1969.

The School's physical expansion continued with the opening of the redeveloped Plowden building by HRH The Prince of Wales in 1983. The Queen's Award for Export Achievement followed in 1992, in recognition of the School's growing international standing. Its portfolio of courses continued to expand and, in 1993, it further enhanced its reputation for leading the way in international business education by launching the Masters in Finance programme.

In 1986, the School was granted a Royal Charter by the Privy Council in recognition of its national and international stature in management education.

Taunton Place, the latest addition to London Business School's campus, was completed in 1998. This building houses the library and sports centre.

Product

London Business School has three main areas of activity: post-graduate degree programmes in management (MBA, MSc and PhD), non-degree courses for business executives, and research.

The school's full-time MBA course is a 21-month programme with an annual intake of around 320 students. The internationally-focused course, which is especially strong in the areas of finance, leadership and entrepreneurship, attracts participants from over 70 countries.

Our Vision

It is the **Vision** of London Business School to be the pre-eminent global business school, nurturing talent and advancing knowledge in a multi-national, multi-cultural learning environment.

The world-renowned Masters in Finance programme is designed for those planning or already pursuing careers which require an in-depth knowledge of finance. It is taught by the School's finance faculty and can be completed in two years part time or ten months full time. The programme is not available at any other top international business school and is widely regarded as a 'must have' for finance professionals around the world.

London Business School is also famous for its Sloan Masters Programme (MSc). This course is unique in Europe and is offered at only two other institutions in the world, Massachusetts Institute of Technology and Stanford in the US. The course is designed for more experienced participants (average work experience pre-programme fourteen years) from ethnically, geographically and professionally diverse backgrounds.

The School's Executive MBA Programme (EMBA) is a two-year course which students take while remaining in full-time employment. It is highly practical and allows students to apply newly-learnt knowledge and skills to their work. In 2001 the School launched its EMBA-Global programme as part of a strategic alliance with Columbia Business School in New York. Participants spend time studying at both schools.

The School's PhD programme has graduated over 300 candidates, and admits fifteen new students each year. The programme attracts the highest calibre candidates from around the world and is one of the most highly regarded in Europe.

For non-degree courses, the School offers around twenty general management and specialist executive programmes, including the acclaimed four-week Senior Executive Programme, which celebrated its 50th programme in 2003. The Accelerated Development Programme for middle managers and the Young Professionals Programme for high-potential people who are making the transition into their first managerial role. Over 1,500 executives attend open enrolment programmes at London Business School every year.

The school also offers company-specific courses from its Centre for Management Development, designing and delivering tailor-made programmes for a range of multinationals, including a joint programme with Columbia Business School for Deutsche Telekom.

London Business School is well known for the excellence of its research. In 1996, the School was awarded the highest possible rating for the quality of its research by the Higher Education Funding Council for England. This has helped the School attract over £12 million in research funding since 1999. All faculty members undertake research as well as teaching, publishing on average a total of 400 papers, books and articles every year.

Recent Developments

Executive Education is developing virtual learning concepts in partnership with clients together with the introduction of a new 'discovery process', provoking new insights and acting as a catalyst for leadership and strategy development programmes.

Among the fund-raising successes of the last year was a pledge for £2 million from Adecco SA to endow the Adecco Professorship in Business and Society. Through the outstanding efforts of the Adecco Chairman and London Business School alum John Bowmer, the School won the support and confidence of Adecco and its many stakeholders to create this newly endowed chair.

2002 was undoubtedly a tough year for global business. Future growth in the world economy is likely to come from emerging markets such as China, India or Brazil. The School's Centre for Emerging Markets is running a major project on foreign direct investment, looking at the factors leading firms to enter in particular ways: 'greenfield', joint venture or acquisition.

The School's new Centre for Hedge Fund Research and Education addresses some of the key business issues in the complex world of capital markets: how do hedge funds generate returns? What kinds of risks do they take and how do these differ from traditional funds? The centre is rapidly becoming the leading academic authority and focal point in Europe for new thinking and educational activities in this exciting field.

Promotion

London Business School's internationally high profile is built by word of mouth, through business school rankings, at trade fairs and through information sessions for potential students.

The School also makes effective use of press and public relations, using the School's core assets – its faculty, students and alumni – to build an ever-growing list of opinion-forming contacts in the press. The press office's strongest relationships are with journalists who cover economics, finance, business, technology and management issues all over the world.

Brand Values

London Business School is the pre-eminent global business school, nurturing talent and advancing knowledge in a multi-national, multi-cultural learning environment. The School is at the centre of a dynamic and diverse global network of leading business thinkers and practitioners, as well as the corporate leaders of the future. Its desire for pre-eminence is reflected in the scale of its work; those whom it reaches; the difference it makes in the world and the leadership it demonstrates and inculcates in those who learn at the School.

London Business School is a global business school founded on the assets which its position in London provides: the diversity of its culture, the global business capabilities of its graduates and its ability to network with its stakeholders and beyond.

Constant communication and the sharing of up-to-date thinking and knowledge is vital. London Business School's global networks and experience mean that global knowledge quickly becomes part of its educational programmes.

www.london.edu

Things you didn't know about London Business School

The School has over 19,000 alumni located in more than 109 countries, linked by a network of 37 international alumni clubs.

The School's Dean, Laura Tyson (pictured above), served in the Clinton Administration as the President's National Economic Adviser and was the highest ranking woman in the Clinton White House.

Famous alumni from the world of business and finance include Tony Wheeler (Founder and CEO of Lonely Planet guides) and Merlyn Lowther (Deputy Director and Chief Cashier of the Bank of England).

Gurus on the School faculty include Sumantra Ghoshal, Professor of Strategic and International Management; Lynda Gratton, Associate Professor of Organisational Behaviour and one of the world's leading HR gurus; Elroy Dimson and Paul Marsh, Professors of Finance, founders of the FTSE 100 index and authors of 'Triumph of the Optimists', a ground-breaking study of the last hundred years of investment returns.

Market

LYCRA® is a fibre that since its invention 40 years ago has become an integral part of the fashion industry. Invented by DuPont, the fibre gives fabric added comfort and flexibility in a wide range of clothes across all garment categories. Although LYCRA® has been around for over 40 years, demand for the product from clothing manufacturers continues to grow. Leading designers claim fibre technology to be their most fundamental inspiration as they strive to make garments with the flexibility and high performance values needed to match the lifestyle of the twenty first century consumer. People today expect more from their clothes than style alone; market research highlights that comfort, ease of care, durability, breathability and lightness are all extremely important. Today LYCRA® is the leading brand within the brand portfolio of INVISTA, a wholly owned subsidiary of DuPont.

In September 2003 INVISTA was launched as the new name of DuPont Textiles & Interiors (DTI). The name change represents the company's next step towards separating from the parent company DuPont.

Achievements

A fabric ingredient and not a fabric itself, the fact that LYCRA® is such a well-known name all over the world, bears testament to INVISTA's marketing efforts. LYCRA® boasts a global awareness of over 90% and, according to Interbrand, is among the top ten clothing and textile brands in the world, sitting alongside names like Levi's and Armani.

LYCRA® is not just a famous name – it is also an invention of great significance, being cited by the Council of Fashion Designers of America as one of the twentieth century's most important fashion innovations.

Over the years, INVISTA has constantly kept abreast of developments in fashion and fibre technology, launching products that have maintained the fame and market-leading position of LYCRA®. Where some brands die when fashions change, INVISTA has consistently reinvigorated and reinterpreted LYCRA® to answer changing consumer needs especially in the ever changing world of fashion.

History

LYCRA® was invented in 1959 by a team of scientists at DuPont, originally as a replacement for rubber in corsetry. Before LYCRA® was invented, consumers endured saggy, baggy, stretched and bunched clothes. But when the DuPont scientist Joe Shriver perfected a revolutionary new fibre – code named K – that all changed.

In the 1960s LYCRA® revolutionised the way in which fabrics could be used. In beachwear it replaced thick and heavy swimsuits with light, quick-drying garments like the bikini. In 1968, the medal-winning French Olympic ski team became the first high-profile sports personalities to wear ski suits with LYCRA® – a trend that soon spread to other sports. By 1972 Olympic swimmers swore by the sleek, lightweight suits contoured with LYCRA®. The fibre soon became an integral part of performance wear for millions of amateur and professional athletes.

In the 1970s, the brand started to make an impact on the fashion scene, as disco fever and interest in fitness made leggings and figure-hugging leotards the look of the moment. Leggings and stretch jeans with LYCRA® are among the defining looks of the decade. By the mid 1980s, over half of all women's hosiery and underwear relied on LYCRA® for a close, comfortable fit.

During the 1990s, the position of LYCRA® in the sports market strengthened through the development of hi-tech fibres such as LYCRA® POWER compression shorts which help reduce athletes' muscle fatigue. This decade also saw the rising popularity of the fibre not just in women's fashion but in men's too. President Clinton gave the brand an important endorsement by sporting a suit made with LYCRA®, not to mention the interest sparked by the England football team's decision to sport business suits made with LYCRA®.

Product

LYCRA® is a man-made elastane fibre, invented and produced by DuPont. Never used alone, but always blended with other fibres, it has unique stretch and recovery properties. LYCRA® adds comfort, fit, shape retention, durability and freedom of movement. This is achieved thanks to the unique properties of the fibre, which can be stretched up to seven times its initial length before springing back once tension is released.

There are no natural or man-made clothing fibres that cannot be mixed with LYCRA®. Very small amounts of LYCRA® can transcend the performance of a fabric – the amount of LYCRA® in a material can be as little as 2%. There are various ways of integrating LYCRA® with other fibres to provide fabrics for all needs.

INVISTA carries out continual research and development in fibre technology. This is supported by an understanding of the market and ever changing fashion trends coupled with an awareness of developing consumers wants and needs.

An example of this brand development was the launch in 2001 of the campaign Jeans with LYCRA®. This garment marketing concept brought enhanced fit and freedom to denim and was welcomed by designers and manufacturers who were looking for new directions in which to develop Denim in a race to gain market share and brand recognition. The denim market has gone from strength to strength in recent years.

In 2001, LYCRA® set the scene for the future of leather with the launch of breakthrough technology: Leather with LYCRA®. Using proprietary techniques, the technology fuses layers of leather with layers of LYCRA®. This new structure gives the

natural leather a 'memory' which enables it to stretch and recover without losing any of its original quality or natural appearance.

Leather with LYCRA® was launched to the fashion world by Randolph Duke in Los Angeles, Carlos Miele in São Paulo, and Lawrence Steele in Milan who all featured collections which showcased the versatility of LYCRA®.

INVISTA has also made important contributions to the hosiery sector in recent years. LYCRA® Curves are designed to flatten the stomach and lift the bottom comfortably. The LYCRA® LegCare range has been proved in tests to help prevent tired and swollen legs – a common symptom among busy women who spend their days standing and walking. LegCare hosiery has a 'massaging' effect, which allows the blood to flow more easily in the leg, reducing swelling and feelings of heaviness and fatigue.

INVISTA has continued to innovate to keep LYCRA® at the cutting edge of sports and fashion technology. Other innovations, include LYCRA® POWER which is specially designed to reduce muscle fatigue and increase endurance. Soft Comfort LYCRA® offers improved comfort for hosiery garments and LYCRA® 3D is a knitting technique that further improves appearance, comfort and fit.

Recent Developments

In 2003 INVISTA launched a collection of innovations that deliver specific well-being benefits in clothes – Body Care by LYCRA®. The Body Care collection uses textile finishes and specially engineered yarns to deliver freshness, moisturising and massaging benefits to clothes. Freshness is delivered by technologies that inhibit the growth of odour-causing bacteria as well as trapping odour causing molecules that are then released in the next wash. Micro-encapsulation means moisturising agents are stored in the fibre structure which break open and release their contents to continuously hydrate the skin. Compression technology and temperature management in high-tech hosiery yarns offers massaging action.

Another significant recent development is the launch of LYCRA® elastic fibre T-400. This brand new fibre under the LYCRA® umbrella has a dimensional stability which gives it superior dyeability and colourfastness. It is ideal for applications such as denim, shirts and other woven fabrics that

require moderate stretch.

INVISTA's ability to drive innovations to the market and therefore to the consumer is partly due to the role it plays in the supply chain. The introduction of the 'Online Fabric Library' has revolutionised the process of sourcing fabrics for garment manufacturers all over the world. This 24 hour-a-day, seven day-a-week virtual library includes over 20,000 fabrics from 400 mills in over 40 countries.

INVISTA has also introduced a revolutionary new scanning technology to safeguard the LYCRA® brand against fraud. LYCRA® BrandScan™ is a sophisticated scanning system to determine whether a fabric or garment labelled as containing LYCRA® really does.

Promotion

The promotional strategy of LYCRA® is essentially two-pronged. Its most important audience comprises the business partners who include the fibre in their clothes and fabrics. But to do this, designers and retailers have to be convinced that there is strong consumer demand for clothes containing LYCRA®. Consequently, INVISTA invests US $1 million annually in research to understand consumer behaviour, better target its audience, and generate LYCRA® demand at retail.

INVISTA co-ordinates trade and consumer advertising to increase awareness of the brand among trade partners and end-users alike.

INVISTA has always invested heavily in marketing the LYCRA® brand, a fact which explains why it continues to enjoy such strong awareness among business and consumer customers. In 2002 INVISTA launched a US$40 million global advertising and promotion campaign, part of a US$200 million three year investment in the brand. The 'Has It' campaign illustrates the benefits of LYCRA® by associating the brand with a confident and stylish lifestyle attitude – 'you either have it or you don't'. The aim of the campaign is to engage consumers with the LYCRA® brand in order to motivate them to actively look for garments with the LYCRA® label. INVISTA has also introduced

new brightly coloured LYCRA® Has It hang tags to further drive awareness in store.

In April 2003 INVISTA launched Hotel LYCRA® in São Paulo, Brazil. Now one of the hottest venues in São Paulo, Hotel LYCRA® does not provide accommodation, instead it features a fashion store, gallery and restaurant. This innovative concept brings consumers face-to-face with the brand, giving them a total brand experience. Hotel LYCRA® also provides the LYCRA® brand with an interactive opportunity to showcase new products, gather consumer feedback and test new marketing concepts.

LYCRA® is set to take ownership of 'style' in 2003 with three impressive celebrity fashion awards; The LYCRA® British Style Awards, the

HAS IT.

When lingerie has LYCRA®, you get curves you never knew you had. (If the tag doesn't say "has it", it doesn't have it.)

You either have it or you don't.

LYCRA.

China LYCRA® InStyle Awards and the LYCRA® MTV Style Awards in India.

All three are highly prestigious in their own markets celebrating the best in fashion and style. Further, the LYCRA® British Style Awards is positioned as the Oscars of the global fashion industry and attracts international celebrities from the fields of fashion, music, sport and film.

Brand Values

INVISTA's marketing for LYCRA® focuses on a key product promise – that LYCRA® equals comfort, fit, shape retention and freedom of movement.

Whilst this is the functional brand promise, recent marketing has aimed to establish the brand's lifestyle appeal. Projects like Hotel LYCRA® will enhance the brand image amongst consumers, allowing them to experience the brand and establish LYCRA® at the forefront of style and fashion.

www.lycra.com

Superbrands

MEDIACOM
closer ●● to clients

Market

MediaCom is the market-leader in the UK media agency sector, with billings of £665 million (in a market worth £9 billion). Historically, media agencies provided media planning and buying services for advertisers; but today, MediaCom's role has expanded to embrace a wider communication role including consumer research, brand consultancy, econometrics, sponsorship, direct response and many other areas that help advertisers engage with their target audiences more efficiently and more effectively.

Achievements

When MediaCom was formed via a merger four years ago, the resulting company was the sixth biggest player in the market. Since then it has doubled in size – an unprecedented level of growth in the media agency sector.

The brand's growth has been matched by equally unprecedented levels of acclaim amongst independent consultants and the trade press. Since the merger in 1999 MediaCom has been named Media Agency of the Year by both Campaign and Marketing magazines; it has been voted the best media agency for Value for Money in a survey of clients conducted by Marketing Week, and has come out clearly on top in the Ocean Consulting Media Agency Monitor every year to date. A recent front page headline of another trade magazine, Media Week, asked simply 'Are MediaCom the best in the business?' The answer was 'yes'.

In the most recent Ocean Consulting Survey, MediaCom came top in four categories namely; Agency which consistently delivers the most impressive strategic planning; Most admired for all round professionalism and commercial performance; Agency with most impressive external communications and PR output and Agency most receptive to innovative ideas and approaches.

Also in 2003, MediaCom was chosen as one of the Top 100 Best Companies to Work For in the UK by the Sunday Times. MediaCom was also named one of the top ten companies for staff having faith in the senior management.

Over the past twelve months MediaCom has gained a further £50 million of new business in one of the toughest downturns the industry has known.

History

The present-day MediaCom was formed from the merger of two existing media agencies: MediaCom and The Media Business Group plc.

The Media Business was one of the first wave of media independents that emerged in the late 1970s and early 1980s, when senior personnel from top advertising agencies split away to set up companies that were specifically designed to handle the media planning and buying function. The Media Business was one of the key players as the industry underwent a transformation that saw most of the media planning and buying teams leaving ad agencies to find a home in this new sector.

The major advertising agency groups responded by splitting their media planning and buying functions into stand-alone companies. MediaCom was the Grey Group's media division.

Before the merger, The Media Business had established a reputation as one of the fastest growing media agencies in the country, but did not yet have the global presence to work with the biggest advertisers. MediaCom, on the other hand, was a part of a global network which had experience working with major advertisers such as P&G and Mars. A merger therefore made perfect sense.

Product

MediaCom's core skills are communications planning and buying. It is one of the world's largest media agency networks, with a major presence in all key regions. In Europe for example, MediaCom is one of the top three networks with clients including Procter & Gamble, Nokia, IKEA, Universal, Volkswagen, Shell, Masterfoods, Glaxo SmithKline and Oracle. MediaCom promises global clients 'everything everywhere', meaning the same level

of service, media expertise, buying power, planning process and research and evaluation tools in every market. Its extranet system allows its global clients immediate desktop access to media plans and relevant data from anywhere in the world.

MediaCom's buyers are the most powerful in the UK media market. As the biggest buyers across virtually every media, the brand has more negotiating clout than any of its competitors. MediaCom is the biggest buyer in TV, national press, magazines, regional press and is partnered

with the biggest buyer in outdoor and ambient.

As a result it is in the proud position of never having failed to meet any buying commitments that it has made to its clients. As most of its business is audited by media consultancies, its buying track record is independently vouched for.

MediaCom's communications planning department has pioneered an exciting revolution in the modern communications industry – the move towards integrated communications planning (ICP). With this system, all of MediaCom's clients' communications – from above-the-line advertising through to point of sale – is integrated around one clear strategic platform, bringing greater focus and therefore greater effectiveness to all the work. MediaCom was the first UK media agency to embrace ICP as a way of working, and continue to handle significantly more ICP business than any other agency. The ICP process that MediaCom has developed is called Real World Communications. It has been designed to ensure innovation, accountability and cut-through in all MediaCom's work.

MediaCom's biggest ICP client is Masterfoods, and it has achieved significant results for Masterfoods brands ranging from the pet food Frolic through to the classic MARS bar. Because ICP is channel-neutral, it tends to lead to work where media is deployed in innovative and therefore more impactful ways, with creativity being at the heart of the operation. MediaCom's recent work for the launch of the Audi A8, which included the UK's biggest ever online banner campaign (in a sector where TV would usually be the lead medium), is one example of its creative approach.

MediaCom was also the first media agency to develop a major direct response division. It is now the market leader in direct response media – more than twice the size of its nearest competitor with billings of £140 million per annum, and consequently has more insight into how media actually works than any other agency. The learnings from its direct response work is fed back into its brand work as well, helping MediaCom to offer greater accountability to all clients.

Its research function is split into two main areas: Consumer Insight and Effectiveness.

To offer its clients insight into the behaviour and attitudes of their target audiences, MediaCom runs a series of regular surveys and email panels to ensure that it has an ongoing dialogue with all the key audiences. Beyond this, its clients can find out the answer to any question they may have in a matter of days using the email panels. As well

as media research, clients have taken advantage of this facility to test out creative ideas and even to ascertain the viability of new product launches.

MediaCom's effectiveness team is the largest econometrics unit in the sector with fourteen statisticians in total; combined with its direct response expertise, it allows MediaCom to offer clients extremely high levels of accountability, both in demonstrating the effectiveness of previous campaigns and in modelling the impact of future activity. As a result, MediaCom has been able to offer clients valuable advice on pricing, stocking levels, call centre staffing levels, regional distribution, and on the 'halo effect' that one brand's advertising has on other brands.

Among MediaCom's many specialist teams is the Entertainment Media Group. EMG specialises in working for clients in the entertainment field – records, videos, games – and is particularly skilled in working to extremely tight deadlines.

Recent Developments

The media industry is in a constant state of evolution, and so MediaCom is constantly adding new skills and new divisions.

The biggest change the industry is currently going through is the arrival of ICP – discussed earlier. To ensure that it remains the leading player in ICP, MediaCom undertakes intensive training not just of all its planners, but also for its buyers. And because ICP is a highly collaborative process, MediaCom also

trains its clients and their third party agencies.

In recent years, MediaCom's sponsorship division SponsorCom, has become increasingly important, and its new event marketing arm has hit the ground running; already creating valuable events for clients such as the Snickers Game On street sports and music event which has given the brand a renewed salience with younger consumers.

It has also recently set up MediaCom Career which is a specialist resource to handle recruitment advertisers.

Promotion

In the July 2003 Media Agency Survey conducted by Ocean Consulting, MediaCom's marketing and communication was voted the best in the business – three times better than the nearest rival. An especially pleasing result given that for many years MediaCom was considered to be a 'low-profile' agency.

This seeming contradiction is explained by the fact that MediaCom has always rejected the idea of promoting a few high-profile stars, in favour

of communicating the company's core brand statements directly to its target audience.

Essentially therefore, MediaCom targets marketing directors and marketing departments, as well as anyone else who may be involved in the decision to appoint a media agency such as chief executives, finance directors, procurement directors, and media auditors.

It is also of importance to MediaCom that it regularly communicates with media owners; but it tends not to place much emphasis on marketing activity that will only be seen by its peers.

The brand's communications channels include SMART – a regular quarterly magazine, which keeps clients up to date with developments in the media world as well as developments at MediaCom. John Billett, who is a leading industry figure, recently said that SMART was the "best piece of communication I have ever seen from a media agency."

The New Beetle Cabriolet.

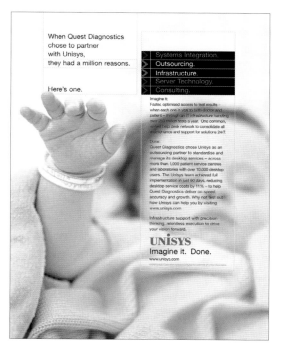

In addition, MediaCom holds Client Open Days – devoted to particular areas of interest, for example ICP, sponsorship, digital media and it also offers a general overview for interested clients.

Other activities include ongoing PR in both trade and national press.

Brand Values

MediaCom sights its brand values as being 'passion', 'accountability', 'ahead of the game', 'creativity' and 'straight-talking'. As a constant reminder, its meeting

rooms are named after its brand values. While its values shape the way the organisation does business, it also has one central brand statement that it believes sums up what makes MediaCom different from its competitors – 'closer to clients'.

www.mediacomuk.com

Michael Page

INTERNATIONAL

Market

Michael Page International is renowned for performing well during both bull and bear economies and this has again been proven true in the current market where many of its competitors have lost market share through office closures. The company has steadily increased its market share and developed internationally while also heavily investing in its support network and infrastructure, thereby reinforcing its position as a world leader in the recruitment of qualified and skilled professionals for organisations across a broad spectrum of industries and professions.

Over the past five years the internet has had an immense impact on the recruitment industry by providing a cost-effective alternative route to market. Yet whilst Michael Page International has embraced this technology to develop its business, the company fully realises that the industry remains very much a relationship-based experience for clients and candidates alike. It is this personal approach that has helped Michael Page International to a healthy slice of the multi-billion pound recruitment consultancies market worldwide.

Achievements

Michael Page International has grown from a small London consultancy to become an international company based in sixteen countries, with 107 offices and nearly 2,400 staff. In its 27 years of operation it has consistently aimed to be a market leader and can now lay claim to a considerable number of notable achievements.

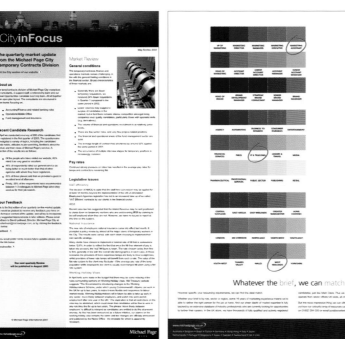

Whatever the brief, we can match it.

It was, for instance, the first executive recruitment firm to be floated on the London Stock Exchange. The company also established a bespoke consultant training programme covering the operational and management aspects of the business. Michael Page International was the first in the recruitment industry to develop an international computerised applicant network – a system that provides consultants with instant access to a database of job vacancies and applicants the world over.

State-of-the-art computerised recruitment systems have enhanced the company's specialist knowledge and bolstered its strong client relationships. The company has invested heavily in the development of these systems, which are considered to be among the most innovative in the business.

It was also the first to develop a pan-European network in which nationals of the specific countries were instrumental to expansion. And in the national press, Michael Page International has consistently been a major advertiser – a fact particularly emphasised by the company's dominant presence in the Financial Times.

The company also now has twelve specialist divisions – a reflection of its sheer market presence and breadth of industry expertise. And to communicate

all of its activities, Michael Page International has created its own in-house Marketing Department.

History

Its eponymous founder and Bill McGregor, who came from the oil and brewing industries, established Michael Page International in 1976. Bill McGregor remains part of the management team today.

The company was founded in London, principally to recruit accountants for industrial clients. Within ten years it had built a network of offices throughout the UK and continental Europe, and had expanded to cover recruitment in the finance, legal, marketing, sales, consultancy, taxation, information technology, engineering, human resources, retail, corporate treasury and banking sectors. It has now expanded to have offices in Australia, the Far East and the US.

Other milestones in the company's history include the establishment of Accountancy Additions in 1992, the implementation of an East European Division in 1995, the creation of Michael Page Human Resources in 2000, the opening of offices in Tokyo in 2001 and being awarded the accolade of Business Superbrand (professional recruitment) since the award began.

Product

The product of Michael Page International is based on the 4 Cs: consultants, candidates, clients and care.

Michael Page International wholeheartedly believes that professional consultants come first, without them nothing can be achieved. This is wholly reflected in the organic growth of the company whereby nearly all the current management is the result of internal promotion. And to ensure that consultants are professional in the way they work, they are not paid by commission.

The company believes that if you provide a sincere and genuine service to candidates everything will fall into place. Michael Page International has long realised that the creation of loyalty stems from finding out about a candidate's career aspirations and then showing them how they can realise their vision. Many candidates come to the company's door by way of referral or recommendation, or often, they already have a history of being placed into previous roles via the consultancy.

Michael Page International also recognises that by having a pool of quality candidates, clients will be drawn to the business. Coupled with this, the provision of a personal service to all clients, taking the time to find out how they can provide a bespoke recruitment solution, creates a powerful incentive to secure repeat business.

Finally, care and consideration always has a way of rewarding you in the future.

With the 4Cs as guiding principals, Michael Page International has developed its brand to

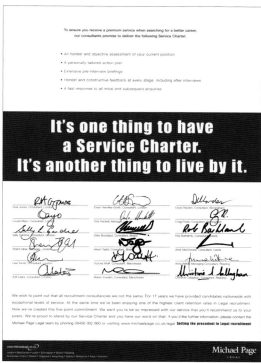

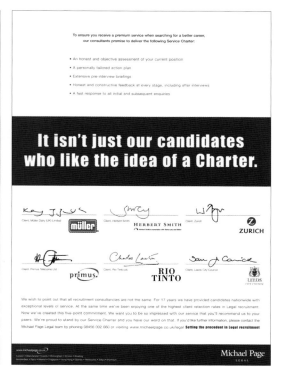

signify efficiency and quality in recruitment services. The brand has been developed along two central and associated fronts. Firstly, the company has focused on developing specialist consultancy teams to recruit for the disciplines in which they are often personally qualified. Thus the company has bankers recruiting for banks, salesmen recruiting sales professionals and so on. Secondly, the business operates on a global basis to facilitate the international movement of skilled management.

Its people are clearly the company's most important asset and have helped Michael Page International to achieve an unrivalled level of expertise and market penetration.

Recent Developments
Although the company continues to expand its terrestrial network, with new offices in Stockholm, Sweden, and Brussels, Belgium, the most exciting and important development has been the rollout of a new global IT recruitment system, commencing in 2003 and continuing throughout 2004. Such initiatives are typical of the company; even in periods of tough trading it continues to invest in its office network and computer systems.

The ongoing evolution of the company's third generation website has also been a significant

development. Since the relaunch of all of the company's global websites in June 2002, Michael Page International has continued to listen to the needs of its users and to undertake improvements where appropriate. In the UK, for example, there has been a reduction in the amount of time it takes to sign up for My Page (a service which allows candidates to receive job alerts, track applications and save searches). Many leading clients have a branded presence on the website and there is now also an advice section that offers a comprehensive selection of informative and topical articles from recruitment experts and award winning journalists to help

candidates and clients make the most of job searching and the recruitment process.

Since the relaunch, visitors to the UK site have increased by 66%. The UK site receives an average of 200,000 visitors and 20,000 applications per month.

Looking forward, Michael Page International will continue to deliver an online service with a 'human touch'. The focus will remain on the users' needs, with the endeavour to develop an ever-more intuitive, easy-to-use site that offers a high volume of quality opportunities and specialist content and advice.

Promotion
The recruitment industry, while rapidly adapting to the digital revolution, continues to utilise traditional methods of recruitment. Recruitment advertising in the press and other printed media remains its main element. Michael Page International is a market leader in the classified advertising pages of the national and trade press worldwide. In the UK it is the industry's biggest advertiser, significantly ahead of its nearest rival. It also holds a leading position in Australia, France and the Netherlands.

The superior quality and creative content of Michael Page International's advertising and publications have been important factors in promoting the company's principal objective of providing excellent service. The praise that its work has received reflects its professionalism and innovation.

The company's global office network, which has established close relationships with local organisations, also promotes the recruitment services of Michael Page International to a wide audience. This regional presence helps the company to achieve an extremely high level of local market penetration. The internet also helps the company to target new candidates, especially in places such as South Africa where it has no offices.

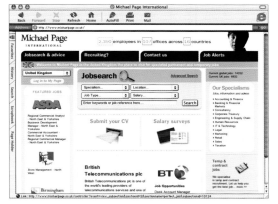

The website is an extremely useful resource for candidates in those countries looking for international job opportunities.

As www.michaelpage.co.uk grows, the company will forge further alliances with other high quality brands to ensure that Michael Page International continues to be promoted to a well-targeted international audience.

Brand Values
The quality and expertise of its consultancy and support staff are the best expression of the brand values of Michael Page International. The company's policy is to recruit and train its staff to be the best in the business – to be passionate about their work and make the best matches possible between candidates and clients – and above all, to uphold the philosophy of the 4Cs.

The Michael Page International brand is identified as a specialist brand with individual businesses operating in specific markets and disciplines. It is a global brand, which sets common standards of service excellence, entrepreneurial spirit, continuity and operational effectiveness throughout its worldwide operations – a network of offices that operate at national, regional and local levels.

www.michaelpage.co.uk

Things you didn't know about Michael Page International

In 1978 the company's first office outside London was opened in Manchester. The board minutes state: 'It was decided to open an office in Manchester solely on the basis that if we can be successful there, we can be successful anywhere.'

Michael Page International receives an estimated 100,000 unsolicited applications every year from would-be job seekers.

In 2002 Michael Page International facilitated around 20,900 permanent placements and 22,400 temporary positions.

The company works with all of the FTSE 100 companies.

At any given time, Michael Page International has around 80,000 candidates on its books.

The Michael Page website in the UK receives at least 7,000 visitors a day.

MINTeL

Market

After three decades of business, Mintel has become both a business and a household name. Accurate market intelligence is key to a successful business: knowing ones customers, market, competitors and their products as well as accurately predicting what the future holds is paramount. Mintel supplies this knowledge and does so consistently and reliably to a global client base and the need for these answers has propelled Mintel into phenomenal growth in new markets across the Far East, North and South America and Europe, as well as consolidating its leading market position in the UK.

However, the best information is useless without the best delivery mechanisms. Mintel constantly develops and deploys the latest technology to satisfy its clients' demand for instant information. A reputation for high quality, reliable market, consumer, product and media research, coupled with the most effective delivery mechanisms, has earned Mintel Business Superbrands status consistently since the award began.

But the market is changing again – clients now expect the best, continually updated information instantly as well as having other needs, such as being able to manipulate the data further and tailor it to their own business requirements. Mintel no longer sells one-off publications, it supplies live pieces of information that are updated using the latest news developments and analyst commentary. It sells a complete information solution.

Mintel's sales approach has evolved to become more consultative, through listening and learning from its clients and giving them the tools to take its analysis further. The brand views its clients as a community of users, many of whom are fantastic ambassadors for Mintel as they are responsible for improving its profile throughout their organisation.

Achievements

One could mention Mintel's 20% compound sales growth over the last ten years – virtually all organic and self-funded, however, it is more inspiring to look at the constant product development and employee growth that underpins the brand's success.

Consistently high levels of service, clear branding and a focus on quality have resulted in unprecedented client growth and investment. Expansion has been exceptional, with the US operations leading the way. Staff turnover is low, with today's more mature company based upon organic growth and experience. While the group has retained its head office presence in London and Chicago, Mintel has an established satellite office in Sydney and a successful sales agency in Belfast (with another office in Cork soon to open).

Mintel's core reports range is now interactive, meaning that updated information and analysis are continuously pushed through the website and onto its clients, so that at any point the data they use is both topical and relevant. In addition, Mintel now supplies clients with graphing, analytical and presentational tools to ensure its data is used comprehensively throughout its clients' organisations. Its more detailed consumer analysis highlights why people do what they do, when they do it and how best to reach them from a marketing perspective.

Mintel's US operation now has a reports portfolio of almost 200 titles to add to the existing 400 in the UK and European range, covering every aspect of consumer expenditure.

The brand's Global New Products Database (GNPD) is populated with over 450,000 fmcg product launches across 53 countries, with access to a global network of 4,000 country representatives. Recent developments include packaging data for all new products launched, as well as the opportunity to view the latest TV and radio adverts for products.

Comperemedia, the US direct mail and print advertising monitoring service, has enjoyed continued success in a tough economic climate. Product extensions have included specific services for financial intermediaries and marketing service suppliers.

Other key divisions such as POS+, Services and Consultancy have increased in value as

always in fashion

(and food, fitness, finance...)

www.mintel.com

MINTeL

Mintel strives to offer its clients a complete 'information solution' – meaning that any of the products or services can be developed further or tailored specifically to clients' needs.

Mintel's well-established UK relationship with the media has provided an excellent platform for increasing international awareness of the brand. Constant mentions of Mintel in the press are no longer unique to the UK, with the US press office now receiving a stream of media exposure. Furthermore, the company boasts leading analysts in the retail, leisure, consumer and finance arenas. Many are speakers and consultants who enjoy regular media exposure.

Quoted in many company brochures, Mintel is regularly used as a source in presentations and government and trade publications. The company is also frequently cited for PR purposes, since its objective market assessments guarantee trade credibility. Mintel has also assisted the flotation of several major companies, with data included in various prospectuses.

History

Over the past three decades Mintel has gained recognition as a leading international research supplier. Originally a provider of fmcg food and drinks reports in the UK, the company has progressively expanded its product range and geographical coverage, with the result that the company is now recognised as a leading supplier of market, media, product and consumer intelligence.

Its brand guardians, that include all of the company's employees, have played a major part in the brand's success. Within the organisation it is seen as a welcome challenge to predict and surpass client needs, while always remembering that any contact or experience with Mintel must reflect its core values and reputation.

The continuing support and loyalty of its clients, many of whom had their first Mintel experience while studying at university and have maintained that relationship throughout their working life, is obviously an integral part of its branding success. Mintel has rewarded that loyalty with constant innovation and improvement to the product and level of service.

Product

Central to Mintel's brand is the Mintel market report. Each report includes market size and trend data, together with a detailed segmentation analysis. Reports highlight participating companies within the industry, as well as market shares. The future of the industry is assessed and users are supplied with exclusive forecast data. Unique to every Mintel report is the primary consumer research, which helps to provide an in-depth understanding of consumers. The research is reactive and often highlights topical industry issues. As well as standard reports, Mintel is also well known for its lifestyle range, which examines the nation as a whole: our attitudes, hopes, fears, intentions and desires, across a wide range of topics.

Product and media research is provided in the form of the GNPD, Comperemedia and the sales promotions database POS+.

GNPD is a database monitoring worldwide product innovation in consumer packaged goods markets, offering coverage of new product activity for competitor monitoring and new product development. Featuring pictures, ingredients, details and descriptions of all key new products, the database provides users with daily updates and an email alert service. Mintel also facilitates product audits and retrieval around the globe, from Aruba to Zanzibar and from Burkina Faso to Tahiti.

POS+ is another service used by manufacturers, retailers and marketing/advertising agencies, to determine on-pack and on-shelf fmcg, food

"shhhhhhh...
i'm using mintel"

in 1998 saw Mintel exporting a number of existing product ranges to the US market. US development has been rapid, and there are now as many US-based employees as there are UK and European.

Mintel uses constant client feedback to ensure that it tailors and develops all of its products to meet client expectations and stay well ahead of any competitor offering. Varying economic conditions in core markets have necessitated a focus on ensuring that Mintel's products are used effectively and constantly throughout the client organisation while marketing and IT support have been paramount in successfully maintaining the client base.

As mentioned previously, a more consultative sales approach has underpinned Mintel's high client retention and ability to develop new business areas. It provides clients with usage statistics and strategies to ensure that its products are used throughout the organisation.

A further development has been a focus on recruiting and retaining the best employees.

group marketing ensure a consistent brand message. All marketing and PR is carried out in-house by an established and integrated team.

A series of workshops have been introduced across Europe to promote the brand and continue to be successful in terms of brand-building as well as providing sales opportunities.

Electronic marketing has however dominated Mintel's promotional activity over the last two years – a focus on tools such as email campaigns, strategic weblinks and online advertising, always directing users through to the established Mintel website have been utilised.

Mintel also forges links with leading trade associations and industry bodies, such as the Chartered Institute of Marketing (CIM), providing further confirmation of Mintel's status as an authority on consumer research. A sponsor of the CIM's national conferences for the last four years, Mintel also works with the CIM to promote the importance of market intelligence in any industry.

Brand Values
Mintel's core brand values include providing quality global research, that is top of the range, with the best delivery, detailed methodology and timeliness. Three decades of experience and data

collection with the most technologically advanced delivery methods have ensured that the Mintel name is synonymous with these values. Mintel's dynamic sales team and consultants focus on the application of information, rather than just supplying facts and figures.

Mintel's philosophy is to ensure that it either educates its clients or helps them make profits – ideally both.

www.mintel.com

and non-food promotional activity adopted throughout the UK's retail stores.

Meanwhile in the US, Comperemedia tracks products, offers, incentives and creative techniques across two types of media: direct mail and print advertising. With access to over 250,000 households in the US and 40,000 in Canada, Comperemedia collects all the direct mail sent to a rolling sample of 10,500 households and 1,200 businesses every month, enabling it to undertake competitive analysis of direct mail and advertising across 42 market sectors.

Mintel's Consultancy offers an extensive range of tailored solutions including an information centre that has a rapid response helpdesk. A team of consultants have extensive experience in strategic analysis and forecasting, as well as qualitative and quantitative consumer research. The Consultancy also includes a newsgathering service, which provides a daily email news alert digest service.

Recent Developments
Globalisation has been at the heart of Mintel's expansion, with the most significant company developments having occurred within the past five years. The opening of Mintel's US office

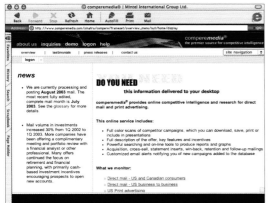

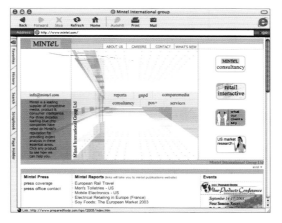

Internal recruiters in both London and Chicago ensure that as the business grows, there is a constant supply of suitable new candidates who possess key characteristics and drive to take the business even further. Internal communication has become key as the organisation has grown, as has constant nurturing and development of the talented staff base.

Promotion
Mintel's continued Business Superbrands success is testimony to the strength of its brand. Every external contact, whether paper, electronic or face to face must promote its brand consistently and effectively.

In the UK the use of the Mintel yellow and black logo is subtle and reflects its high brand recognition, while in the US and Europe where the brand's profile is still being developed, it is much bolder. Strict house styles plus centralised

---

Things you didn't know about Mintel

Mintel produces so many reports that one could read two current Mintel reports a day, and still never read the same one twice for over a year.

According to Mintel's Comperemedia division, US households received over five billion pieces of mail about credit cards in 2002.

Over 500 new fmcg product launches are added to the Global New Products Database each day.

In 2002 Mintel polled nearly half a million people in the UK and US.

In the UK we spend £3.3 billion on our pets, with over a fifth of UK pet owners buying them gifts, including Christmas and birthday presents.

Mintel has clients in more than 100 countries, including exotic locations such as French Polynesia and the Maldives.

NatWest

Market

The UK financial sector is intensely competitive and diverse. Apart from the 'big four', the market has expanded exponentially over the last decade with the arrival of new, low-cost entrants, especially 'virtual' brands, offering branchless banking over the internet. Without the 'bricks and mortar' cost of supporting a branch network, web-based operators have been able to achieve substantially lower delivery costs.

The market has also become further crowded by the entrance of non-traditional banking brands, such as supermarkets and retailers. This, combined with the demutualising of building societies, means that the borders of the financial services sector have become extremely blurred, with the result that all players now compete against each other in almost every sphere.

This has not only made the UK banking market much more price competitive, but also contributed to other factors, such as a sharp decrease in brand loyalty, as customers shop around for the best deals. This has resulted in a fundamental change in the relationship between a customer and their bank. The relative value of a face to face relationship, versus an arms-length virtual relationship over the internet is a hot issue. Many banks have closed branches to focus on telephone and internet banking, while others, including NatWest, have sought to balance web-based and telephone services with the provision of 'traditional' personal services which many customers still prefer. In today's market, banks have to go to great lengths to keep their more demanding and fickle customers happy.

Having said that, there is an increasing incentive to do so, as the growing prosperity of the UK population means we are 'consuming' more and more financial products and services. In 1975, just 44.6% of the UK population had a current account, but by 2000, that figure had grown to 87.6%. Similarly credit card ownership has grown from 13% to 53% and savings account holders from 27% to 59% (Source: TGI/BMRB).

Even though the sector has become more complicated and fragmented, NatWest still enjoys a high profile. It has eight million current account holders in the UK and a 16% market share.

Achievements

NatWest has become a true Superbrand – not just of the financial world, but in all senses, it is a brand woven into the fabric of the country. With 1,643 branches and 3,400 automatic teller machines around the UK, NatWest's presence is all around. It's not surprising that research shows that 94% of British adults instantly recognise its brand.

But scale and recognition is not everything. NatWest has performed commendably in adapting its business to suit the changing climate of modern financial services, not only broadening its scope of operations, but also doing so while maintaining high levels of service and customer satisfaction.

This is reflected in the broad range of awards picked up by the bank across numerous different areas of its activity. Its Business Banking service came top of an NOP Opinion Formers Poll in March 2002 and Best Bank for Small and Medium sized businesses in the Chartered Institute of Management Accountants awards of 2001.

Its mortgage products have won awards, with NatWest Mortgages Direct voted Best Direct Lender for four years running by Your Mortgage Magazine. In November 2002, the same magazine's awards voted it Best Bank for Mortgages. Financial Adviser magazine voted it 'Best Overall Lender'.

Its marketing and communications have also attracted plaudits, especially its 'Another Way' advertising campaign, which showed the bank still cared about keeping branches open and offering personal service at a time when its competitors were being criticised for doing the exact opposite. The campaign was runner-up in the 'Campaign of the Year' category at the Money Marketing Financial Services Awards in 2001.

But it is not just the high-profile advertising aspect of its communications strategy which has been praised. NatWest's online marketing saw it reach the finals in two categories of the prestigious Revolution Magazine awards and NOP Opinion Formers Research said the bank 'provides the best guides and information packs'.

History

In 1968 National Provincial Bank and Westminster Bank merged as National Westminster Bank. Together these banks could trace their history back to the 1650s.

The process of integration was completed in 1969 and National Westminster Bank commenced trading on January 1st 1970, with the famous three-arrowheads symbol as its logo.

The new bank, with its many branches, developed a wide range of new services, including the bank's first credit card, Access, in 1972, and computer-linked cash dispensers, Servicetills, in 1976. Deregulation in the 1980s, culminating in 'Big Bang' in 1986, also encouraged National Westminster Bank to enter the securities business. County Bank, the Group's merchant bank, acquired stockbroking and jobbing firms to create NatWest Investment Bank. Meanwhile, the International Banking Division looked to provide international banking services to large companies and to focus on expansion in the US, the Far East and Europe.

In the 1980s new services were developed such as telephone banking and touch-screen share dealing to assist the government's privatisation programme. The 1980s also saw the National Westminster Home Loans established as well as the Small Business Unit in 1982. The Switch debit card extended the electronic transfer of money to point of sale in 1988. In the 1990s financial services markets worldwide underwent massive change and in response the bank refocused its activities, exiting from a number of markets and adopting the title of NatWest.

In March 2000, The Royal Bank of Scotland Group completed the acquisition of NatWest in a £21 billion deal that was the largest take-over in British banking history. NatWest is now part of a financial services group which is the second largest bank by market capitalisation in the UK and in Europe and ranks fifth in the world.

Product

NatWest, which is a subsidiary of The Royal Bank of Scotland Group, offers retail and mortgage banking services, as well as online banking and brokerage capabilities to individuals and small business customers. Other activities include insurance, asset management, lease financing, international banking and private equity funding.

It offers a full range of current accounts, from the basic to specialist accounts for children and students. For higher net worth customers who desire a more personalised approach to their services, the bank has the Advantage Gold and Advantage Premier accounts. It also offers a full range of business current accounts.

Its range of savings accounts includes basic notice to specialist Bonds, ISAs and Business Deposit accounts. NatWest's loans and overdrafts are designed to suit all sorts of different needs, including Professional Trainee loans, numerous business finance products, MBA loans and College of Law loans.

NatWest is also a big player in the mortgages sector, and in assurance and insurance, offering life assurance, travel, car and home insurance and business insurance covering such things as public and employers' liability, assets and money.

It offers a vast array of credit cards, including specialist business and commercial charge cards. Other products specifically designed for the corporate world include financing, investing, payments and cash management, international services, global banking, currency accounts and risk management.

NatWest has recognised that customers want to interact with the bank in the way of their choosing, so as well as the full internet and telephone banking options for personal, business and corporate customers, it also offers a personal service by offering 'relationship banking managers'.

Recent Developments

As part of its effort to constantly refresh its image and offering, NatWest recently embarked on a massive investment programme to refurbish its network of branches. Everything that carries the NatWest brand will be updated, from signage, literature, advertising and account products like cheque books, paying-in books and plastic cards. From early 2003, every branch started to receive new external signage, merchandising and interiors. The new look is designed to reflect a warmer, friendlier and accessible way of doing business.

The new interiors will pay close attention to improving accessibility for disabled customers, including lower-level counters, wheel chair ramps and automatic or power assisted doors. Audio induction loops at all till positions plus an audio

visual queuing system will help people who are visually impaired or deaf.

Staff will receive a new uniform to complement the new identity, which has been developed with a poly-wool material enriched with LYCRA® to keep the wearer looking smart but feeling comfortable throughout the day.

Promotion

NatWest's marketing has been among the best produced by the banking sector in recent years, especially the 'Another Way' campaign, which was released in July 2000 to convey the company's new approach to banking.

At the time, the main high street banks were all facing mounting criticism, particularly for cutting services whilst increasing profits. Widespread branch closures, particularly in the country, left many communities feeling abandoned and underserved. This feeling was exacerbated by the banks' increasingly depersonlised services, with an emphasis on using call centres and the internet.

NatWest appreciated how frustrating these changes were and began to swim against the tide, reversing its own branch closure programme, ensuring that customers could speak to a real person – not just a machine – 24 hours a day, and putting Business Managers in place for a minimum of four years.

These and other measures collectively represented 'Another Way' of doing banking and this underlined the bank's entire marketing and business strategy adopted in the summer of 2000.

Three years on, the bank continues to spearhead new initiatives that focus on customer service and accessibility. The advertising strategy has evolved to reflect how the bank thinks from the perspective of its customers and, rather than focusing on individual loan rates or specific product offers, it conveys how the whole ethos of banking is handled more efficiently at NatWest.

Brand Values

The essence of NatWest's brand is that it aims to think like a customer, not a bank. This central thought is linked to its communications, which aim to convey that NatWest does things another way – the customer's way. It also gives the brand a clear personality, of being straightforward, experienced, real, upbeat, insightful and friendly.

www.natwest.com

npower

Market

The UK energy retail market is today worth £25 billion (Source: DTI). It is dominated by seven major suppliers of which npower is consistently ranked in the top three by industry analyst Datamonitor.

The market has gone through radical change since deregulation began in 1992. Previously electricity was provided by twelve regional suppliers while gas was supplied, nationwide, by British Gas. Customers could not choose their supplier and prices were set by the regulator.

Following deregulation we now have a fiercely competitive national energy market. Energy prices have gone down, but opportunities for companies to grow a loyal customer base by offering energy products and home and business-related services, have increased.

The business energy sector is particularly complex. Large industrial and commercial customers' needs and buying patterns differ vastly from those of small and medium sized enterprises (SMEs) who, at the low end are more akin to domestic customers. Meanwhile there is a large overlap in the middle-market which includes, for instance, big single site customers, or small groups.

Deregulation brought challenge as well as opportunity. Companies with an eye on the long game needed to establish scale to survive. Around five million customer accounts was seen to be the minimum for most companies to succeed. This meant both through organic growth and acquisitions. It also meant keeping existing customers happy and loyal.

Pace of change led to a volatile market and huge integration challenges for merged companies. Along with the organisational and HR issues, decisions had to be taken regarding the IT systems for storing huge customer databases and swapping customers between suppliers. Designed in isolation, these now needed to be integrated or to communicate with each other.

In the market today these practical hurdles still exist alongside tough strategic questions about branding. Energy companies are still grappling with issues like the value of existing regional brands, versus the value of adopting and building a single, new national brand. Equally important is the issue of how 'broad' a brand can stretch beyond traditional energy, without snapping.

Achievements

In less than four years npower has integrated five companies into a single, national whole. It now employs around 8,500 people and has over six million residential customer accounts and

provides gas, electricity, conveyancing, household insurance and central heating maintenance. It holds 20% of the business-to-business energy market – serving over half a million customers from the likes of BT down to the local pub or fish and chip shop.

To achieve this npower has had to become very adept at change management and growth, but the key to success has been keeping the customer as the centre of attention. In a commodity market, price is always a key factor, but the careful development of the npower brand, in a traditionally low-interest sector, has been vital in maintaining customer relationships.

In only three years the npower brand has gone from 0 to 90% national awareness. The brand has successfully shed heritage associations with regional monopoly supply, but maintained the loyalty of the customer bases it has acquired. It has avoided the 'fly-by-night' tag attached to many new brands that can put off risk-averse customers, and it has developed the flexibility to allow expansion beyond the core products of gas and electricity. In 2002 an independent study by research company Brand Finance estimated the value of the npower brand at £200 million.

Along the way npower has picked up a number of awards including: Utility Week's Marketing Achievement of the Year in 2000; the FT Global Energy Award for Overall Marketing Campaign of the Year, 2001 and the Sports Industry Awards' Best Sports Sponsorship 2002.

This success has been achieved in a market comprising, at one end, aggressive 'low cost' new entrants and at the other British Gas – a company which began the deregulated era with an enormous customer base and was gifted a massive head start in terms of brand development.

History

In 1999 the domestic electricity market fully opened up to competition and the company National Power began to build a 'retail' business with the purchase of gas company Calortex and the Midlands Electricity Board.

In October 1999 it created the npower brand as a collective name

for its customer businesses. In 2000 it added new entrant Independent Energy to the npower stable. Later that year National Power demerged into International Power and Innogy plc. Innogy kept npower along with power generation, trading and engineering assets.

In 2001 Innogy plc acquired the Yorkshire Electricity Group bringing customer numbers to over five million. In September the same year Innogy swapped the distribution business (the wires) of Yorkshire Electricity for the customers of Northern Electric and Gas. npower's customer numbers now topped 6.5 million, including half a million business customers.

In May 2002 Innogy was acquired by the German multi-utility company RWE which includes Thames Water amongst its subsidiaries.

Product

Energy is a low interest product which is difficult to differentiate. At the most basic level the pricing is the product, but npower took the view that marketing needed to be more innovative than a series of pricing skirmishes. These would be counter productive and costly, encouraging customers to come and go regularly with maximum disruption and minimum return.

npower believed simple clever product innovations would help attract loyal customers. Examples of this include an unprecedented partnership signed with Greenpeace to develop and sell 'npower Juice', a domestic, non-premium priced green electricity tariff linked to the company's North Hoyle offshore wind farm off the North Wales coast. Although, a niche product for now, 'npower Juice' attracts users who are significantly more loyal than mainstream electricity consumers.

A further innovation helping cement loyalty has been npower's diversification into home moving products via a joint venture with The Move Factory. These range from providing simple home move information through to conveyancing, with online progress tracking and seven days-a-week telephone access.

On the business-to-business front product innovation has tended to mean introducing flexibility to help meet the needs of business customers which vary widely in their consumption habits and patterns. At the SME end this will never stray far from the basics of accurate and timely billing, but npower has looked to develop size and sector specialisms (your average grocery chain owner considers himself a grocer, not an SME). A classic and popular example of a simple improvement on multiple billing is a collated service for group

sites where head office receives collated statements and a summary invoice, while individual sites receive energy statements.

At the industrial and commercial end of the spectrum the financial stakes are incredibly high. In the current market structure, predicting demand and tracking consumption are vital for major energy users. npower has met this trend with a Half Hourly Online product which allows customers to track usage securely via the internet, and receive alerts when consumption is breaking pre-set thresholds.

Meanwhile npower's Renewables and Consolidation Service helps major business customers bear the growing burden of statutory environmental obligations, and protects them from the market risk of over-reliance on a single power generator.

Recent Developments

npower has recently instigated a programme of workshops based on market research principles and held at various locations around the country. These 'Pow wow groups' involve a range of staff in the business and domestic divisions of npower, beyond the core brand and marketing teams. They examine customer perceptions and address specific business issues and challenges. This helps ensure the brand is anchored to the real concerns of both staff and customers.

High on the list of concerns for large business

customers have been industry technology glitches. npower has recently announced it is to move further into metering and data collection to help take unnecessary links out of the chain that makes up the complex billing process.

In 2003, npower added to the momentum created by 'npower Juice' with the launch of a trial solar power 'account' which could enable householders and businesses to offset energy costs by selling daylight generated electricity back to npower. The company is also stepping up the 'green' offer to businesses offering 100% green energy which enables customers to offset environmental taxes. By 2004 npower will be offering green electricity to all business customers.

The second major area of social responsibility for npower surrounds the issue of vulnerable customers. 2003 saw the successful expansion of npower's Health Through Warmth scheme – a £10 million programme helping to eradicate 'fuel poverty'. As many as 40,000 people die every winter from cold related illnesses. Health Through Warmth trains NHS healthcare workers and home visitors to spot the signs of poor energy efficiency in the homes of the vulnerable. It then puts these people in touch with sources of grant aid to make improvements.

Promotion

npower's approach to promotion and marketing has evolved with the company. At launch npower was a challenger, competing with established brands like British Gas and Powergen.

The immediate goal was to gain awareness and promote the, still novel, idea that energy customers had a choice of supplier. From the outset it was clear that mass marketing was needed to put npower on the radar for business customers as well as domestic users.

Early television advertising included a campaign using the strapline 'There are some things in life you can't choose, your energy supplier is not one of them'. A controversial execution featuring a ginger-haired family was instrumental in putting npower on the map. Awareness was sustained and improved through a simple but daring two-year sponsorship deal with ITV's 'The Bill' and associate sponsorship of the FA Premiership.

A real watershed in npower's brand development was achieved with its decision to take over sponsorship of English Test Cricket from long-term incumbent Cornhill. The cricket sponsorship built the stature and reputation of the brand by linking it with an established, national, experience. The demographics of cricket followers meant the sponsorship registered from the outset with business users – something npower capitalised on by extending its sponsorship and developing business-to-business marketing tie-ins with the successful county cricket Twenty20 Cup competition, launched in 2003, promoting 'after work' fun for business customers.

In the residential market npower then built on widespread awareness with sponsorships linking the brand to 'home'-related properties, for instance the Daily Mail Ideal Home Show and Channel 4's strand of home programmes which included 'Location, Location, Location', 'Property Ladder', and 'Britain's Best Home'.

For business customers the mass-marketing approach was supported by bespoke communications. npower broke new ground with the award-winning customer magazine 'The Hub' aimed at major business users, mixing business and lifestyle features. Alongside the Hub npower also produced 'Insider' – an objective round up of topical energy issues supporting the

'industry expertise' positioning valued by specialist energy buyers.

At the SME end of the market npower has struck a balance between sector-focused marketing, for instance title sponsorship of the Pub Show in 2003, and building links with business 'communities of interest'. Tie-ins with Durham University's SME research department and with the Sunday Times Enterprise Network, for example, helped position npower as an expert in the growing 'middle market' business sector and guaranteed regular national media exposure as well as valuable access to SME databases.

Brand Values

npower has been created from a variety of companies, each of which joined with a specific culture and a different business plan. The creation, and more importantly adoption, of a clear and specific set of brand values was as vital in guiding the company's internal behaviour as it was in creating a personality for the brand. With literally millions of customer interactions per year, npower's brand values had to be demonstrated in daily dealings with customers as well as in headline marketing activity.

With that in mind npower focused on making the values an integral part of everyday working life. All members of staff work to npower's 'Customer FIRST' vision, the initials standing for: Customer obsession; Focus; Innovation and challenge; Responsibility; Straightforwardness and

Team success. These are directly linked to staff appraisals and bonuses.

Externally the values are reflected in the feel of npower, which market research consistently indicates is fresh and innovative, without sacrificing the warmth element needed to build loyalty. In Millward Brown's influential BrandZ survey npower, a three year old brand, ranked third out of fourteen established household name service brands for its ability to establish a firm bond with its customers.

www.npower.co.uk

Superbrands

O₂

Market

O₂ UK, a subsidiary of mmO2, is one of five licensed operators competing in the UK's mobile communications market. O₂ competes principally against Vodafone, Orange T-Mobile and 3.

Some twenty years after liberalisation, the mobile market is still intensely competitive, hugely challenging and full of surprises.

In a competitive market, where emphasis on the delivery of new products and services is critical and provides short-term differentiation it is important to always remain focused on the customer. O₂'s strategy is one based upon customer centricity, putting the customer first, at the heart of the business and then delivering products and services based upon their needs.

O₂ has recognised that whilst voice services remain a key driver in the use of mobile handsets, customers are increasingly comfortable and interested in mobile data services. This started with simple texting, but is now moving towards more innovative applications such as media messaging (MMS), mobile games and video services. These services are still in their infancy; however early signs are encouraging and it is widely agreed that demand for mobile multimedia services will increase as people find uses for the services from dating to catching sight of a celebrity walking down the road and sharing it with their friends.

The introduction of services over 3G has been much discussed amongst the press. O₂, takes a cautious and measured approach; underpinned with the aim to launch such services when both the technology and handsets, and the customers, are ready. In O₂'s case this has meant pursuing

o2.co.uk/business

Talk to a person not a recorded message

Join Best for Business 0800 781 02 02

O₂

revenues from services with proven appeal, such as SMS text messaging, whilst at the same time introducing businesses and consumers to the future of personal and group communications through the seeding of a range of next generation multimedia applications such as music and video over the existing mobile network.

Achievements

A comparison of the awareness ratings achieved by O₂ in the spring and summer of 2002 illustrates just how rapidly O₂ has built its identity in the business world. In April 2002, O₂ had yet to establish its credentials, trailing Vodafone on corporate awareness of its brand by around 24%. By June the two companies were positioned virtually neck and neck. O₂ is one of the smallest spenders compared to the big three. The key to its success is a very focused approach to marketing concentrating on the customer and executing campaigns that engage the customers in an exciting and fresh way.

As well as building its brand identity, O₂ has turned out a strong operational performance, fulfilling the key strategic goals that the company identified for itself when it demerged from BT. In particular, O₂ has made gains in the under-developed, but strategically crucial, market for mobile data services. So much so, that by March 2003 mobile data contributed over 17% of O₂'s European revenue, ahead of target.

O₂ has made progress on many other fronts too. During the course of 2002, the UK business acquired around one million new customers, taking its total customer base to approximately twelve million. Significantly, many of the newer customers have chosen to sign contracts with O₂, instead of opting for the less profitable pre-paid service.

Aside from furthering its operational objectives, O₂ has continued to demonstrate a strong commitment to corporate responsibility. This includes establishing a corporate responsibility advisory council to provide an external check on internal policies and practices, launching a programme to put mobile technology to greater social use and undertaking a major review of its approach to diversity and human rights. As a consequence of these factors, O₂ now features in several of the main sustainability indices and funds, such as the Dow Jones Sustainability Indexes, the FTSE4Good Index Series, and the new UK Business in the Community Corporate Responsibility Index.

History

O₂ was officially launched on May 1st 2002, following the demerger of mmO2 from BT the previous November. mmO2 comprises a number of wholly owned European subsidiaries, formerly belonging to BT's wireless portfolio and now trading collectively under the O₂ brand. These include O₂ UK, (formerly BT Cellnet), O₂ Germany (formerly Viag Interkom) and O₂ Ireland (formerly Esat Digifone). The group has operations in the Isle of Man (Manx Telecom) and owns a leading European mobile internet portal, formerly known as Genie, now trading under the O₂ brand.

Product

Whatever the fine detail of the approach, an objective, shared by most mobile operators is to attract high value customers, and to encourage them to take up mobile data solutions. However, before moving the customer through to using data, it is important that they're comfortable and confident both with using their mobile and with the company. That is why, in 2003, O₂ ceased to use IVR for all their small business and corporate customers. So that a much more personal service can be provided, quickly and efficiently so problems and queries can be rectified and the customer can get on with their day and making the most out of the mobile services provided by the company.

According to industry analysts, businesses generate 40% of the revenues associated with voice communications – but a mere 11% of the revenues deriving from non-voice services (Source: Analysis Mobile Data Solutions for Businesses July 2003).

O₂ is a leader in mobile data and has focused its data strategy on developing exciting new mobile data services whilst maintaining its lead in SMS and online services.

In the business market O₂ has provided valuable market differentiation through the provision of mobile internet and email on the move. Two business focused services stand out – the BlackBerry® and the Xda.

One early success for the company was the launch, in late 2001, of BlackBerry®, a wireless 'always on' email device that integrates with a corporates IT systems. BlackBerry® enables users to send and receive their email whilst on the move – without ever having to dial in to retrieve email messages. Following on from this, in May 2003, O₂ began trialing a modified service aimed at small businesses and professionals. The new solution, which offers the same benefits as the corporate model, operates as a stand-alone device, dispensing with the need for a back-end server.

The second new product performing well for O_2, is the Xda, a personal handheld device, which combines the capabilities of an advanced mobile phone with a touch screen personal digital assistant, internet and email access allowing customers to carry one handset instead of two. The Xda, which is playing a key role in O_2's drive to get business customers using mobile data, has had excellent market reviews, winning Connect Magazine's product of the year award in 2002. It is also performing well in the corporate market, where a number of organisations are using the Xda to build closer relationships with their customers.

Building on this success, O_2 has recently developed an Xda II, an enhanced version of the original, incorporating some new and potentially business critical features. The Xda II is triband, enabling seamless use to the US. It can also be used in Europe, Australia and Asia due to O_2's extensive GPRS roaming capability. Bluetooth is standard, enabling seamless connectivity to Bluetooth enabled headsets or PCs. The removable battery enables power users to swap the battery whilst on the move for added flexibility.

As well as introducing new services, O_2 is becoming adept at customising its products to reflect the needs and interests of different segments of the business market.

For example, the company recently got together with Reuters to pre-configure a run of Xda handsets with Reuters' 3000 Xtra Companion market information service.

Recent Developments

In addition to the launch of new data products O_2 is developing a whole range of customised mobile voice and data solutions for small businesses. The launch of the Best for Business campaign is an important example of O_2's understanding of the needs of the small business market. O_2 understands when technology can help someone and when it is important to speak to a person so that any queries can be solved quickly and easily. With Best for Business package Small Businesses can be assured that they will always speak to a person, never a recorded message.

Before this campaign, O_2 developed the '2 Minute Challenge' which lay down the gauntlet for small businesses to call to find the best mobile solution for them. Rather than using a specific tariff, the campaign looked at the business need and put the customer at the heart of the business proposition. The campaign has been O_2's most successful to date and has increased the company's market share within small businesses to 24%.

This has allowed the company to segment the market and move its offering into new areas that include manufacturing and construction, business services and local government, as well as retail and wholesale suppliers.

Promotion

Since its launch in May 2002, O_2 has moved rapidly to generate strong awareness of the O_2 brand, with an emphasis on reaching the sorts of high value, technology-accepting business and personal customers that it most wants to attract.

To coincide with the launch, O_2 ran a high-profile brand building campaign, centred upon the theme 'a new current in mobile communications'. It was during this initial period, that the company used, for the first time, the visually striking, oxygen bubbles in blue water image that has become its trademark symbol. By the end of the launch phase, which involved advertising across TV, print and poster media, supported by direct marketing, O_2 had become a well-known brand, achieving levels of recognition on a par with its rivals.

In the business sector, following on from the corporate launch, O_2 ran product-based

advertising, promoting the Xda and BlackBerry® solutions. It has also run thematic advertising, including the '2 minute challenge' and 'talk to a person not a machine' campaigns, emphasising the fresh, uncomplicated and demystifying approach to technology that it has made its own.

As well as advertising, O_2 has worked hard at stimulating positive editorial, loaning its flagship products, such as the Xda, to business and technology journalists in a variety of trade and business publications. O_2 also engages in sponsorship to build awareness of the brand and, more unusually for a sponsorship deal, to stimulate immediate use of its products. A classic example of this is the range of text alerts, sports-related news updates and interactive quizzes that O_2 developed to complement its partnerships with Arsenal Football Club and the England Rugby Squad.

Take the 2 minute business challenge.

0800 781 02 02

O_2

Brand Values

Branding involves more than simply projecting a new image. For service businesses in particular, it means changing the inner world – how people on the inside of the business see the brand, how they think and how they behave. This was the challenge that faced O_2, when it parted company with BT – to reinvent the brand both internally and externally.

Two years on, O_2 possesses a new and optimistic sense of self – a fresh and distinctive personality, resting on the four core values that have been set out to define the brand.

Firstly, O_2 is bold, a company that is full of surprises, continually coming up with ideas that are practical and relevant, opening up a world of exciting possibilities. Secondly O_2 is clear and straightforward, a company that has the knack of turning highly complex technology into products that are easy to understand and easy to use. Thirdly, it is open and candid, a brand that tells it as it is. Finally, O_2 is trusted by its customers, a responsive brand that listens to people, is accurate and truthful and does not over-claim.

Above all else, O_2 is a brand that makes things possible – a brand with a 'can do' attitude to life.

Today, barely two years into its new life, O_2 is on course to achieve what Cellnet was unable to achieve in two decades – project a modern, attractive and internationally persuasive brand identity, rivalling the brand power of Orange, and at last capitalising on its extensive networks, depth of experience and customer knowledge.

www.O2.co.uk

officeangels
RECRUITMENT CONSULTANTS

Market

The UK recruitment market is growing rapidly year on year and is currently worth £24 billion – marking an 8% increase in the permanent and 7% increase in the temporary sector since 2000 (Source: REC, Annual Recruitment Industry Survey 2001/02). Agencies big and small are not only vying for the best clients, but the finest candidates. To succeed in such a competitive marketplace demands a unique offering and Office Angels believes that it excels in delivering such a service.

Office Angels is the UK's leading recruitment consultancy specialising in secretarial and office support staff for temporary and permanent positions. A multi-site company with 64 branches and a rapidly expanding network of satellite offices, Office Angels is an authority on recruitment issues and is distinct in the services it offers to both clients and candidates. Each week, it finds 8,000 people temporary assignments and places more than 9,000 people in permanent positions every year.

The business boasts a prestigious range of clients, including 90% of The Times top 100 companies in the UK. Office Angels help organisations grow their businesses from scratch or realise their ambitious expansion plans.

Achievements

Office Angels is recognised as the UK's leading secretarial and office support recruitment consultancy because it has earned the reputation of offering the very best recruitment solutions.

Six years ago, Office Angels coined the term 'Executary', to give recognition to senior secretaries and PAs, as well as highlighting the increased responsibilities within their role. Supported by The Guardian newspaper, the Office Angels Executary of The Year Award has become a high profile national event, achieving recognition and prestige for both winners and their companies.

Office Angels has been praised for a progressive approach to age diversity in its placement of both over 45's and the younger generation of school and college leavers in work. Previous winners of the 'Age Positive' Recruitment Award of Excellence,

Office Angels acknowledges that today's workforce is made up of a diverse range of age groups and therefore embraces a non-discriminatory approach to recruitment.

The brand enjoys a highly creative and effective national and regional PR campaign that results in a higher media profile than any other recruitment consultancy. In 2002 alone, Office Angels generated 935 media hits, reaching 783 million people. Office Angels has maintained and developed its position as an authority on human resource issues and has generated stories on what makes workers happy, summer office withdrawal syndrome and how managers communicate to their teams. The brand also analyses human interest and work-related stories through a range of press

The Recruitment Agency With Balls!

officeangels
RECRUITMENT CONSULTANTS
34 WEST STREET, BRIGHTON
01273 737554
www.office-angels.com

releases including first day 'clangers', how to survive killer questions, after office hours drinking habits and the impact of winter blues on working life.

This combined range of activity ensures that recall of the Office Angels name is significantly higher among job seekers and clients than any other recruitment consultancy.

History

Established in 1986, Office Angels has expanded to 64 branches nationwide, employing over 600 people.

The brand has built its reputation on putting people first, by matching individual skills to individual needs. The Office Angels mission is to offer the very best recruitment solutions to clients and job seekers by enabling their employees to make it happen.

Office Angels is part of the Ajilon Group of companies, a global leader in consulting,

managed services and speciality staffing. Its associate businesses – OAexec, Computer People, Ajilon Executive, Ajilon Finance, Jonathan Wren, Ajilon Consulting, Roevin and Ajilon Learning – provide an integrated approach to company-wide resourcing.

Product

Office Angels' areas of expertise enables clients to use one supplier for all their office support requirements. Both temporary and permanent staff are assigned across a range of secretarial, administrative, financial, call centre and customer service positions.

All Office Angel's consultants undergo intensive training and development throughout their career, to ensure they are equipped with first class skills to work in the 'people business'.

The service provided to job seekers is free and each candidate follows a thorough and formal procedure from registration through to assignment, which includes an in-depth interview and skills evaluation.

To assess candidates' skills, Office Angels uses Ajilonresult, a bespoke skills evaluation system, which allows consultants to assess the fundamentals, like standard PC packages, but can also create tailored tests to reflect a client's exact requirements. Additionally, because Ajilonresult is web-based, Office Angels are able to email assessments to candidates for a quicker turnaround.

Through working closely with candidates and providing them with continued support, Office Angels lives by its belief that it is in the business of finding 'jobs for people' rather than 'people for jobs.' Taking a holistic approach to candidates' training needs, provides the foundation for this relationship and has resulted in Office Angels running a variety of vocational skills seminars.

Office Angels are committed to promoting diversity across the business, not only as an employer but also as a supplier of staff to its clients. The company is improving awareness by explaining how diversity impacts on business performance. As a member of Race for

Opportunity (RfO), Office Angels has participated in a UK-wide benchmarking exercise on its current race initiatives and will use the results of the survey to shape future equality and diversity initiatives.

In May 2003, Office Angels' 'Perfect Presentations' seminar was supported by the Evening Standard and was attended by over 200 individuals. Summer 2003 saw Office Angels' corporate social responsibility programme engage branch expertise to help educate school leavers about career opportunities. Nationwide, in-school

Friday lunches help ensure that candidates are rewarded for their dedication and professionalism.

For clients, it is Office Angels' ability to provide both 'bigger picture' authoritative business insights and understanding the necessity for everyday attention to detail that distinguishes the brand from its competitors.

Business seminars help Office Angels' clients identify and react to key recruitment issues while the commissioning of original business research helps them understand on-going employment dynamics.

sponsorship, corporate social responsibility, internal communications, research, the internet and an extensive programme of client and candidate care.

The business also has regular link-ups with leading consumer brands for local and national promotions including Filofax, Saks, Amazon.com, Red Letter Days, Henry J Beans, Twinings and Paper:Mate.

Office Angels are committed to conducting regular research studies and publishing reports on a range of employment-related issues including flexible working, employee benefits and managing communications in the modern office. These gain editorial recognition in both the national and regional press, as well as broadcast, recruitment and lifestyle media.

Brand Values

The maverick style and personality of the Office Angels brand attracts both clients and candidates alike. Office Angels has a passion for recruitment and is dynamic and forward thinking. Its clients are not industry or sector specific as they buy 'personalities' rather than 'processes' and therefore want an attentive, personal service. Clients are also keen to discuss issues, as they have the assurance that the Office Angels name signifies that there will be a real difference in the service they receive.

www.office-angels.com

It's New! It's Pink! It's the Office Angels... Smoothie! "mmm!"

training sessions were attended by 16-18 year olds who benefited from gaining a deeper understanding of the diversity of skills needed in the current job market.

Office Angels' 2003 'investing in the future' youth research will once again enable its clients to benefit from Office Angels' thought-leadership credentials. Conducted among 1,000 16-19 year olds, this research will identify their educational, financial and emotional aspirations and will serve to help clients assess ways to communicate opportunities within their organisation to encourage future employees to join them.

Integral to Office Angels' commitment to its temporary staff is its ongoing candidate care programme. Initiatives such as regular social and networking events, Temporary of the Month Awards, savings schemes, competitions, training and free

Recent Developments

The Office Angels website (www.office-angels.com) has been redeveloped to enable candidates to register quickly with the branch of their choice and view current vacancies and temporary assignments online. Importantly, this facility is not a substitute for the personal, one-to-one service that is the corner stone of the Office Angels philosophy. Rather, it is designed to help potential and existing candidates and clients access information quickly and efficiently.

Promotion

Office Angels have developed a highly effective marketing strategy which aims to capitalise on the brand's position as an industry leader. Activity encompasses press, outdoor and radio advertising, direct mail, event marketing, public relations,

Things you didn't know about
Office Angels

A survey conducted by Office Angels in 2003 revealed that amongst 1,500 office employees and employers, nearly three-quarters (73%) of office workers admit that the start of the new year inspires dreams of finally ditching the rat race in favour of their ultimate 'escapist' job.

Working closely with the Royal National Institute for the Blind (RNIB), Office Angels is trialling the use of technical testing equipment that blind and visually impaired candidates can use to give them access to work opportunities with clients.

Each year the 600 staff of Office Angels nominate a charity to be the main focus for fund-raising in its 64 branches.

Office Angels has a broad spectrum of candidates, of which one in four are male, one in five are over 45, and nearly one in three are women returning to work after a career break.

Office Angels research has found that 71% of employees rank a 'job clinching' interview as one of the 'most dreaded' experience of their adult lives – more so than meeting a partner's parents (16%) or a wisdom tooth extraction (13%).

Superbrands

Market

Only a decade ago, investment in IT was a relatively low priority for businesses, but today's robust IT is regarded as being essential to conducting business.

Accordingly, business spend on technology has grown exponentially, driven by wave after wave of developments, such as the explosion in mobile business, the growth of e-commerce and m-commerce, continued improvements in processor speeds and new technology, such as 3G mobile communications and broadband internet.

This rapidly-changing technology landscape means that businesses are constantly changing their IT requirements to keep pace with their more demanding, technology-aware customers. As such, IT plays an increasingly central role in business, and has become a market worth £15 billion (Source: UK IT Expenditure Trends and Forecasts 2003).

Competing against other well-known brands and value-added resellers, PC World's dedicated business-to-business arm, PC World Business has become one of the key brands serving the IT needs of UK businesses.

Achievements

PC World has grown to become Britain's largest chain of computer superstores, with sales in 2002/3 in excess of £1.400 million.

The company now boasts 140 stores in the UK and four in the Republic of Ireland, with more stores opening across the UK and Europe.

PC World (PCW) is also the only computer retailer to provide 24 hour helplines, 365 days a year, supported through one of the largest technical support centres in Europe.

The company's success has been recognised with numerous awards. In 2002 it was voted Retailer of the Year by What Laptop magazine and Best Computer Equipment store by Computeractive Magazine.

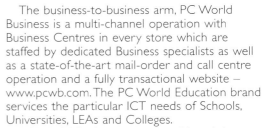

The business-to-business arm, PC World Business is a multi-channel operation with Business Centres in every store which are staffed by dedicated Business specialists as well as a state-of-the-art mail-order and call centre operation and a fully transactional website – www.pcwb.com. The PC World Education brand services the particular ICT needs of Schools, Universities, LEAs and Colleges.

PC World Business recently achieved the position of number one reseller of IT to the UK SME market.

History

PC World was founded in November 1991, when a company called the Vision Technology Group Ltd, founded by Jan Murray, opened the first PCW Superstore in Croydon.

The 24,000 square foot store specialised in the sale of PCs and computer related products. With PC ownership just beginning to take off, the concept soon proved popular and a second 23,000 square foot store was opened the following year at the Lakeside Retail Park in West Thurrock.

Two further stores followed, at Brentford and Staples Corner in north London. At that point, in 1993, Vision Technology Group struck a deal to sell its four PC World Superstores to the Dixons Group plc (DG).

Throughout the 1990s DG continued to expand the PC World portfolio of stores rapidly. In 1996 it acquired DN Computer Services plc,

It has broken new ground in the industry, with innovations such as introducing a PC Clinic into every store. Managed by fully trained technicians, trained in association with Microsoft and Intel, offering on-the-spot diagnostic advice and service both for consumers and for business customers, PC World is the only computer retailer to offer this service.

In addition, PC World offer the Component Centre. These consist of self-service one-stop shops for consumer or business customers with more technical knowledge providing a vast choice of PC components and upgrade products. The range can also be accessed online at www.pcworld.co.uk/pccomponents.

a direct computer reseller business, operating out of Bury in Lancashire.

This gave DG the infrastructure it needed to launch PC World Business Direct in September 1997 – a new business-to-business IT mail order service incorporating the brand strength of PCW and the sector expertise of DSG. A fully functional transactional website – www.pcwb.com – followed in 1999.

In March 2001, as PC World Business, the company moved into a brand new £13 million headquarters building and Operations Centre in Bury, Lancashire to meet the growth in demand from the business market.

In October 2001 PC World Business was accepted to become

an accredited GCat (Government Catalogue for IT supply) Prime Contractor to the Public Sector.

In May 2002 PC World Business won two major multi-million pound contracts as a lead supplier and enabler of the Scottish Parliament's (The Scottish Executive) new 'Digital Inclusion Programme' aimed at giving every individual in Scotland better access to online services.

Also in 2002 the group acquired Genesis Communications – a specialist Business Telecoms reseller – to strengthen its business-to-business offering.

PC World Business also strengthened its product offering in 2003, with the introduction of a new finance package called SmartPlan. This product, a unique offering in the UK, allows businesses to spread the cost of their larger IT purchases in the form of a lease agreement.

Product

PC World stores offer consumers and business customers more than 5,000 product lines, covering not only PCs but laptops, printers, software, peripherals and accessories across all the major brands. These include many products which are exclusive to PC World – e.g. the award winning Advent range of PCs and laptops.

PC World Business has an extended range of over 30,000 products to businesses offered via its 852-page Definitive Buyers Guide. Now in its nineteenth volume, this catalogue is produced three times a year.

In addition, these 30,000 products are available for next day delivery from the www.pcwb.com website, where prices and stock levels are constantly updated in real time.

PC World's after-sales service operation includes the largest distribution network of its kind in the UK. This includes a field sales force of 250 fully qualified engineers, of which 82 are dedicated to business customers, undertaking over 165,000 on-site visits per year.

Through its strategic alliances with the world's premier IT vendors and the buying power of its parent – Dixons Group – PC World Business aims to help businesses deliver consistent value and get the most from their IT budgets.

As well as products, PC World Business can supply services and solutions from selling telephone software support for one PC to managing a business's whole network remotely. The company aims to be able to offer all sizes of business and public sector organisations complete IT solutions, from an individual PC to an entire network.

Dedicated business-to-business account managers and business specialists, both in-store and at the end of the phone, are always available to help deliver cost-efficient IT solutions for customers.

Through PC World Business companies can open a Business Account which gives them preferential terms of trading. To date, around 250,000 businesses have done this.

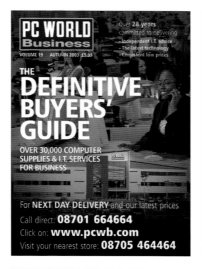

Recent Developments

The opening of the new headquarters and operations centre in Bury in 2001 was a major step forward for PC World Business, demonstrating the Group's commitment to servicing the needs of businesses.

The centre incorporates the latest telephony, IT infrastructure and working facilities, and has provision for up to 1,000 staff, recruited from the local community. Now the stores are following suit with a major refit programme of all the in-store Business Centres to make them more accessible, modern and easier for small businesses to do business via their local store.

Promotion

PC World Business has experienced extraordinary growth over the last few years – against market trends. This is not only due to its investment in infrastructure, but also in a powerful integrated customer-led marketing strategy.

Direct marketing plays a key part in this, exemplified in The Definitive Buyers Guide

catalogue, distributed free to regular customers and updated three times a year. The company also runs a monthly mailing programme to business customers, highlighting key deals on products and services.

A high level of personalisation is used to tailor messages and offerings to the various businesses, dependent on their size and market sector.

PC World Business always aims to go the extra mile to add value where appropriate. For example, when they wanted to better understand the IT needs of the Education sector, they invested in recruiting a panel of independent experts from different areas of the teaching profession, to advise on all education matters.

It also produces a termly newsletter for the Education sector, called Learning Curve. This is written by teachers for teachers, helping them make more informed decisions about their IT requirements.

Direct marketing works in tandem with the Business Specialists, either in-store or on the phone, keeping in regular contact with customers. This helps PC World Business to remain front of mind and be there when the need arises.

A sophisticated online portal system keeps in-store staff informed of what mailings have gone out to whom so they can follow those customers up with a sales call.

Additional in-store and point of sale materials match these mailings to ensure consistency of the business brand and messaging.

Brand Values

PC World's objective is to deliver a competitor-beating service that exceeds customers' expectations, whether they be consumers or business customers.

It aims to offer the UK's largest range of products, with the UK's lowest prices, backed by expert and professional service.

It also has the most extensive after sales support of any UK retailer, with 24-hour helplines, 365 days a year, twelve months free of charge in-home service, and free annual PC Healthchecks.

Although still a young brand – little more than ten years old – PC World's rapid growth – from a four-store chain in 1991 to a nationwide chain of 140 stores today – is due in no small part to its commitment to those core values.

www.pcwb.com

PRICEWATERHOUSECOOPERS

Market

In the global business community, PricewaterhouseCoopers LLP (PwC) stands at the forefront of the professional services market. In an industry that continues to be highly competitive PwC remains the leader, not just in terms of size and fee income, but also through innovation, contribution to society and leadership on business and professional issues. The largest of the world's 'Big Four' professional services firms, PwC retains an unparalleled client list that includes many of the world's major corporate bodies, alongside nationally and regionally significant private sector companies and public sector organisations.

PwC operates in sectors where the leading players must be of a size and global reach to meet the complex requirements of the clients they serve, while still providing service at a local level. With a presence in 142 countries and employing 125,000 people, the depth and breadth of PwC's resources, encompassing both industry and business competencies, allow the firm to deploy specialist expertise to help solve client problems and issues wherever in the world they are needed. But PwC is not just interested in the large multinationals. In the UK, it is the leading firm in the mid tier and has an extensive regional network with offices in 36 locations.

PwC contributes to the creation of legislative and policy solutions in many marketplaces, and helps encourage the development of new standards in social and ethical accountability. Mirroring this stance is its own rigorous adherence to high principles; PwC is the first professional services firm to implement a Code of Conduct and Framework for Ethical Decision Making.

Achievements

In the past twelve months, the percentage share of the FTSE Global 100 audits held by PwC has risen to 47%, significantly ahead of its rivals. It audits 33% of the FTSE Mid-250, 29% of the FTSE Small Cap and 33% of the FTSE All share. Further afield it audits 29% of the FT Euro 500, 33% of the FT Global 500 and 30% of the Fortune Global 500. In each category PwC is the market leader.

Equally significant is the extensive client base in non-quoted companies and public sector organisations that also benefit from the firm's broad range of services.

PwC's ability to deliver exceptional service is based on the high calibre of individuals who work in the firm at all levels. Their professionalism has resulted in several important awards being made to PwC over the past year. Amongst these were

Accountancy Age's 'Big Four Firm of the Year', Butterworth Tolley's 'Tax Team of the Year' and 'Financial Due Diligence Firm of the Year' by Acquisitions Monthly.

PwC was nominated as 'UK and European Pensions Accountant of the Year' by Professional Pensions, named 'Service Provider of the Year' at the British Insurance Awards 2003 and won 'Best Tax Website' at the LexisNexis Tax Awards.

The firm's expertise in Public Private Partnerships is widely recognised and resulted in six successes in the Public Private Finance Awards 2003, including 'Best Transport Project' and 'Best Local Government Project'.

PwC leads the way in helping shape the professional services industry. This is evidenced by the fact that six of the firm's partners featured in Accountancy Age's Financial Power list, significantly more than any other firm. In addition, PwC is represented on many influential bodies, for example, the Government's new Human Capital Taskforce, the Chartered Institute of Taxation, the Institute of Chartered Accountants in England and Wales, the Financial Reporting Council, the Turnbull Committee and others.

The firm's commitment to its people is clear, with a series of employee focused programmes. Success was underlined when The Times/High Fliers 'Top 100 Graduate Employers' 2003 survey ranked PwC first in the accountancy sector and third overall. This continues the trend for the third year in succession that PwC has been in the top three for best employer.

PwC's award-winning Careers website had 2.5 million hits in 2002. The 2003 Universum survey of UK undergraduate business students ranked PwC – the country's biggest private sector employer and trainer of graduates – as employer of choice in the professional services sector. Quarterly internal research supported this, with 93% of PwC people proud to work for the firm.

The firm has an active Community Affairs programme, designed to act as a catalyst for positive social change whilst developing the skills and insight of its people. During the past year

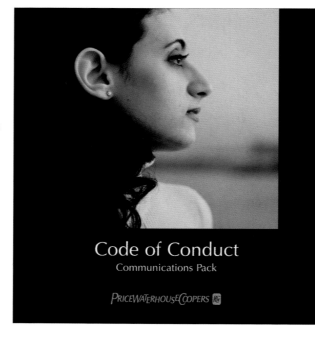

Code of Conduct
Communications Pack

PRICEWATERHOUSECOOPERS

over 900 PwC volunteers shared their skills and gave more than 9,000 hours of time and expertise to community projects.

PwC has a reputation as a leading example of corporate social responsibility and good corporate citizenship. One of its community programmes, which addresses educational under-achievement, was a London winner in the 'Community Impact' category of the Business in the Community Awards for Excellence. Additionally, PwC is a founder member of Leeds Cares, which won the BitC Award for Excellence for Collaborative Action and PwC Manchester, as member of Greater Manchester Cares, was also a regional example of excellence.

History

PricewaterhouseCoopers has its origins in the mid nineteenth century.

In 1849 Samuel Lowell Price set up business in London. Price, Holyland and Waterhouse joined forces in 1865 and nine years later Price, Waterhouse & Co was created.

William Cooper established a practice in London in 1854, which became Cooper Brothers. In 1957, the UK firm of Cooper Brothers and Co merged with McDonald, Currie & Co of Canada and Lybrand, Ross Brothers & Montgomery of the US to form Coopers & Lybrand.

In 1982, Price Waterhouse's international expansion saw it form the Price Waterhouse World Firm. In 1990 Coopers & Lybrand pursued a similar goal, merging with Deloitte Haskins & Sells in several countries around the world.

In 1998 the merger of Price Waterhouse and Coopers & Lybrand created PricewaterhouseCoopers – the world's largest professional services firm.

Following a unanimous vote by partners, the UK firm adopted LLP status on January 1st 2003.

Product

PricewaterhouseCoopers delivers effective solutions for its clients through lines of service and industry groups. The firm's principal lines of service include the following;

Audit and related advisory services – PwC is best known for the reliability and rigour of its statutory and regulatory audit services. Also offered is accounting and regulatory advice, reviews of treasury and finance operations and verification of both financial and non-financial data.

Risk Management Solutions, provides advice for clients on managing their risks and are active in performance improvement.

Tax services – PwC's expert tax specialists advise on domestic and international tax issues and tax compliance.

Corporate Financial Advice provides independent financial advice on reorganisations, mergers, acquisitions, and rationalisations to publicly listed private equity and venture capital companies.

Human Resource Services – as one of the leading firms in the industry,

PwC aims to create value for businesses through people by advising on issues including; restructuring, pensions strategy and communications.

The firm's industry groups, deliver solutions based on knowledge of best practice and global experience in these areas and include; Financial Services, Technology, Communications and Entertainment, Consumer and Industrial Products & Services, Public Sector and Public-Private-Partnerships.

Recent Developments

Major structural change in the last year has seen PwC sell its consulting business, PwC Consulting, to IBM while Exult purchased the firm's Business Process Outsourcing unit. In an innovative move, PwC outsourced all its IT support services to Cap Gemini Ernst & Young.

PwC is at the forefront of the accountancy profession in defining the way forward for corporate reporting post Enron. In the latter part of 2003 PwC published, for the first time, a UK annual report and accounts, complementing its Global Annual Review which was produced in November 2002.

The firm's commitment to recognising the best in corporate reporting is demonstrated further by its decision to launch the first 'Building Public Trust Awards'. The awards, presented in September 2003, focus on the quality of the reporting of the largest 350 companies in the UK. In its 'World's Most Respected Companies Survey', run in association with The Financial Times, PricewaterhouseCoopers identified the top UK and global businesses setting the pace in building reputational capital.

Client publications, such as Sounding Board and Sustaining Public Trust, explain to clients corporate and accounting reforms such as the Smith Report.

The PwC DrivingAmbition campaign continues to provide ambitious independent companies with access to the breadth and depth of ideas and solutions available from PwC. Pace Notes, a quarterly newsletter launched this year features discussions on current hot topics on the Board's agenda and insightful case studies.

PwC Inform, the firm's online resource for UK and international financial reporting, offers users access to real time information 24 hours a day, and a time-saving single source for all their accounting and auditing research and training requirements. It has secured circa 7,000 registered users. A further 16,000 have subscribed to the new PwC Portal, which offers clients direct online access to PwC experts, solutions, tools, research and analysis.

Promotion

PwC has an excellent reputation for innovative marketing and communications, strongly promoting the PricewaterhouseCoopers name as the world's foremost professional services brand.

The firm has a formidable public relations reputation. It consistently captures an appreciably greater share of voice in the UK national and regional press than any competitor, as measured by MB Precis, a leading independent media analysis group.

Creative communication plays an important role, with advertising in daily newspapers and business publications, on radio, billboard posters as well as through the award winning website. Many have been created by PwC's design studio, EC4.

Human Resource Services ran a campaign in conjunction with The Financial Times to promote its 'Mastering Leadership' series, using outdoor posters, radio and press advertising. The content of this series, dealing with the key elements of business leadership, is currently being developed as a book.

Business sponsorship continues to play an important role in promoting the PwC brand via a range of B2B initiatives such as the Fast Track annual surveys in conjunction with The Sunday Times.

These include the Fast Track 100 and Profit Track 100 league tables. These identify the fastest growing and most profitable UK independent companies. Also in the series, Tech Track 100 analyses the fortunes of hi-tech businesses.

Other business sponsorships include annual events like the PLC Awards. These awards recognise excellence in the smaller quoted company sector, and are run in association with The Financial Times and the London Stock Exchange. It is one of several high profile partnerships that enhance the reputation of the PwC brand.

The first part of 2003 saw the launch of a major campaign, Good Business. Its aim was to communicate that PwC brings about good business by helping clients develop more successful, sustainable and trusted businesses. 'Good Business' speaks of PwC's relationships in the business community and the quality of

people who deliver solutions. It was launched nationally at the time of the Chancellor's Budget in April 2003 and was followed by regional coverage throughout the UK in the press, outdoor poster sites and at events.

Recognising that successful brands need to evolve, the second half of 2003 saw the introduction of a new global brand positioning for the firm: Connected Thinking. It demonstrates how PwC connects its network, experience, industry knowledge and business understanding to build trust and create value for clients. This programme will extend into 2004 and beyond.

Brand Values

The three core values of the PwC brand are; excellence – the brand delivers what it promises, teamwork – the best solutions come from working together, with clients and colleagues and leadership – leading with clients, leading with people and leading with thought.

PwC aims to deliver what it promises and add value beyond what is expected. It is committed to building a culture of client service and product innovation. It aims to be the leading professional services organisation, solving complex business problems for clients in global, national and local markets.

www.pwc.com

Market

Though seldom noticed, adhesives are everywhere, and we use them virtually every day of our lives, from the notes we stick to our computer screens to the strips of brown gaffer tape used to secure parcels. Packaging, furniture, clothing, and even microchips all rely on adhesives of one sort or another.

Over recent years, environmental concerns have put pressure on adhesive manufacturers to avoid using solvents, leading to a growth in water-based products. Pritt, one of the best-known household adhesive brands in the world, is a solvent-free glue – made from everyday items such as starch, sugar and water.

Henkel, the maker of Pritt, is the number one name in the stationery adhesive market. This sector is worth £56 million in the UK alone, and Pritt has a total share of over 50% – and more than 75% of the specific stick market.

Achievements

Can you remember a world without Pritt – well there was one – pre 1973. At this point, the market was dominated by liquid glues that were awkward and messy to use. Along came Pritt with the revolutionary new and innovative solid glue stick. It could do everything its traditional liquid rivals could do, but it was cleaner, quicker and easier to use. Since then it has achieved the status of entering everyday language as a widely recognised generic term for glue.

Pritt regularly wins design and innovation awards. In recent years it has been named Spicers Supplier of the Year, and it has a major presence in most of the outlets where it is sold. These include Tesco, Woolworth's, Asda Walmart, Staples and WH Smith. Plus lets not forget the traditional corner shop. And given its popularity with children, it is inevitably the brand of choice for many schools. In total, over twenty one million Pritt sticks are sold every year.

History

The Pritt brand is part of the Henkel Group,

which was started by the 28-year-old Fritz Henkel and his two partners in Aachen, Germany on September 26th 1876. Its first product, rather than being a glue, was a washing powder which was one of the first to be sold in packets rather than loose.

Henkel has seen significant growth over the years and the company now employs over 50,000 people

worldwide and its headquarters are in Dusseldorf, Germany. The proportion of the workforce employed outside Germany is about 75%, making it one of the country's most internationally aligned companies.

The group operates in four business sectors: Homecare, Personalcare, Consumer and Craftsmen Adhesives and Technologies. Through its adhesives

business sector, Henkel develops, produces and markets adhesives for use in the home and office as well as for craftsmen. It is the largest manufacturer of adhesives in the world, with sales in excess of 9.6 billion euros in 2002. It supplies more than 3,000 different adhesives and sealants, by far the broadest product portfolio in this market.

Alongside Pritt, Henkel offers an extensive range of product brands for the household, office, do-it-yourself home improvement and Trade markets. Its other brands include the household names UniBond, Loctite, Solvite, Sellotape and Copydex. For professional craftsmen it provides adhesives and sealants for construction, flooring, roofing, decorating, renovation, and home furniture, to name a few.

The company invented the glue stick in 1969, basing its revolutionary design on the lipstick tube. Legend has it that a Henkel scientist had the brainwave after watching his secretary apply lipstick. The idea was to create solid glue that could do everything a liquid adhesive could, contained in a user-friendly, twist-open tube. Advertised as 'the non-sticky, sticky stuff' – a phrase that still pops into the minds of successive generations whenever the brand is mentioned – Pritt quickly found its way into the hands of the nation's children. With its no-mess, no-fuss application and its obvious utility for scrapbooks, photo albums and collages, Pritt Stick soon became part of everyday language – joining the list of generic products like Sellotape and Hoover. In 2003 Pritt celebrated its 30th anniversary in the UK.

Product

Available in four sizes – to cater for every kind of user, Pritt is the number one branded glue stick in the UK. It is water-based, solvent free (making it safe for children), and washes out of clothing easily at 30°C. A surface coated with glue from a Pritt Stick can be repositioned for up to two minutes, allowing for more precision. As well as the stick, Henkel also makes rollers for adhesive, correction and highlighting purposes under the Pritt brand name, and Pritt Sticky Pads and Sticky Tac.

SAFE, SOLVENT FREE & EASY TO USE

Pritt

ADHES... STICK

Clean, Quick...

EASY, CLEAN & WA...

Pritt

...ck Sück S...

SAFE & SOLVENT FREE

IDEAL FOR STICKING PAPER & CARD

Recent Developments

An innovative brand extension, Power Pritt, was launched in June 2003. Instantly distinguishable by its silver sleeve, this multipurpose product, is more powerful than any other glue stick on the market, can stick wood, leather, photos, felt, fabrics, metal, card and some plastics. Again in Pritt tradition it's safe, easy to use and solvent free.

Also in 2003, Henkel launched an entirely new range of products which include Pritt Sticks and associated art and craft accessories called Kids Art. Aimed at children between four and twelve, the range aims to make art and craft fun, and has been designed to appeal to the sought-after 'tween' market, with flashy packaging and bright colours. Entirely washable and safe, the range includes: traditional PVA glue; a glue stick that goes on blue and dries clear; gold, silver and festive glitter; and Glitzy Bitz, brightly coloured lettering and shapes. Henkel has made all of these available at 'pocket money prices'.

Promotion

Thanks in part to its original advertising slogan, 'the non-sticky, sticky stuff', combined with a determined distribution strategy that has placed it in the UK's leading retail outlets, Pritt has a brand awareness of 85%. The plastic stick has developed a brand identity in its own right, evolving into the plucky Mr Pritt animated and fun character.

In recent years, the Pritt name has been broadened to cover an entire range of adhesive and correction roller products, from sticky pads and tack to Correct-It pens.

In 2003 promotion mainly concentrated on the 30th anniversary of the Pritt Stick. Public relations among consumers was backed up by a print campaign in the trade press, aimed at wholesalers, the dealer network and office suppliers, as well as buying groups for the education market. Consumers were encouraged to take advantage of several anniversary promotions and added-value packs – which have all proved to be strongly received by the consumer.

Pritt's marketing activity regularly utilises in-store displays, and 'dump bins' containing examples of the product, which are regularly placed at till points, encouraging last-minute purchases. As it is popular among young users, Pritt is also marketed with school children in mind – the company organises 'Mr Pritt' days, with an accent on art and craft, featuring a full-sized Mr Pritt who visits classrooms.

Pritt has a strong level of recognition in the UK and an 85% unprompted awareness, but does continue to use TV advertising frequently. Its Power Pritt TV campaign, which was launched in September 2003, has been a significant and exciting move for the brand.

The established Mr Pritt character was brought to life by the Oscar winning animation company Aardman Animations as part of the worldwide launch of Power Pritt Stick. However, this is not the only occasion that Aardman Animation has worked with the brand, having also animated the Pritt Correction Roller.

For the Power Pritt ads, the original Mr Pritt has been given muscles to reflect the 'extra strength' properties of the new product. Three executions have been developed to introduce the product, then to reflect the properties of the product with the final ad showing how the product is different from the competition, illustrating how many extra uses Power Pritt has. At the end of each ad the strapline 'Another great idea from Pritt' is used.

Power Pritt could even be described as a more 'adult' version of the Pritt Stick, sitting on the desks and in the tool kits of those who have grown up with the brand and feel comfortable having it in their lives. It is the first time the Pritt brand has been extended beyond paper-oriented products toward the professional user and also to the increasingly important DIY sector.

Brand Values

Henkel constantly strives to create products that make people's lives 'easier, better, and more beautiful'. It submits the Pritt stick as a typical example of an innovation that is not only easy to use, but also fun, helpful, creative, clean, and environmentally friendly. Continuing the theme, the Pritt roller correction devices – which dry instantly, allowing users to rewrite text straight away – are another example of a product that eliminates fuss and waste from an everyday task.

Henkel is customer-driven, innovative, and aspires to excellence in quality. The average number of employees engaged in research, product development and application engineering at Henkel worldwide is around 3,000. Expenditure on research and development at the Henkel Group amounted to 259 million euros in 2002.

New extra strong Power Pritt

Power Pritt

There's nothing in the UK quite like new extra strong Power Pritt. Felt, fabric, heavy card, PVC, metal, wood and ceramics. You name it, Pritt will stick it. And all this from a solvent-free, safe to use glue stick. Our national TV campaign including GMTV and satellite starts on 22nd September plus it will be supported in national press.

For sales support call 01707 289 017 or email: order.service@henkel.co.uk

This corresponds to an R&D ratio in relation to sales of 2.7%.

While preserving the tradition of a family company, it is committed to generating shareholder value, as well as being dedicated to sustainability and corporate social responsibility.

www.prittworld.com

Superbrands

Prontaprint
■ DIGITAL DESIGN PRINT COPY

Market

With current developments in digital print, design, and copy technology, there is no doubt that the business print world is changing. As the largest and the best-known brand in the print-on-demand market renowned for quality, value and service, the role of Prontaprint is also evolving in line with market trends and technological developments.

Now more than ever, businesses today must understand the needs of clients and be in a position to satisfy a greater proportion of their requirements. Prontaprint is enjoying continued success through its close working relationship with both small to medium sized businesses and corporates. The brand is positioned as a strategic partner, helping clients address business communication challenges through print and electronic media.

By taking a totally client-focused role, the Prontaprint network is strongly positioned to capitalise on major changes within the business-to-business marketplace. Prontaprint recognises that people buy from people, and has geared its offering around delivering exceptional standards of client care and relationship management.

In recent years, clients themselves have become increasingly digitally enabled and web smart. Prontaprint's forward-looking perspective means that clients can now send in work direct from their desks via email, ISDN and the internet. Innovative new products and services include affordable short-run, full-colour digital printing, large format digital colour printing, variable data printing, scanning, archiving, and retrieval.

Prontaprint's position at the forefront of the print-on-demand market has been maintained through continual investment in cutting edge digital technology. Prontaprint continually seeks and develops new opportunities for the benefit of clients and Franchisees alike.

Prontaprint offers significant opportunities in a growth market for those with a desire to run their own franchise business. With the value of the current European market for print-on-demand set to grow to £17.9 billion by 2004 (Source: Cap Ventures), Prontaprint is well positioned for the future.

Achievements

Established over 30 years ago, Prontaprint has grown to become the largest brand within the print-on-demand market and was the first print brand to be acknowledged as a Business Superbrand by The Brand Council. The company has a fully integrated national network of nearly 200 digitally linked centres across the UK and Ireland. Prontaprint employs over 1,100 people and has an annual turnover in excess of £50 million.

Prontaprint was a founder member of the British Franchise Association (BFA) and played a crucial role in establishing a regulatory body for the franchise industry. The company remains a strong and active supporter of the BFA. Prontaprint is also affiliated to the British Print Industry Federation and the British Association of Printers and Copy Centres, the Institute of Printers and XPLOR International (the Electronic Document Systems Association). These links ensure that Prontaprint remains at the forefront of the

YOU HAVE THE HEAD FOR BUSINESS...

...WE HAVE THE HAT THAT FITS!

As the clear brand leader in the Print-on-Demand market, we are seeking our next generation of franchisees to rapidly develop established centres or open new centres. If you are capable of developing local business to exceed £1 million turnover, contact us to arrange a serious discussion on

Major towns and cities available

08457 626748

Prontaprint
■ DIGITAL DESIGN PRINT COPY

www.prontaprint.com

industry and keeps abreast of technical advances and changes in the marketplace.

Prontaprint has a strategic global alliance with Sir Speedy, the premier US-based quick print franchise. The alliance enables Prontaprint to offer clients central purchasing and digital transfer of documents to more than 1,600 locations in over 28 countries, for local printing and distribution.

Prontaprint was the first national print-on-demand network to sign a formalised licensing agreement with the Copyright Licensing Agency. This allows licensed copying of specified material within agreed limits. Prontaprint is able to offer clients advice on copyright issues and help protect businesses from potential copyright infringements.

History

The first Prontaprint centre, in Collingwood Street, Newcastle-upon-Tyne, opened its doors in 1971. Co-founders Edwin Thirlwell and Ken Clement were determined to overcome the high prices, large minimum orders and long lead times associated

Business Communication Services

Prontaprint

with traditional commercial printers. This approach helped form Prontaprint's ongoing ethos of high quality in design, printing and copying at affordable prices, with rapid turnaround times coupled with excellent client care.

Following the signing of the first Franchise Agreement in 1973, the Prontaprint business model went from strength to strength. The key drivers in the print-on-demand market – fast turnaround, short run lengths, good quality colour capability, coupled with Prontaprint's 'Total Solutions' approach, were to become core strengths within the growing network. Over the years the company has expanded widely across the UK, as well as into various international markets, and in 1996 it became part of Adare Group.

Today Prontaprint has the largest network of digital design, print and copy centres in the UK and Ireland. Prontaprint offers a comprehensive advice and support package to Franchisees in many areas including, marketing, IT, field-based business management, centralised purchasing, franchise sales, legal and estate matters as well as initial and ongoing training.

Even as a mature franchise business, Prontaprint has many opportunities available to prospective Franchisees throughout the UK and Ireland. With further expansion plans on the horizon – and with some Franchisees nearing retirement age – Prontaprint is currently seeking the next generation of Franchisees. Prontaprint is also looking to open new centres in partnership with Franchisees who have the drive, ambition, and sales skills to succeed.

Product

Prontaprint offers a comprehensive portfolio of business communication services to both small and medium-sized businesses (SMEs) and corporates. These include creative design, traditional printing, copying, digital and large format printing, facilities management solutions, colour presentation and document finishing. The company aims to be at the forefront of the design, dissemination and production of business documents either as hard copy or digital format.

Prontaprint provides a complete solutions approach to business print, from concept design, through to print, finishing and delivery. Prontaprint centres feature the latest digital black and white, colour, and high volume print equipment. Centres also have both digital and traditional print capabilities. Through the national network, every centre has the capacity to handle any job, large or small, to the most exacting standards.

Prontaprint is committed to an ongoing programme of investment in the latest digital technology to improve and develop its products and services. Prontaprint centres are able to accept work on a variety of disk formats, ISDN and email. This allows clients to order what they require, whenever they require it – a good example of the changing print-on-demand concept, reducing the need to hold stock, minimising wastage and requiring less up-front investment.

With many documents now produced digitally, clients' original designs can be easily enhanced, updated, and amended. Work can also be stored electronically at Prontaprint centres, where it can be quickly and easily called up.

The versatile nature of the Prontaprint digital network means that material can be supplied to one centre and sent out digitally across the network to be produced at different centres simultaneously, simplifying distribution and increasing capacity and efficiency. This not only saves the client time and money with reduced wastage and storage costs but also improves competitive advantage by enabling clients to respond to market opportunities quickly.

As part of Adare Group, who provide print,

Recent Developments

Proud of its brand heritage, Prontaprint remains focused on new opportunities and new horizons. The company is committed to identifying new products and services to 'take to market'. Prontaprint has embraced the internet to strengthen existing client relationships and help develop inroads to local, regional, and corporate accounts.

Clients now have access to Prontaprint via the web 24 hours a day, seven days a week. Prontaprint's new e-commerce solution offers clients an efficient buying experience saving considerable time and resource via online ordering of regularly requested items. Additionally, clients can obtain fast quotations for work and track the progress of jobs online from anywhere in the world.

Document management is a key success factor in running an efficient and effective business in today's fast-moving business environment. The storage, timely access and retrieval of electronic documents is therefore paramount in improving efficiency as well as reducing administration, storage and transportation costs. The Prontaprint Quickfind system enables the conversion of paper documents into digital images, accessible from anywhere in the world via the internet, intranet or CD Rom. Clients have instantaneous access at their fingertips coupled with robust file security and integrity of data enabling the easy transfer of files to approved recipients.

and PR, ensuring that Prontaprint communicates key messages to its target business audience.

Brand Values

Consistent quality, service, value for money, innovation and professionalism are all key elements of the Prontaprint brand. It views Franchisees collectively as the custodians of the brand and has established a strong reputation by carefully guarding its core brand values of quality, reliability, added value and technical expertise.

Ultimately, Prontaprint's principal asset is its people – its Franchisees and their staff – who are responsible for consistent delivery of the brand promise.

www.prontaprint.com

Archiving & Retrieval enters the digital age...

mailing, and data management solutions to Blue Chip organisations throughout the UK and Ireland, Prontaprint is able to access Group-wide expertise and resources when providing on-demand print solutions to major corporate businesses as part of wider communication solutions – for example as part of the Adare Print Management Solution.

Promotion

Since its inception in 1971, Prontaprint has continually invested in the promotion of its brand on a local, national and international level. Over the years it has been transformed from a general high street print and copy shop into a very well known print-on-demand brand in the business-to-business sector.

Prontaprint has maintained its position as market leader through a sustained and structured approach to business planning and marketing strategy at macro and micro level. Marketing activity is based on extensive client feedback and market research.

Prontaprint believes that consistent and regular sales and marketing activity is central to profitable sales growth and is focused on the development and retention of existing clients as well as attracting new business. Prontaprint provides Franchisees with a wide range of central sales and marketing tools and resources to enable them to grow their businesses locally. This direct sales and marketing activity at local level is supported by national advertising

REED

●●●

Market

Reed enjoys a leading position in the UK recruitment, training and HR consultancy sector at a time when people are recognised to be the key component of any organisation's success. Valued at approximately £24 billion, the UK recruitment market now supports over 14,000 different recruitment companies. While providing temporary and permanent staffing are core areas, Reed's services now extend to training, HR consultancy and outsourcing across every stage of involvement between an employer and employee. Reed enjoys a leading position in each one of these areas.

At a time when global competition is intense, labour market flexibility is a prerequisite for commercial success. People are the oxygen of business and organisations that seek to be world-class will only succeed in becoming so if they recruit and retain world-class talent. At times of greater uncertainty managing this people resource as effectively as possible also becomes a key competitive differentiator for organisations. This means that the way an organisation chooses to approach its sourcing, development and deployment of people at every level will have a critical bearing on its future success. Reed is committed to working in partnership with all its clients to help them gain enduring competitive advantage as a result of the range of staffing services and solutions the company can deploy.

The internet and other new technologies are transforming the entire recruitment market, and Reed is leading this change through its recruitment site www.reed.co.uk and the development of electronic managed services and electronic procurement and payment software.

Achievements

Perhaps Reed's greatest achievement is that from modest beginnings in the 1960s the company has grown organically, and not by acquisition, into one of the UK's largest private businesses with over 2,400 employees and 280 branches that now generate sales of £400 million per year. At the time of its delisting from the London Stock Exchange in April 2003, Reed was valued at £62.6 million.

Its growth is attributed to providing clients with the right people. It has won a growing number of clients by continually innovating and improving the service it has to offer. It is committed to delivering 'The Intelligent Response', which has been a consistent theme since the company began.

Reed was the first recruitment company to offer specialist recruitment services. This began with the creation of Reed Executive, Reed Accountancy Personnel and Reed Nursing Personnel in the early 1960s. At least another dozen specialist niches have been developed since. Reed's move into specialisation fundamentally changed the UK recruitment market.

Following its first decade of success, the company was floated on the London Stock Exchange in 1971. In 2001 the healthcare operations were demerged as Reed Health Group plc, and this business continues to flourish as a separately quoted company using the Reed brand. In 2003

Reed Executive once again became a private company, reflecting the Reed family's continued belief in the business, and their commitment to the core values that underpin it.

To this day the founder's entrepreneurial spirit is fundamental to the company's culture and to its approach to the market. Reed prides itself on being an organisation that continues to innovate and to specialise, and on being one that will rise to meet challenges, however great.

In today's sophisticated markets, many of the best achievements are gained through an in-depth partnership between Reed and its clients. One example of this is Reed's work with a multi-site government department. The Environment Agency

![Screenshot of the reed.co.uk website homepage showing job search options and featured sectors]

are responsible for protecting and sustaining the environment, operating from over 100 offices spread right across the length and breadth of the UK. The often rural, remote nature of their locations poses considerable issues in sourcing over 400 temporary staff every day. Reed's Managed Agency offering provides solutions to these problems – unparalleled brand recognition backed up by partner agreements with local agencies ensures maximum fulfilment of the roles.

The company prides itself on taking an active role in creating and leading positive social change. For example, Reed in Partnership specialises in developing people and their communities through the delivery of Government and EU programmes. It brings fresh thinking, new ideas and Reed's commercial experience to the challenge of helping people break the cycle of benefit dependency and make the step from welfare to work. Since 1997, the company has

won contracts across the country. Another example is Reed Education, which has introduced a range of innovative new services to the supply of teachers into schools, including two Local Education Authority (LEA) contracts. The Lancashire Teaching Agency and the Cheshire Supply Service are ethical partnerships that are responsible for the cost-effective deployment and development of the counties' supply teacher workforce, whilst providing a better fill rate at a lower cost.

Underpinning many of these achievements is Reed's leading position online – its website having been established in 1995. Today, visitors can make use of innovative tools such as saved searches, where they can be sent details of jobs matching their specific criteria via email or SMS. Other popular features include CV Builder and Client Profiles. Over 39,000 recruiters use Reed's services through the site and there are over 100,000 temporary and permanent jobs on the site for jobseekers to search, attracting a projected 31.8 million visits in 2003. Reed currently has over 1.3 million jobseekers registered online and through the branch network.

Above all Reed attributes its success to the quality of its employees, whom it refers to as Co-Members. It has developed a programme of Co-Member training and development and offers all of its Consultants the opportunity to study for a Certificate in Professional Recruitment Services accredited by the University of London. Trainees are also given the opportunity to gain prestigious industry qualifications with the Chartered Institute of Personnel and Development. As well as full programmes of recognition and reward, there

sectors. Finally, Reed Connections Ltd delivers information technology solutions and financial and accounting services to both internal and external customers.

Recent Developments

Reed has continued to develop its Starburst Strategy, first announced by Chief Executive James Reed at the beginning of the new Millennium. This reorganised the group into smaller, more versatile business units. This alongside the strategy that underpins it have created an even more customer focused business that is capable of moving quickly to meet client needs and that is able not just to adapt to, but to lead an ever changing market.

The Starburst Strategy also continues to deliver many more opportunities for people within Reed to take the initiative and develop their own areas of operation. The company pursues a Venture Peoplist business model, which means that it continues to invest in and pursue new business opportunities that centre on people and people resourcing.

More recently, Reed has developed the Working Life Cycle model, which views each person at work as undergoing an inevitable seven-stage process of involvement with their employer. Beginning with Attraction, this process ranges through Recruitment, Induction, Development, Reward, Retention and – finally – Release. Reed's bespoke PeopleAudit service is just one of the targeted ways in which the HR Consultancy team offers expertise to help organisations maximise their effective management of people at every stage of the process.

Promotion

Reed's most consistently visible presence in the recruitment market comes from the physical locations of its 280 branches that operate across the UK and Ireland. This physical network is supported by an electronic network that is centred upon its website. The availability of Reed's

established services through the extensive online and offline network enables Reed as a major recruiter to offer a market-leading recruitment service. Indeed, independent research from Hitwise.co.uk indicates that the word 'Reed' is one of the UK's ten most searched for recruitment terms on the internet, and that its website is one of the top three recruitment sites in the UK.

Over the years the weighting of the media mix and of the advertising spend has varied considerably, but care is taken to ensure that the brand always remains front of mind of both employers and job-seekers. This investment means that Reed retains high awareness even at times when advertising has been relatively light.

Reed's advertising expenditure is supported by an active approach to public relations and the company's work is often featured in the national and regional press. The company regularly publishes information on the state of the labour market and frequently surveys the opinions of its clients and candidates. Reed is therefore well positioned to provide a very up to date perspective on all that is happening in the world of work.

Word of mouth communications are especially important to Reed, not least because the majority of the company's customers – candidates and clients – state that they first made contact with Reed as a direct result of a recommendation and what they know of the company's reputation. Reed is well aware that there is no better promotion than customer promotion and the company is determined to build on this bedrock of goodwill by continuing to improve its services to clients and candidates in the future.

Brand Values

Reed is, and always has been, passionate about people. In a 'people' service business, it is Reed's 'Co-Members' who embody the brand.

Central to Reed's brand values is its role in creating and leading positive social change. Reed believes work to be a social good and therefore the group's focus is on improving people's working lives, and making the labour market both fairer and more efficient.

Reed's philosophy is that 'People Make the Difference', and its promise is to 'Deliver the Intelligent Response'. Its purpose is to be 'First Choice for People', which means being first choice for Clients, Candidates and Co-Members alike.

The Reed brand combines reliability and tradition with innovation and adaptability.

www.reed.co.uk

are also opportunities to have fun. One example is the party James Reed held for all Co-Members and their families in July 2003 at the Reeds' Cotswolds home.

It is because of this commitment to Co-Members that this year Reed has been independently judged one of the Best 100 Companies To Work For by the Sunday Times.

History

Reed began on May 7th 1960 when James Reed's father, Alec Reed, then aged 26, opened the first Reed branch in Hounslow, West London. He started with just £75 and worked alone for a year. Reed celebrated its 40th birthday on 7th May 2000.

Product

Reed's growth has been dramatic and the company's stated ambition is to grow the business substantially in the future. Reed has been organised into five separate operating companies to make this happen. The largest of these is Reed Solutions plc, which delivers bespoke and general staffing solutions through the Reed Employment network of branches, and HR consultancy and outsourcing through Reed Managed Services. Reed Personnel Services plc focuses on specialist recruitment services across professions such as accountancy, law, engineering, insurance and IT. Reed in Partnership plc provides outsourced services to the public and private sectors, while Reed Learning plc supplies learning, training and education services, again to the public and private

RESEARCH INTERNATIONAL

Market

In today's world where previous definitions of consumers and markets are increasingly irrelevant, where global communications mean there is nowhere for corporations to hide, and where the next big idea in global marketing is as likely to come from a teenager in Texas as a board room in Birmingham, knowledge is power.

Market research is the fuel of this knowledge economy. It has long supported decisions made in marketing – understanding people in order to provide them with products and services that they need at a price they will pay. This has led to a burgeoning demand – the global market research industry is estimated to be worth approximately US$15 billion annually. But research has moved beyond support in tactical decisions to helping companies define their business strategies, manage knowledge and seize the opportunity to thrive and gain competitive advantage.

In response to this, Research International works hard to differentiate itself. By focusing on the delivery of marketing knowledge, rather than data or intelligence, it provides both detailed, specific answers faster than ever before, but also provides 'the big picture' to give a deeper understanding.

As the world leader in custom market research services Research International is a truly global company with offices in over 55 countries. This lends itself to creating a vast knowledge base about consumers around the world. It has global knowledge bases by sector, business issue and research technique and uses sophisticated knowledge management systems to support them. Research International has been researching more customers for longer and in more places than any one else. All of its work is designed in response to individual client needs. This means it works as partners with many familiar brands and companies the world over – helping clients solve problems, and develop the knowledge to create successful brands and businesses as well as gain a better understanding of consumers and customers.

Clients include manufacturers of cars, planes, white goods (washing machines etc), brown goods (TV, hi-fi etc), computers, mobile phones and a wide range of food, alcoholic and non-alcoholic drinks. It also works with a number of the big banks and building societies as well as the makers of trainers, big hotel chains, postal companies, transport bodies, major retailers, IT and telecommunications.

Achievements

Research International was the first market research agency to understand the value to clients of a global network. Well before other agencies, it established offices – the majority wholly owned and not only associates or affiliates – in over 50 countries, in order to ensure the consistent delivery of fast and accurate knowledge all over the world. The largest Research International companies are now in the UK, the US, France, Germany, Japan and Sweden. All offices offer the same range of services; are thoroughly trained in all the research techniques the brand uses, and its sophisticated internal knowledge-sharing systems ensure quality and the interchange of ideas.

Research International Qualitatif is the world's leading qualitative network – a truly integrated community of research professionals.

Furthermore, it is acknowledged as the leading 'thinking' market research agency. Its offices are supported by leading edge marketing science centres (Research International has specially trained teams to do this) in Europe, the US and Asia and its directors are recognised experts invited to speak regularly on areas such as branding, pricing and innovation. Over the years the company has built large databases of normative data against which clients can assess their position and progress.

As a result, wherever a client company is in the world (or wherever they want to be) Research International is on hand to deliver the same dedicated service and knowledge.

Research International is a recognised Investor in People. It was the first major marketing research agency, and remains the only one of the top global players to bear this accreditation. In addition to its human resources network, it has a dedicated team of seven learning and development professionals, based in London, collectively called The Learning Zone. Research International is a recognised leader in this area, placing great emphasis on the training and development of its people. In January 2001 it became the first to receive an accreditation from the MRS (Market Research Society) for its graduate trainee development programme. In conjunction with the trade publication Research magazine, it launched the Talent Magnet Awards in 2003 – to find and nurture the best young talent in the research industry. This resulted in two young researchers being presented with awards at the Market Research Society's Conference in March 2003.

Research International has won many awards over the years; most recently in many categories of the Atticus awards. These awards were set up in 1994 by WPP, of which Research International is a part, to recognise and reward exceptional work by WPP company people across all disciplines. In 2003 Research International won the overall Market Research category with 'Death of an Idea' – a presentation which refutes the suggestion that market research kills good new product ideas.

It was also awarded a Merit for its work based on findings from its global (47 countries worldwide) qualitative study 'International Branding: Resolving the Global-Local Dilemma'.

Also in 2003, Research International in the Netherlands was voted the most highly appreciated marketing research agency, as awarded by an independent study among marketers and company marketing researchers.

History

Research International grew out of the market research departments of Unilever and its marketing companies/advertising agencies around the world. In 1972 these companies were brought together under the 'Research International' name. In early 1987 Unilever sold the Research International organisation to The Ogilvy Group and in 1989 The Ogilvy Group – and with it Research International – was acquired by WPP.

At the end of August 2001 the company redesigned the way it worked for clients, training all its staff in new client service approaches and restructuring the organisation.

As a reflection of the changes, Research International adopted a new identity symbolising how it now works for clients which combines images of a wave and a drop. The drop represents how the company delivers detailed answers to business problems, and the ocean represents the 'big picture' – the stream of strategic knowledge the new strategy provides to clients.

Product

Research International specialises in research in Consumer Understanding, Branding and Communications, Innovation, Channel Management, and Customer Relationships. It has developed research techniques to support its work – such as Equity Engine℠, MicroTest℠ eValuate℠ and Locator℠ and has large, globally validated databases that gives clients benchmarks for their performance in all these areas.

Its team of qualitative and quantitative 'Consumer Understanding' experts gathers information from consumers, and interprets often complex patterns in a way which is easy to understand and easy to apply. Their brief is to work with clients to provide the knowledge and underlying insights to aid building consumer knowledge required to develop a brand's strategy, anticipate trends and future opportunities as well as plan for long term growth.

Research International is recognised as a leader in the area of branding. If it is true that

Heliathus annuus.
Average seeds
per flower: 435
(Increase of 12%
over last year's yield)

Good news for the
low-fat spread sector

When we asked clients what they need from market research, the message was clear. "We want things done differently. We want the detail - sharp, focused answers - faster than ever before. And we need the big picture - marketing knowledge and consumer insight to inspire and guide strategy."

So we changed the way we work, to create a new kind of market research company. One that is equipped to meet the new challenges. One that works closely with clients as proactive partners to deliver both the detail and the big picture.

To find out more, call Colin Buckingham on +44 (0) 20 7656 5000 or knowyourworld@research-int.com

RESEARCH INTERNATIONAL

brands now represent the most important business assets for very many companies, then defining and monitoring the value of those assets is critical.

Research International aims to understand what creates brand strength. What drives value in a particular market and what people want, how well its clients' brands are seen as meeting these needs and what benefits do people associate with them.

Much of its work with brands addresses the so-called 'soft' benefits – the brand's personality, and the emotional and self-expressive payback that the consumer gets from the purchase. But it also focuses clearly on the underlying product and service characteristics and the 'hard' benefits that these deliver in a competitive context. It is the interaction of these emotional and functional benefits that creates equity. Research International's Equity Engine℠ model allows it to understand the interplay of these elements. The resulting database of international brands and additional metric, Brand Edge℠, means it can predict whether a brand is likely to gain market share over time. In addition, Locator℠ gives clients a detailed understanding of their brand in the market together with the knowledge of how to optimise their positioning and monitor brand health over time.

The area of innovation has always been a major

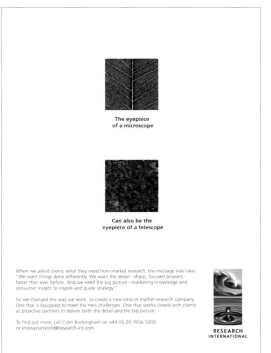

The eyepiece
of a microscope

Can also be the
eyepiece of a telescope

When we asked clients what they need from market research, the message was clear. "We want things done differently. We want the detail - sharp, focused answers - faster than ever before. And we need the big picture - marketing knowledge and consumer insight to inspire and guide strategy."

So we changed the way we work, to create a new kind of market research company. One that is equipped to meet the new challenges. One that works closely with clients as proactive partners to deliver both the detail and the big picture.

To find out more, call Colin Buckingham on +44 (0) 20 7656 5000 or knowyourworld@research-int.com

RESEARCH INTERNATIONAL

part of Research International's business. With over 30 years' experience across sectors it helps clients develop and launch new products and services, using a portfolio of qualitative and quantitative approaches. It uses its extensive, international database with over 20,000 concepts to identify emerging consumer influences and trends. From this it understands what factors increase success rates for new products. Research International offers an integrated and seamless innovation journey, from gaining inspiration, identifying new consumer needs or platforms via ethnographic research, stimulating idea creation and assisting with idea development using specially trained creative consumers Super Group®, to understanding market potential using MicroTest℠ through to launching in the market and tracking the results.

Research International's global community of channel management knowledge specialists meets regularly to share knowledge and learning. It also has direct access to the wealth of expertise available from The Store – the retail expertise of WPP. It provides the knowledge of customers' behaviour, motivations and needs that enables both retail and manufacturer businesses to navigate through the whirlwind of change.

Customer relations is not just about collecting survey data about your customers, nor is it about analysing databases full of customer information. The definition of customer relations has changed over the years. Now we know that in order to have good relationships companies must manage 'the experience' their customers have with business.

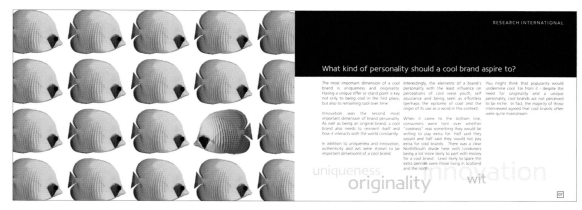

What kind of personality should a cool brand aspire to?

uniqueness originality innovation wit

Recent Developments

In 2003 a new globally validated index of universal consumer needs was launched – needs that drive people the world over, which Research International refers to as the universal needs inventory – UNI for short. Most organisations talk about understanding the needs of their consumers and admit that this is fundamental to their business. But it is very hard to do. To put people at the heart of marketing, it has developed a new approach – one that enables brand owners to uncover unmet needs and target 'white space' more effectively. Research International believes that linking those needs to the world in which brands communicate gives marketers clear direction for brand activity going forward.

In addition there have been two major new developments in innovation at Research International in the past year. First of all Fifteen20℠ has been established as an early stage innovation practice and secondly the company has seen great success with its new concept screening tool eValuate℠.

Both these developments are key because they have addressed the most important issues facing the company's clients at the moment – the problem of coming up with breakthrough innovations, and the problem of ensuring the right ideas are brought to market. In the past, market research has been used as more of a check on concept development and innovation; Fifteen20℠ breaks this mould by generating the concepts in the first place. And market research is often criticised for killing new ideas (the old

adage that consumers only like what they know, so asking them about radically new concepts inevitably leads to rejection). eValuate℠ deals with this problem by using early adopters in the screening process, to understand those ideas that are truly viable.

Promotion

The marketing strategy at Research International supports its client relationships by delivering new and relevant knowledge. Valued clients are invited to a series of seminars – The Marketing Knowledge Exchange programme – where new research and learnings are shared. Research International also provides clients with a regular newsletter – The Issue – which takes an in depth view of a current issue of relevance to marketing and business and looks at it from several different angles. Both The Issue and the Marketing Knowledge Exchange programme are rolled out worldwide. Its research and development programme generates a lot of interest in the marketing, trade and national press and the brand is frequently asked to contribute features or to present at conferences. Its website also drives the knowledge exchange programme with regular articles, updates and news from across the Group.

Approximately every other year, its qualitative network regularly undertakes a large, multi-country study – the Research International Observer (RIO), which looks in depth at an issue or trend of global relevance. Recent RIOs have included consumer attitudes to Global Brands, eCommerce and Men in the Millennium.

Brand Values

Research International is at the heart of decisions about businesses and brands, helping clients understand people and anticipate and shape their future.

www.research-int.com

REUTERS
KNOW. NOW.

Market

Reuters, the global information company, provides information, trading and analytic tools tailored for professionals in the financial services and media markets. It provides fast, accurate and unbiased information that can be integrated into the decision-making processes of its customers.

Reuters is best known as the world's largest international multimedia news agency, supplying news – text, graphics, video and pictures – to media organisations and websites across the globe. However, more than 90% of its revenue comes from its financial services customers. Nearly 500,000 financial market professionals around the world rely on Reuters services, which provide them with the information and tools they need to make decisions and trade.

Achievements

Reuters has been at the forefront of innovation in information technology ever since it made some of the earliest use of telegraph cables in the late nineteenth century.

It pioneered the use of radio to transmit news around the world in 1923, the use of computers to transmit financial data internationally in 1964 and was the first to use computers to display real-time foreign exchange rates in 1973. It was also the first company in the private sector to send news via satellite.

In 1981 it launched the Reuters Monitor Dealing electronic broking service for international traders – a system through which half of the trillion dollar-a-day spot foreign exchange volume is now traded. In 1992 its Dealing 2000-2 product became the first automated broking service.

Reuters news reporting achievements are equally impressive. It was the first to report the assassination of President Lincoln in 1918, the first with the news of the World War I Armistice, and in 1989 it broke the story that the Berlin Wall had fallen. Reuters also had one of the largest teams of journalists in Iraq in 2003. Coverage of the war and subsequent events has won plaudits for media and financial services customers across the globe.

History

Reuters was founded by Paul Julius Reuter, who began transmitting stock exchange prices and news by carrier pigeon from Aachen in Germany in 1849. He set Reuters up as a news agency in London in 1851, taking advantage of the new telegraph technology.

By 1858, Reuters had opened offices all over Europe following the wider installation of telegraph cable. The company quickly established a reputation for unbiased, speedy reporting of international news.

During the 1970s, Reuters was transformed when it pioneered a new range of electronic information products for the world's rapidly growing financial markets. Its computer terminals providing real-time financial data revolutionised foreign exchange dealing, as did its introduction of electronic transactions in 1981. These developments made Reuters a force in the international financial information market.

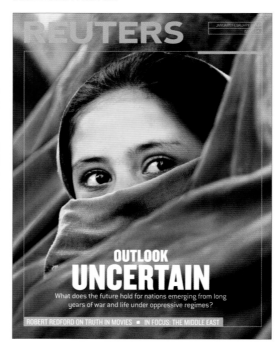

Over the years, a number of strategic acquisitions have strengthened Reuters position in key markets. In 1986, it bought Instinet, an electronic securities broking company, which now accounts for much of the dealing on the NASDAQ market. More recently, in 2001 Reuters bought Bridge Information Systems, acquiring a large customer base among US institutional investors as well as trading and order-routing technologies.

Product

Reuters has shaped its business to reflect the way its customers work. The company operates through customer segments and associated sales and customer support channels to create, sell and support its products. The company's core strengths lie in providing the information, analytics and trading capabilities needed by financial professionals.

In Treasury Services, Reuters has a long history of helping customers operate more effectively in the foreign exchange and money markets. Customers work in banks, brokerages, exchanges, corporate and institutional treasuries. Key customers in Investment Banking include global, regional and boutique investment banks, brokerage and venture capital firms. Reuters Asset Management customers include the top 50 asset management firms around the world and range from institutional fund managers and hedge funds to private banks and retail broking houses.

Reuters open technology, based on industry standards, enables its customers to bring together Reuters own information with content from other sources, helping financial professionals act faster at work. Reuters also provides customers with specially designed tools to help them manage risk, distribute and manage the ever-increasing volumes of market data, and also offers bespoke trading products.

Reuters has become the world's leading news agency, providing news, film, pictures and graphics to media owners around the world. The media business is directed towards serving the needs of the world's newspapers, television and cable networks, websites and consumers. Retail customers are also offered direct access to Reuters news and data through branded websites such as www.reuters.com.

Recent Developments

The competitive market in which Reuters operates demands continual product innovation to meet the needs of financial markets professionals. The company recently launched an innovative messaging service and the next generation of information and trading products aimed at financial markets professionals. Reuters also has a track record of making successful acquisitions to support its own

products, a recent example being the addition of comprehensive US data and analytics with the purchase of Bridge Information Systems Inc.

The financial services market has undergone rapid and significant structural changes in the last two years. In response to this, Reuters stepped up the pace of its business transformation programme known as 'Fast Forward'. The goal of this programme is to ensure Reuters leverages its core skills, scale and brand to deliver the right products at the right price and provide customers with innovative products that truly represent the day-to-day activities of a financial market professional. In addition to the creation of new products, the company is making a significant investment in a single technical and data distribution architecture and business operating model. This in turn will assist Reuters customers in managing their costs more efficiently.

Reuters is committed to delivering great customer service and has boosted the pace of investment in its service initiatives: increasing the number of customer support staff, implementing a global CRM system and introducing new help desk technologies in Reuters four customer relationship management centres, based in London, Sydney, Chicago and Geneva.

Promotion

Recognising the growing importance of a strong brand identity and clear positioning in the increasingly competitive financial services and media markets, Reuters is increasing promotional activity with a new advertising campaign due to break in the Autumn of 2003. Given the very specific nature of the financial services target audience, the choice of media is largely B2B financial.

Reuters also uses its own assets to raise brand awareness. Reuters Infopoint (see picture bottom left) is installed on the trading floors of many financial institutions globally, with plans to introduce the service in public places such as airports and train stations. The award-winning Reuters Magazine showcases the expertise and insights of Reuters global network of journalists. Business TV channels such as CNN International and CNBC deliver pre-packaged news reports direct from Reuters journalists, which is supported by brand advertising.

RULE #3:
OBTAIN VERIFICATION
Are you in or out? Reuters double checks its facts so you can make a call with confidence. **REUTERS**

With a 4,000-strong sales and service organisation, Reuters focuses much of its promotional activity on supporting a global programme of customer events. These activities help the company develop closer client relationships and ensure customers and prospects are exposed to Reuters new products.

Reuters uses its sponsorship activities to promote its values of speed and accuracy through long-term relationships with Formula One (as sponsor of the BMW-Williams F1 team) and European Tour golf (as sponsor of the official performance statistics).

A global direct marketing programme focuses on building loyalty amongst key customer groups, and generating awareness and interest from industry prospects.

Brand Values

The Reuters brand is one of great heritage and authority as the leading source of financial information and news in the financial service and media markets. Reuters has always been committed to delivering fast and accurate information. More recently, the company has built on this brand value to give financial markets professionals and the world of the media the right insight and tools exactly when they require them; so that in turn they can act faster and be successful in their jobs.

Reuters commitment to independently managed 'Trust Principles' has helped build its reputation for the delivery of unbiased, impartial, factual information. Reuters is passionate about always representing both sides of any issue and delivering the same opportunities and level of service to customers regardless of their scale or geographic location.

Reuters prides itself on its global reach with nearly 500,000 financial markets professionals using its products to find the best execution or best distribution for a deal. Reuters dedication to open standards is unparalleled in the professional financial markets. Customers have always been able to rely on Reuters to deliver technological solutions that can be integrated into the heart of their business, so services can be tailored to users' needs.

Reuters people are key to the delivery of its brand values and there is a focus and determination within the company, driven by the 'Fast Forward' programme, to ensure that the delivery of the brand values and products are always to the direct benefit of the customer.

www.reuters.com

RULE #6:
HAVE MORE REPORTERS ON THE GROUND
Reuters has more people in more global locations to hunt down the stories that matter. **REUTERS**

www.reuters.com/knownow

RIO TINTO

Market

As one of the biggest names in the mining industry, Rio Tinto produces a broad range of metals and minerals, sold in a variety of markets with differing characteristics and pricing mechanisms. Markets for metals and minerals reflect business cycles in the global economy. Metal prices, for example, are set every day by the London Metal Exchange, and these provide the basis of prices for metals sold all over the world. Fluctuations in prices inevitably affect Rio Tinto's financial results, though the company in recent years has enjoyed record profits in spite of unfavourable conditions.

In 2003 Western markets remained weak, but had stabilised in the expectation of a recovery, the timing of which is uncertain. A flagging economy in the West has been compensated for by strong sales of metals and minerals into China, which is undergoing a major phase of infrastructure development. In addition to difficult market conditions, a major challenge has been society's growing expectations for all businesses in areas such as the environment, community affairs and corporate governance. As a result the global minerals industry is undergoing a gradual metamorphosis; to better understand and respond to community expectations.

Achievements

Rio Tinto owns long life operations producing coal, copper, gold, aluminium, industrial minerals and iron ore. In addition, it continues to research and develop new projects, and has a clear and focused exploration programme to seek out opportunities for further expansion.

When we go shopping, almost everything we buy can be traced back, either directly or indirectly, to the mining industry – and often to Rio Tinto itself. The company provides the minerals and metals that are the building blocks of everyday life, including iron, copper, aluminium, titanium dioxide, borates, gold, diamonds, coal, uranium, nickel, zinc, silver, lead, and salt.

Rio Tinto is also a significant energy producer, providing low-sulphur steam coal to power stations that supply homes, businesses and industries in the US, Australia and Asia. It provides metallurgical coking coal to iron and steel mills in Asia and Europe. It also mines the uranium oxide that, when enriched into fuel rods, enables nuclear power stations to generate electricity in Europe, the US and Asia-Pacific. Growing internet use and ever more sophisticated forms of consumer electronics are increasing the demand for power in the developed world, as is electrification in developing countries.

Rio Tinto has a consistent record of outperforming its sector in total shareholder returns. Indeed, the company points out that in the period from 1993 until the end of December 2002, it made more money for its shareholders than any of its industry peers. Rio Tinto's performance is also reflected in the HSBC Global Mining Index, in which it has outperformed the index by a compound average of 7% a year throughout the last decade.

Rio Tinto also has the highest credit rating in the mining sector: Standard & Poor's A+, and Moody's Investor Service Aa3.

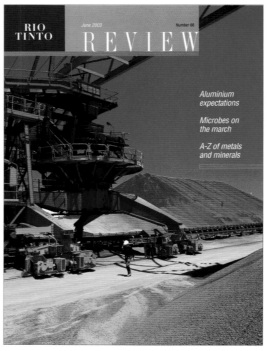

History

British entrepreneurs founded Rio Tinto in 1873 to buy and reopen an ancient copper mine in Rio Tinto, southern Spain which the Spanish Crown was willing to sell to provide much needed money for a country weakened by 50 years of civil strife. The payment was made in gold bars, transported to Madrid by train and oxcart in wooden cases. The founding Spanish business was however later sold to fund expansion elsewhere.

In 1905, another company, The Consolidated Zinc Corporation, was created to treat zinc-bearing mine waste at Broken Hill in New South Wales, Australia – later expanding into mining and smelting there and in the UK. The British parents of these two companies merged in 1962, creating Rio Tinto plc. At the same time, the Australian interests of both companies were merged, creating Rio Tinto Ltd. The pair effectively operated as separate entities until 1995, when they finally became a single company.

After the 1962 merger, Rio Tinto plc embarked on a number of new mining projects, extracting copper at Palabora in South Africa, uranium at Rössing in Namibia, and copper and tin at Neves Corvo in Portugal. Between the late 1960s and the mid 1980s it also developed significant interests in cement, chemicals, oil and gas, and manufactured products for the construction and automotive industries.

However, after a major strategy review in 1988, the company decided to refocus on its core mining and related activities. In the late 1980s and early 1990s it sold off non-core businesses, while acquiring more mining interests.

In parallel, its sister company Rio Tinto Ltd grew through the development of important mineral interests, such as iron ore in Australia, copper in Papua New Guinea, bauxite and aluminium smelting in New Zealand and Australia, as well as coal, diamonds and gold in Australia and Indonesia.

Since the two sister companies merged in 1995, Rio Tinto's exploration and technology efforts have been refocused to guarantee efficiency and exploit the Group's full potential. Capital expenditure has been at record levels as it develops its wide range of projects. Rio Tinto completed US$4 billion worth of acquisitions in 2000, covering aluminium, iron ore, diamonds and coal, and adding further strength to an already exceptional base of resources.

Product

Rio Tinto's mines provide some of the world's most vital materials, from the superstars of the commodities industry – like iron, copper, silver, diamonds and gold – to little-known yet vital substances like ilmenite, rutile, zircon, bauxite, and boron.

Ilmenite, for example, with its ability to scatter light, imparts brilliance and opacity to paints, plastics and paper. Rutile is used in the manufacture of titanium metal, which is used to make jet engines. Zircon is a mineral used in the production of ceramic tiles and sanitary ware. Refined to zirconia, it is used in advanced ceramics, computers, spacecraft, clothing, jewellery and electronics. As an ingredient of TV screens and computer monitors, it protects us from harmful

x-rays. Rio Tinto is one of the world's leading suppliers of these vital minerals.

Bauxite is refined into alumina, which is smelted into aluminium. Rio Tinto is a major producer of all three.

The Group is also a top supplier of boron. Boron-based minerals are called borates, a vital ingredient of many home and garden products. Rio Tinto Borax's mine in California's Mojave Desert is the world's largest borates mine.

Rio Tinto's gold production comes mainly as a by product of copper mining. The Group produces 7% of world copper, ranking it fourth in the world, and 4% of mined gold, making it the fifth largest producer.

Gem diamonds share the stage with gold as a luxury commodity. With the opening of the Diavik diamond mine in Canada in 2003, Rio Tinto is able to offer diamond products across the colour spectrum, including the most spectacular flawless whites.

Rio Tinto is among the world's largest producers of iron ore with production of about 74 million tonnes per year. In energy, Rio Tinto accounts for 7% of traded thermal coal and 13% of uranium, ranking the company fourth and third respectively in world terms.

Recent Developments

Rio Tinto has a number of projects under construction, representing an increased interest in certain commodities. The US$900 million Diavik diamond mine in northern Canada produced its first diamonds in early 2003. Diavik is expected to deliver the greatest value, per tonne of ore, of any diamond mine in the western world.

The US$750 million Comalco alumina refinery project at Gladstone in Australia will make Rio Tinto a major player in the traded alumina market. Alumina is an intermediate product for the manufacture of aluminium. The new refinery will start in 2005 with an initial capacity of 1.4 million tonnes per year and with options to expand to 4.2 million tonnes.

In energy products, the US$255 million Hail Creek project in Australia, together with the expansion of its existing Kestrel mine, will make Rio Tinto a significant supplier of hard coking coal. The first shipments of coal were expected in October 2003.

Also in Australia, in April 2002 Rio Tinto committed itself to the construction of a commercial size iron smelter at a cost of US$200 million. Using new technology, it is more efficient than conventional processes and reduces greenhouse gas emissions.

A wholly owned Rio Tinto subsidiary, Kennecott Utah Copper in the US, owns 37,000 hectares of land adjacent to its mining and smelter complex at Salt Lake City. It has formed a spin-off company, Kennecott Land, to develop 4,000 hectares for residential use. The first stage, Project Daybreak, is costing US$50 million.

Rio Tinto is also in the process of expanding and developing many of its existing mining projects, and raising production to meet market demand.

Rio Tinto's Chairman, Sir Robert Wilson, retired in October 2003 after 33 years with the Group, seven of them as executive chairman. His replacement is Paul Skinner, who takes on the role of non-executive chairman. Skinner joined the board of Rio Tinto as a non-executive director in 2001. He was group managing director of Royal Dutch/Shell in London, from which he retired at the end of September to take up the chairmanship of Rio Tinto.

Promotion

Rio Tinto recognises the importance of maintaining a spotless reputation, while being seen as a leader in the field of sustainable development. All activities linked to this area are grouped under one line manager, the head of communication and sustainable development – who reports to the chief executive.

The department's communications are primarily aimed at shareholders, opinion leaders and key media. Among other duties, it conducts corporate auditing and reviews for 'The way we work', Rio Tinto's statement of business practice. This statement is crucial to the company's conduct, as it describes the manner in which it works closely with local communities and adopts safety and environmental policies that go beyond requirements. 'The way we work' has been translated into eighteen languages to spread the word, including Oshidonga (Botswana), Farsi (Iran), Welsh, Japanese, Russian, Chinese, Indonesian and Zulu.

In addition, the communication unit works closely with Rio Tinto's health, safety and environment (HSE) department, which plays a key role within the Group. Building from a foundation of compliance with existing health and safety rules, Rio Tinto seeks to improve its performance by setting targets, implementing effective management

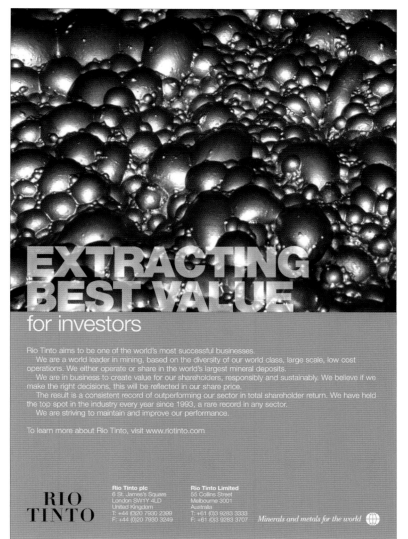

EXTRACTING BEST VALUE
for investors

Rio Tinto aims to be one of the world's most successful businesses.

We are a world leader in mining, based on the diversity of our world class, large scale, low cost operations. We either operate or share in the world's largest mineral deposits.

We are in business to create value for our shareholders, responsibly and sustainably. We believe if we make the right decisions, this will be reflected in our share price.

The result is a consistent record of outperforming our sector in total shareholder return. We have held the top spot in the industry every year since 1993, a rare record in any sector.

We are striving to maintain and improve our performance.

To learn more about Rio Tinto, visit www.riotinto.com

RIO TINTO

Rio Tinto plc	Rio Tinto Limited
6 St. James's Square	55 Collins Street
London SW1Y 4LD	Melbourne 3001
United Kingdom	Australia
T: +44 (0)20 7930 2399	T: +61 (0)3 9283 3333
F: +44 (0)20 7930 3249	F: +61 (0)3 9283 3707

Minerals and metals for the world

systems, and operating the best possible practices. Its goal is zero injuries in the workplace and the elimination of occupational disease.

Brand Values

The company's strategy has been substantially unchanged for well over a decade. The underlying principle is simple: it is in business to create value for its shareholders, in a responsible and sustainable manner.

In order to deliver superior returns to its shareholders over many years, it takes a long term, responsible approach to all its activities. It helps meet the global need for metals and minerals that contribute to improved living standards, as well as making a direct contribution to economic development and employment in those countries where it invests.

Rio Tinto seeks world class, large-scale, low-cost operations. It does not invest on the basis of product or geographical location. Instead, it looks for projects that will create shareholder value and generate strong cash flow, even when prices are depressed. By consistently pursuing this strategy over many years, Rio Tinto has established a spread of commodity exposures that serve this goal well.

www.riotinto.com

Things you didn't know about
Rio Tinto

- In 1873, £400,000 in gold bars was smuggled by oxcart over the Pyrenees through lines of warring factions to the hard-pressed Spanish government in Madrid. British businessmen sent the bars as a down payment on the Rio Tinto copper mines, suggested to have been the original 'King Solomon's Mines'.

- British managers at the Rio Tinto mines introduced football to save Spanish workers from the taverns and brothels, and thereby founded Spain's oldest football club, Recreativo de Huelva, now in the first division La Liga.

- Rio Tinto operations around the world (43 in 2002) hold annual bird watching events for staff and families in partnership with BirdLife International. Participants gather information about bird species relevant to environmental management.

- Talc from different deposits has such a variety of textures that Christian Dior alone uses more than twenty different Rio Tinto talcs in its formulations.

- Sodium borohydride, derived from the mineral borates mined by Rio Tinto, is being used to develop technology that can safely store hydrogen fuel in emission free cars.

Rolls-Royce

Market

Rolls-Royce is a global company providing power for land, sea and air. The brand operates in four distinct markets: civil aerospace, defence aerospace, marine and energy, where its gas turbines are used to power aircraft, drive ships, provide electricity, pump oil or compress gas.

Rolls-Royce has offices, service centres and manufacturing bases in 48 countries and customers in more than 160. There are now some 54,000 Rolls-Royce gas turbines in service and these generate high-value services throughout their operational lives. An aero engine can be in operation for 40 years or more and as such the aftermarket is an extremely important area of the brand's customer relationship. The services business of Rolls-Royce is growing with a global overhaul network and innovative e-business products being launched to monitor engines as they operate. Furthermore, a range of complete engine management services on behalf of customers called TotalCare has been introduced.

In 2002 the company had a turnover of just under £6 billion and an order book of £17 billion. It employs 37,000 people around the world, with major employment centres in the UK, US, South America, the Nordic countries and Germany.

The core technologies of Rolls-Royce are used in all of the markets it serves and in the last five years the company has invested more than £3 billion in research and development.

The markets it operates in demand the use of cutting edge technology to develop the latest systems and products, the brand's achievements are based on the development of ground breaking technology.

Achievements

Rolls-Royce has been at the forefront of British engineering excellence for the past 100 years.

More than 500 airlines, 4,000 corporations, utility aircraft and helicopter operations, 160 armed forces and 2,000 marine customers use Rolls-Royce power. In the last decade the company has established itself as the second largest supplier of engines to the civil and defence aerospace markets and is the number one marine systems supplier in the world.

Rolls-Royce has won over 23 Queen's Awards for innovation and for export, including in 1998 being the first company to win awards in all three categories in a single year.

In addition, the Trent engine family is now the market leading large engine for the new generation of airliners. The Trent 800 powers the Boeing 777, while the Trent 700 powers the Airbus A330 and the Trent 500 has recently entered service on the long-range Airbus A340. The latest Trent, the '900' is in development for the new double-decker Airbus A380 and has already secured a major share of the market for powering this aircraft.

In the defence aerospace business Rolls-Royce is part of major new programmes such as Eurofighter and the US/UK Joint Strike Fighter aircraft which has a requirement for up to 3,000 airframes.

History

The names Rolls and Royce could hardly flow together more appropriately, however when the two men first met 100 years ago in May 1904, one would not have thought of them naturally as business partners. Rolls was the Hon Charles S Rolls, the son of a wealthy landowner and Henry Royce was the hard working, brilliant engineer who came from a very humble background.

Rolls was looking for a British engineer who could build him the best car in the world and Royce was looking for a partner who could help him bring his car and his talents to market.

The car business was of course how it all started and from where the reputation of the company was formed but it was not long before the major part of the company's work turned to air power. In World War I the country turned to its most talented engineers to make the first aero engines and of course Royce was among them.

The Rolls-Royce name was subsequently linked to many of the great air

World-leading integrated marine systems.

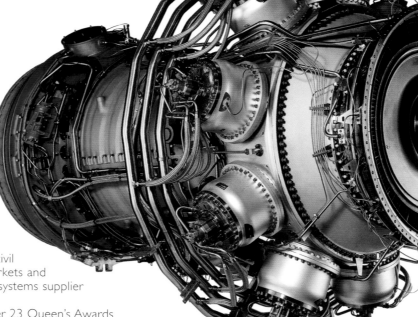

achievements of the last 100 years. Famously, the Merlin engine for the Spitfire and working with Sir Frank Whittle to develop the first jet engine, the Welland. Rolls-Royce also went on to power the Comet, the world's first commercial jet aircraft, then came others such as the world's only vertical take-off aircraft, the Harrier. A Rolls-Royce engine powered Concorde, the TriStar, the Boeing 747 and many others up to the current, most modern airliners. Today the company is one of only three major aero engine makers in the world, the other two being based in the US.

As for the car, it has not been made by Rolls-Royce plc since 1971. It had a long period of ownership under Vickers but more recently the BMW Group has acquired the rights to use the brand in the automotive industry and in 2003 launched its new version of the Rolls-Royce car, The Phantom.

Product

The core product in each market sector is the gas turbine. This is a compact power unit which can be used in different applications. The company philosophy is to design and develop once, and use many times. Therefore if an engine is first developed for powering an aircraft it may also be converted for use in the marine market or for producing environmental and efficient electricity. Aero derived gas turbines produce enormous power from relatively small units and so are attractive for offshore oil and gas platforms or for power stations where they can be built easily and cost-effectively on relatively small plots of land.

Recent Developments

The Trent family of large aircraft engines is utilising core technology for use in all major new air frame

programmes, ensuring that the brand's customers are offered the choice of Rolls-Royce, whenever they buy new aircraft.

The power behind 160 of the world's armed forces is evidence of the brand's strong position in the Defence aerospace market, and its unrivalled experience in vertical take-off technology is establishing its position on the major future development programmes, including the F-35 Joint Strike Fighter.

Rolls-Royce is the world's largest supplier of integrated marine systems and as such, the goal is to continue to build a complete solution capability. Its marine technology is used in all aspects of marine application, in civil and military vessels, and the adoption of its aerospace technology in large scale marine propulsion units is further enhancing the brand's reputation for providing proven reliable power solutions.

Furthermore the adaptation of the Rolls-Royce gas turbine technology in the energy market is providing more opportunity for realising the potential of its core capability. Gas turbines are used to generate electricity or for power on offshore oil and gas platforms.

In all of its markets Rolls-Royce continues to embody its reputation for embracing innovation and pursuing new areas of development. The presence of its brand values, namely reliability, integrity and innovation, in all that Rolls-Royce does, ensures that its reputation for striving for the excellent standards remains a goal for the company.

Rolls-Royce believes that its founders would be proud that the company bearing their name is taking their traditions of quality to new levels today and looking forward to the future. What started as two men with a vision, has now become a multi-billion pound organisation, which despite its size, appreciates the values that are core to the brand. To quote Henry Royce, "Small things make perfection, yet perfection is no small thing".

In 2004, Rolls-Royce will be celebrating a century of innovation, from the time the company's founders first met.

Promotion

The Rolls-Royce name is synonymous with quality, it always has been, and with good reason. With the car being a consumer brand, it is inevitable that there is confusion between this and Rolls-Royce plc. The challenge therefore in its promotion is not to build awareness of the name, after all, it is one of the most recognisable marques in the world, but instead to ensure the goodwill and credibility that is associated with the name is present in all of the company's current and future activities. The proven heritage of Rolls-Royce is no substitute for its need to deliver to its customers day by day. The brand believes that it is vital not to rely on its past achievements to secure its future success.

Consistency is key to all of the brand's promotional activity. Its single brand strategy ensures that confusion of the name is minimised and the impact of its messages is maximised.

The target audiences of Rolls-Royce are extremely small for a company so large. There are only 500 airlines in the world who are potential customers, therefore the brand's best form of marketing is direct marketing. And it is very direct – face-to-face meetings are held in order to build strong, trusting relationships and develop customer solutions which are bespoke to individual requirements. In the marine area, commercial customers are spread throughout the world and although they have different product requirements, they demand similar assurances. In the defence and energy activity Rolls-Royce operates with government agencies and military offices, which poses different requirements and often unique approaches.

Therefore, the messages are seen by a succinct audience, who require assurances throughout the product life. The brand's communications always try to be transparent, open and above all honest in order to maintain the brand's image as a knowledgeable, professional and accurate organisation.

As an employer of over 37,000 people worldwide, Rolls-Royce also appreciates its responsibilities to the communities within which it operates. A programme of regional development and participation in many community activities is its way of building lasting relationships with communities and expressing its gratitude for the help that they provide to its facilities.

With such targeted audiences, Rolls-Royce does not pursue mass media promotional campaigns. Trade and regional advertising campaigns reinforce the brand messages, with sponsorship and donations emphasising the brand's commitment to providing help and assistance where it can.

Brand Values

The brand values of Rolls-Royce, reliability, integrity and innovation, help guide its operations and activities and provide a conscience that demands the extra effort that its customers expect. These values are present in all that the brand does and drives it forward in the never-ending quest for excellence. The organisation is positioned under the brand message, 'Trusted to deliver excellence'. The pedigree and success of Rolls-Royce has been underpinned by this ethos.

As previous generations have done before, Rolls-Royce is cautious not to dilute its effect. The company does not use sub-brands and product brands. The brand message is clear and concise, and all its products and subsidiary companies benefit from the values that are inherent throughout the company.

www.rolls-royce.com

The best reason in the world for choosing a window seat.

Every day the Rolls-Royce name is a welcome sight to millions of airline passengers all over the world. For our customers we provide the most advanced engines available, powering the widest range of commercial aircraft. The unparalleled performance and reliability of our engines is key to our growing customer base of more than 500 airlines, including 39 of the world's top 50. We also power 4,000 corporate and utility aircraft and helicopter operators and 160 armed forces. A truly global company that is built on reliability, integrity and innovation, the best reasons for choosing Rolls-Royce. **Trusted to deliver excellence**

www.rolls-royce.com

 Rolls-Royce

Market

Royal Mail has a massive and diverse customer base – every single person in the UK who sends or receives something in the post is a customer of Royal Mail.

The brand operates in the market for distribution of physical text and packages for non-guaranteed and express delivery. Both markets are growing with volumes rising 1-4% each year dependent on sector. Around 90% of mail originates from businesses and the majority is sent to consumers. Of the various applications for which mail is used, financial transactions are the biggest in terms of volume, followed by Direct Mail (which is also the strongest growth area for mail) and goods distribution.

The market is currently undergoing massive change. Alternative media, such as fax, email and mobile phones, have created significant competition in the letter and packet delivery sector. Developments in e-commerce in recent years have also changed the distribution market.

External factors such as globalisation, the advent of the regulator and European cross-border mail liberalisation are shaping the marketplace and demanding that Royal Mail adapts to meet the changing needs of current and future customers. Most of the UK market will be opened up by 2004, several years ahead of the rest of Europe. The regulator has announced plans to abolish all restrictions on market entry by April 2007.

As well as Royal Mail's core market in the UK, it also has an international customer base. As one of the world's largest carriers of international mail, Royal Mail despatches mail on over 1,400 scheduled flights every week to over 280 postal gateways worldwide.

Achievements

Royal Mail's greatest achievement is the way in which it collects, sorts and delivers the nation's mail in a 24-hour process, which continues all year round. Royal Mail consistently delivers nine out of ten First Class letters the day after posting.

Less well known is Royal Mail's capability in warehousing and customer return logistics where its services are state-of-the-art. Up to 35,000 bar-coded items can be picked, packed and dispatched daily enabling business customers to realise the cash tied up in the customer returns channel.

The opening of the world's most technically advanced international mail centre in early 2004 puts Royal Mail in a strong position. The new centre is situated five minutes from Heathrow airport. At an investment of £150 million, the 'art mail centre' is a 24-hour, 365-day operation and can process ten million letters and packets a day.

In 2002, following the success of the 2001 £1 million First Class Christmas promotion, Royal Mail developed a campaign leveraging the scale and topicality of 'The Lord of the Rings: The Two Towers' film property. This was the first

time that Royal Mail had partnered with such a big entertainment property. The objective was simple: to stimulate more people to buy more First Class Christmas stamp books. Christmas stamp sales (measured over November and December) have increased by £19 million+ during the last two years, generating incremental sales in what was previously a static market.

Keen to maintain mail's position as the third largest advertising media, Royal Mail has set up the Mail Media Centre, a one-stop shop for advertisers, offering specialist information, help and advice on the development and use of direct mail. Royal Mail is a partner in the Postal Preference Service which helps improve

the targeting of mail. Response uplifts of between 20-400% have been achieved using this data compared with traditional lifestyle data files.

In response to customers' preferences, self-adhesive stamps have now been rolled out in First and Second class stamp books across the

UK, combining stamp manufacturing technology with the distinctive values of the traditional postage stamp.

History

Royal Mail is one of the most trusted brands in the UK. It is a valuable asset which has evolved and grown since 1635 when the service of accepting and handling mail by the Royal Posts was opened to the public by Charles I. This royal proclamation and the establishment of the General Post Office in 1660 began the crucial social change which put the postal service at the centre of the community and heralded a communications revolution. Letters were originally collected from households and handed to the local postmaster. Occasionally he would arrange onward delivery, but this was not granted to all until Queen Victoria's Jubilee Declaration in 1897. This face-to-face contact began the relationship for which Royal Mail is well known today.

The awareness of Royal Mail grew considerably once the Mail Coach service was introduced in 1784, launching the national postal network. New postal routes were opened and mail volumes increased dramatically with the introduction of the uniform postage rate in 1840. The first road-side post boxes were introduced in 1852. The 150th anniversary of post boxes was commemorated in 2002 with a set of special stamps featuring post boxes from the 1930s and 1960s.

Around the middle of the nineteenth century, mail carriages began to use the words 'Royal Mail' for the first time alongside the Royal cypher. The term 'Royal Mail' is steeped in history and has been in use since the seventeenth century, but Royal Mail has only been established as a business since 1986 with its own identity following three years later. The Cruciform logo now used includes the royal crowns – St Edward's for England and Wales and St James's for Scotland. Stamps, postmen and postwomen, vans and postboxes continue to symbolise the Royal Mail brand. Its heritage provides a solid foundation for what is now the most far-reaching communications network in the UK.

Product

Royal Mail's core offering centres around a range of physical distribution products for both consumers and businesses, as well as an increasing portfolio of electronic and internet solutions.

Mail is increasingly used as part of the business communications mix to attract customers and nurture business relationships as well as strengthening brands. A range of services is available to business customers, including Mailsort, Presstream, Packetpost and Special Delivery and significant savings can be made on standard postal rates depending on how the customer pre-sorts mailings.

Despite the advent of fax, telephone and internet, direct mail volumes continue to grow strongly and now represent nearly 14% of all advertising revenues. Royal Mail's direct marketing products aim to transform the way businesses advertise using the mail by making it easier for them to price, plan and control their mailings. There are also a range of tools available online at www.royalmail.com/dmonline to help smaller businesses with their mailing campaigns.

Royal Mail Stamps are renowned for their patronage of both English art and design and design in general. Stamp collecting remains a popular pastime and a way of collecting a little bit of history. One of the most popular new ranges of Special Stamps is known as 'Smilers', which can be personalised with a photograph printed alongside the stamp to celebrate a variety of occasions. The new range of stamps for 2004 includes, Classic Locomotives, Lord of the Rings and Royal Society of Arts.

Recent Developments

In common with all industries, the distribution market has been significantly affected by the opportunities represented by e-commerce. Royal Mail has seized these opportunities and developed a presence in this marketplace. In a nation with a relatively high internet penetration, Royal Mail has maintained an extremely high level of growth through its activities.

Royal Mail is working closely with a number of online businesses, most notably Amazon.co.uk, eBay and bol.com, for whom it is the contracted delivery arm. Online retailers face the challenge of creating a real brand in an e-world and this is where Royal Mail can add value to the experience of many brands by becoming the trusted carrier for online customer orders.

Royal Mail is investing a great deal in its flagship product, Special Delivery. The product offering has recently been expanded to include a guaranteed by 9am delivery, complimenting the already established guaranteed by twelve noon service. Independent research conducted by NOP confirms that, Special Delivery has been proven to continually beat other courier services on both price and reliability. A collection on demand service has also been introduced for all UK businesses.

One of Royal Mail's newest products, SmartStamp, is a new online service that generates postage electronically from a personal computer that can be printed directly on to envelopes or labels. There is also space next to the postage impression where a company logo or an image can be included giving the opportunity to apply brand or add advertising messages to their mail. SmartStamp offers a more convenient and efficient way to deal with mail, and from the comfort of an office.

In the biggest shake-up of delivery services for many years, Royal Mail is introducing the national roll-out of a single delivery every day across the UK which will mean one million more First Class letters should hit their delivery target every week. Business customers will be able to have their mail delivered from 6am with the

Timed Delivery Service. Royal Mail is also planning to trial other variations to its standard delivery service including the choice of re-delivery in the evening or an option to collect mail from delivery offices.

Promotion

Much of the continued growth in mail volumes is attributed to a carefully planned and well executed marketing communications strategy. Even though the Royal Mail brand is one of the most well known in the UK, it does not rely on this alone to ensure continued growth. Good marketing communications help strengthen the brand and enable reinforcement of the core brand essence of 'reach'. Promotional activity spans both businesses and consumers and actively seeks to guide customers through the many mailing options available.

For consumers, promotions focus on useful information such as how to find the correct postcode and the latest recommended posting dates for Christmas. Sales promotions encourage active participation using innovative techniques which engage the nation.

For Christmas 2002, the First Class promotion was based on a partnership with the feature film 'The Lord of the Rings: The Two Towers'. This high profile partnership saw Royal Mail venture into the world of movies for the first time. The promotion offered customers buying books of First Class Christmas stamps the opportunity to 'Find the One Ring and Win £1 million'.

For Christmas 2003, Royal Mail linked up with TV production company Celador International Ltd to use its 'Who Wants To Be A Millionaire?' property to deliver a £1 million promotion. Customers received a scratch card with every purchase of twelve First Class Christmas stamps, instantly finding out whether they have the chance to win one of a number of cash prizes, including the £1 million top prize.

In 2002 a new management team took responsibility for what is arguably the biggest corporate turnaround in British industry and as a result will be developing as a true service brand driven by its people.

A key element in this strategy was the marketing, which needed to tap into the latent goodwill towards the brand and turn it into an active choice for both business customers and the general public.

The first step on this journey was in October 2003, to launch a new campaign across all media, with the aim of refreshing the Royal Mail brand and reasserting the spirit of how the brand does business.

The advertising campaign focused on the dedication of the Royal Mail postmen and women, and the approach they take to their work, summed up by the advertising endline 'with us it's personal'.

The campaign incorporates Special Delivery, Royal Mail's hero product, which benefits from its own commercial, focusing on the new 9am service. The new service was also announced and supported by a through the line campaign.

Recognising the importance of new media, Royal Mail continues to develop its online presence in line with customer needs. The site has consistently achieved industry recognition as a well designed and customer focused site. It provides online information about products and services, as well as interactive services. 'Postcode Finder' allows customers to type in an address which then displays the relevant postcode.

Brand Values

The essence of the Royal Mail brand is built on reach. This is firmly rooted in the fact that Royal Mail has the most far-reaching network in the UK. Only Royal Mail reaches 99% of UK addresses every day. It reaches deep inside businesses and targets exactly the right customers.

The most important capability within Royal Mail's brand essence is its human reach. Royal Mail is a people business whose primary aim is to enable physical communications with other people. On behalf of businesses, it is in touch, in person, every day, everywhere.

The personality of the brand is straightforward, human and bold. Royal Mail is supremely confident in its ability as postal communications market leader and strives to build relationships with its customers which are responsive, co-operative and flexible. Royal Mail believes that its people live the brand by taking pride in their personal concern for the collection and delivery of mail.

www.royalmail.com

Market

In today's hi-tech world, electronic goods seem to help us with everything we do at home and at work. The companies that help us function in this technology-led society have become global giants, but the balance of power is shifting.

Samsung Electronics, the flagship of the wider Samsung Group (which is also active in areas as diverse as finance, chemicals and heavy industry), is currently one of the biggest and fastest-growing electronics companies in the world.

Established as the world's largest memory chip-maker (with a 32% market share), its DRAM chips are the most widely used computer-memory chips in the world. It is the market leader in a host of other areas, such as thin film transistor liquid crystal displays (TFT-LCD), colour monitors for TVs and computers, video recorders, microwave ovens and CDMA hand-held phones.

Samsung is now also a major manufacturer of mobile handsets. In 2001, it overtook Siemens to become the world's third largest mobile phone manufacturer, behind Nokia and Motorola. When it comes to DVD players, Samsung is striving to supplant Sony as the market leader. According to the Financial Times' survey of the world's largest companies, Samsung is already ahead of Sony in terms of capital value with a market capitalisation of US$40.4 billion, compared to US$33.7 billion for Sony.

It is just as well that Samsung is broadening its range of expertise, as the line between conventional electronics, telecommunications, entertainment and the internet is increasingly blurred. This radically changes the market landscape for Samsung and its closest competitors.

Achievements

From its modest beginnings in 1938 as a provincial 'general store', Samsung has evolved into Korea's most profitable enterprise and a pioneer in global industries such as semiconductors, digital media, telecommunications, consumer goods, shipbuilding and heavy equipment.

A stunningly successful policy of shedding its 'cheap brand' image and moving upmarket into higher-end products with an emphasis on stylish design and cutting-edge technology, Samsung has become the recent success story not only of the global electronics industry, but international business as a whole. In 2003, its brand value reached US$10.8 billion and it was recognised by Interbrand as the world's fastest-growing global brand.

While the electronics industries of Europe, the US and Japan are in decline, with factory closures and job losses, Korea's – driven by Samsung – is thriving. In 2002, the company tripled its profit compared to the previous year, to US$5.8 billon. This is an astonishing recovery. In 1997, in the midst of the Asian economic crisis, Samsung made a profit of just US$131 million. At the time, Korea's economy was in serious trouble, but now Samsung's success epitomises the recovery of Korea itself.

The company's amazing turnaround has earned it the respect of the global business community. Samsung Electronics was by far the best Korean company in the first annual Investor Relations Magazine Asia Awards and it came a close second to Sony in the category of best Asia Pacific company in the US at the Investor Relations Magazine US Awards 2002.

A survey by PricewaterhouseCoopers of over 1,000 top executives revealed that Samsung was the world's third most respected company in the electronics sector, the 42nd most respected company overall, and Samsung's chairman, Lee Kun-Hee, was voted the 32nd most respected business leader in the world.

Samsung's products have also won plaudits. Most recently, the company received five design awards in the annual Business Week IDEA Design Awards. It was also recently named Best Mobile Manufacturer in the UK Mobile News Awards.

History

Samsung's history dates back to 1938 when 'Samsung General Stores' opened in North Kyungsang Province, Korea. It continued in this trade business until the 1950s, when it became a producer of basic commodities such as sugar and wool and also diversified into the insurance business.

In the 1960s, Samsung became one of the first Korean companies to expand overseas as it broadened its manufacturing business to include paper and fertiliser. It also strengthened its retail operations and insurance operations and moved into the communications sector, establishing a newspaper and broadcasting company.

Substantial investment was made in the company during the 1970s, which proved crucial in shaping the present-day Samsung. It moved into the semi-conductor, information and telecommunication industries, and also into heavy manufacturing, by venturing into shipbuilding, construction and aircraft manufacturing.

In 1987, the current chairman, Kun-Hee Lee took charge of the company. He set about fundamentally changing the management philosophy of the company in order to keep up with the rapidly changing global economy. The company's rigid hierarchy was dismantled, making it more responsive, streamlined, globally focused and responsive to the needs of the market.

Today, the group's core businesses are electronics, finance and trade and services. It has more than 285 overseas operations in 67 countries.

Product

Samsung is divided into several different subsidiaries with different specialisations. The best-known and most profitable part of the Group is Samsung Electronics, established in 1969 and which

Flawless refrigeration

Side-by-side refrigeration with unique CoolSelect Zone™ from Samsung

DigitAll *accessories for the home*

SAMSUNG DIGITall
everyone's invited™

DigitAll *temptation*

Samsung widescreen TFT-LCD flat panel television

SAMSUNG DIGITall
everyone's invited™

now employs 63,000 people in 47 countries. It manufactures a wide range of products, including audio/visual, computer-related and telecommunication products, such as mobile phone handsets, monitors, memory chips and VCRs.

Another unit, Samsung SDI, is a global leader in digital and mobile display technology, manufacturing items such as cathode ray tubes, liquid crystal displays and plasma display panels. With the growing popularity of flat TFT screens for personal computers and audio-visual displays, this latter area is of increasing importance for the company. South Korea is now the world's biggest producer of TFT-LCD displays, thanks to the efforts of Samsung and competitors also making them in the country, such as LG Philips.

Samsung's TFT-LCD displays are among the company's impressive portfolio of 'world-best' products – namely those with a market-leading position in their sector. Others include DRAM chips, the most widely used computer memory chips in the world. Samsung's SRAM chips (ideal for portable computers and mobile phones) are also market leaders.

Other world-best products include Samsung's CDMA mobile phone handset – the smallest, lightest and most compact on the market – and its range of VCRs, microwave ovens, floppy disk drives and colour monitors.

Some of the lesser-known areas in which Samsung has also built market leadership include industrial solvents (made by Samsung Fine Chemicals) and flame-retardant resin, used in a variety of applications, including automotive, toys and cameras.

Samsung hopes to extend this list of seventeen world-best products to 30 by 2005. Doing this will require continued investment in R&D – a dedication to which has long been a hallmark of the company's success. In 2002, Samsung invested US$2.4 billion in R&D, equating to approximately 7% of its revenue. The focus of this huge programme is centred in six research centres located in Korea and a further nine worldwide. Some 17,000 researchers – 34% of Samsung's total workforce – work to ensure Samsung's remains at the forefront of innovation.

Recent Developments

In June 2003, Samsung Electronics announced a US$16.75 billion plan to build a new plant to make flat panel displays for computer monitors and televisions.

The investment demonstrates Samsung's desire to increase its share of the fast-growing global market for TFT-LCD displays.

The new factory in Asan, 80km south of Seoul, will take seven years to complete and will increase Samsung's number of TFT-LCD production lines from six to eleven.

The project is the latest in a series of heavy investments by Samsung. It is also aggressively working to boost its share of the mobile phone, introducing a host of exciting new products, such as a new camera phone introduced into the UK in January 2003 featuring a unique swivel lens. In Korea, Samsung recently introduced a 'TV phone', allowing users to view real-time TV broadcasts on their handsets.

Other recent product launches include the Samsung X10 laptop PC. This ultra thin DVD/CDRW notebook has a battery life of up to 4.5 hours, weighs only 1.8kg and is 23.8/28.3mm thin.

Promotion

As well as a focus on R&D and product design, Samsung can also thank its investment in marketing for its stunning turnaround of recent years. Three years ago, Eric Kim was appointed EVP Global Marketing and set on a mission to change the world's perception of Samsung's products, from cheap and cheerful to premium, desirable and cutting-edge. Some US$400 million has been invested in global marketing campaigns to communicate Samsung's new positioning, based around the company's promise to provide a 'DigitAll Experience'. According to Kim, this new emphasis on marketing illustrates the company's first attempt to be at the leading edge, rather than following its competitors.

The policy has paid off, with the value of the Samsung brand rising from US$3.2 billion in 1999 to US$10.8 billion in 2003.

In 2003 Samsung embarked on its biggest ever single concerted marketing campaign. The brand worked closely with Warner Bros to promote the film Matrix Reloaded. Marketing support for up to six different products stretched across sixteen European countries, both above and below-the-line work was carried out with a consistent theme. In a three month period, US$50 million was invested in the Matrix Reloaded marketing campaign and globally, a total in excess of US$100 million was spent.

Brand Values

Samsung's current slogan, 'DigitAll – everyone's invited', aims to communicate the inclusivity that is at the essence of the Samsung brand. It is a brand that is at the epicentre of the digital revolution, enabling people to make the most of what the combined technologies of the internet, telecommunications and audio/visual have to offer.

Featuring the best in product design and technological innovation, Samsung aims to inspire the 'wow' factor in anyone that encounters its products. The personality of the brand is as an explorer, leading the way in digital convergence.

www.samsungelectronics.co.uk

Market

Adhesive tape is often associated with the home and office where products like Sellotape Original are commonplace. However the adhesive tape market has grown and now encompasses applications specially developed for the DIY and industrial markets.

Demand for natural adhesives, including tape, continues to increase because of a growing environmental consciousness among manufacturers with a desire to conserve resources and to use renewable raw materials where this is economically viable.

The total European clear sticky tape market is worth an estimated US$335 million annually, with the Sellotape brand recognised in all sectors. The brand's competitors include 'own brand' tapes that have increased in numbers over recent years.

Achievements

Sellotape was launched in the stationery sector in the 1930s. Such is the brand's success that the word 'Sellotape' has been synonymous with clear adhesive tape for generations. Furthermore, the product even has its own entry in the Oxford English Dictionary.

Consumer awareness of the brand is very strong. In the UK where Sellotape enjoys 89% spontaneous recognition as a brand of clear tape, research has found that seven out of ten consumers claim that they would buy Sellotape in preference to other brands of sticky tape (Source: RSG Marketing Research 2003). Additionally, the brand is the favourite cellulose tape throughout Europe and it is the clear brand leader in New Zealand and number two in South Africa.

Sellotape film is biodegradable and has received an environmental award from the British Office Systems and Stationery Federation (BOSSF) every year since 1996. The company's emphasis on performance measurement has earned it supplier accolades from ASDA Walmart, Homebase and Kingfield Health.

The company has also won a Good Sales Promotion Award in the B2B category for its National Lottery promotion.

History

The earliest reference to tape can be found in Thomas Mace's Musick's Monument published in 1676 where lute makers used 'little pieces of paper, so big as pence or two pences, wet with glew' to hold the thin strips of sycamore in place during construction of their musical instruments.

The first use of 'pressure sensitive' tape, which is how Sellotape Original is described can be found in 1845 in a US patent taken out by Shecut and Day where a natural rubber, pressure sensitive adhesive was used in the manufacture of sticking plasters.

In the midst of the American Civil War, it is known that sticky bandages were first used.

However, real progress was not made in this field until the mid 1920s when Henry Ford pioneered the industrial uses of adhesive tapes. Masking tapes were used in the spray-painting process, where different coloured cars – aside from the ubiquitous black of the time – were assembled.

The Sellotape brand dates back to 1937 when Colin Kininmonth and George Gray coated cellophane film with a natural rubber

resin, creating a 'sticky tape' product which had been based on a French patent. They registered their product under the name 'Sellotape'. Manufacturing soon commenced in Acton, West London.

On the outbreak of hostilities in 1939 the company was put on war work and made cellulose tape for sealing ration and first aid packs and a cloth tape for sealing ammunition boxes. A product was also developed for covering windows as protection from shattering glass.

In the mid 1960s Sellotape became part of the British paper and packaging conglomerate, Dickinson Robinson Group (DRG). In the late 1990s DRG was broken up and the transformation of Sellotape began. Sellotape was restructured and

investment in new plant and systems followed. In 1995 the brand was relaunched and the company started to expand and extend its product portfolio to new sectors with offerings such as the Sellotape Office.

Today, Sellotape products are highly popular and used widely in offices and homes worldwide. It is sold in a wide variety of retail outlets from corner shops and post offices to high street stationers and DIY stores as well as through mail order stationery company's which specifically target the office market.

Sellotape is a truly international brand and is a registered trademark in 119 countries with manufacturing sites in Europe and Asia Pacific. In 2002 the company was purchased by Henkel Consumer Adhesives, part of the Henkel Group which employs 50,000 people worldwide. Henkel brands and technologies are available in 126 countries and operates in three strategic business areas – Adhesives, Sealants & Surface Treatments, Home Care and Personal Care.

Product

Sellotape Original is Europe's biggest selling clear cellulose pressure sensitive tape. A pressure sensitive tape is defined as any adhesive tape that will stick to a variety of clean dry surfaces, requiring only a minimum amount of pressure being applied. Other properties are that it is ready to use and does not need to be activated by water, a solvent or heat.

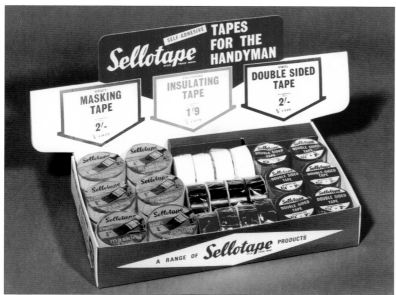

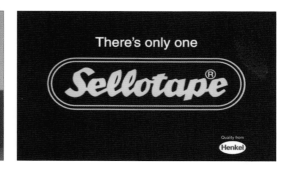

This kind of tape consists of a relatively thin flexible backing or carrier, coated with an adhesive that is permanently sticky at room temperature. The tapes can be manufactured with adhesive coating on one or both sides of the carrier.

Sellotape Original contains the only completely biodegradable film in the European market. It is made from cellulose a natural wood pulp product. Its natural origins provide a number of intrinsic benefits over rival products which make it naturally static-free for no tangle handling as well as making it easy to tear by hand.

Constant innovation has resulted in extensive development of both the consumer and office product ranges beyond the clear sticky tape with which the Sellotape brand is identified.

The Sellotape range has been expanded in recent years to include tapes for a variety of jobs. Products such as Invisible, Double Sided and Sticky Hook & Loop give consumers a wider range of solutions to their needs.

The company has carried out extensive research to design a range of more than 70 products to suit every 'sticky' need around the home, office, garage and garden with applications as diverse as binding books to repairing a broken hose.

Despite wide awareness, the brand has never been complacent and has kept abreast of the latest trends and technological developments, and now that it is part of the Henkel portfolio the brand can expect even more support and New Product Development (NPD). It is clear that the strength of the brand is fast becoming as significant for the business sector as it is for the domestic market.

The 'Sellotape Office' brand provides a range which targets the needs of the office market including the 'Small Office Home Office' (Soho) sector with new products packaged with upbeat graphics and a creative promotional programme.

Sellotape has expanded its product range beyond actual tape with a range of innovative tape dispensers. The New Wave dispenser, for example, allows the user to dispense and cut tape in one, while the fashionable chrome dispensers provide a stylish and useful desk accessory. One of Sellotape's recent successes has been in Hook & Loop products, as this area has witnessed real growth. These include Sticky Fixer, double sided foam pads and strips which provide a swift and easy way to display and hang objects.

Recent Developments

Sellotape continues to innovate. In 2003 it introduced Spellotape, a funky purple adhesive tape printed with creative words designed to get children's imaginations flowing. The new tape, offered with blister packs of Sellotape Original, is suitable for pencil cases or even the kitchen draw.

Promotion

In April 2003 the brand returned to television after a 25 year absence to reinforce its position as the UK's best known sticky tape brand. The campaign took advantage of Sellotape's generic status to remind consumers to look out for and choose the brand. In the commercial a mind reader tells viewers he is about to show them an object and then asks them to describe it with the first words that spring to mind. He holds up a roll of sticky tape for a few seconds before telling his audience: "I know what you're thinking." The ad closes with a pack shot and the endline 'There's only one Sellotape'.

Innovative and creative promotional concepts have become central to Sellotape's marketing strategy, with the aim of adding value to the brand and generating customer demand.

In the commercial stationery market the company often runs promotional campaigns to support its trade customers, encouraging office staff to specify Sellotape as their preferred office tape.

The brand's biggest office promotion, which launched in autumn 2003, featured £38,000 worth of prizes including luxury safari holidays and spa weekends. The promotion on four packs of Sellotape Original featured a 'savannah' or grassy plain with hidden products. Buyers were instructed to 'text to win' by sending the co-ordinates of the hidden prize on the map, plus the individual pack number.

This kind of support activity enables Sellotape to sell at premium prices and generate strong sales for its trade customers. Indeed, EPOS data shows that Sellotape promotional packs achieve the highest stock turns of any supermarket stationery product and are among the highest of any non-food product during the Christmas period.

Brand Values

Sellotape products are high quality, reliable, efficient and very solution oriented. The brand's success attests to the fact that a distinct and honest proposition can enjoy long term popularity with the consumer and build itself a prestigious, highly valued brand name that produces high customer loyalty.

Sellotape's customer service is also taken very seriously. Delivery performance is measured weekly and monthly in several operating countries to ensure targets are met.

www.sellotape.co.uk

Things you didn't know about
Sellotape

Sellotape was first launched into the stationery trade in the 1930s.

Devised in conjunction with teachers, the Sellotape Education Pack has been designed to stimulate discussion and learning amongst Key Stage Two pupils about the importance of the environmental responsibility and sustainability.

Sellotape was among the emergency implements used to save a passenger's life in an emergency mid-air operation between Hong Kong and London.

The amount of Sellotape Original rolls sold each year is enough to stretch to the moon and back.

Market

Shell operates in a massive, global energy industry that does not involve oil alone but also natural gas and coal (although Shell does not produce coal). These three sources together provide around 85% of all the energy we consume. According to the World Energy Council, global demand for energy will double by 2020, driven by increased consumption in the developing economies of Latin America and Asia.

Natural gas has become a major energy source in homes and businesses throughout Britain and now supplies around one third of the UK's total energy needs. Demand for gas is already growing rapidly, up 75% in just the last decade, due to increasing use in electricity generation.

Oil is the biggest energy source, driving an industry worth over £500 billion in annual revenues and there is certainly no sign of a slackening in the demand for motor fuel. According to a recent report by Mintel, in the UK alone, there are now 25.9 million privately owned cars. And the car still remains the most popular way to travel, with the average UK citizen notching up 5,354 miles per year by automobile, compared with only 368 miles by train.

Oil and gas will inevitably play an important role in meeting the world's energy demands in the future, but other fuels are emerging. Renewable energy sources including solar, hydrogen and wind power will be part of the long-term solution. Shell is committed to exploring all of these options.

Achievements

From humble beginnings as a nineteenth century business in London, importing oriental seashells, Shell has developed into one of the world's biggest brands. It is a global group of energy and petrochemicals companies, operating in over 145 countries and employing more than 115,000 people. In 2002 it had earnings of US$9.2 billion.

Shell is one of the most instantly recognisable brand identities in the world, recently voted the sixth most influential logo of the last century by the FT. The famous pecten seashell image has become so familiar that, in 1999, the company decided that this should stand alone as the symbol of the brand, without the need to incorporate the word 'Shell' itself.

Building a brand like this demands extraordinary achievements. For example, Shell has invested over £10 billion in oil and gas exploration and production facilities since the North Sea fields became active in the 1960s. The development of the Brent oil

field, the biggest discovery in the UK sector of the North Sea, is acknowledged to be one of the greatest technical feats of British private enterprise.

Shell has also led the way in being more accountable to society for its actions. Following widely reported controversies in the early 1990s, a top to bottom re-engineering of the business around the three dimensions of financial, environmental and social performance was initiated in 1998 and communicated in a worldwide programme called Profits and Principles. The results of this activity show how effectively Shell has changed. In 1997, a MORI poll gave Shell a favourability rating of 48% among global opinion formers, with 40% expressing a neutral view and 12% being negative. By 1999, the former figure had jumped to 69% with just 23% remaining neutral.

The company is also a leader in the search for sustainable energy sources to supplement and replace oil and natural gas, and has committed billions of dollars to solar, wind and hydrogen energy research. In 2002, Shell was ranked top of the energy sector in the Dow Jones Sustainability Index.

History

Shell's origins go back to 1833, when Marcus Samuel opened a small shop in London's East End dealing in antiques, curios and oriental seashells. His trade in shells – a fashionable item in Victorian households – became so profitable that he set up regular shipments from the Far East. Before long this had turned into a general import-export business.

The connection with oil was not established until early 1890, when Marcus Samuel Jr started

exporting kerosene to the Far East, sending the world's first oil tanker through the Suez Canal. Samuel named the kerosene 'Shell' in recognition of his father's original business. In 1897, Samuel named his enterprise Shell Transport and Trading Company and chose a pecten seashell emblem to give the name visual emphasis.

In 1907, Shell Transport merged with a Dutch rival also active in the Far East – Royal Dutch Petroleum – forming the group of companies still known as Shell today. Gradually an international network of oil exploration, production and marketing facilities was established and the advent of the motor

car literally fuelled Shell's growth for decades to come.

By the late 1950s, oil had become the world's major energy resource. Supply and demand both boomed, and during this period Shell supplied almost one seventh of the world's oil products. During the 1960s, there was a similar boom in the market for natural gas, leading to the exploration and production of natural gas in the North Sea. Shell also started diversifying into a new growth area – producing chemicals from petroleum products. Over the next twenty years, its chemical product range grew enormously, and manufacturing plants were established in 30 locations around the world.

Product

Shell's core businesses are Exploration and Production, Oil Products, Chemicals, Gas and Power, Renewables and Hydrogen.

Shell's Exploration and Production companies have interests and ventures in over 40 countries. One of them, Shell Expro, managing Shell's exploration and production activities in the North Sea, produces over 500,000 barrels of oil a day and has been a leader in developing the UK's oil and gas reserves for over 30 years. It has created an extensive infrastructure in the North Sea, producing 21% of the country's oil and 13% of its gas.

A key feature of Shell Gas and Power is its pioneering development of the global liquefied natural gas (LNG) industry, in which it has a leading market position. Gas is the cleanest hydrocarbon fuel and is used extensively in electricity production, and as an industrial and domestic fuel.

Shell's Oil Products companies operate in almost all countries in which Shell has a presence, and provide the primary point of contact with Shell's customers, whether consumers or businesses. Its Retail business, for example, has 55,000 Shell service stations, making it the largest and most widespread single brand retailer in the world.

Oil Products encompasses all the activities that transform crude oil into Shell products for customers. It has an interest in more than 50 refineries worldwide and markets fuels for the automotive, aviation and marine sectors, along with heating oils, industrial and consumer lubricants, speciality products such as bitumen and liquid petroleum gas (LPG) and technical services – all massive businesses in their own right. Shell Aviation, for example, provides fuel, technical and financing solutions for the aviation transport sector globally. It has been a major supplier of fuel, lubricants and technical services to the aviation industry since the earliest days of flight, and has recently been awarded Armbrust 'World's Best Jet Fuel Marketer' for the third time in five years.

Shell Chemicals carries out the chemicals operations of the Royal Dutch/Shell Group, with a multi-billion dollar annual turnover and significant investments in manufacturing assets around the world – both direct and through joint ventures. The end products of the petrochemicals industry are everywhere – in homes, shops, work places, schools, cars, boats and planes. Such petrochemicals have transformed countless aspects of the modern world.

Shell Renewables and Shell Hydrogen are both small, but fast-growing businesses investing in making renewable and lower-carbon energy sources competitive for large-scale use.

Recent Developments

As part of its overall commitment to sustainable development, Shell recently announced it would not explore for, or develop oil and gas resources within any natural World Heritage Sites, it is the first energy company to publicly do so.

Shell has also consistently sought to be at the cutting edge of fuel technology development. Current applications of this include its development of low sulphur diesel and its optimisation of performance motor gasolines, e.g. Optimax, based on its technical relationship with Ferrari, its exploration of biofuels, such as ethanol, as fuel components in order to reduce greenhouse emissions, its development of gas to liquids technology to produce super-clean liquid fuels from natural gas, and most recently its development of hydrogen fuel technology.

As part of its environmental programme, Shell has invested in Iogen Energy, a Canadian company with a promising technology that could lower the cost of converting plant waste into ethanol.

In its commitment to sustainable development, Shell is leading the way in the development of hydrogen fuel technology. Set up in 1999 to explore the commercial applications of hydrogen, Shell Hydrogen opened in April 2002 the first Shell-branded hydrogen station worldwide in Reykjavik, Iceland. It was used to refuel three DaimlerChrysler fuel cell buses run by local bus company Straeto. Private hydrogen vehicles are expected to arrive on the city's streets in the near future.

In March 2003, General Motors and Shell Hydrogen announced they are combining resources to help make hydrogen fuel cell vehicles a commercially viable reality. Also in 2003, Showa Shell opened the first hydrogen refuelling station in Tokyo. The station provides liquid and compressed hydrogen to a fleet of prototype fuel cell vehicles.

Promotion

The core of Shell's corporate promotional activity is the Listening and Responding programme. This global communication initiative is designed to educate Shell's business partners, employees, investors, the media and the general public about its business practices. It was developed when research suggested that these audiences didn't know enough about

Shell's policies and practices; particularly in terms of environmental responsibility, social investment and Shell's commitment to sustainable development.

As well as the annual publication of the 'Shell Report' – an audit of its economic, environmental and social activity – Shell has an extensive website (www.shell.com), which encourages feedback and addresses criticism in a frank and detailed manner.

The initiative also led to a recent advertising campaign called Living the Values, which through a series of TV, press and online ads, allows viewers to meet real people putting Shell's business principles into practice.

In its oil marketing activities, Shell's communications processes have been increasingly integrated through its sea-branding concept, to create a single unique consistent visual territory across all audiences.

Over the past few years, Shell has increased the profile of its global sponsorships, especially Ferrari, where Shell, with its cutting edge research, has become an integral part of their technical team. Shell's sponsorship of the Ferrari Formula One team dates back to when Enzo Ferrari first started making cars, and the technical relationship has provided powerful endorsement for Shell's launches of performance fuels worldwide.

In order to ensure that its communications and actions are 'in tune' with its various and diverse stakeholders, Shell has increasingly made use of extensive and systematic market research; the core of which are Shell's Global Brand Tracker, run annually for the past six years in some 50 countries worldwide to cover motorists. There is also the annual Shell Reputation Tracker, covering corporate stakeholders and business partners and the Shell People Survey, covering employees.

Brand Values

Shell describes its core values as honesty, integrity, and respect for people. These values are as relevant to customers as they are to corporate stakeholders and have been embodied in Shell's

Shell

V-Power

Instant thrill
Endless energy

Fill up with Shell V-Power and feel the force of the only petrol developed with Ferrari. It delivers performance the moment you need it, putting you in control of an unparalleled wave of power and acceleration.

More power is available at your nearest Shell petrol station.

shell.com

Business Principles, which since 1997 have included a commitment to human rights and to contribute to sustainable development.

Group-wide policies cover health and safety and the environment, and Shell has global standards for such matters as diversity and inclusiveness, environmental management, emission from its sites, and brand management. In order to monitor whether it is living by its principles, the company asks the head of each Shell operation to assure the committee of managing directors every year, in writing, that his or her organisation has acted in line with corporate policies and standards.

In addition, Shell is a charter member of the Global Reporting Initiative (GRI), supporting the greenhouse gas reporting protocol being developed by the World Business Council for Sustainable Development and the World Resources Institute. In 2002 it strengthened its measurement and reporting of potential environmental threats by combining quantitative measures with in-depth reporting from specific sites. Both KPMG and PricewaterhouseCoopers LLP advise the company on its reporting procedures, bringing external audit to all three performance dimensions – financial, environmental and social.

www.shell.com

SIEMENS

Market

For over 150 years, the Siemens name has been synonymous with technology. From its headquarters in Germany, the company has evolved into a global business, active in more than 190 countries worldwide. Today, around two-thirds of Siemens employees operate outside Germany, forming a vast knowledge network spanning the globe.

Siemens' core expertise lies in electronics and electrical engineering and its products and services are found everywhere. From mobile phones to power stations, trains and light bulbs to medical scanners, the company's technological know-how is continuously at work, touching all of us every day of our lives. The company is not only a global manufacturer of innovative products but, in the UK, more than half of the 18,000 employees are involved in service businesses such as meter reading, data processing and financial services.

With total sales in 2002 of 84 billion euros, Siemens is Europe's largest electronics and electrical engineering firm by a wide margin, and third in the world behind General Electric and IBM. Other leading players in the sector include Hitachi, Sony, Hewlett-Packard and Matsushita.

In common with others, Siemens has been hit by the global economic slowdown, compounded revenue in research and development (R&D), Siemens has consistently been amongst the world's top three R&D investors, outspending all of its competitors in developing the technologies and applications that shape our future.

Achievements

For as long as it has been in business, Siemens has been at the forefront of technological innovation. With some 150,000 patents to its name, and an output of more than 30 inventions per day, intellectual property has become one of the company's major assets, contributing significantly to its financial value.

Siemens has been responsible for some of the world's most influential inventions. From the early days, these include the first automatic-dial telegraph in 1847 and the first alarm bell system to warn railway workers of approaching trains. Siemens' discovery of the dynamo-electric principle in 1866 was the starting point for electrical power engineering, giving us power generation and electric motors. Siemens built the world's first electric train and, in 1883, the first public electric railway, designed by Siemens, was opened on Brighton sea front.

Over the years, Siemens achieved numerous other firsts for Britain. In 1881, Siemens provided transport systems – that sound like science fiction, not reality. Yet bizarre as they may sound, these ideas contain the seeds of our future, a future that someday we will take for granted.

History

Werner Siemens established the company as a partnership – Siemens & Halkse – in 1847. Set up to take advantage of the latest advances in communications technology, Siemens quickly established a reputation for itself as an innovator.

Siemens established a London office as early as 1850, under Werner's brother, William, who had arrived in the UK 160 years ago, in 1843, armed with his first patent for a revolutionary electroplating process. The UK business grew rapidly and played a vital role in the improvements in the age. In 1873, it laid the first transatlantic undersea cable, spawning an exciting new age of communication. As a result William Siemens, by now a British citizen, was knighted by Queen Victoria in 1883.

Thanks to its pioneering work in electricity generation, Siemens grew as quickly as the electrical industry and by the time World War II broke out, it was the world's largest electrical company. However, by the end of the war, the company's

by the dramatic collapse of capital spending in telecommunications, the company's largest customer group. Nevertheless, within the context of these difficulties Siemens has performed well, maintaining a healthy balance sheet and producing a net income of 2.6 billion euros in 2002.

Siemens has a reputation for sound financial management. Staying true to this policy has enabled it to weather a turbulent market better than many of its competitors. In particular, the company has been rewarded for keeping a level head during the telecoms bubble of the late 1990s, and by its refusal, unfashionable at the time, to win business through liberal financing deals. Another factor in Siemens' favour is its international diversity and broadly-based portfolio which has minimised the repercussions for the group of recent economic events.

For all its legendary prudence, Siemens has its sights fixed firmly on tomorrow. Nowhere is this more apparent than in its commitment to innovation. Investing around 7% of its annual the first electric lighting for a theatre, at the Savoy, and in the same year installed the world's first electric street lighting, in Godalming, Surrey.

Siemens was at the forefront of early radio, television and aviation, and pioneered electric locomotive design in 1930. Another landmark was reached in 1958, with the world's first pacemaker built by Siemens.

More recently, it was behind the first 1MB memory chip to go into production, the world's fastest neural computer and the first GSM mobile phone with colour display. Today, the company is still innovating at a phenomenal rate, solving practical problems for businesses and supplying Britain's hospitals with advanced medical equipment, such as three-dimensional scanners, enabling radiologists to view images of the heart with breath-taking precision.

And there is more to come. Scientists at Siemens UK research centre at Roke Manor in Hampshire, and around the world, are constantly working on innovations – such as robot-powered public operations – especially in Berlin – were in tatters. It lost 80% of its foreign assets and all of its patents and trademarks.

During the 1950s, the process of reconstruction saw Siemens shift its headquarters from Berlin to Munich and claw back its export business. In 1966, it concentrated its operations under one name – Siemens AG. At this stage, the company had recovered from the wartime damage, employing 257,000 people worldwide and with sales of £2.4 billion. Nowadays, Siemens constantly reviews its wide portfolio divesting in some areas and expanding in others as market conditions dictate.

Product

Siemens' portfolio comprises seven business areas: Information and Communications, Automation and Control, Power, Transportation, Medical, Lighting and Financial Services. Within these areas individual groups are responsible for their own profitability.

Information and Communications (IC) is by far the largest business area, offering voice, data and business services for all kinds of applications and industries. As well as a leading supplier of networks, Siemens is a major provider of mobile telephones, wired, cordless and ISDN phones, server systems, call centre technologies, IT and e-business solutions. Not only one of the top three mobile handset providers in Europe, Siemens Mobile is also playing a key role in creating Hutchison 3G's network in the UK.

Through Siemens Business Services, the company offers IT consultancy, systems integration and operates and maintains infrastructure as well as business services for businesses such as the UK Passport Service and high street banks. The networks business provides a full range of technology and service solutions, from simple telephony through to managing entire telecommunications networks for organisations such as the UK's Met Office.

Siemens has been a major force in the energy sector since the nineteenth century. Nowadays it operates across the complete energy chain, building and maintaining power stations and providing the technology that transfers electricity to homes and businesses as well as reading meters and processing data for billing purposes – it is the largest independent supplier of such services to the UK utility industry. The company also offers a range of instrumentation, monitoring and control systems to ensure that plants are both efficient and safe.

Automation is boosting productivity in every walk of life. Siemens is a leader in this field, supplying the controls that keep traffic flowing around our towns and cities, goods manufactured, processed and distributed efficiently and buildings safe and comfortable to work or live in.

Transportation is another important sector. For the rail industry, Siemens manufactures and designs rolling stock, powers electric railways

and provides the latest signalling, safety and communication systems. In the automotive sector, it provides electronic components and technologies, such as engine management systems, reducing running costs and making vehicles safer and more environmentally friendly. Other Siemens' products, such as tyre pressure monitoring and navigation systems, help to reduce the number of road accidents.

Healthcare is also a major growth area, with hospitals around the world depending on a host of Siemens' applications for clinical workflow to diagnostic imaging, radiotherapy, ultrasound machines and digital hearing aids.

Through its Osram subsidiary, Siemens is a major player in the lighting sector, supplying energy saving lighting to customers such as the British Library. Through its Financial Services arm the company provides business funding and equipment leasing to a wide variety of sectors for IT, telecommunications, plant, office and healthcare equipment.

Recent Developments

Siemens has aggressively expanded its international business, with overseas markets now accounting for around 80% of sales. Latterly, the company has focused on the US, its largest market worldwide. Having boosted its presence in the region – in part through acquisitions – one of Siemens' top priorities is to make its US operations more profitable.

2002 also saw Siemens making substantial gains in Asia Pacific, another part of the world that it views as a strategic priority. This included the building of a gas turbine power plant in Maura Tawar on the outskirts of Jakarta, an order valued at around 230 million euros. In 2002, the UK became the third largest sales performer in the Siemens' group, a considerable achievement topped by the award of further major contracts, including an order worth 2.5 billion euros to deliver 1,200 regional trains to the private railway operator, Stagecoach. Trains on South West Trains routes in the South of England will be serviced and maintained, under a twenty year contract, at a new hi-tech traincare facility where a Formula One 'pit-stop' approach will reduce down time, keeping trains in service

and minimising delays to passengers.

Many recent projects undertaken by Siemens, in the UK, reflect the growing importance of service provision. Linked to this, is the trend towards forming long-term contracts with customers, sometimes extending over several decades. For example, Siemens is involved in a number of private finance initiatives, including a £64 million contract to build and run an extension at Barnet General Hospital in North London. As lead partner in the consortium, Siemens is responsible for installing systems and equipment, and maintaining all of the services for 30 years.

Promotion

Most businesses in the group trade under the Siemens brand. A few, such as Osram, the well-known lighting specialist, retain a separate identity.

Siemens runs some corporate advertising, focusing typically on a few key messages: the company's global reach, innovation-led culture and international employee network allowing ideas and

knowledge to wing their way across the world. Aside from this, most advertising is undertaken by the individual businesses. Information & Communications is the largest advertiser, with ads in national press, including the FT. Other businesses, such as Medical, concentrate on trade press.

Public relations and sponsorship are managed similarly, with a few showcase corporate programmes supported by targeted campaigns, instigated by the individual businesses and regions. At the corporate level, Siemens is a major sponsor of the arts, funding several foundations and prizes, including the highly regarded Ernst von Siemens Music Prize.

Sports sponsorship, particularly Formula One, mountain biking and football, is becoming increasingly important to Siemens. One recent deal, which put the Real Madrid team into jerseys bearing the Siemens Mobile logo, has been particularly successful, boosting awareness of the brand in Spain and amongst Real Madrid's large following in other countries. Awareness will be further enhanced with the signing in summer 2003 of David Beckham to Real Madrid.

Siemens describes many of its significant sponsorship deals as 'partnerships'. This highlights the importance that it attaches to sponsorship, and the way in which it uses the medium, strategically rather than tactically, to further its long-term goals in growth markets around the world. A good example of this is China, where Siemens Mobile has become the title sponsor of the Chinese football league and a partner to the country's national team.

Brand Values

First and foremost, Siemens is about innovation, developing and applying ideas from around the globe, to make the world a better, safer and more pleasurable place. Underpinning this simple proposition are five corporate principles to articulate the company's core beliefs and what it expects of itself and its employees.

The five principles comprise: a commitment to making Siemens' customers more competitive, innovating to shape the future, generating profitable growth for sustainable success, empowering Siemens' employees to excel and embracing corporate responsibility.

www.siemens.com

Market

The Stanley knife is one of the most recognised hand tools in the world. The Stanley Company however, which employs nearly 16,000 people is one of the world's largest hard goods manufacturers, producing more than 50,000 different tools, hardware, decorating and door products for professional, industrial and consumer use. The brand, which is headquartered in Sheffield, enjoyed worldwide sales of US$2.6 billion in 2002 and is particularly strong in Europe where it derives 30% of its total revenues. In the UK, Stanley accounts for fourteen of the top twenty selling hand tools commanding an overall 27% share of the sector and total UK sales in 2002 totalled US$151 million. The UK DIY market as a whole has shown consistent growth in recent years. Indeed the market is estimated to continue its healthy growth and reach an estimated value of £9.58 billion for 2002 (Source: Mintel 2003).

Achievements

Stanley is one of the oldest tool manufacturers in the world and passionately believes in the strength of the brand. Over the years, the company has produced some of the most innovative and useful tools ever made. Among these tools are the Bailey Plane, the Surform, the PowerLock tape rule and most recently the FatMax line of products. The company's philosophy of ingenuity combined with excellence has resulted in a string of firsts; from patents on new products or improvements to existing products. Stanley's solid heritage has gained the loyalty, trust and respect of consumers. It has won plaudits from the industry for advertising creativity, product innovation and design. For example, Stanley received what may have been the very first patent issued for ergonomic tools and introduced the world's first retractable blade knife, the Stanley 99E. The product not only became a twentieth century design icon but also remains the world's best selling knife.

The fact that many Stanley hand tools have become status symbols among professional tradesmen testifies to the quality of

the product. Some tools have even become collector's items. Today, more than ever, Stanley continues to be an industry leader in tool innovation. As a direct result of this commitment to excellence, the brand continues to earn numerous awards and prizes. For example, for two years running it was awarded the prestigious Golden Hammer Award in 2000 and 2001. It has also won a clutch of medals in The Business Week/IDSA Awards.

History

Mention the Stanley Knife and most people normally associate the steel-made product with Sheffield, traditional home of the UK steel industry. Paradoxically the brand is an American thoroughbred. In 1843 two Americans, Frederick T Stanley and his younger brother William, founded a company which they called New Britain, Connecticut. It began life in a humble one-storey wooden building producing door bolts and hinges. Despite its modest beginnings, The Stanley Bolt Manufactory soon gained a reputation for quality and value. Expansion was inevitable but wisely the brothers, reluctant to risk all their resources in one concern, pooled their funds with a group of investors and on July 1st 1852 formed a corporation, The Stanley Works. This remains the company's official name today.

In 1920 the company acquired the Stanley Rule & Level Company, another New Britain

business, which had been founded by Henry Stanley, a distant family member. The product range included rules, levels, planes, carpenter's squares and hammers, gradually evolving into the famous Tool Division of Stanley which produces innovative and practical equipment such as the Bailey plane, the Powerlock rule and the Surform shaper.

However it was not until the acquisition of the Sheffield-based steel and fine tools manufacturer J A Chapman in 1937, that Stanley began manufacturing in the UK. The company was based at Woodside and despite expansion elsewhere, continues to produce a range of products including the Yankee Screwdriver.

Following a £1.4 million investment in 1998,

Stanley announced that its Hellaby plant near Rotherham would become a manufacturing centre of excellence. The plant is the producer and supplier of knives, blades, chisels and screwdrivers to all the brand's markets worldwide.

Drakehouse, the brand's UK commercial base, which also serves as the site of its sliding door manufacturing plant, is in the Waterthorpe area of Sheffield. But recognition of the brand is so high in Sheffield that the Post Office redesignated Stanley's postal area as Drakehouse.

Product

In the UK the Stanley name is most closely associated with hand tools where sales totalled US$151 million in 2002. According to a recent survey, 87% of consumers and 97% of professionals owned at least one Stanley product, indicating a brand adoption level of 95%.

Hand tools are not however the only products encompassed by Stanley. It produces a range of decorator's products which include paint brushes, rollers, stripping knives and seam rollers. There are also sliding doors, fastening systems, mechanic's tools and accessories and storage units including toolboxes. All these Stanley products carry the brand's 160 year-old hallmark of quality and design.

Recent Developments

A steady stream of new products is the lifeblood of this company. Following the success of its Discovery Team programme in the US, Stanley started rolling out the programme in Europe in 2000. The teams, known as the eyes and ears of the business, have worked with US professionals on site since 1997, enabling Stanley to evaluate the development potential of tools. Stanley believes that innovative products developed in response to actual practical experience are better placed to meet the needs of professionals and enthusiasts, making their jobs easier, quicker or simpler. The FatMax tape rule, featuring the longest blade standout in the industry, has garnered plaudits for its original design, as well as being the forerunner of a range of branded products which stand for the ultimate in performance and features.

In the US, Stanley has worked with the ErgoCenter, part of the University of Connecticut Health Center, to develop a range of cutting edge tools. One result has been an anti-vibration hammer specifically designed to combat repetitive strain injury. Elsewhere it has produced a range of decorator's cutlery,

featuring ergonomically designed bi-material handles.

Stanley launched a range of new hand tool products for the UK market in 2003 including the Universal, JetCut and FatMax saws, the VDE and MaxSteel pliers and the eight metre Powerlock tape. Other products included new Stanley screwdrivers, the Sports Utility knife, the Steelmaster Axe and the Bailey Chisel set. Expansion of the power tools sector

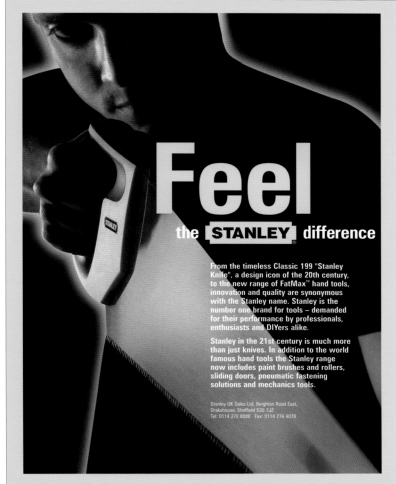

was marked with a 3.6v cordless drill and the Intellisensor, a device which enables users to locate wood and metal within walls prior to drilling.

In the sliding wardrobe doors product category, new designs have taken the concept to a younger consumer. It is part of Stanley's ongoing drive to cement the brand in this sector and make it synonymous with excellence.

Promotion

Since 1998 more than 325 products have been introduced and 26 licensing agreements signed for ancillary products such as worked gloves, torches and power tool accessories. Appropriately representing this active period of product innovation, Stanley unveiled a new advertising campaign in 2002. The push featured many of the brand's best selling products and deployed the strapline 'Feel the Stanley Difference'. Underlying the campaign was the assurance that Stanley is one of the world's most trusted names and that its products are suitable for professionals and enthusiasts. The campaign underscores Stanley's

philosophy that its commitment to the consumer extends beyond providing a range of products by its belief in continuous product innovation which encourages and enables the end user to work efficiently and effectively.

Brand Values

Stanley's strength lies in its heritage of quality, innovation, knowledge and integrity. The world-class products that Stanley has developed have been designed for professionals and those who think like professionals. Stanley's brand vision is to inspire and motivate consumers to realise fully their skills, vision and creativity and by so doing, to be the brand leader for the hard goods industry.

Stanley's brand vision and strategy comprises of three elements; growth, positioning and competitiveness. Its commitment to continuous innovation has created a steady stream of new products and business opportunities worldwide. Innovative products have been developed to make the professional's job easier and more productive, and a push into new or previously untapped market segments has created additional needs and demand for Stanley products. The brand realises the key to winning a strong retail position is to have innovative products merchandised effectively. Targeting the professional user, it complemented this strategy by repositioning the brand with a single look and feel, which was achieved through consistent product colours and packaging design. The brand also believes that key enablers of growth are competitiveness and exceptional customer satisfaction, both of which depend on simplicity, standardisation and systemisation.

www.stanleytools.com

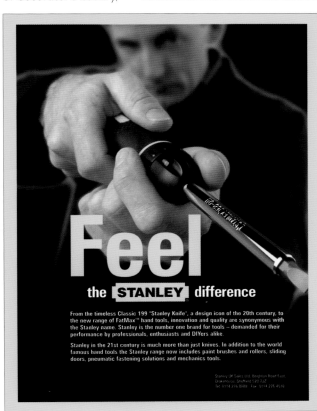

Market

Information is the bedrock of business. Access to timely and accurate market intelligence can make the difference between success and failure in the twenty first century. As a result of client demand the market information sector has witnessed rapid growth over the last decade and is today worth an estimated US$18 billion. The main growth drivers have been the globalisation of demand as more companies go down the multinational route, the impact of technology, outsourcing and the continuing development of new industry sectors. TNS is the third largest information company. Its main competitors include ACNielsen, Ipsos and NOP.

The brand's aim is to deliver up-to-the minute information to help its clients stay ahead of the competition. Expert teams in specialist sectors around the world combine in-depth market knowledge with the latest research techniques and sophisticated technology to provide immediate and informed market measurement, analysis and insight. TNS thinks creatively to help its clients interpret this information into innovative business solutions enabling it to develop more effective relationships with its customers. In July 2003 TNS completed the acquisition of NFO Worldgroup Inc. The enlarged company has more than 14,000 employees worldwide and boasted a turnover of £926.7 million in 2002 (based on combined 2002 revenues of £618.9 million for TNS and £307.8 million for NFO).

Achievements

TNS frequently achieves industry recognition. On an international level, the brand has been ranked third in the world by The Honomichl Global Top 25 research industry review in recognition of its work in the sector. The President of Mexico, Vincente Fox, has

publicly praised the brand for its willingness to embrace a government programme aimed at tackling ageism.

In 2003 TNS won Marketing magazine's Research Award for a project for Northcliffe Newspapers, the UK regional newspaper chain. The eighteen month long project which encompassed nine of the group's regional evenings by surveying 12,000 readers was designed to identify ways of better engaging readers and increasing their enjoyment of newspapers whilst also providing an insight into reader perception

If only money grew on trees

of newspapers. Elsewhere in the UK, Aegis Media signed a deal with TNS to use the pioneering television audience analysis system InfoSysTV. The system not only increases the speed at which television and audience research

can be analysed but enhances the planning and buying of airtime.

TNS' Media division, along with the BBC, won the IPA Award for Best Paper at the Media Research Group Conference in Budapest in November 2002.

TNS also conducted the first ever opinion poll live during the programming of the FIFA World Cup. This was conducted in real time and broadcast nationally on the Sony Entertainment Television Channel.

History

TNS has expanded rapidly since 1997 when UK listed company Taylor Nelson AGB acquired the French operation Sofres. Through a series of strategic acquisitions it has reinforced its global network and strengthened its specialist sector presence and now operates from more than 70 countries. In April 2003 the operation, which was known as Taylor Nelson Sofres, rebranded as TNS. Then in July 2003 TNS completed the acquisition of NFO Worldgroup Inc further strengthening its existing network in North America, Europe and Asia Pacific. Its membership of the Gallup International Association, means it has partner offices in a further sixteen countries.

TNS has introduced a wide and increasingly sophisticated range of products to enable it to make use of the latest technological developments and experience significant growth.

Product

TNS provides market measurement, analysis and insight in more than 70 countries. By working with national and multi-national organisations, it helps clients develop effective business strategies and enhance relationships with their customers. TNS prides itself on its customer commitment and consultative capabilities. By understanding

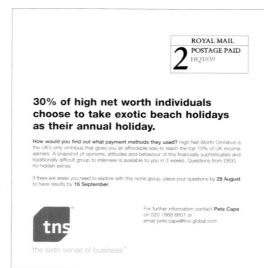

ROYAL MAIL
2 POSTAGE PAID
HQ1039

30% of high net worth individuals choose to take exotic beach holidays as their annual holiday.

How would you find out what payment methods they used? High Net Worth Omnibus is the UK's only omnibus that gives you an affordable way to reach the top 10% of UK income earners. A snapshot of opinions, attitudes and behaviour of this financially sophisticated and traditionally difficult group to interview is available to you in 3 weeks. Questions from £800, no hidden extras.

If there are areas you need to explore with this niche group, place your questions by 28 August to have results by 16 September.

For further information contact **Pete Cape** on 020 7868 6601 or email pete.cape@tns-global.com

the sixth sense of business

Did you know?

the need to adapt to market and sector changes on both a local and global level, it is able to surpass the traditional methods of market research and add value by using the latest research techniques and technology to deliver in-depth findings containing data and reasoning. This enables clients to enhance their business plans by having a better understanding of their customers needs. TNS works with companies in a range of areas enabling them to segment their markets and evaluate new products as well as conduct pricing studies. It also works with companies helping them to test and track the effectiveness of advertising and promotional campaigns, assess customer loyalty and satisfaction and conduct corporate image studies. Additionally TNS has expertise in evaluating brand equity and public opinion polling. TNS has focused on a combination of increasingly sophisticated product and technology developments to bring added value to its research and analysis, and thus add insight to its client's business decisions.

Through its consumer panels sector the brand measures consumer behaviour across a range of markets and outlets worldwide. It uses the best tools and technology to give the most advanced consumer insights available and is continually investing to develop new value added services which in turn leads to entry into new sectors.

TNS Telecoms division is a global provider of strategic and tactical business analysis and information for telecoms service providers, equipment manufacturers and government regulators. Through its comprehensive range of solutions and its consultative capabilities TNS is able to meet the challenges faced by the industry.

The brand's information technology arm boasts more than 25 years of experience and is one of the world's largest customised IT market information groups supplying a range of services to multinationals. More than 100 former IT industry employees and world-class IT research specialists provide insight into customer attitudes, motivation and behaviour, helping companies meet their customer's needs.

TNS Healthcare uses its industry knowledge and expertise to conduct specialist research for most of the world's leading pharmaceutical companies. Continuous disease and drug monitoring services supplement a full range of research in areas including HIV, Asthma/COPD, Lipids, CVD Metabolics and Antibiotics.

The brand's hospitality and leisure division focuses exclusively on delivering worldwide research to leading hospitality organisations. For more than a decade its dedicated team of researchers has been advising hotel and restaurant groups, food service operators, health and fitness operators, airlines, cruise-lines and tour operators, in order to provide cost-effective, value-added research and insights into the industry. The findings have been beneficial in helping companies optimise operations, improve human resource management, develop and enhance brand image and advertising strategy and improve client and customer retention.

TNS's television audience measurement systems are designed to meet the challenges of digital,

cable and satellite viewing. Value-added audience analysis is delivered by the innovative InfoSysTV software, used to enable companies to evaluate the success of the programmes they make or buy, as well as helping them make investment decisions about future programmes and allowing them to schedule their inventory of programmes effectively.

The interactive division provides leading-edge research solutions to clients seeking to maximise the opportunities of the internet across specialist market sectors. By combining in-depth market knowledge with the latest research techniques and sophisticated use of internet market research technology it gives clients immediate and informed market analysis, insight and innovative business solutions.

On an international basis the media intelligence group is a leading source for proactive and comprehensive media solutions across all media. It provides advertising expenditure tracking, creative advertising and editorial monitoring

services for TV, radio, cinema, the internet and print. It also provides sports sponsorship evaluation.

Operating a skilled team of research professionals the automotive division specialises in addressing the complex information needs of the industry's major manufacturers and component suppliers. Through its expertise the division brings a wealth of industry knowledge and insight to each project.

Finally TNS offers a portfolio of branded research solutions which enable clients to address international marketing issues more consistently and cost effectively. Areas covered include advertising evaluation, tracking, brand equity, customer satisfaction and employee research, market segmentation and brand portfolio analysis.

Recent Developments
Recently TNS has been expanding its global network. The acquisition of NFO WorldGroup Inc from Interpublic boosted TNS to third place globally in the market information sector. The brand has also expanded into Central America with its acquisition of Data Advanced Research, one of the region's leading market information companies. The deal means TNS can offer clients additional

insights into the strategically important markets of Guatemala, El Salvador, Costa Rica, Panama, Honduras and Nicaragua.

Promotion
TNS uses a variety of marketing vehicles to raise awareness and generate business opportunities for its products and services worldwide. These include advertising, public relations, direct mail and e-marketing as well as attending trade shows, delivering papers at conferences and sponsoring or organising key industry events.

The brand has also been raising its awareness through a partnership with television news channel CNN as well as Time magazine. The deal provides feedback on current affairs and world issues which feature in CNN programmes as well as featuring as regular news items in the European edition of TIME magazine.

Brand Values
TNS sees itself as being 'the sixth sense of business'. The brand is the eyes and ears of business, looking beyond the numbers, beyond the trends and reading between the lines. TNS believes that this 'sixth sense' of business enables it to understand the world in which clients operate, interpreting the opportunities and dangers they face and providing them with a window on the future. It means understanding what is happening today and what will happen tomorrow by providing intelligence that cuts through the noise and clutter of the twenty first century. The company's brand values are summed up in four words: wit, intelligence, attitude and imagination.

www.tnsofres.com

UNISYS

Market

Unisys is a dominant force within the IT sector and has a global presence, operating consistently in more than 100 countries. Unisys worldwide client-base includes 2,200 financial services clients, 1,500 government agencies, 100 communications providers, 200 airlines and more than 200 newspapers.

Unisys sits at the heart of the economy – acting as an engine that keeps people and businesses talking and transacting with each other. Anyone who writes cheques, leaves voicemail messages, makes an airline reservation, has a mortgage, invests in the stock markets or contacts emergency services could well be using a Unisys system. In the UK, for example, it is estimated that an average person interacts with a Unisys system around 5-6 times a day – frequently without knowing it.

Unisys differentiates itself in this competitive marketplace through decades of experience serving the financial services, public sector, communications, transportation and publishing markets. It prides itself on its ability to facilitate information transactions.

Unisys is able to achieve this leadership position by providing business and government with vital technology, outsourcing, managed services and multi channel delivery systems. Every day, Unisys combines an intimate understanding of each core vertical market in which it operates with unrivalled expertise in outsourcing, systems integration, network services and multi-channel support.

Achievements

Unisys has received many awards and accolades over the years. In June 2003, it was rated number 53 in BusinessWeek's InfoTech 100 best performing technology companies.

In 2000, Unisys was ranked sixth among service companies in Upside magazine's e-Biz 150. In the same year it came 27th in eWeek's FastTrack 100 innovators in e-business networking.

In addition, in 2002, Computer Business Review's 'IT Services Top 50 Companies' rated Unisys fourteenth. Recently, major outsourcing projects in the UK for clients such as Woolwich Building Society and Abbey Life have won awards from The Banker magazine and the Management Consultancies Association, endorsing Unisys' ability to devise, create and manage the most complex services arrangements. The 2,200 patents that Unisys has been awarded over the years are a symbol of its technological understanding and leadership.

History

Unisys was formed in 1986 through the merger of two organisations – Sperry Rand and Burroughs Adding Machine Co. However, the history of these organisations dates back some 100 years.

The American Arithmometer Co was founded in 1886 to manufacture and sell the first commercially viable adding and listing machines, invented by William Seward Burroughs. In 1905 the company changed its name to Burroughs Adding Machine Co.

The company was responsible for many innovations over the succeeding years including the invention of the first adding-subtracting machine in 1911; the introduction of the direct multiplication billing machine in 1923; and the pioneering use of magnetic ink character recognition (MICR) in 1959.

Sperry Rand has an equally innovative history. The company was formed in 1955 through the merger of Remington Rand and Sperry Gyroscope Co, which was founded in 1910 to manufacture

![ROSEVILLE OPERATIONS — SPERRY UNIVAC COMPUTER SYSTEMS]

and sell navigational equipment. The Remington Typewriter Co, that had been founded the previous year, produced the first 'noiseless' typewriter, as it was initially known. In 1925 the company produced the US's first electric typewriter.

In 1949 the company began production of the 409 – the world's first business computer. The 409 was later sold as the Univac 60 and 120 and was the first computer used by the US Internal Revenue Service and the first computer installed in Japan.

In 1945 Remington Rand created the world's first digital computer (ENIAC), which was followed in 1950 by the launch of Univac, an important forerunner of today's computer. In 1951 Univac was used by the US Census Bureau and in the 1960s a new generation of Univac computers became the standards for mainframe systems and secured Unisys's success in technology. NASA gathered the world's largest collection of Univac computers and this technology played a key role in putting the first man in space in 1969. Unisys continues to develop industry-leading technology that supports the most demanding business environments, such as the much-acclaimed Unisys e-@ction ES7000 server which is at the heart of many vital data centres. Customers include Abbey National, the Nasdaq stock exchange and AT&T.

However, as customer demands change, so does Unisys. In 1992 a unit to deliver IT services was introduced and by 1994, services and solutions had become the company's single largest business unit. Services now account for some 75% of total Unisys revenues.

Today, drawing on the expertise and knowledge accumulated over the years, Unisys solutions process millions of transactions across the globe every day, supporting crucial systems at the heart of financial institutions, governments and airlines, as well as the worlds of telecommunications and publishing.

Product

Unisys is a global supplier of information services and technology to large, complex organisations in business and government. It provides IT solutions to companies in the finance, travel, telecommunications and publishing sectors, as well as to central and local government and justice and safety organisations. Increasingly its solutions are based around services, whether systems integration, consultancy, business process outsourcing or other managed services; over two-thirds of its revenue comes from this area. Unisys will also supply specialist software – its own or its partners – and high-end hardware for the most demanding environments. Its technological abilities and heritage mean that the company is able to offer true end-to-end support to its customers, from identifying the business issue, designing the IT strategy to solve it, through to designing, manufacturing and implementing the technology that makes the strategy come to life and deliver results. Unisys aims to build lifetime partnerships with its customers, in many cases seeing them through generations of business cycles.

Recent Developments

Unisys is well positioned for growth. Against tough trading conditions, the company has remained profitable, with its strategy of focusing on outsourcing and other managed services reaping dividends.

The last year has seen Unisys refine its focus even more sharply, moving away from low margin areas of business and building up skills where customers are demanding them, such as in higher end consulting and systems integration as well as outsourcing and managed services.

Promotion

As a global company selling to large, complex organisations, Unisys uses a full range of marketing communications disciplines to promote the brand; from advertising, media relations and the web, to direct customer contact and sports sponsorship. Communications are designed specifically to reach the business audience, because Unisys does not operate in the SME or consumer arenas.

Unisys promotion targets the board level decision-maker, a vital audience as IT plays an increasingly central and strategic role within business and government. However, IT management is crucial to the decision-making process, and so advertising and media relations at Unisys are directed towards the IT press as well as major national and business titles. To support its clear focus on selected vertical markets, Unisys will also reach out to vertical media in finance, telecoms, public sector, media and transport.

For over twenty years, Unisys has been present in sports in two ways – as a sponsor and as an information technology supplier. Unisys works with prestigious events such as the European PGA Tour, the US Open and the British Open, providing the vital scoring systems as a live demonstration of its technological abilities. Golf offers an excellent opportunity to reach key audiences around the world. A major sporting event has all the information technology demands of running a large business or government agency, and possibly more.

Information must be delivered fast, accurately and in a format useful for decision making, but at a split-second pace, to audiences not just on the event site but globally, and frequently whilst working in inclement weather at the 'hostile environment' of the event site. Live TV adds intense pressure, requiring computer-generated graphics plus statistical information for commentators.

Brand Values

Unisys takes the view that the credibility of the brand depends on consistent behaviour at many levels – each encounter builds the brand experience.

Unisys has a worldwide image as a clear, sharp brand that it works hard to maintain. Research has shown that to customers, the brand stands for tenacity, creativity, technical excellence and doing the right thing – in other words, the actions and attributes of Unisys employees. The Unisys brand comes alive through building a service culture whose success is reflected in strong relationships that endure and evolve over time. Unisys is committed to the importance of customer service and sponsors the Unisys Management Today Service Excellence awards, a UK programme to encourage organisations to meet the highest standards in creative customer service.

Unisys strives to be a responsible corporate citizen, whether through its environmental stewardship programmes, supporting the charitable work of its employees, involvement in education programmes or in emphasising work-life balance. In the UK, Unisys puts efforts into charities where employees have an opportunity to get involved, such as Outward Bound, bringing benefits to the organisation and the voluntary sector alike. The Vision ON programme, launched by Unisys in the UK in January 2002, is designed to create a supportive environment for its people, helping them contribute fully and bring imagination and intelligence to bear on their work. At the same time, Vision ON also focuses on Unisys corporate responsibility in the community. One example is the development of volunteer teams in each Unisys office – the Vision On Location Teams (VOLTs). Each VOLT is manned by staff at all levels of the organisation, keen to make an impact on their environment. Every location team is given an annual budget of £10,000 to spend on improving their surroundings and to support the charitable causes of their choice. In each case, the VOLT's involvement went well beyond the funding, with staff actively engaged in helping out.

Around the world, Unisys runs a comprehensive ethics training programme which all employees go through every year, covering topics like behaviour to fellow employees and ethical business dealings with customers and suppliers.

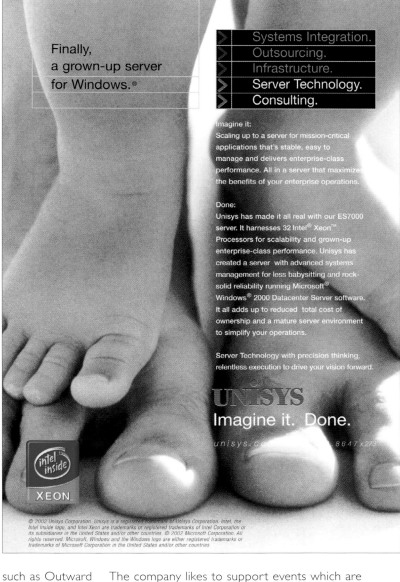

The company likes to support events which are opportunities for the whole family to participate, such as motor racing at Goodwood, meaning that busy Unisys employees, as well as its customers, can minimise disruption to home life and involve their families in leisure time activities.

www.unisys.com

Things you didn't know about Unisys

Unisys systems handle the passenger reservations for more than 200 airlines around the world.

Half the world's cheques are processed by Unisys.

More than 1,500 government agencies around the world use Unisys services.

Unisys systems and people operate in diverse areas ranging from handling all of BT's Callminder services nationwide to successfully processing and facilitating all NASDAQ stock market transactions.

Worldwide, Unisys has deployed more than 100 million voice/fax messaging mailboxes.

Unisys runs the Metropolitan Police's 999 emergency response service.

More than 200 newspapers – from The Wall Street Journal to Italy's IL Sole 24 Ore – rely on Unisys to serve millions of readers worldwide. Unisys Publishing Solutions help publishers manage editorial workflow, pagination, advertising, archiving and web publishing.

Unisys holds nearly 2,200 technology patents worldwide.

UNIX 03

Market

The UNIX operating system sits at the heart of Information Technology (IT). Generally known as 'servers', UNIX® systems excel in the tasks of running medium and large sized businesses, including many governments, in an ever-growing market. Businesses that utilize large databases, transaction systems, accounting operations, customer resource management, enterprise resource planning – or a myriad of other applications – are all supported by UNIX systems.

Analyst sources such as Gartner and IDC, who track sales of such servers, have calculated the UNIX system market as being worth close to US$20 billion per annum. They credit industry heavyweights Hewlett Packard, IBM and Sun Microsystems with taking the lion's share of this market with HP being quoted as having between 34-36%, Sun 36-40% and IBM around 27%.

Each of these companies has a range of systems – all certified through the UNIX certification programme – from small systems suitable for small businesses or departments, through to (in IBM's case) traditional, very large mainframes. Other companies who have certified UNIX systems include Fujitsu, Fujitsu Siemens Computers, NCR, NEC, SCO, and Silicon Graphics.

The cost of developing applications software is considerably greater than the cost of the hardware on which the applications run. The idea of 'open systems' came about because of the growing need for organisations to maintain investment in their critical applications; while having the ability to mix and match platforms as hardware costs fall. The UNIX certification programme has reached a position where it is widely recognised as the international symbol of assurance in open systems. By the end of 2002, the value of procurements of open systems referencing the Single UNIX Specifications exceeded US$55 billion.

Achievements

In September 1993, a group of 75 leading system and software sellers agreed to back an initiative to ask X/Open Company (now The Open Group) to standardize the specifications of the UNIX operating system to create a single, standard operating system. In a parallel move, Novell Inc announced that it would transfer the UNIX trademark, which it owned, to X/Open Company Limited.

In a matter of weeks, the computer industry put behind it over 25 years of policy differences

and technical incompatibility to concentrate on delivering a single specification for the UNIX system. The aim was to create greater application and information portability and flexibility, as well as freedom of choice for customers. All major vendors agreed that they would ensure that their operating system products would meet a single comprehensive standard.

This industry initiative worked through the proven processes of X/Open Company to develop a set of specifications by broad industry consensus, supported by a certification and testing programme, that would deliver commonality across multiple implementations of the UNIX system. The early specification, took into account the interfaces utilised by the most widely used UNIX system applications to ensure older applications would also be compatible.

The Single UNIX Specification now defines what it means for a product to be called UNIX, and is backed by a comprehensive certification programme run by The Open Group. With the Single UNIX Specification, there is a single, open, consensus specification that defines a product. They also carry the UNIX brand name, so products that conform to the Single UNIX specification can be easily identified. Both the specification and the trademark are now managed and held in trust for the industry by The Open Group.

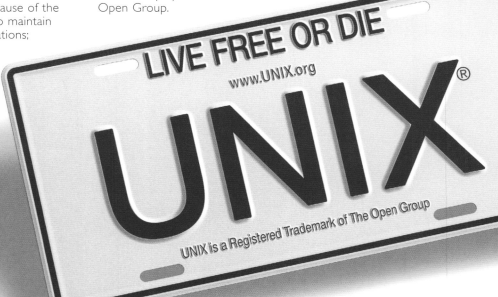

With more than US$55 billion in procurements mandating products that conform to the Single UNIX Specification, it is clear that customers see the value in the achievements of The Open Group too.

Everything from computer-aided design, manufacturing control systems, laboratory simulations, even the internet itself began life with and because of the UNIX system. Today, without UNIX systems, the internet would come to a screeching halt. Most telephone calls could not be made and electronic commerce would grind to a halt. Furthermore, modern filmmaking would have none of the special effects we now take for granted.

History

Licensees of UNIX system code began developing their own variants following its 'escape' from the AT&T Bell Laboratories in the early 1970s. Universities, research institutes, government bodies and computer companies all began using the powerful system to develop many of the technologies which are part of today's world. In the early 1980s the market for the UNIX system had grown sufficiently to be noticed by industry analysts and researchers. The question was no longer 'What is the UNIX system?' but 'Is the UNIX system suitable for business?' In 1984 a group of vendors, concerned about the continuing domination of their market by larger companies' proprietary systems, developed the concept of 'open systems'. The idea was that such systems should meet agreed criteria. This development led to the formation of X/Open Company Limited, forerunner of The Open Group, with a remit to define a comprehensive open systems environment. The UNIX system was chosen as the basis for open systems that would save on costs, attract a wider portfolio of applications, and foster competition on equal terms.

In 1987 in a move intended to unify the market, AT&T announced a deal with Sun Microsystems, the leading proponent of the Berkeley derivative of UNIX system code. The rest of the industry, however, believing that their own markets were under threat, clubbed together to develop their own open systems organisation, The Open Software Foundation (OSF). AT&T/Sun formed UNIX International as a response. The ensuing 'systems wars' divided the vendors between AT&T's System V and the rival OSF/1, with X/Open Company holding centre ground where it continued the process of standardising the Application Program Interfaces necessary for an open operating system specification.

During this time, X/Open not only developed a certification programme based on vendor guarantees and supported by comprehensive testing, but also continued to broaden the scope of open system specifications. As the benefits of the certification programme became popular and understood, many large organisations began using it as the basis for their procurements. By 1993, over US$7 billion had been spent on certified systems. Four years later the figure stood at US$23 billion, and by 2003 the amount had topped US$55 billion.

In 1993 AT&T sold its UNIX System Laboratories to Novell.

The UNIX trademark and specification was transferred to X/Open Company as stewards on behalf of the entire community. In 1995 the UNIX 95 brand for computer systems was introduced. This was a critical development because, for the first time, a UNIX system did not have to be built from the original AT&T source code.

Today the UNIX certification programme has achieved critical mass, and all key vendors in this market have products that meet the demanding criteria of the certification programme. UNIX 98 (the second update of the programme) has been superseded by UNIX 03 to ensure that the brand responds to customer needs and technological advances.

UNIX has always been closely linked with open systems, and The Open Group continues to develop and evolve the Single UNIX Specification and associated certification programme on behalf of the IT community.

Product

UNIX certification is part of The Open Group's internationally recognised portfolio of open systems certification programmes that encompass three primary attributes.

First, there are widely accepted and freely available specifications that describe the software interfaces between components of a computer system such as: the operating system, networks, applications and desktop screen environment.

Second, computer systems can be built to meet the standards and the needs of specific markets.

Finally, a neutral, open certification process gives the assurance that products meet agreed specifications and conformance requirements.

The UNIX certification programme creates more market choice for computer system buyers. Furthermore, it reduces cost and time to market for suppliers and stimulates competition in a larger, unified market for computer system products clearly identified by the UNIX brand.

The Single UNIX Specification benefits the entire IT industry. From a user's perspective, products carrying the brand's certification provide a powerful open platform for the development, implementation and management of 'mission-critical' computer systems. The specification broadens choice across the widest range of systems, thereby protecting the buyer's investment in software and data.

For sellers of software, the brand unifies a previously fragmented market and offers the ability for all to compete on equal terms, while reducing engineering and maintenance costs.

System vendors have a standard specification that underpins a widely recognised brand name through which they can market their certified UNIX system products.

Quality assurance inherent in UNIX certified products is aided by a suite of software testing tools developed by The Open Group to cover all aspects of the Single UNIX Specification: core system calls, commands and utilities, extensions and networking interfaces.

Recent Developments

The introduction of UNIX 03 in 2003 marks the latest upgrade, although work on the project started in 1998. The approach towards the

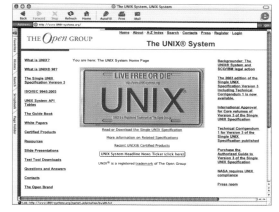

development of the latest specification was one of 'write once, adopt everywhere'. This development brings together three specifications –POSIX, ISO and UNIX – which all had similar coverage but were managed by separate groups. This revolutionary move combined industry led efforts and formal standardisation activities into a single protocol by including a wide range of participants from academia, government, commerce and the open source communities. The core of UNIX 03, known as the 'Base Specifications', was developed and is maintained by an industry-based committee known as The Austin Group.

This achievement is a real demonstration of the value of The Open Group: it is the place where customers and vendors meet to openly discuss, address, and resolve issues and future needs of information systems. It is the place where industry standards and formal standards can be brought together to enable real products that meet buyers needs; where markets are enabled because customers can be assured that the products they buy conform with the standard.

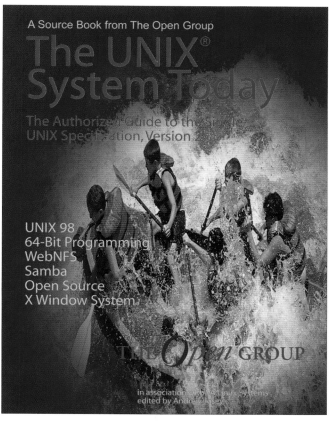

Promotion

The Open Group has three key elements in its strategy towards optimising the value of trademarks: Protect, Police, and Promote. Each trademark is protected in key trading countries around the world, normally in classes associated with computer systems, publications and services.

Once protection is secured, The Open Group monitors usage of the mark and takes action whenever a conflict is spotted. Initially it seeks to use education and persuasion to obtain correct usage and attribution of the UNIX trademark. Only in the most rare of cases is it necessary to resort to legal action. With such a well-known and widely used trademark, this is a tough ever-continuing job and, like painting the Forth Bridge, never ends.

Most UNIX trademark promotion is done through certified products. Licensed computer system vendors promote the fact that their products are guaranteed UNIX systems alongside their own brand names.

Brand Values

It is very important to IT buyers that the UNIX brand is represented accurately at all times. Therefore, every product certified with the UNIX trademark is warranted by the vendor to conform to the specifications and certification requirements, at all times and under all circumstances. If it doesn't, for any reason, the problem must be rectified at the vendor's expense within an agreed amount of time.

The UNIX brand is the visible sign of the promise that the product conforms to standards, and will therefore support the applications needed by the buyer, interoperate with existing and future systems and cost less to own and operate.

In this way, the brand's integrity and value is maintained and UNIX certified products offer a more comprehensive and valuable warranty to buyers than any other system.

www.opengroup.org

virgin atlantic

Market

The airline industry was affected more than most by the tragic events of September 11th 2001. There was an immediate and significant reduction in passenger demand, particularly across the North Atlantic, and a number of airlines became bankrupt. Since then, the trading environment has continued to be extremely challenging as a result of the combination of global downturn, the war in the Middle East and the impact of SARS.

It is clear that in order to survive and compete in this challenging environment it is vital for airline companies to adapt and evolve, focusing on controlling their costs while also capturing the market with an ever-improving range of services. Airlines with strong brand leadership, like Virgin Atlantic, will emerge from the challenge strengthened.

Achievements

Since its launch in 1984, Virgin Atlantic has been regarded as one of the most forward-thinking and innovative companies in the market. As a result, it quickly became the UK's second largest long haul airline and the first to succeed in breaking British Airways' dominance of transatlantic routes by capturing a 20% market share.

Right from its launch, Virgin Atlantic set new standards for customer care by introducing a number of innovative products and ideas that other airlines strove to emulate. The airline quickly became renowned for its consideration of all passenger needs, both during the flight and at the airline's airport facilities. Virgin Atlantic's own in-flight surveys reveal that 98% of passengers in Upper Class would fly with Virgin Atlantic again and would recommend the service to others.

Virgin Atlantic has won numerous prestigious annual awards. In 2002 alone, Virgin Atlantic won a whole host of awards including Best Long Haul Scheduled Carrier from Travel Trade Gazette, Best Transatlantic Airline from Travel Weekly, Best Business Airline from The Guardian and Observer and Conde Nast Traveller and Best Airline to the Far East from Official Airline Guides.

The result of this success is that in April 2003, at the end of the financial year, the Virgin Travel Group announced that, in a very difficult time for all airlines, it had not only achieved a profit but also a turnover of £1,401 million carrying over four million passengers – a far cry from the 125,000 passengers carried by the company back in 1984.

History

In the early 1980s, transportation – rather than customer care – was the top priority of the airline industry. When Virgin Atlantic burst on to the scene

offering not only better service and lower costs for passengers but also a commitment to put the customer first, the effects were radical.

The company was set up in 1984 when an Anglo-American lawyer, Randolph Fields, approached Richard Branson – the young and unorthodox chairman of the Virgin Group – with an idea for a new airline that would fly between the UK and the US. Better known at the time as the leading light in the world of pop and rock music, Branson was enthusiastic about the opportunity to diversify. His characteristic energy and enthusiasm meant that within three months the airline leased its first planes and June 22nd 1984 marked Virgin's inaugural flight from London to New York.

Virgin Atlantic has since pioneered a string of industry 'firsts'. Abandoning the traditional structure used by other airlines, it was the first to offer just two flight classes: Economy (a choice of Premium Economy and Economy) and Upper Class, a first class service at a business class fare. Other 'firsts' included individual TV screens for all passengers, on-board automatic defibrillators and

cabin crew trained to handle cardiac problems. Virgin Atlantic's Upper Class was the first to offer a dedicated sleeping cabin for business class passengers and a sleeper service with flexible meal options. It also remains to this day the only carrier with an on-board bar and on-board beauty therapists offering treatments.

From the outset, Virgin Atlantic's mission was to provide the highest possible level of service for all classes of air travellers at excellent value for money.

Now based at both London's Gatwick and Heathrow airports, it operates long haul services from Heathrow to New York (Newark and JFK), Los Angeles, San Francisco, Washington, Boston, Tokyo, Hong Kong, Johannesburg, Cape Town,

Shanghai, Delhi, Miami and Lagos. Virgin operates services from Gatwick to Orlando, Barbados, St Lucia, Antigua, Grenada, Tobago, Las Vegas and Port Harcourt. Virgin Atlantic also operates a service between Manchester and Orlando.

In December 2000 Richard Branson signed an agreement to sell a 49% stake in Virgin Atlantic to Singapore airlines to form a unique global partnership. The company has codeshare agreements with Continental Airlines, Singapore Airlines, Malaysia Airways, Nationwide, bmi British Midland and Air India. Virgin Atlantic's sustained success derives from the fact that despite huge growth and a solid reputation, the service still remains customer driven with a continued emphasis on value for money, quality, fun and innovation.

Product

Virgin Atlantic Airways is based at Heathrow, Gatwick and Manchester and carries over four million passengers per year. Virgin Atlantic operates departure lounges at Heathrow – the flagship Clubhouse – in addition to lounges at New York (JFK and Newark), Boston, Washington, San Francisco, Hong Kong and Johannesburg and provides lounge facilities at each of its gateways. The company opened an arrivals lounge, Revivals, at Heathrow in 2000.

Virgin's Upper Class is marketed as a first class service at a business class fare and therefore competes with other carriers' business class products. Since its launch in 1984 it has won every major award in the travel industry and has changed the face of business travel.

At a time when many airlines are withdrawing from the first class market, Virgin Atlantic is investing £50 million in a new product – the Upper Class Suite. The product consists of a reclining leather seat for take off, a place to sit and eat a proper meal opposite your partner, the longest fully flat bed in the world with a proper mattress for sleeping on, a private on-board bar to drink at with your friends and four limousines per return trip, plus the Freedom menu which allows passengers to eat what they want when they want and a private massage room – all at a price thousands of pounds less than other airlines' first class. The new bed is the longest in any airline's first or business class flying today.

Premium Economy is aimed at cost conscious business travellers and offers facilities and services more comparable to a traditional short haul business class with its own check-in, a separate cabin on board, and comfortable spacious seating – thanks to the 38 inch seat pitch. For the price of a fully flexible ticket, passengers also enjoy a priority meal service,

duty-free and baggage handling and complimentary pre-take-off drinks and newspapers.

Virgin Atlantic's Economy service focuses on maximum value for money and was the first to provide every passenger with a seat-back TV screen broadcasting Virgin's in-flight entertainment system with over 200 hours of video-on-demand entertainment, fifteen computer games and SMS text messaging to mobile phones and email addresses. Passengers also receive an amenity kit including a non-disposable headset and complimentary drinks.

The safety, comfort and entertainment of children in all classes is catered for through an 'unaccompanied minors programme', baby changing

by American Express cardholders.

Virgin Atlantic was the first airline to recognise the different needs of economy travellers.

Recent Developments

In recent years, Virgin Atlantic has extended its network of routes around the world and captured market share from the leading players in the industry.

In April 2001, Virgin Atlantic ordered six Airbus A380 superjumbos due to come into service in 2006. The airline was also the launch customer for the Airbus A340-600 – the longest aircraft flying today. The airline took delivery of the first in July 2002 and its inaugural flight took place to New York on August 1st 2002.

an integrated media strategy to promote its brands, including television, newspapers, posters, promotions, direct mail and the internet, often to wide acclaim.

Virgin Atlantic's advertising aims to be stylish and classy with an individual twist. A selection of strip advertisements emphasising Virgin Atlantic's Upper Class services and comfortable facilities featured in the UK press and won several leading marketing awards.

Brand Values

Virgin Atlantic strives to provide the best possible service at the best possible value. It is a distinctive, fun-loving and innovative brand which is admired

facilities on all aircraft, special meals and snack boxes, KiDS packs, and a dedicated children's TV channel.

Virgin flying club – previously Virgin Freeway – is one of the most generous frequent flyer programmes available and was the first to offer air miles for travel in all classes. Designed to build passenger loyalty, the scheme operates on three levels: red, silver and gold. Miles and rewards can also be earned with Virgin's partner airlines and

In February 2003 the airline launched twice weekly services to Port Harcourt, Nigeria and in May launched weekly services to Grenada and Tobago taking the number of destinations the airline flies to 22.

Promotion

The greatest and best known advertisement for Virgin is Richard Branson himself. Branson is often perceived as the 'consumer's hero', an entrepreneur operating in a very personal style with Virgin's brand values reflecting his own personality. At the same time he is one of the UK's most admired businessmen, and his daredevil antics, such as ballooning across the Atlantic, have given the Virgin brand additional publicity. Branson also keeps a shrewd eye on promotional opportunities. For example, when he heard of British Airways' decision to remove the Union Jack from their plane exteriors, he capitalised on the change by actually introducing the Union Jack on Virgin planes.

Virgin Atlantic has proved an astute advertiser over the years and has implemented

for its intelligence and integrity. Its core brand values include honesty, innovation, caring, value for money and fun. Judging from the results of a poll conducted by the research agency NOP World, the public also associates it with friendliness and high quality. In the 2002 (based on research by NOP World) Business Superbrands Awards Virgin Atlantic won the 'Brand most perceived to keep its promises' award.

www.virgin.com/atlantic

Things you didn't know about
Virgin Atlantic

The average age of Virgin Atlantic's fleet of aircraft is around five years.

The Upper Class Suite is 33 inches wide and 79.5 inches long making it the longest flying today.

The Upper Class Suite is arranged in a revolutionary 1-2-1 configuration meaning all passengers have an aisle seat and half of all passengers get both a window and an aisle seat.

In the next two years, Virgin Atlantic in-flight beauty therapists will perform over half a million massages.

Virgin Atlantic serves approximately 2.5 million ice cream bars and 120,000 bottles of champagne each year.

YELLOW PAGES™

Market

Yellow Pages competes in the classified advertising market with other producers of classified and local advertising, as well as local, regional and national newspapers and classified advertising magazines. Yellow Pages is part of Yell, a leading international directories business, and the biggest player in the £4 billion UK classified advertising market (Source: The Advertising Association 2001). Today Yell publishes 88 regional Yellow Pages editions in the UK, containing more than 1,000,000 advertisements, with almost 28 million directory copies distributed each year.

Yell has an integrated portfolio of products including printed, telephone based and online directories. Its business proposition is putting buyers in touch with sellers through a range of simple-to-use, cost-effective advertising solutions.

Achievements

Yellow Pages' achievements are evident in the brand's ubiquity, with 97% of adults having a copy of the Yellow Pages at home (Source: Saville Rossiter-Base 2003). Through close communication with advertisers and their audiences, Yellow Pages maintains a reputation for comprehensiveness and reliability.

Yellow Pages has achieved Business Superbrand as well as Consumer Superbrand status through its longevity as a household name. For more than 35 years, the directory has been a part of everyday life and both consumers and advertisers trust Yellow Pages to deliver the results they require year after year. Consequently, Yellow Pages is used an estimated 1.2 billion times a year, and over £240 million is generated daily for businesses appearing in the directory (Source: Saville Rossiter-Base 2003).

Yellow Pages and its parent Yell are very aware of environmental and social issues and their impact on the wider community. To reduce the impact of the printing of directories on the environment for instance, Yellow Pages works with local councils to encourage the recycling of old directories. By 2003, 82% of UK councils had the facilities to recycle Yellow Pages directories, and 46% of people said that they recycled their directories.

In April 2002, Yell won a prestigious Queen's Award for Enterprise for its integrated approach

to sustainable development. It demonstrated outstanding commercial success whilst at the same time ensuring work practices which benefit society, the environment and the economy.

In 2003, Yell was awarded a BIG TICK from Business in the Community and was a finalist in the 'Business in the Environment' category at the Business in the Community Awards for Excellence. The BIG TICK recognises companies that have reached a measurable standard of excellence in the field of corporate responsibility.

CALL THE NEW YELLOW PAGES 118 24 7 PHONE SERVICE | **YELLOW PAGES 118 24 7**

LONDON CENTRAL 2003/04

YE1LOW PAGES

History

The first directories were actually produced well before Alexander Graham Bell invented the telephone. In Elizabethan times, street directories were published detailing the names and addresses of local residences and businesses. By the 1840s, Kelly's London Post Office directories had begun to emerge.

The growth of the telecommunications industry

offered further potential to publishers of directories. Yellow Pages first appeared in 1966, when it was bound into the standard Brighton telephone directory. By 1973, Yellow Pages had been rolled out across the UK and existed as a product in its own right. In 1979 it became a registered trademark.

Over the years Yellow Pages has continued to improve and enhance its product, as well as extending into new areas to keep up with the developing directories industry. In addition to Yellow Pages, Yell's products in the UK also include:

Business Pages, introduced in 1985, a specialist directory covering business-to-business suppliers.

Yellow Pages 118 24 7, a new telephone-based information service providing in-depth classified business information, business and residential listings. The Talking Pages service was introduced in 1994, and following deregulation of 192 directory enquiries the service was replaced and enhanced in 2003 by Yellow Pages 118 24 7.

Yell.com, the UK's leading online directory service, enabling people to search for businesses and services on the internet, was launched in 1996.

In August 1999, Yellow Pages expanded into the US with the US$665 million purchase of Yellow Book USA, the largest independent classified directory publisher in the US. In June 2001, Yell was sold by BT for just over £2 billion to a private equity consortium made up of investment funds advised by Apax Partners and Hicks, Muse, Tate & Furst.

Since then there has been further substantial expansion in the US, the most significant development being the US$600 million purchase of the McLeod directories business in April 2002. With the additional US$69 million purchase in December 2002 of National Directory Company, Yell has consolidated its position as the largest independent publisher of Yellow Pages directories in the US. The two acquisitions have more than doubled Yell's geographic US footprint to cover 41 states and Washington DC.

In July 2003, a new milestone in Yell's development was heralded with the company's listing on the London Stock Exchange – the biggest flotation in the London market for two years.

Product

Yellow Pages is committed to supporting the growth and development of businesses in the UK, and

embraces innovation to keep pace with the changing needs of its advertisers. Yell's UK sales force of more than 1,700 ensures that the needs of each business are identified and suitable advertising programmes developed. From a free line entry in a single directory to full-page, colour insertions in all 88 directory editions, Yellow Pages provides value for money, effective advertising packages for UK businesses. 89% of Yellow Pages advertisers consider their advert to be good value for money (Source: Savile Rossiter-Base 2003).

All businesses in the UK can benefit free of charge from line entries in Yellow Pages, Yell.com and Yellow Pages 118 24 7, meaning that potential customers can reach them whether they are at home, at work, on the internet or on the move. Yell's sales teams advise businesses on advertisement design, and place them in the most appropriate classifications in the directories, helping them to communicate more effectively to their target audience. Today there are more than 2,340 classifications in the Yellow Pages directory and these are reviewed on a regular basis to ensure that customers can choose the most relevant and up to date headings for their business.

Since its launch in 1996, Yell.com has established a strong identity. It now features approximately 1.7 million listings, searchable by business type, name and location. During March 2003, the site was visited 4.4 million times and generated 39 million page impressions. The information that Yell.com provides can now be accessed via three channels: the web, mobile and interactive TV.

Yellow Pages 118 24 7 offers callers business and residential directory listings information, and gives advertisers the opportunity to provide extra details about their business, such as opening hours and store locations. This classified information can be updated at any time, making the service an ideal way to promote seasonal and special offers. Callers to Yellow Pages 118 24 7 can choose to have the number read out to them, sent to their mobile via SMS, or be connected straight through to the business.

Yellow Pages has extended its support for its advertisers and the business community as a whole, becoming a friend and partner to those starting out in business and to Small and Medium-Sized Enterprises (SMEs) by providing business advice to help owners and managers run their businesses more efficiently. A 'Director's Briefing' booklet, which gives advice to established businesses, is available to existing Yell advertisers, whilst new business start-ups can receive 'Business Insight' and 'New Business Planner' briefings.

Recent Developments
Yellow Pages is constantly looking at new and innovative ways of attracting new advertisers and retaining existing ones, as well as ensuring the directory is easy to use and relevant to local needs.

In October 2001, full-colour advertisements were published in the Yellow Pages for the first time. It is an innovation that has proved to be popular with advertisers, allowing them more flexibility in the style of their advertisement. Each Yellow Pages directory includes a 'Living in Your Area' guide, which contains helpful information on local leisure and community subjects.

The Guides encourage people to make the most of leisure and tourism opportunities in their own area with ideas for shopping, days out, health and fitness activities, and nightlife. In 2003, a new Insurance Guide was also introduced, containing helpful information and advice alongside insurance listings and advertisements.

As a general policy, Yellow Pages regularly reviews the traditional geographical boundaries of its directories to ensure that users can find the information that is most relevant to them. Where necessary, and only if there is overwhelming local support, boundaries will be redrawn to split an area into separate, new directories.

Promotion
Yellow Pages has consistently used strong advertising campaigns to build and reinforce awareness of the brand. The famous JR Hartley TV advertising, where an elderly man used Yellow Pages to search for a book that he had written years before, aimed to remind consumers that Yellow Pages is 'not just for the nasty things in life'. The advert won a British Television Silver Award in 1983, and in 2000 'Fly-Fishing' came thirteenth in a Channel 4 poll of the '100 Greatest TV Ads of all Time'. Award-winning and memorable advertising campaigns have kept Yellow Pages at the forefront of consumers' minds for many years since. For instance, the memorable 'Cleaners' advert was awarded a British Television Gold Award in 1998.

The latest wave of Yellow Pages TV advertising features James Nesbitt of 'Cold Feet' and 'Murphy's Law' fame, who turns to Yellow Pages in a variety of humorous real-life situations. James Nesbitt has also fronted a radio advertising campaign for the new Yellow Pages 118 24 7 service. This active promotion of Yellow Pages has proved highly successful with the Yellow Pages directory being used more than 100 million times a month (Source: Saville Rossiter-Base 2003).

Existing and potential advertisers are kept up to date with new product and pricing initiatives. Businesses taking out advertising for the first time are offered favourable rates and are subsequently offered the chance to increase their advert size, allowing them to see how Yellow Pages advertising and an enhanced presence can work for their business at a discounted price. Payment plans also mean that advertisers do not have to start paying for their advertising until it has been published and the advertising has started to work for them. The cost of their advertising can then be paid in ten monthly instalments, interest-free.

Brand Values
In today's competitive environment, Yellow Pages plays a crucial role in people's everyday lives, both at home and in the workplace. More than 35 years' experience has enabled Yellow Pages to offer an unparalleled service to suppliers and buyers, and it has become a trusted and familiar

source of information. In keeping with the brand's friendly and helpful personality, Yellow Pages' involvement with charity and environmental projects reflects its concern with issues that affect individuals and communities throughout the UK.

Yellow Pages has worked with Marie Curie Cancer Care since 1999, supporting the annual 'Daffodil Campaign', which has raised more than £8 million for the charity.

Yellow Pages' support of The Directory Recycling Scheme (DRS) forms part of the company's ongoing commitment to the environment. A major schools recycling initiative – The Yellow Woods Challenge – was launched in October 2002 with the aim of educating children about recycling, conservation and to encourage them to recycle old Yellow Pages directories.

www.yell.com

ZURICH

Market

Zurich Financial Services is an insurance-based financial services provider with an international network that focuses its activities on its key markets of North America, the UK and Continental Europe. Founded in 1872, Zurich is headquartered in Zurich, Switzerland. It has offices in more than 50 countries and employs approximately 64,000 people.

Basing its business on a tradition of innovative financial solutions, Zurich is one of the world's major players in insurance and offers its customers a broad range of insurance-related products.

Using local expertise backed by an international network, it provides insurance and risk management products and services for small to medium sized enterprises, corporations and multinational companies. Zurich also offers a comprehensive range of insurance products for individuals – such as property, travel and car insurance – as well as financial products such as life cover, investment and pensions.

The UK is one of the Group's three core markets and a significant contributor to Zurich's overall profits, and is often looked to for best-practice models and trailblazing innovations.

In the UK, Zurich works across many market sectors, either selling direct to customers or distributing its products and services through intermediaries. In most of its markets, it is a top-five player and in many it leads the way.

Achievements

As an indication of Zurich's success in its chosen markets, in 2002 gross written premiums, policy fees and insurance deposits for the group as a whole rose by 19% over 2001, reaching a total of US$62 billion. In the same period business operating profit increased fivefold to US$1.1 billion. In the first half of 2003 Zurich reported continuing operating improvements and a net income of US$701 million.

Zurich is a regular winner of industry awards around the world. And whilst they aren't the focus of the work the brand does, they are an excellent means of measuring Zurich's success in its chosen markets.

In the UK in 2003, it won 'Insurance Provider of the Year' and 'Service Provider of the Year' at the Insurance Age awards. Added to this is Zurich's achievement in 2002 of being a finalist for a record-breaking thirteen times for the UK Insurance Times Awards.

Zurich achieved further recognition in 2003 by winning the Underwriter of the Year Award at the British Insurance Awards. A panel of industry leaders, influencers and commentators vote on these awards and Zurich is extremely proud to achieve its endorsement and recognition. It was also recognised for giving 'Service Beyond the Call of Duty' at the 2003 Investment Life and Pensions Moneyfax Awards.

In addition to this, Zurich's various efforts to create a more accommodating work environment for its employees have received praise.

Zurich's shares have been included in funds that use various criteria of corporate responsibility, including commitment to employees, community contribution and environmental management. It has also qualified for the Dow Jones Sustainability Group Index, one of the leading indexes tracking the performance of companies committed to responsible business and long-term durable growth from the day it began.

Charity work plays a big part in everyday lives at Zurich UK. In fact, Business in the Community has awarded its Dementia, INclusion and India programmes with the coveted BIG TICK mark for three consecutive years for programme impact. Zurich received the 'Community Initiative of the Year Award' in the Insurance Times Awards in 2001. The company's charity arm – Zurich Community Trust – was also awarded an 'Excellence in

Partnership Award' at the House of Commons for its work with the Gloucester Neighbourhood Project Network.

History

The roots of the Zurich Financial Services Group go back to the nineteenth century, with the founding in 1872 of Zurich Insurance Company. Within eight years of its founding, the company was already servicing a large clientele beyond Switzerland.

This growth continued, with business reaching all continents by the end of the 1970s. The asset management business became a major part of the company's strategy in the 1990s.

Zurich Insurance began operations in the UK in 1922, offering a wide range of personal, commercial and international insurance products, primarily through a nationwide network of intermediaries.

In September 1998, Zurich Financial Services Group was created from the merger with the financial services business of BAT Industries plc – bringing together Zurich, Allied Dunbar, Threadneedle, Sterling and Eagle Star under one roof in the UK – together with major consumer and small business insurer, Farmers, in the US. Following business transitions, the majority of activities in the UK now come under the Zurich banner.

The insurance business is often influenced by the welfare and social policies of the country it operates in. Zurich has had to make major adjustments over the years to respond to these changes. Whole lines of business can be destroyed or created by a stroke of the legislative pen.

Zurich's historical agility and adaptability has served it well as it has found opportunity in change.

Product

Zurich UK offers a wide range of products within each of its market sectors.

Its commercial insurance and services products help businesses – from sole traders to large commercial businesses – to keep running if the unexpected happens. Some products are suitable for a wide variety of businesses – such as fleet insurance, employers' liability cover and property insurance – while others are tailored to specific types of businesses. For example, Zurich has a wide range of products and services aimed at businesses operating in the construction industry.

'The London market' serves the needs of FTSE 250 and FTSE 100 multinational companies that need an insurance company that can manage relationships and deliver multiple products and services similar to above but on a global scale.

Zurich's insurance for professionals offers professional indemnity plans, which cover the advice given by solicitors, accountants and other people in service professions.

Zurich's 'risk services' includes audits, surveys and advice to help customers reduce the levels of risk within their business. It focuses particularly on the areas of health and safety, property protection, motor fleet risk, business continuity, occupational health, strategic risk, engineering and environmental risk.

Zurich has tremendous expertise in helping sort out public sector risk management and insurance needs. That includes helping those involved in education, health, social housing, community services and local authorities.

Zurich helps customers through its range of personal consumer products protect themselves and their possessions (through car, boat, travel and home insurance) as well as planning for their long-term financial future (through pensions, investments, mortgages and life insurance).

Many of Zurich's products are sold through intermediaries and the brand offers extensive support in recognition of their importance to the business.

In its position as the UK's fourth largest general insurer, it is no surprise that the brand offers high levels of support to general insurance brokers working in a variety of markets, both personal and commercial. This support focuses on building relationships with brokers and their customers, and making sure they find it easy to do business with the company.

Zurich, via its franchised adviser network, provides face-to-face advice on a range of financial services including mortgages from its panel of mortgage lenders, such as Halifax and Nationwide. It helps create a complete financial package to suit individual needs. As franchises, these businesses are run by the franchisee with the support of Zurich. This includes regulatory, training, business development and marketing support.

Zurich also supports independent financial advisers (IFAs), who can recommend products from all financial services providers.

As well as distributing its products through intermediaries, Zurich also deals directly with business customers in the public and private sectors. Again it goes further than just selling its services, by offering information and assistance.

Zurich has worked with a number of strategic partners to develop products specifically for their target audiences – those partners include Alliance & Leicester, Bristol & West, Bradford & Bingley, Market Harborough Building Society and Newcastle Building Society.

Recent Developments

Zurich continually looks to develop its product set and services offerings. Recent developments include Riskline, a 24-hour telephone helpline offering expert risk management advice not just a reiteration of legislation, for the cost of a phone call.

Zurich has also launched a unique product for the Fine Art and Specie market, which combines both commercial business cover and specialist stock insurance in one policy. Fine art and specie includes paintings, antiques and collectibles as well as precious metals and stones, cash, securities and other high value items.

The brand's commercial business website has also recently been revamped, which makes it easier and quicker for brokers to conduct business online.

Meanwhile, Zurich's newly launched IFA Advantage+ programme, brings together a unique range of added-value services for IFAs. These services include training, online investment information and personal support services.

The Zurich Mortgage Network is a new service which provides a one-stop-shop facility for advisers to provide their customers with highly competitive residential and commercial mortgages, conveyancing, accident sickness and unemployment insurance as well as award-winning home contents and life protection products.

In response to Financial Advisors desire for products that can provide their customers with greater certainty, Zurich has designed the

Guaranteed Account offering a 100% capital guarantee regardless of the movement of the FTSE 100 Index.

Promotion

Zurich uses a range of media to promote itself. Its UK flying pigs TV campaign was very successful at driving awareness, image and consideration of Zurich.

By adopting the well known saying 'pigs might fly', Zurich's research confirmed that consumers acknowledge the brand as being 'in tune' with their views on financial services while at the same time warming to the refreshing attitude.

The campaign has helped to differentiate and position Zurich effectively and has contributed greatly to its overall presence and regard in the market as well as assisting greater business generation.

Obviously, financial services can't be seen or touched, so there are also many benefits in developing an association with something 'real' – in Zurich's case rugby union was chosen as it is a high-profile national activity that is 'part of the fabric of the nation'.

The aim was to associate the brand with a newsworthy message to gain consistent, cost-effective national coverage in a range of media including radio, press, TV and the internet. Further to which, as the sponsors of the Zurich Premiership, the brand name is visible across the country and it lends itself to hospitality opportunities to build relationships with intermediaries and business customers.

The rugby audience is a key one for Zurich, as the profile of rugby fans is similar to the target market for insurance and financial services. Furthermore, findings from sponsorship image research show that those who are aware of TV and sponsorship activity very clearly think more highly of Zurich. In rugby, the brand has found what it views as its perfect match – it targets the right audience for the brand, fits with the brand and provides an excellent opportunity to make people aware of who they are across the UK.

In terms of the sport itself, the sponsorship has allowed the game to flourish and develop from grass roots to its upper levels, with greater exposure and improved competition creating an exciting sporting package.

Zurich often produces marketing material for intermediaries to use to generate new business leads and make the most of their existing customers. These can be based on

specific products and offers or on more general areas of financial planning. In fact Zurich was one of the first insurers to support brokers with above-the-line activity. Such support is ideal for Zurich's intermediaries as, in short, it makes it simple for them to do more business.

Zurich achieves its promotional goals in various ways including technical articles and advertising in specialist trade press, industry representation at government level, membership of industry bodies, event sponsorship, newsletters and websites. This sort of activity allows it to share its expertise with customers and represent their views.

Brand Values

The Zurich brand in the UK has been built around five attributes namely 'personal' which manifests itself in treating people as individuals, offering them relevant products and services and always looking for ways to help them. Zurich is a credible, experienced and knowledgeable brand that offers a professional service at all times, this is summed up in the second brand attribute 'expertise'. 'Convenience' is also key and reflects the accessible, easy to deal with and efficient nature of the brand. This includes giving business customers exactly what they need to do their jobs more efficiently. In today's frantic digital world, Zurich views offering its customers 'choice' as highly important. They can therefore choose the method of contact, relationship, and product that is right for them. Finally, being 'trustworthy' is also key to Zurich. This encompasses the reliable, dependable, fair, open and honest nature of the brand.

www.zurich.co.uk

3M

PIP FRANKISH
General Manager, Corporate
Marketing & Communications

Pip Frankish is general manager, Corporate Marketing & Communications for 3M's UK/Ireland operations and previously held other B2B communications roles at Texaco and ABB as well as within 3M. In her current assignment, she is responsible for the protection and enhancement of 3M's corporate reputation, including all brand assets.

Accenture

JAMES MURPHY
Global Managing Director
Marketing & Communications
In addition to his current role, James is chairman of Accenture's Marketing Management Committee as well as being a member of Accenture's Executive Committee and Global Leadership Council. James joined Accenture in 1993, prior to which he was chairman and chief executive officer of the US operations of Burson-Marsteller.

TERESA POGGENPOHL
Partner and Director
Global Brand, Advertising
and Research
In addition to her current role, Teresa is a member of the organisation's Marketing Management Committee. She also serves as the Marketing & Communications lead for Accenture's Executive Brand Steering Committee – a senior leadership team providing oversight for major strategies and investments.

American Airlines

KIM DE PAOLIS
Regional Marketing Manager

Kim joined American's sales group in 1989 with a background in customer service. In 1992 she became UK Marketing Manager and Regional Marketing Manager in 1995. During that time Kim has been involved in the implementation of a corporate marketing database, the introduction of brand advertising specifically for the UK and most recently the launch of websites across Europe.

Barclaycard

ALISON HUTCHINSON
Marketing Director

In her current role Alison is responsible for the marketing of Barclaycard UK, Company Barclaycard, Barclaycard Merchant Services and Barclaycard International. Previously, Alison was Chief Executive Officer for Barclays B2B Ltd where she led the turnaround and transformation of the company, which had been set up eighteen months earlier as a '.com'. Prior to joining the Barclays group she worked in a variety of roles for IBM, most notably as Global Director for Financial Solutions.

Barclays

SIMON GULLIFORD
Marketing Director

Simon was appointed Barclays Marketing Director in May 2001. He is responsible for all marketing planning and execution throughout the Group.
Prior to this, in an extensive career spanning seventeen years, Simon gained a considerable reputation at the highest levels of strategic marketing at EMAP plc, Sears plc, his own consultancy and at Ashridge Management College.

BASF

JOHN RANDLE
Director Corporate Services,
BASF UK & Ireland
John has spent over 30 years in the chemical industry in many different functions. He is currently responsible for all the risk and reputation issues of BASF in the UK & Ireland. This includes corporate communications, media relations, government affairs and environment, health and safety.

CHRIS WILSON
Corporate Communications
Manager
Chris has been helping to promote and protect BASF's corporate brand for 26 years. His current role involves media relations and managing a high profile corporate advertising campaign in the UK. A former journalist, he moved into PR with a new town development corporation before joining BASF in 1977.

BBH

NIGEL BOGLE
Chief Executive Officer
Nigel founded BBH with John Bartle and John Hegarty in London in 1982. The three met eight years previously when they started the UK office of TBWA. After TBWA was voted Campaign magazine's first ever Agency of the Year, they decided to go it alone. Nigel has overall responsibility for the strategic direction of the business as well as remaining closely involved with several of the agency's clients.

JOHN HEGARTY
Chairman & Worldwide
Creative Director
John started in advertising as a junior Art Director at Benton and Bowles, London in 1965. After they fired him, he joined a small Soho agency, John Collings & Partners. In 1967 he joined the Cramer Saatchi consultancy which became Saatchi & Saatchi in 1970, where he was a founding shareholder. One year later he was appointed Deputy Creative Director. John went on to co-found TBWA, London as Creative Director and in 1982 he started Bartle Bogle Hegarty.

Blue Circle

MIKE LOMAX
Marketing Communications Manager

Mike has been in Marketing and Brand Communications for 25 years, working with blue-chip brands such as Pilkington, GE and GEC, Baxi and Owens Corning. Since May 2001, Mike has been in charge of Marketing Communications for Blue Circle cement products. Blue Circle is a brand of Lafarge, the largest building materials manufacturer in the world.

British Airways

SUE MOORE
Head of Brands
Sue joined British Airways in 1987 from Unilever and following roles in Brand Management, Relationship Marketing and Corporate Strategy became Head of Brands in 1997. Sue's responsibilities include designing and specifying the customer experience for all BA's cabin brands from FIRST to Euro Traveller, new product development and the Executive Club.

JILL MCDONALD
Head of Global Marketing
& Inflight Business
Jill joined British Airways in 1990 from Colgate Palmolive and has worked in a number of departments including Brand Management, Advertising and Sponsorship as well as heading up Sales & Marketing for BA in East Asia. Jill's current role includes responsibility for the BA Masterbrand, Global Marketing Communications, Market Research, Design Management and Inflight Retail and Entertainment.

BSI

FRANK POST
Group Marketing Director
Frank has responsibility for the brand and marketing strategy development of the BSI Group.
Prior to this he was the Global Sales & Marketing Director of BSI Management Systems worldwide which encompasses some 40,000 clients. Frank joined BSI in April 1999 after a career that included senior sales and marketing positions with Williams plc and Chubb plc.

PUNIT SHAH
Group Marketing Manager
Punit is responsible for the implementation of BSI's global branding strategy, relaunching the BSI brand across 110 countries in 2002. Punit started his career agency side and joined the BSI Group in 1997. He became Group eBusiness Manager in 2000 leading the team that developed BSI's highly successful online presence.

Casio

TOMOKI SATO
Director, Corporate Strategy
Tomoki is currently responsible for product planning, marketing and strategy at Casio in the UK. Having joined the company in 1992, he has spent the last eight years in Europe moving from product planning to managing strategic partnerships with Siemens and Vodafone. In his current role, he is charged with re-invigorating the Casio brand.

CNBC Europe

MICK BUCKLEY
VP & Commercial Director
Mick has worked in commercial TV for fifteen years. He joined CNBC Europe in March 2003 in a new role overseeing all commercial aspects of the business within sales, marketing and public relations.
Prior to joining CNBC Europe, Buckley was at Turner Broadcasting Systems Europe, where he was Executive VP, TBS News Networks and UK Managing Director. He held a series of distribution and sales roles for a number of Turner channels including CNN and its entertainment properties.

RICHARD COTTON
Chief Executive Officer
Rick Cotton took over as CEO of CNBC Europe in January 2001, developing the channel from the fledgling European business channel in 1998 to what is now the leading pan-European real-time business and financial TV channel. Prior to joining CNBC Europe, he was NBC's executive vice president and general counsel from October 1989, where he reported to Robert C Wright, President and Chief Executive Officer of NBC.

Compass

PAUL KELLY
Corporate Affairs Director
Paul Kelly is responsible for reputation management, corporate social responsibility, government relations, competition and regulatory affairs and crisis management.
Paul took up his current position following Compass' acquisition of Granada's hotel and hospitality interests in 2001. At Granada he was Brand Development and Marketing Director for Granada's restaurants division. Prior to joining Granada he was a management consultant specialising in branding and communications for the leisure and hospitality industry.

IAN DALY
Senior Vice President
Select Service Partner Global
Since Ian Daly joined Compass Group in 1994, he has been one of the leading advocates of Brands within the Group. He has been responsible for developing and creating Compass' owned consumer brands; such as Upper Crust and Caffè Ritazza, and for creating often exclusive partnerships with Brand-owners like TGI Fridays and Burger King.
In addition he has played a key role in the development and implementation of Compass' client facing brands e.g. Eurest, Medirest, Scolarest.

Conqueror

SARAH FLOWER
Conqueror Brand Manager
Following an honors degree in French from the University of Exeter, Sarah held a number of international sales and marketing roles within ArjoWiggins before taking on the role of brand manager for their flagship brand, Conqueror: Recent achievements include a major repositioning of the brand, responding to the needs of today's digital office environment.

ILAN SCHINAZI
Sales & Marketing Director,
ArjoWiggins Fine Papers
With a broad international background, Ilan has held several senior roles within both the B2B and B2C sectors. His current appointment to ArjoWiggins Fine Papers has seen him as champion of a significant brand rationalisation project for the division – implemented alongside the continuing development and support of the world famous Conqueror brand.

DHL

JOHN GEDDES
Commercial Director
DHL UK
John has worked for DHL since 1989. His first eight years were spent in and around the Middle East, including spells in Saudi Arabia, Oman and Pakistan where he held senior management positions. In 1997 John returned to the UK becoming Commercial Director in 2002.

MICHAEL DENT
General Manager Marketing
DHL Express UK
Michael joined DHL in 1989 and is now back in London after spells in Brussels to run the Market Segmentation project and in Fort Lauderdale to head up the Latin American marketing team.
Prior to joining DHL Michael worked as a consultant with Coopers & Lybrand, specialising in Travel and Distribution. He received his MSc from City University and an MPhil from London Business School.

DuPont

TONY JORDAN
Public Affairs Manager,
DuPont UK
Tony has been in B2B communications most of his professional career.
He held senior communications roles in several major international corporations including SKF, Bosch, ICL and ICI before joining DuPont in 1993. He is a member of the Institute of Public Relations, The Chartered Institute of Marketing, and the Marketing Society.

JUAN F 'KIKO' SUAREZ
Brand Manager,
DuPont Europe
Kiko joined DuPont in 1991 at Asturias, Spain, after running his own startup company for about three years. His background is in information technology and business communications. Kiko undertook various assignments in Europe and the US, where he led the renewal project for the corporate website, dupont.com, and various global initiatives related to the company bicentennial. In September 2002, Kiko was appointed Corporate Brand Manager for DuPont Europe, Middle East and Africa.

Earls Court and Olympia London

DEBBIE THOMAS
Director of Communications
In her current role Debbie is responsible for all marketing, media, staff and political communications activity. Reporting directly to the Chief Executive, Debbie has a team of four (and a half) of which two are responsible for marketing. Debbie joined EC&O in March 2002 following nine years in a range of communications roles with airport operator BAA and two and a half years in consultancy.

ANDREW MORRIS
Chief Executive
Andrew has spent seventeen years in the exhibitions industry, firstly as Managing Director of the Business Design Centre in Islington, which his family brought back to life after years in the wilderness as a neglected former agricultural hall. Following this, he led the family's venture capital-backed purchase of Earls Court and Olympia from shipping company P&O in 1999.

easyCar

STELIOS HAJI-IOANNOU
easyGroup Chairman
Stelios is the serial entrepreneur who founded easyCar. He is also the chairman of the easyGroup which owns such additional brands as easyJet, easyInternetcafe and easyCinema.
He remains chairman and principal brand guardian of easyCar but, as with former companies, when easyCar becomes a public company he intends to delegate the running of the company to its board in order to concentrate on his younger, private companies.

JAMES ROTHNIE
easyGroup Director of
Corporate Affairs
James is responsible for media relations, brand, corporate image and lobbying for all the private easyGroup companies. He originally worked for easyJet and then moved to the easyGroup as it was founded in order to extend the brand into other industries. Prior to any of the easyGroup companies James worked for Disneyland Paris.

FT

ZACHARY LEONARD
Managing Director, Europe,
Middle East & Africa
Formerly UK Director, Zachary was appointed to his current position in July 2003 and is responsible for all commercial operations for the EMEA region. As Chief Operating Officer for FT.com, he led the division's drive to Q4 2002 profitability and its successful launch of subscription services. He previously launched and managed both FT YourMoney, the personal finance portal, and FTMarketWatch.com, for which he served as Chief Executive, which became Europe's leading website for private investors.

JOANNA MANNING-COOPER
Director of Communications
Joanna Manning-Cooper is Director of Communications. Her global remit covers corporate communications, media relations, brand PR and internal communications for the Financial Times Group, including the FT newspaper and FT.com.

Heathrow Express

DIANE GLASSFORD
Head of Marketing

Diane Glassford has been spearheading the marketing of Heathrow Express for two years. Leading the creation and development of successful integrated marketing and advertising campaigns, Diane has been instrumental in the growth of Heathrow Express' market share, making it the market leader for people traveling from central London to Heathrow Airport.

Hill & Knowlton

MARIE LOUISE WINDELER
Chief Executive, Hill and Knowlton UK

Marie Louise joined the consultancy in 1985, and was promoted to Chief Executive in March 2001. Assisted by a Senior Management Committee of ten and a Board of Directors totalling 34, she leads and directs the day to day running of Hill and Knowlton UK. Marie Louise also remains Executive Chairman of the Marketing Communications Division, which she has led since 1985.

PAUL TAAFFE
Chairman & CEO

Paul Taaffe is chairman and CEO of Hill & Knowlton, Inc and chairs the firm's Worldwide Executive Committee. His current clients are primarily international companies engaged in communications across borders and include Kellogg's, American Express and GE Capital. He was previously president of Hill & Knowlton in Europe, Middle East and Africa, and prior to that, chief executive of Hill & Knowlton UK.

Intel

DAVID MITCHELL
Head of Brand Marketing

David Mitchell is Head of Brand Marketing for Intel in the UK. He is responsible for all Intel's brand activities in the UK, including the advertising on TV, print, outdoor and web.

Since joining Intel in 1996, David has worked in a variety of marketing roles addressing both the retail channel and PC Manufacturers.

Prior to Intel, he worked as a sales manager at Compaq and Dell in the UK, after starting his career with a number of years as an account director in retail marketing agencies.

IoD

ANDREW MAIN WILSON
Chief Executive

Andrew Main Wilson has twenty years experience building and transforming premium quality service-industry brands, as Marketing Director of Thomas Cook and Sales & Marketing Director of Citibank Diners Club. Andrew joined the Institute of Directors in 1996, to transform the brand, commercial activities and significantly expand membership. Membership has since increased 50%, to 55,000, and revenues have increased 100%.

J Walter Thompson

NICK BELL
Executive Creative Director

Nick joined JWT as Creative Director in July 2003. His career has seen him win the Cannes Grand Prix, as well as seven Cannes Golds and two D&AD silvers for clients such as Mercedes-Benz, John West, Heinz and McDonald's. One of the creative industries' leading figures, Nick is currently President of D&AD.

SIMON BOLTON
CEO

Simon started his professional life at Ogilvy & Mather in London. In 1995 Simon joined FCB Worldwide as regional director of South East Asia. In 1998, he was asked to lead FCB's major office on the West Coast. Simon joined JWT as Group Chief Executive of its five component companies in April 2001. His ambition is to make JWT the most respected communications agency in the UK.

Kall Kwik

JOHN BLYTH
Head of Marketing

John has been Head of Marketing at Kall Kwik UK since 2000 where his remit is to guide and protect the brand. A repositioning of the business based on its ability to deliver tailored solutions has increased its salience to corporate clients, and reinforced its market leading status.

SANDRA FITZGERALD
Commercial Director & General Manager

Sandra joined Kall Kwik UK as Sales Promotion Manager in 1990. She is now Commercial Director and General Manager, giving her overall responsibility for the strategic direction and management of the business, which consists of sixteen staff at Kall Kwik UK and nearly 170 print, design and copy Centres nationwide.

London Business School

LAURA D TYSON
Dean

Laura D Tyson began her term as Dean of London Business School in January 2002. She was formerly Dean of Haas Business School at the University of Berkeley, California. From 1993 to 1996 she served in the Clinton Administration, during which time she was the President's National Economic Adviser. She is an Economic Viewpoint columnist for Business Week, and writes regularly in The Washington Post, The New York Times, and other US and internationally-syndicated newspapers and magazines.

DAVID LANE
Communications Director

David Lane heads a communications team of six responsible for London Business School's press and PR, e-communications, internal communications and brand management and publication production. David joined the School in 2003 from the Export Credits Guarantee Department at the Department for Trade and Industry where he was Director of Marketing and Customer Relationship Management. Prior to that, David was Head of NatWest Brand Communications and Customer Marketing at Royal Bank of Scotland Group.

LYCRA®

LINDA W KEARNS
Global Apparel Communications Director, INVISTA

Linda W Kearns is currently the Global Apparel Communications Director for INVISTA. She joined DuPont in 1984 as a marketing research analyst in the Corporate Business and Marketing Group of External Affairs. Linda graduated from the Massachusetts Institute of Technology with a BS degree in mathematics and holds a Masters Degree from Princeton University. She and her husband, Tom, live in Newark, Delaware, and have two children, Emily and Jake.

DENISE SAKUMA WERTZ
European Apparel Communications Director, INVISTA

Denise Sakuma Wertz was appointed to her current role in 2001. Ms Sakuma joined DuPont Brazil SA in 1994 as a Ready-to-Wear marketing representative in the LYCRA® business group. She was subsequently named marketing specialist in 1996, account manager circular knitting and fashion in 1997 and LYCRA® brand manager for South America in 1998. In 1997, she was instrumental in DuPont receiving the MTV Fashion Award for LYCRA®.

MediaCom

NICK LAWSON
Joint Managing Director

Nick joined The Media Business in 1991. In October 1997 he was promoted to the Board as Marketing Director where he was responsible for the agency's new business and also defining the MediaCom brand. In August 1999 he became Joint Managing Director and still holds key responsibility for IKEA.

KAREN BLACKETT
Marketing Director

Karen joined The Media Business 1995. In October 1999 she was promoted to the Board. Her client portfolio includes Audi, IPC Media, Metropolitan Police and Wrigley. Karen was recently promoted to Marketing Director at MediaCom and was named as one of the Top 35 women under 35 by Management Today.

Mintel

Everyone at Mintel, from production to direct sales, is an ambassador for the brand. It is not fair to focus on any one individual within the group.

NatWest

STEPHEN DAY
Head of Brand Strategy

Stephen joined NatWest in November 2002 from GE Consumer Finance, following a spell as Marketing Director with First National Consumer Finance. Prior to his career in financial services Stephen worked at Guinness for eleven years, in a variety of marketing roles, within Great Britain and Worldwide. His career started at Bass.

npower

DAVID ANDREW
Director of Brand Development
David joined npower in October 1999 as Marketing Director and has held key roles including Director of Residential business, with over six million customers. Before joining npower, David was Vice President Marketing UK & Ireland for Hilton International. Prior to this, David worked in brand management, marketing and operations management in the brewing industry, at Grand Metropolitan Brewing and Bass plc, financial services at N&P and The Leeds Building Society and the launch of Guardian Direct Insurance.

KEVIN PEAKE
Head of Brand
Kevin joined npower in May 2000 as Head of Brand. His responsibilities include brand strategy, internal marketing, market research, advertising and sponsorship. Previously he worked in marketing and brand at Comet, TSB and Abbey National. Kevin is instrumental in the npower cricket sponsorship.

O₂

CATH KEERS
Marketing Director, O₂ UK

Cath Keers became O₂ UK Marketing Director in February 2003 having spent two years as Director of Consumer Business leading the rise in O₂'s performance in the consumer market place.
She directs all of O₂'s marketing activity in the UK for both business and consumer sectors with P&L responsibility for these areas.
Cath successfully launched the O₂ brand in the UK, including the development of the innovative interactive sponsorship of Big Brother which firmly positioned O₂ as the leader in text messaging.
Previously, Cath was General manager of Customer Care in Cellnet and moved into Marketing as Director of Prepay before assuming her role as Consumer Director.

Office Angels

SARAH EL-DOORI
Head of Marketing & Public Relations, Ajilon UK

Sarah was promoted to her current position in May 2002, following the formation of the Ajilon Group. She manages all elements of the marketing strategy for the nine brands in the Ajilon portfolio, including Office Angels, Computer People, Jonathan Wren, Ajilon Finance, Ajilon Executive, OAexec, Roevin, Ajilon Consulting and Interskill Interactive.

PC World

DEREK LLOYD
Managing Director
Derek took on his role in 1997 with the remit of overseeing all of the company's UK operations. He has quickly taken the company to a turnover of £200 million and has grown the workforce to more than 540 people.
Derek has also led the re-branding of the company to PC World Business, as well as the development and implementation of both the acclaimed Definitive Buyers Guide and the pcwb.com e-commerce strategy.

RICHARD MILLMAN
Marketing Director
Richard oversees marketing across the company's UK operations, as well as supporting PC World Group stores throughout Europe. He directs a team of 85 marketing and service professionals, controlling an annual marketing budget in excess of £7.5 million.
Since joining PC World Business in 2000, Richard has been responsible for developing and executing a revised customer-led marketing strategy, resulting in the company achieving the position of the UK's number one reseller of IT to the SME market in 2002/03.

Prontaprint

KEITH DAVIDSON
Head of Marketing

Keith Davidson was appointed Head of Marketing at Prontaprint Limited in 2000 and oversaw a major rebranding exercise designed to reflect the company's positioning as the premier provider of print-on-demand, business-to-business communication solutions across the UK and Ireland. Two years on, Prontaprint became the first print industry brand to be acknowledged as a Business Superbrand. Davidson, who is responsible for all aspects of marketing and brand management within Europe's largest print franchise, has worked in the marketing function of Prontaprint Limited for over fourteen years and has also held positions within all the key support departments.

Reed

KATY NICHOLSON
Marketing & Communications Director
Katy started out in publishing, then joined Reed as Marketing Manager for professional divisions in 1989, becoming Group Public Relations Manager in 1996. In 1998 she left Reed for the PR Agency world, working on brands including BT, Cisco, RAC, Dixons, and Tesco, before returning to her current position in 2000.

JAMES REED MA, MBA
Chief Executive
James was appointed Chief Executive of Reed Executive PLC in February 1997. His early career was spent with BBC Television, Help the Aged, Saatchi & Saatchi PLC and The Body Shop PLC. He is committed to providing innovation, value and continuous improvement to all Reed clients.

Research International

COLIN BUCKINGHAM
Chairman & CEO
Colin joined Research International in 1996 as Global Marketing Director, in which role he oversaw the agency's relationships with international clients. In April 2000 he was appointed CEO of Research International in the UK (retaining his membership of the Research International Group Board and overall responsibility for the Group's marketing and some of its largest global clients). Before joining the company, he worked for AC Nielsen and has over twenty years experience in the marketing research industry.

LUCY DAVISON
Director, Marketing Communications
Lucy joined Research International in May 2000. She is responsible for the marketing strategy and its implementation for the Group as a whole. Lucy first joined the company to develop and manage its rebranding programme, resulting in a new identity, which was launched in September 2001. Before joining RI she ran her own business providing media relations and marketing consultancy, and freelance copywriting services to a range of marketing service and design companies.

Reuters

ALEXANDER HUNGATE
Chief Marketing Officer
Alex Hungate assumed the role of Chief Marketing Officer for the Reuters Group Worldwide at the beginning of 2002. He is responsible for protecting and leveraging the Reuters brand, communicating value propositions to customers, gaining insights about customers, markets and competitors and managing commercial policy. Before assuming his current role, Alex was President of Focus Group Accounts, responsible for sales to the largest global customers worldwide.

AMANDA WEST
Director, Global Marketing Communications
Amanda joined Reuters in 1987 and following various roles as a Director of Product Management was appointed to her current role in 1998. Marketing Communications manages all global customer communication campaigns. In 2001 the role was expanded to include the development and communication of the Reuters brand.

Rio Tinto

CHERRY DEGEER
Manager Corporate Communications
Cherry DeGeer joined Rio Tinto in 1997 and is responsible for Rio Tinto's corporate communications activities and global visual identity, promoting design, editorial and brand consistency across the company's business units.
Cherry's role includes the co-ordination of all internal and external corporate communication projects: websites, intranet, video, multimedia, advertising, printed literature and she is also editor of Review, Rio Tinto's corporate magazine.

ANDREW VICKERMAN
Head of Communication & Sustainable Development
Andrew Vickerman has overall responsibility for corporate communications, health, safety and environment activities for Rio Tinto. His corporate communications responsibilities encompass media, sustainable development, public affairs and community relations in addition to communications strategy and brand management. Andrew has a BA, MA and PhD from Cambridge University and prior to joining Rio Tinto in 1991 he worked as a development economist and as a consultant for international organisations, including the World Bank.

Rolls-Royce

COLIN DUNCAN
Director - Corporate Communications
Colin joined Rolls-Royce in January 2002. Colin has overall responsibility for the communication of the Rolls-Royce brand around the world, and has been instrumental in the alignment of both the parent and motorcar brands. Previous positions at BNFL, BP and British Gas has given him considerable experience working with international brands.

DAVID HOWIE
Head of Brand & Communications
Head custodian of the Rolls-Royce brand, David's responsibilities involve maintaining the integrity of all branded communications.
David began his career as a Press Officer at Rolls-Royce in 1982, he left to join a Marketing Consultancy for five years returning to the company in 1992, and has enormous experience of working with and more recently directing the Rolls-Royce brand.

Royal Mail

TOM HINGS
Head of Brand & Advertising
Tom Hings began his career in advertising at Cogent Elliott and then at Lintas. In 1990 he joined Allied Breweries and relaunched Castlemaine XXXX. As Marketing Manager at Carlsberg-Tetley, Tom was responsible for Carlsberg's sponsorship and advertising programmes. As Marketing Controller for Lagers, he re-launched Carlsberg and Carlsberg Export. He joined Royal Mail in 2002.

PAUL TROY
Head of Marketing Services
Paul Troy is Head of Marketing Services. He has held marketing management positions in Smithkline Beecham, Allied Domecq and Weetabix. More recently he has been a Brand Marketing Director with Cadbury Schweppes, and LloydsTSB.

Samsung

YOUNG CHO KIM
President of Samsung Electronics Europe HQ & UK
Young Cho joined Samsung Corporation in 1973. He is now Head of the European and UK operations of Samsung Electronics. Prior to this, he was head of Samsung Electronics' CIS and European Semiconductor operations. Increasing the Samsung brand power further in Europe is one of Young Cho's key objectives and he is focusing his organisation and efforts on achieving this target.

HADRIAN BAUMANN
Senior Manager, European Marketing
Hadrian was appointed to his current position in 2002. He is responsible for implementing the company's European brand and retail marketing strategy. Extensive working experience with Samsung Electronics in Korea, a two-year stint at a consultancy and an MBA provide Hadrian with a strong background to help building Samsung into a household name in Europe.

Shell

VENETIA HOWES
Global Brands Strategy Manager
Venetia Howes has responsibility for the strategic development of the Shell brand. Her experience includes B2B marketing in chemicals, shipping and lubricants, and she was previously the Marketing Manager for Shell's global aviation business. She took the CIM Post-Graduate Diploma mid-career and is an active member of the Worshipful Company of Marketors, as well as being a school governor.

RAOUL PINNELL
VP, Global Brands & Communications
Raoul Pinnell developed an early interest in business whilst at school, Bradfield College, leaving to pursue Business Studies, subsequently followed by a post-graduate Diploma in Marketing. Following seventeen years with Nestlé, five years at Prudential and three years at NatWest, Shell International appointed him to the post of VP, Global Brands & Communications in 1997.

Stanley

CLIVE MEARS
Commercial Director – Europe
Clive joined the Stanley Tools organisation in 1980 as a Sales Representative, becoming National Sales Manager in 1994. In 1997 Clive became the UK Commercial Director and consolidated the separate businesses in the UK (Hand Tools, Decorating Products, Sliding Doors, Fastening Solutions and MAC Tools) into one marketing and selling organisation to provide a greater focus on the specific needs of customers within the UK region. Clive is currently extending this successful approach across the whole European region.

Zurich

CHARLOTTE THURSZ
Brand Development Director
After a decade of classic domestic and international consumer marketing with fmcg giants P&G, GSK and The Coca-Cola Company, Charlotte joined Zurich in 2001 to take up the even greater challenge of marketing in the financial sector where she is responsible for the development of the Zurich brand within the UK..

JAMES HILL
Corporate Marketing Director
James is a marketing graduate, Chartered marketeer and holds an MBA in strategic marketing.
For the last ten years his responsibilities have been in corporate marketing.
As Zurich's Corporate Marketing Director James manages all central aspects of brand development. This includes advertising and sponsorship, corporate hospitality and events, corporate identity, research, brand portfolio positioning and transition projects and aspects of the businesses web interface.

3M
3M United Kingdom PLC
3M Centre
Cain Road
Bracknell
Berkshire
RG12 8HT

Accenture
Accenture
60 Queen Victoria Street
London
EC4N 4TW

American Airlines
American Airlines
23-59 Staines Road
Hounslow
Middlesex
TW3 3HE

Barclaycard
Barclaycard
Barclaycard House
1234 Pavilion Drive
Northampton
NN4 7SG

Barclays
Barclays Bank PLC
54 Lombard Street
London
EC3P 3AH

BASF
BASF plc
PO Box 4
Earl Road
Cheadle Hulme
Cheadle
Cheshire
SK8 6QG

BBH
BBH
60 Kingly Street
London
W1B 5DS

Blue Circle
Lafarge Cement UK
Manor Court
Chilton
OX11 0RN

bmi
British Midland Airways Ltd
Donington Hall
Castle Donington
Derbyshire
DE74 2SB

British Airways
British Airways plc
Waterside
PO Box 365
Harmondsworth
UB7 0GB

BSI
BSI Group
389 Chiswick High Road
London
W4 4AL

BT
BT Group plc
BT Centre
81 Newgate Street
London
EC1A 7AJ

Casio
Casio Electronics Co. Ltd
Unit 6
1000 North Circular Road
London
NW2 7JD

CNBC Europe
CNBC Europe
10 Fleet Place
London
EC4M 7QS

Compass
Compass Group PLC
Compass House
Guildford Street
Chertsey
Surrey
KT16 9BQ

Conqueror
Arjo Wiggins
Fine Papers House
PO Box 88
Lime Tree Way
Chinehamd
Basingtoke
RG24 8BA

DHL
DHL International (UK) Ltd
Orbital Park
Great South West Road
Hounslow
Middlesex
TW4 6JS

DuPont
Du Pont (U.K.) Limited
Ermin Street
Brockworth
Gloucester
GL3 4HP

Earls Court & Olympia London
Earls Court & Olympia Group Ltd
Earls Court Exhibition Centre
Warwick Road
London
SW5 9TA

easyCar
easyCar (UK) Ltd
The Rotunda
42 Gloucester Crescent
London
NW1 7DL

Eurostar
Eurostar
Eurostar House
Waterloo Station
London
SE1 8SE

Fidelity Investments
Fidelity Investments
Kingswood Place
Millfield Lane
Lower Kingswood
Tadworth
Surrey
KT20 6RB

FT
Financial Times
Number One
Southwark Bridge
London
SE1 9HL

Goodyear
Goodyear Dunlop Tyres UK Limited
88-89 Wingfoot Way
Erdington
Birmingham
B24 9HY

Heathrow Express
Heathrow Express
Macmillan House
Paddington Station
London
W2 1FT

Hill & Knowlton
Hill & Knowlton Ltd
20 Soho Square
London
W1D 3QW

Intel
Intel Corporation UK Ltd
Pipers Way
Swindon
Wiltshire
SN3 1RJ

IoD
Institute of Directors
116 Pall Mall
London
SW1Y 5ED

J Walter Thompson
J Walter Thompson
1 Knightsbridge Green
London
SW1X 7NW

Kall Kwik
Kall Kwik Printing UK Ltd
106 Pembroke Road
Ruislip
Middlesex
HA4 8NW

London Business School
London Business School
Regent's Park
London
NW1 4SA

LYCRA®
INVISTA (International) S.A
2, Chemin du Pavillon
PO Box 50
CH-1218
Le Grand-Saconnex
Geneva

MediaCom
MediaCom
180 North Gower Street
London
NW1 2NB

Michael Page International
Michael Page International
39-41 Parker Street
London
WC2B 5LN

Mintel
Mintel International Group Ltd
18-19 Long Lane
London
EC1A 9PL

NatWest
National Westminster Bank Plc
135 Bishopsgate
London
EC2M 3UR

npower
npower
Oak House
1 Bridgwater Road
Worchester
WR4 9FP

O₂
O₂ UK
260 Bath Road
Slough
Berkshire
SL1 4DX

Office Angels
Ajilon Group
The Triangle
5 Hammersmith Grove
London
W6 OQQ

PC World
PC World
Dixons House
Marylands Avenue
Hemel Hempstead
HP2 ZTG

PricewaterhouseCoopers LLP
PricewaterhouseCoopers LLP
1 Embankment Place
London
WC2N 6RH

Pritt
Henkel Consumer Adhesives
Apollo Court
2 Bishop Square Business Park
Hatfield
Herts
AL10 9EY

Prontaprint
Prontaprint Ltd
106 Pembroke Road
Ruislip
Middlesex
HA4 8NW

Reed
Reed Executive
145 Kensington Church Street
London
W8 7LP

Research International
Research International
6-7 Grosvenor Place
London
SW1X 7SH

Reuters
Reuters Limited
85 Fleet Street
London
EC4P 4AJ

Rio Tinto
Rio Tinto plc
6 St James's Square
London
SW1Y 4LD

Rolls-Royce
Rolls-Royce plc
65 Buckingham Gate
London
SW1E 6AT

Royal Mail
Royal Mail Group plc
Royal Mail House
148 Old Street
London
EC1V 9HQ

Samsung
Samsung Electronics
Samsung House
1000 Hillswood Drive
Surrey
KT16 0PS

Sellotape
Henkel Consumer Adhesives
Apollo Court
2 Bishop Square Business Park
Hatfield
Hertfordshire
AL10 9EY

Shell
Shell International Petroleum
Company Ltd
OMM/3 Shell Centre
York Road
Waterloo
London
SE1 7NA

Siemens
Siemens plc
Siemens House
Oldbury
Bracknell
Berkshire
RG12 8FZ

Stanley
Stanley UK Sales
Drakehouse Plant
Beighton Road East
Drakehouse
Sheffield
S20 9JZ

TNS
TNS
West Gate
London
W5 1UA

Unisys
Unisys Ltd
Bakers Court
Bakers Road
Uxbridge
Middlesex
UB8 1RG

UNIX
The Open Group
44 Montgomery Street
#960
San Francisco
California 94602
USA

Virgin Atlantic
Virgin Atlantic Airways Ltd
The Office
Crawley Business Quarter
Manor Royal
Crawley
West Sussex
RH10 9NU

Yellow Pages
Yell
Queens Walk
Reading
RG1 7PT

Zurich
Zurich Financial Services (UKISA) Ltd
22 Arlington Street
London
SW1A 1RW